ARCHAEOLOGY AND ETHNOHISTORY OF IXIMCHÉ

Maya Studies

UNIVERSITY PRESS OF FLORIDA

Florida A&M University, Tallahassee
Florida Atlantic University, Boca Raton
Florida Gulf Coast University, Ft. Myers
Florida International University, Miami
Florida State University, Tallahassee
New College of Florida, Sarasota
University of Central Florida, Orlando
University of Florida, Gainesville
University of North Florida, Jacksonville
University of South Florida, Tampa
University of West Florida, Pensacola

Archaeology and Ethnohistory of Iximché

C. Roger Nance, Stephen L. Whittington, and Barbara E. Borg

With Contributions by George Guillemin and Sergio Rodas Manrique

Foreword by Diane Z. Chase and Arlen F. Chase, Series Editors

University Press of Florida

Gainesville/Tallahassee/Tampa/Boca Raton

Pensacola/Orlando/Miami/Jacksonville/Ft. Myers/Sarasota

First cloth printing, 2003
First paperback printing, 2024

29 28 27 26 25 24   6 5 4 3 2 1

Library of Congress Cataloging-in-Publication Data
Nance, Charles Roger, 1938–.
Archaeology and ethnohistory of Iximché / C. Roger Nance, Stephen L. Whittington, and Barbara
E. Borg, with contributions by George Guillemin and Sergio Rodas Manrique; foreword by Diane
Z. Chase and Arlen Chase.
p. cm. — (Maya studies)
Includes bibliographical references and index.
ISBN 978-0-8130-2633-6 (cloth) | ISBN 978-0-8130-8067-3 (pbk.)
1. Cakchikel Indians—History. 2. Cakchikel Indians—Antiquities. 3. Tecpán
(Guatemala)—Antiquities. 4. Tecpán (Guatemala)—History. 5. Excavations
(Archaeology)—Guatemala—Tecpán. I.Whittington, Stephen L. II. Jones-Borg, Barbara E.
(Barbara Elizabeth), 1946–. III. Title. IV. Series.

The University Press of Florida is the scholarly publishing agency for the State University System
of Florida, comprising Florida A&M University, Florida Atlantic University, Florida Gulf Coast
University, Florida International University, Florida State University, New College of Florida, University of Central Florida, University of Florida, University of North Florida, University of South
Florida, and University of West Florida.

University Press of Florida
2046 NE Waldo Road
Suite 2100
Gainesville, FL 32609
http://upress.ufl.edu

For Charles and Lisa,
for Charles and Alice,
and for Becki

Contents

Illustrations

Tables

Foreword

The Highlands of Guatemala are beautiful. Picturesque cities and towns are surrounded by pine-covered volcanic peaks and deeply plunging ravines in an area that is home to a large population of Maya. Not only are the Highlands heavily occupied by the modern Maya, but this area also had substantial Pre-Columbian settlement. However, compared to the extensive research that has been undertaken in the tropical Maya Lowlands, the Guatemalan Highlands are relatively unknown archaeologically. Perhaps the best known Highland site is Kaminaljuyú, located in the outskirts of modern Guatemala City, and a focus of continued, but sporadic, research by individuals associated with the Carnegie Institution of Washington and Pennsylvania State University. Apart from Kaminaljuyú, just a small number of other Guatemalan Highland sites have been the subjects of both intensive research and publication. Zacualpa was investigated by Robert Wauchope and published by the Middle American Research Institute. A series of ethnohistorically known sites have been researched. A summary of excavations at Mixco Viejo was published by Henri Lehmann. The Mam capital of Zaculeu was investigated and extensively reconstructed through the efforts of the United Fruit Company and published by Richard Woodbury and Aubrey Trik. The stone-robbed Quiché capital of Utatlán was the locus of archaeological investigation by Robert Carmack and the State University of New York at Albany. And, George Guillemin, a Swiss engineer by training, extensively excavated the central portions of the Cakchiquel capital of Iximché. A full excavation report on this site, however, never appeared in print because of his untimely death in 1978.

Although Guillemin never fully analyzed or published his data, he did attempt to summarize the investigations in articles. As mapped by

Guillemin, the site center of Iximché contained several secular palaces, each with a religious plaza; these paired architectural units potentially serve as a key to understanding Cakchiquel social and political organization. One of the excavated palaces, reported in this book, was heavily burned and had *de facto* refuse associated with it. Guillemin believed that this represented the part of Iximché that had been burned by Spanish forces on February 7, 1526, almost two years after the initial capture of the city by Pedro de Alvarado in 1524. Guillemin had hoped to use his Iximché excavations to answer questions about the Contact era Maya, questions that remain unanswered today. Unfortunately, however, he did not live to complete the analysis and publication of his research.

Thanks to the authors of this volume, the results of Guillemin's investigations are finally being published. Because of the difficulties of using the data and notes of other researchers, few contemporary scholars are willing to undertake the task. Yet, when the time and effort are expended to breathe life into dormant drawings and documents, the result can sometimes be extraordinary. By using Guillemin's archaeological research, C. Roger Nance and Stephen L. Whittington have succeeded in reconstructing a significant part of ancient Maya history and in resurrecting part of the past grandeur that once characterized the Cakchiquel capital of Iximché. Barbara E. Borg has further amplified these data through her research on the regional ethnohistory. Their hard work and laborious analyses, carried out over a decade, have demonstrated what can be accomplished with archaeological data that have lain abandoned and forgotten, particularly when modern technology and techniques are employed and when such data are placed within a broader ethnohistoric framework. We believe that returning to existing collections will be a necessary and productive path in the future of Maya archaeology. We hope that the conjunctive work of Nance, Whittington, and Borg will inspire others to consider the full potential of extant collections in their efforts to make worthy contributions to Maya studies.

Diane Z. Chase and Arlen F. Chase
Series editors

Acknowledgments

First and foremost, we must express our sincere gratitude to Nelly Guillemin, George Guillemin's widow. It was she who first encouraged Vally and Roger Nance to examine collections at Iximché which had been excavated by her late husband. She later made available to us George Guillemin's field notes, drawings, and photographs, which she had maintained since his death, and then graciously gave us permission to publish these materials. Clearly, many results of the research at Iximché would have been lost had it not been for Nelly's determination to see George's unfinished work brought as close to completion as possible. Copies of his field notes, unpublished manuscripts, and drawings are on file at CIRMA, Antigua, Guatemala.

Except for those in chapter 10, all photographs in this book were taken by George Guillemin and his associates. We would like to thank the Instituto de Antropología e Historia de Guatemala, the Sociedad de Geografía e Historia de Guatemala, and the Société Suisse des Américanistes, as well as editors of the Academic Press, Ltd., and the journal *Archéologia* for their permission to republish photographs which appeared in earlier publications.

This book has been a lengthy and disparate endeavor across three subdisciplines of anthropology: archaeology, physical anthropology, and ethnohistory. For the authors, it has been a group effort in significant ways, but each of us has had to face unique challenges and work with many different individuals. Thus, each of us would like to express our gratitude to those others who have contributed to this work.

My initial work at Iximché was made possible by a Fulbright Fellowship and a faculty appointment during 1986–1987 at the Universidad del Valle in Guatemala City. I thank Marion Popenoe de Hatch, archaeologist and professor at that university, for her encouragement and support. In the early days of the project, when we began the task of rebagging the pottery and other materials excavated from Iximché, we were assisted by friends, family, and students from the Universidad del Valle. We also received a timely grant from the Centro de Investigaciones Regionales de Mesoamérica (CIRMA) which supported the effort.

In 1990, again with Marion's cooperation and assistance, other Universidad del Valle students participated in a joint field school with students from the University of Alabama at Birmingham (UAB). All students spent three weeks washing and cataloguing potsherds from Iximché at a temporary laboratory in Antigua, Guatemala. The field school was supported by a faculty research grant from UAB as well as by a grant from members of the Birmingham community to support student tuition. The students, who performed the tedious work of washing and numbering thousands of potsherds, did so both competently and with good humor. They were Thomas J. Barrientos, Rick E. Bevel, Brian S. Britton, Rachel C. Clark, Edgar F. Godoy Anleu, Maria A. Godoy, Katy Paredes Maury, David P. Port, Mariana C. Sanchez, Cynthia Straight, and Charles G. Weldy. Laboratory space and a small house which became the men's dorm were provided by the Consejo Nacional para la Protección de la Antigua Guatemala, and thanks are due the head of that organization, City Conservator Victor Sandoval. Also, several families in Antigua volunteered to house the women students from Alabama. All of this support in Antigua was arranged by Edna Nuñez de Rodas, formerly director of the Instituto de Antropología e Historia de Guatemala, but at the time of this project the executive director of the Guatemalan office of the Guatemala-Alabama Partners of the Americas. Edna has had a long-standing commitment to Iximché, and without her help at several critical moments over the past 16 years, this study would never have been completed.

Members of the Partners of the Americas organization, based in Alabama and Guatemala, played important roles. Those providing housing to students were affiliated with the Antigua chapter. During most of the summer of 1992, while I studied the ceramics from Iximché in detail, I was hosted by other Partners, Jon and Lorrena Dunn in Guatemala City. In Birmingham, Partner Renata Harder started it all, by writing a letter of introduction for me to her good friend Nelly Guillemin, while another Birmingham Partner, Helen Rivas, assisted in the translation of passages written by Bartolomé de las Casas which are quoted in this volume.

The Instituto de Antropología e Historia de Guatemala was very helpful in providing laboratory space during the summer of 1992 and maintaining liaison with the caretakers of Iximché throughout the project. Thanks especially to Elizabeth Lemus Toledo and Erick Ponciano A., who served in sequence as chiefs of the Department of Prehispanic and Colonial Monuments, and Edgar Vinicio García, regional archaeologist for Chimaltenango.

I am also indebted to Sergio Rodas Manrique for his fine drawings of Iximché potsherds, to archaeologist Fred Bove for providing lab space for Rodas, and to Charles B. Nance and Hans Barnard for other artistic tasks. Thanks also to Jan de Leeuw, who contributed statistical advice and conducted the Correspondence Analysis reported in chapter 7. Marion Hatch and L. H. (Larry) Feldman helped by critically reading portions of my manuscript. I would also like to thank the editors of *Mesoamérica* for permission to republish findings and tables in chapter 8 which appeared earlier in their journal (Nance 1998).

Finally and especially, I am indebted to my wife, Vally. She was involved in this research from the beginning, contributing not only many hours of labor and her good Spanish in Guatemala, but later her sage advice and encouragement, as she read one draft after another of much of this book.

C. Roger Nance

I would like to acknowledge Eugenia Robinson, who opened her home to me in Antigua and helped me gain initial access to collections of human skeletal remains; Edgar Vinicio García, who arranged for me to see skeletons stored at Mixco Viejo and Iximché in 1991 and helped with osteological analysis in 1992; Teresa Robles and Marion Popenoe de Hatch, who helped route documents to the proper people in the Instituto de Antropología e Historia in 1992; Elizabeth Lemus Toledo and

Erick Ponciano A., who granted permission on behalf of the Instituto de Antropología e Historia to carry out skeletal analyses; Donald Ortner, who donated a copy of *Identification of Pathological Conditions in Human Skeletal Remains* for Vinicio García to use; Valerie Haskins, Bradley Adams, Dominic Ebert, Carlos Monzón, Cindy Risley, Hanna Sanders, Pamela Snow, Vicki White, Christine Whittington, and Dan Whittington, who assisted with collecting data in Guatemala as colleagues, students, and volunteers; David Reed, D. Andrew Merriwether, Robert Tykot, and Jason Wilson, who performed specialized analyses of bones and teeth in the U.S.; Laurie Hartzel, Juan Pablo Ruiz, Maricamen Sandweiss, and Daniel Sandweiss, who translated documents and manuscripts from Spanish to English and vice versa; Carolyn Mullinex Tibbetts and Peter Tibbetts, who redrafted some of Guillemin's figures for the book; and Marcella Sorg, who reviewed a draft of chapter 10 and provided expert advice that greatly improved it.

Skeletal analysis at Iximché was funded by grants to me from the Wenner-Gren Foundation for Anthropological Research, Inc.; the Foundation for the Advancement of Mesoamerican Studies, Inc.; and the Faculty Research Fund at the University of Maine. David Reed's analysis of stable isotopes in bone collagen was made possible by funds for equipment provided to Peter Dienes by the National Science Foundation (EAR 85-11549). Robert Tykot's analysis of stable isotopes in tooth enamel was supported by a grant to me from the Foundation for the Advancement of Mesoamerican Studies, Inc.

Stephen Whittington

My research on Cakchiquel ethnohistory was originally supported by a 1982 grant from the Center for International Programs and Studies at the University of Missouri, and was greatly encouraged by Christopher Lutz and William Swezey, co-directors at the time of the Centro de Investigaciones Regionales de Mesoamérica in Antigua, Guatemala. The director and staff of the Archivo General de Central America in Guatemala City enabled me not only to make the best possible use of my research time during 1982, but also to enjoy thoroughly the many hours spent in the archive.

Barbara Borg

1

ᒧᒧᒧᒧᒧ

Introduction

Today the archaeological site of Iximché is a national park and is well known to Guatemalans as the place that gave their country its name. There is no doubt that Iximché, the site, was Iximché, the capital of a powerful Prehispanic state in the central Highlands. There also is no doubt that residents of Iximché were Cakchiquel Maya. Iximché is surrounded by farms and towns of the Cakchiquel and is close to their modern-day center of Tecpán Guatemala (henceforth referred to by its vernacular name, Tecpán). The Cakchiquel have been in this region since before the Conquest. The first dated episode in the region's history was a revolt of the Tukuché, a major branch of the Cakchiquel, against Iximché on May 18, 1493. The event was recorded in the *Annals of the Cakchiquels*, an early Cakchiquel history employing a Long Count calendar similar to that of the Classic Maya (Recinos and Goetz 1953: 31). Later, when the Spanish arrived in Guatemala, Cakchiquel from Iximché joined them in fighting and defeating their traditional enemies, the Quiché, at their capital town of Utatlán. Arriving at Iximché on July 21, 1524, the Spanish then turned on the Cakchiquel, demanding gold from the Iximché kings, Belehé Qat and Cahí Ymox (Recinos and Goetz 1953: 123). The Cakchiquel decline was precipitous. Four days later the Spanish commander Pedro de Alvarado established the first European settlement in Central America at Iximché. Recording the event in a letter to Hernán Cortés in Mexico, he referred to Iximché as Guatemala, employing the Nahua name for the town, Cuauhtemallan (Alvarado 1969: 86). The Cakchiquel abandoned Iximché a month later, and the Spanish left it on September 5, 1524, as warfare began between the Spanish and the Cakchiquel. On February 7, 1526, Iximché was destroyed by fire, burned down by a contingent of deserting Spanish soldiers. The Cakchiquel began to pay tribute to the Spanish *conquistadores* in January of 1528 (Recinos and Goetz 1953: 127), but warfare did not finally cease until 1530 (chap. 2).

The Spanish attempted to establish a more permanent capital at the foot of the volcanic peak Agua in November 1527, but only 14 years later most of this town of Santiago was buried under a mud slide. Today the locality is known as Ciudad Vieja, which is in the vicinity of Antigua (Lutz 1994: 6–7). Iximché was left in ruin, to deteriorate gradually under the impact of weather, hoe cultivation, and the removal of building stone for new construction (Stephens 1969, 2: 153).

The Research

The focus of this study is archaeological excavations carried out at Iximché between 1958 and 1972 by George Guillemin (e.g., Guillemin 1961, 1965a, 1977). Guillemin excavated during eight full field seasons at Iximché and confined his work to the ceremonial/elite precinct of the site. In the process, he cleared or excavated and partially restored structures surrounding four of the principal plazas (fig. 1.1, A–D).

Why have we written a book about Iximché and Guillemin's work there? Many factors contribute to Iximché's stature as a great archaeological landmark. There is the majestic setting in the rugged mountains of the Altiplano, which contrasts with the human scale of the architectural remains: pyramids, ball courts, and platforms carefully laid out around contiguous plazas. There is also the compelling historicity of Iximché. It may be the only Prehispanic site in the New World for which a written history exists, covering events from the founding of the city, through the Conquest, and into early Colonial times. The *Annals of the Cakchiquels* was written by Cakchiquel survivors of the Conquest. Then, there is the devotion to Iximché still held by thousands of contemporary Cakchiquel. Like other Highland Maya, many Cakchiquel are culturally conservative, continuing Prehispanic beliefs and customs to the present day. Their ancestral capital, Iximché, is a kind of cultural hearth stone. On one corner of the site, altars, or religious shrines, are still used for rituals. Cakchiquel from nearby communities frequently visit the park for weekend recreation, and Iximché is an integral part of the modern-day Cakchiquel world.

There were, however, more immediate reasons for undertaking this research. Guillemin dug for years in the ceremonial-political center of the site, generally clearing and restoring entire structures. There is no doubt that visitors to the park of Iximché have benefitted and will continue to benefit from what George Guillemin accomplished. Through his efforts, Guillemin called attention to the site and saved it from further neglect and possibly even complete destruction.

Unfortunately, Guillemin died in 1978 before he could write a planned, comprehensive study of his work. Archaeological excavation itself is by nature a destructive enterprise. After individual rooms, patios, and plazas have been cleared of their contents, they are in most ways stripped of their archaeological value. All that is left is the record of such excavations kept by the archaeologist. Fortunately, Guillemin was trained as an engineer and was an experienced excavator of Mesoamerican sites. He published many of his field observations in articles he wrote on Iximché, yet at his death many more remained unpublished in notes and papers. Some were published in obscure sources, such as a now-defunct Guatemala City newspaper. With access to all of these sources, including many unpublished photographs, we believed it important to make accessible this new or generally unavailable information on the central precinct at Iximché.

Another reason we wrote this book concerns the collections of pottery and human skeletal remains that Guillemin excavated. It was these collections which initially motivated us to undertake this research. When we first observed it in 1985, the entire collection was stored in piles of hundreds of large plastic bags heaped on wooden racks in a shed at the caretaker's house at Iximché. We discovered that many of the thousands of potsherds were from vessels used by Cakchiquel royalty and the religious leadership of Iximché. They had been excavated from the largest palace and what we have interpreted to be the largest religious edifice within the central precinct. Human bone included the remains of two elaborate burials from the central precinct, likely of elite individuals who had lived or worked in these structures. There were also the remains of many sacrificial victims excavated from a plaza adjacent to the palace. These collections were unique and irreplaceable. They could never be replicated through subsequent excavations at Iximché. There is only one central precinct; Guillemin had excavated the two structures and much of the rest of it thoroughly.

Archaeologists base their interpretations not only on field observations but also on systematic assessments of the thousands of excavated potsherds, stone tools, animal and human bones, and other items of refuse picked out of a site's deposits. Although he clearly intended to do so, Guillemin never reached this last level of analysis. It was this problem, then, that moved us to action. Here were archaeological collections which were an essential part of the archaeological heritage of Guatemala, never systematically studied, and in a precarious and deteriorating condition. This book represents our efforts to save essential aspects of these collections in a written and pictorial record. Analyses of these data, reported here, have produced a much altered and more comprehensive view of Iximché and its inhabitants than previously realized.

This research comprises only the second (after the work of John Weeks (1980, 1983)) intensive study of ceramics from a Late Postclassic Highland site (for the period dating between 1250 and 1524 A.D.) and is the first for the Cakchiquel region. Periods of Maya prehistory are delineated in more general accounts such as that by Coe (1999). In abbreviated form, the Preclassic period lasted from 1800 B.C. to 250 A.D.; the Classic from 250 to 925 A.D.; and the Postclassic, altogether, from 925 to 1524 A.D. (Coe 1999: Chronological Table, p. 11). Also, this research provides the first view of a major palace from this epoch and detailed analysis of its ceramic contents. Dealing with smaller collections from many sites, Robert Wauchope (1970), in his pioneering study of Late Postclassic Highland pottery, recorded not only typological affiliations for potsherds, but also detailed attribute data, describing rim form, vessel shape, and other variables. Yet working in the era before computers, he was unable to summarize these data and bring them to bear on problems at hand. The ceramic study reported here breaks new ground for the Guatemalan Highlands: both computerized typological and attribute distributions are employed in efforts to elucidate the functions of key structures at Iximché.

Our analysis of skeletons excavated at Iximché is significant because it is the first published comprehensive osteological study of a large sample with extensive contextual information from a Highland Maya site. It is the first to apply recent developments in stable isotopes to a Highland Maya sample, and one of only a few such applications to any Maya or even non-Maya Mesoamerican sample. As such, it makes accessible important comparative data that will aid researchers in reconstructing diet, disease patterns, and the impact of warfare in Mesoamerica.

Our efforts at Iximché began in 1986, when Roger and Vally Nance, working with volunteers, undertook to salvage Guillemin's collection.

Fourteen to 25 years before, uncatalogued artifacts and bones had been placed in polyethylene bags, and these had become brittle with age. Most of the bags had holes, and a few were badly torn. Provenience labels were found in about half of them. These were small slips of paper or cardboard containing a date and/or brief identification of a particular structure (e.g., "Great Palace II, Patio NE, 15 April 1972"). We placed all material in new polyethylene bags, and, in order to stabilize the collection, we numbered each bag and tied existing proveniences to bag numbers. We found 323 polyethylene bags filled with potsherds and some obsidian artifacts as well as human bones. Vally Nance prepared a catalogue summarizing this information.

The Ceramic Research

The ceramic study commenced during an archaeological field school in 1990 with students from the University of Alabama at Birmingham and Guatemala's Universidad del Valle. Under Roger Nance's direction, 174 bags of pottery containing approximately 45,500 potsherds were processed. All sherds were washed. Of these, 9,508 sherds were catalogued, which included labeling sherds with unique identifying numbers. Bags processed included all of those with some kind of provenience data plus many without. Sherds selected for cataloguing included all rim and decorated sherds plus sherds to some extent diagnostic of vessel shape. After the field school in 1990, Nance sorted the sherds by type. In the summer of 1992, he refined typological assignments, recorded the catalogue number of each sherd by type, and made certain attribute descriptions for each sherd. During 1993, he entered all of these data into the computer to form an SAS data set. (SAS software is a product of the SAS Institute, Inc., of Cary, North Carolina.) The final data set contains information on 9508 sherds.

These ceramic data led to new interpretations of the settlement pattern of the central precinct and the functions of major structures there, pointing to a greater emphasis on the presence and importance of religious leaders at the very center of the Iximché capital. Also as a direct result of this ceramic research the entire layout of the site can now be viewed in terms of a pervasive Maya cosmology, with east the direction of fertility, political ascendancy, and political power, and west the direction of death, religious practitioners, and religious communication with spirits of the deceased. This entire line of thinking would not have developed without recourse to and analysis of the ceramic data set.

Because Guillemin lacked access to systematic data on the pottery and its distribution across the center of Iximché, he based his interpretations of key structures and the elaborate burials he excavated primarily on the ethnohistoric literature. His interpretations, while recognizing the importance of religion and religious behavior in the central precinct, were, nevertheless, generally secular and couched in terms of military and political events and personages. His ideas were reasonable, but in view of the ceramic evidence compiled here, they seem to reflect the biases of the sources he used. In some ways the sources may be misleading. For example, the authors of the *Annals of the Cakchiquels* concentrate on the kings of Iximché and military exploits; they say very little about the priests of Iximché or their role in community life. Neither do they describe day-to-day religious activities of the populace nor any important national ceremony. These writers profess to have been converted to Christianity: "we had lived in utter darkness. No one had preached the word of God to us" (Recinos and Goetz 1953: 135). In reference to their native religion, they wrote of "deceitful idols" (Recinos and Goetz 1953: 49) and worshiping "the devil" (Recinos and Goetz 1953: 82). Likely they either had become devout Christians and looked upon their former religion with abhorrence, or they had decided to misrepresent their true religious feelings. Fear of punishment by Spanish clergy might have led them to produce a less than candid manuscript. Whatever the reason, the subject of their traditional religion was all but ignored.

The *Annals of the Cakchiquels* describes the existence of two co-ruling kings throughout the history of Iximché, and, given his reliance on this source with its inherent difficulties, Guillemin suggests that each of the two largest structures he excavated in the central precinct represented the palace of one of them. However, our detailed typological and attribute analysis of the pottery showed that one of the two may have been a temple or large religious edifice where priests and their assistants might have lived and led Cakchiquels in religious rites. This is a complex issue which is explored throughout this book. The point is that the ceramic research brought an entirely new interpretation or point of view to the archaeology of Iximché. Often in Mesoamerican archaeology ceramic research is limited to chronological concerns. Our research, reported here in chapters 5 to 8, suggests that microceramic assemblages might serve as well to define the functions of various structures, rooms, patios, et cetera, generally present on Mesoamerican sites and that use of the computer allows efficient comparison of ceramic data in this way.

Human Skeletal Remains

The physical anthropology of this project began to develop in 1989 when Stephen Whittington looked to Guatemala as a source of previously unstudied Maya skeletons which might form the basis for a research project. He explored possibilities through the Instituto de Antropología e Historia (IDAEH) and learned of the collection at Iximché in 1991. His initial examination of the Iximché bones indicated that they were remarkably well preserved for the Maya area, and he decided to develop a project focusing on the site. Roger Nance provided an orientation and the catalogue to the reorganized and rebagged collections, and the collaboration of Nance and Whittington, puzzling over field notes, provenience labels, and the totality of the Iximché problem, began at that time.

In 1992, David Reed, then of the Department of Anthropology at the Pennsylvania State University, spent a month with Whittington working on skeletons at a laboratory in Guatemala City. At Penn State, Reed completed the analysis of stable carbon and nitrogen isotopes in bones. Whittington returned for a second month in 1993 with Valerie Haskins, then of the Department of Anthropology at Washington University, and in 1995 for a final six weeks with Bradley Adams, at that time of the Department of Anthropology at the University of Tennessee. Whittington performed the majority of the paleopathological analysis himself with the assistance of these researchers plus students and volunteers. Robert Tykot of the Department of Anthropology at the University of South Florida completed analysis of stable carbon isotopes in teeth in 1999. D. Andrew Merriwether and David Reed of the University of Michigan have undertaken the analysis of mitochondrial DNA in teeth, but their results are not yet available.

The task of studying Iximché bones was much larger than it had originally appeared in 1991. The soil adhering to many artifacts and human skeletons had never been removed. As noted above, bags had broken open, some materials from various contexts must have been mixed together, and tags with provenience information had rotted away or become separated from their bags. Crania which had once been carefully numbered with red water-soluble ink were now marked with pink blotches. Provenience tags did not belong to the crania with which they were found. Numbered bags of postcranial bones were random mixtures of remains from many people. Formerly complete crania had become smashed, with the pieces spread through as many as five apparently unrelated bags.

Many long days spent trying to fit small pieces of bone together led to the creation of larger agglomerations of bones and to the reconstitution of some skulls and even entire skeletons. A few accurate bits of provenience data which remained, as well as clear excavation photos by Guillemin, ultimately allowed an understanding of the context and characteristics of a subset of the entire sample.

Although these problems limited our research, the Iximché findings are still of value, especially for a region so poorly understood. Highland sites are underrepresented in comparison to Lowland sites in the number and scale of published studies of Maya skeletal samples (Danforth et al. 1997). Only osteological studies of 65 skeletons from Mixco (or Jilotepeque) Viejo (Gervais and Ichon 1990), described alternatively as the Pokomam capital (Lehmann 1968) or as an Akajal (Eastern Cakchiquel) settlement (Fox 1978), and more than 250 skeletons from the Mam capital of Zaculeu (Goff 1953b; Stewart 1953) involve samples as large as and consider almost as many varieties of data as does this study of Iximché skeletons. For both Zaculeu and Mixco Viejo, however, data are presented in a way that makes it difficult or impossible to determine frequencies of skeletal indicators of diet, disease, trauma, and cultural modification. Further, neither study involves analyses based on recent advances in stable isotopes, as this Iximché study does. The only other stable isotope analyses based on a Highland sample are recent studies of teeth from Kaminaljuyú (Wright and Schwarcz 1998, 1999). Results of stable isotope analyses have been published for only a dozen Lowland sites and understanding of intersite variation is still very preliminary.

Chapter 10 contains what Whittington and his colleagues have been able to learn about the people buried at Iximché, who they were, what they ate, how they fought, and how they died.

Ethnohistory

By 1997 analysis of material remains from Iximché was essentially complete, but interpretations often involved the ethnohistorical literature for Highland Guatemala with all of its attendant difficulties. Also,

Iximché is a protohistoric site, and a broad picture of its role in the sociopolitical history of the Highlands immediately before the Conquest was clearly needed. This would provide context for the archaeology of the site; it also was an important component of the Iximché story in its own right. Consequently, Barbara Borg's assistance was sought, and she agreed to collaborate as the project ethnohistorian. The ethnohistorical sketch which she wrote (chap. 2) is the first English language synthesis of regional Cakchiquel "history," and it helps place the city of Iximché into a larger context.

As a doctoral student, Borg had become a research associate of the Centro de Investigaciones Regionales de Mesoamérica (CIRMA) in Antigua, Guatemala, shortly after its inception. In consultation with historian Christopher H. Lutz and archaeologist William R. Swezey (then CIRMA's co-directors), Borg mapped out a dissertation proposal for the ethnohistorical study of an area not far from Iximché and within the Cakchiquel region. Emphasis was placed on the native Cakchiquel people known as the Chajomá, who have occupied the Sacatepéquez region near the Spanish Colonial capital (at or near Antigua) from at least the late protohistoric period, through the Colonial period, and into the present. The dissertation thus included the lands of the towns of San Juan and San Pedro Sacatepéquez and their Colonial period dependencies, San Raimundo de las Casillas and Santo Domingo Xenacoj, respectively. As much as was possible, Borg's study was a diachronic one, beginning about a century before and extending approximately two centuries after the Spanish Conquest. As part of this study, she compiled a body of material which shed light upon the protohistoric relationships between the Chajomá and other nearby branches of the Cakchiquels—especially those from Iximché, who a few years before the Spanish Conquest had completed military subjugation of the entire Cakchiquel region. This earlier research served Borg well as she developed the historic sketch of the Iximché Cakchiquel included here.

Although Borg views Iximché and Cakchiquel society through time, a different approach to the ethnohistorical literature is presented in chapter 3. Here Cakchiquel customs and institutions are viewed synchronically, as they might have existed at the beginning of the sixteenth century. Also, the perspective taken, to a large extent, is archaeological. What aspects of the archaeological record can be explained in terms of the early ethnohistoric sources? Conversely, how might archaeological research elucidate enigmas or gaps in the ethnohistorical literature?

Ultimately, the archaeological and ethnohistorical records for Iximché each provide highly limited views of the community which existed there. Yet, when considered together each account enhances the value of the other. The strengths and weaknesses of each form of narrative become more apparent in light of the other, and the reader is left with a more reasonable assessment. As will become clear below, the account by the sixteenth-century chronicler Bartolomé de Las Casas of human sacrifice in the Highlands is supported through archaeological research at Iximché in very specific ways. At the same time, the archaeological record is mute concerning the elaborate ceremonialism surrounding these events, while it is well-described in the Las Casas narrative.

Limitations to the Research

It is important at the outset to specify the limitations inherent in the collections and related documents generated by Guillemin, and the impact these had on our research. We did not study stone artifacts, and they are not included here, except for a few specimens mentioned in Guillemin's reports and field notes. Obsidian blades were generally absent from the large bags of potsherds, and it seems their proveniences were not recorded systematically by the excavators. In one instance, hundreds of blades were stored in a single large bag. Because of this, the research value of the limited number collected for which there are proveniences seemed minimal. Some large stone artifacts were found in the store room, but they were without proveniences of any kind and even accepting them as from Iximché was judged problematical.

For the ceramics, it is important to understand that this study *covers all bags of pottery for which there are provenience data* as well as a good portion of pottery from bags without provenience labels. The only structures with statistically adequate samples of potsherds are Great Palace I and Great Palace II. Great Palace I sherds are considered together, and Great Palace II sherds are reported by patio within the larger structure. All of this is because of the condition of the collection and the content of the labels we did find. In other words, there is no way to return to the potsherds or documents and glean more refined information on original proveniences.

Unlike some archaeologists excavating Lowland Maya sites during the 1950s to 1970s, Guillemin seems to have had an intuitive understanding of the value of human remains for interpreting the past, and he carefully excavated and stored almost all of them. In retrospect, however, his decisions about recording burial information, marking bones, and storing materials from burials were not always up to today's professional standards. His notes were very brief and sometimes cryptic, his photographs were not always marked with identification numbers of the burials they depict, and he made very few drawings. This has resulted in the irretrievable loss of much information in the years between excavation and the present analysis.

It is important to realize, then, that this has been a salvage project; the data described here certainly have their limitations. In some ways, Guillemin was not an exacting field archaeologist. His field notes are brief, usually three to five written lines a day in a small notebook. He did not excavate trenches or other delineated units, or at least no record was found that he did so. He produced several stratigraphic drawings of structures showing different construction phases, but none survives of excavation unit side walls. Virtually none of the provenience descriptions contains information on depth or structural phases; that is, potential evidence for culture change appears to be lacking. Also, we are told very little regarding the immediate context of recovered artifacts, whether they came from midden or structural fill, for example. Finally, the documentation which Guillemin did produce regarding the archaeology of Iximché is incomplete. Mrs. Nelly Guillemin, Guillemin's widow, lent the authors all extant documents, drawings, and photographs, but some had been lost, including most of the important 1972 (daily) field notes of excavations at Great Palace II. This problem further limited the usefulness of the collection. For example, some provenience labels simply gave a date in 1972, presumably the date of excavation, but without dated field notes proveniences for these bags were lost.

On the other hand, Guillemin made meticulous maps and drawings of the restored structure bases. He was dedicated to the archaeology and restoration of Iximché, and the status of Iximché as a national park today owes much to his perseverance. Moreover, the absence of provenience labels from approximately half the bags must be because they disintegrated, given the deteriorated state of labels we did find. In short, distributional trends across the site which did survive in the ceramic data and extant documentation concerning burials from Iximché are certainly the result of the considerable efforts of George Guillemin.

Early Observations and Research on Iximché

In several publications, Guillemin (1965a, b; 1977) cogently summarized early research and references regarding Iximché. Of foremost importance is the *Annals of the Cakchiquels* (Recinos and Goetz 1953), written in the sixteenth century by two Cakchiquel survivors of the Conquest. As mentioned above, this is literally a history of the city from its founding (ca. A.D. 1460–1470; chap. 2), through the Conquest, and into early Colonial times. Its emphasis is on military history and the succession of Iximché kings.

Not only did Pedro de Alvarado write to Hernán Cortés from Iximché in 1524, but Bernal Díaz del Castillo, the famed chronicler of the Conquest of Mexico, visited the city of "old Guatimala" in 1526, where "the natives had assembled to give us a hostile reception, but we drove them away before us and took possession of their magnificent buildings and quadrangles, for the night" (Díaz 1927: 491; cf. Carmack 1973: 93).

Francisco Antonio de Fuentes y Guzmán (Sáenz de Santa María 1969, 1: 333-335) described the ruins of Iximché at the end of the seventeenth century and also produced a stylized map of the site (see map 11.1). Both are important to understanding Iximché and are discussed in chapter 11. Stephens and Catherwood (Stephens 1969, 2: 147–153) visited both Tecpán and Iximché in 1840. A moat which Fuentes y Guzmán had described as dividing Iximché (see chap. 4) was still three yards deep when observed by Stephens. Stephens wrote that on every Good Friday, the Cakchiquel inhabitants of Tecpán walked in procession to Iximché, certainly an indication of the region's strong cultural continuity. As mentioned above, the Cakchiquel regard Iximché as their preeminent historic landmark (Schele and Mathews 1998: 311–317).

The first accurate map of the ruins and vicinity of Iximché was drawn by Miguel Rivera y Maestre in 1834 (map 1.1). The map, as copied by Gavarette, delimits the perimeter of the level ground at Iximché as set off by surrounding gorges and depicts gullying caused by run-off from both ends of the moat (cf. Guillemin's maps, 1959; 1965a: 13; 1967: 26). The four plazas aligned from northwest to southeast in Rivera's map are probably Guillemin's Plazas A, B, C, and Placita C.

If so, the blackened square in the southeastern quadrant would be Great Palace II, still visible in 1834 but, by the 1950s, leveled and buried under the continuous onslaught of hoe cultivation (see chap. 4 for discussion of these features). A later nineteenth-century map by Alfred P. Maudslay (1889–1902: vol. 2, plate 73) shows the six largest pyramids at Iximché (Guillemin's Structures 1–6; see fig. 1.1) and the two ball courts (Structures 7 and 8) but not Great Palace II.

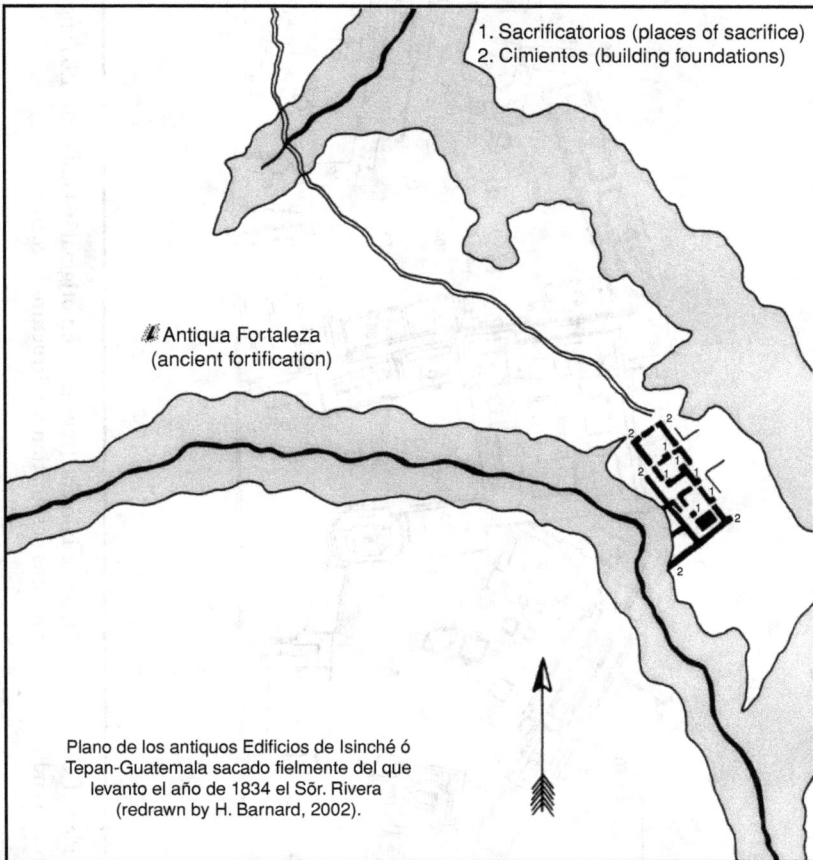

Within the map:
1. Sacrificatorios (places of sacrifice)
2. Cimientos (building foundations)

Antiqua Fortaleza (ancient fortification)

Plano de los antiquos Edificios de Isinché ó Tepan-Guatemala sacado fielmente del que levanto el año de 1834 el Sōr. Rivera (redrawn by H. Barnard, 2002).

Map 1.1. 1834 map of Iximché by Rivera y Maestre (copied as an inset in a map of Guatemala by Juan de Gavarrete dated 1846; original at the Bancroft Library, University of California, Berkeley)

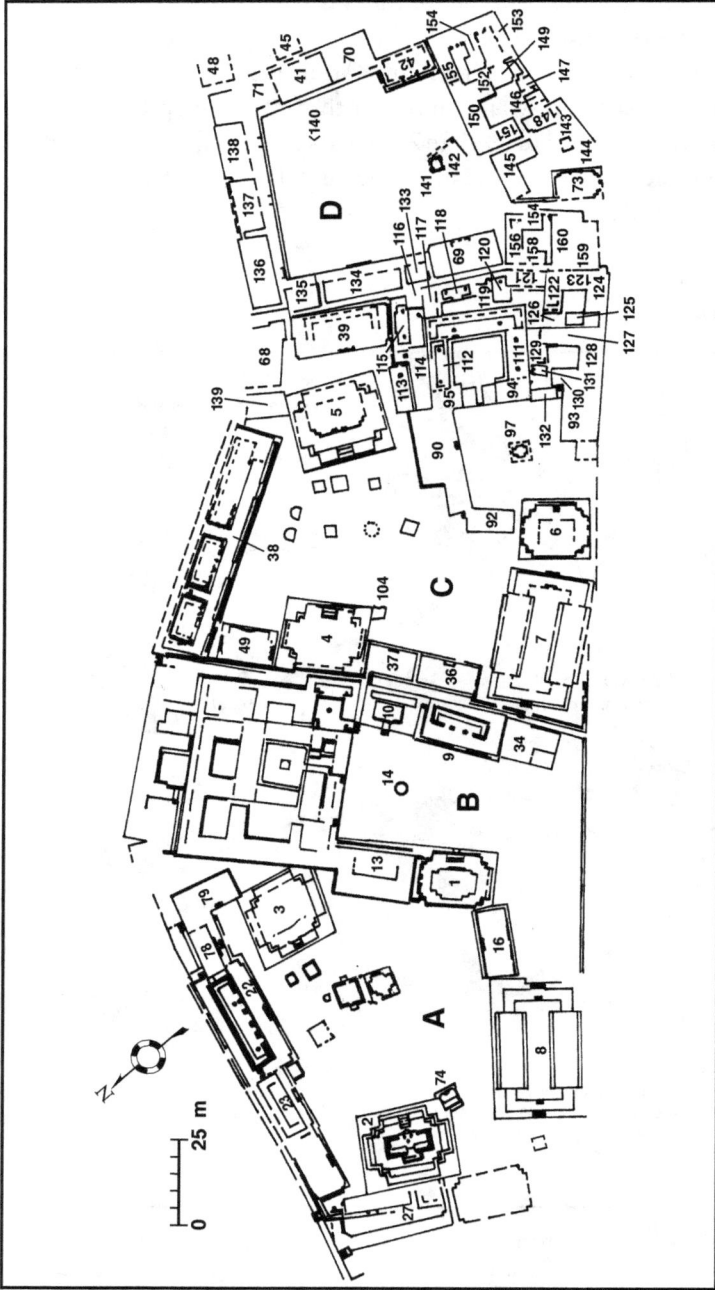

Fig. 1.1. Plan of Ceremonial Center of Iximché (revised from original in Guillemin 1977: fig. 3; modifications: designations for Structures 78 and 79 added; erroneous designation for Structure 13 corrected.)

The only archaeological field work at Iximché other than Guillemin's was by Janos de Szecsy in 1956, but this was never published because of his sudden death (Guillemin 1959: 22–23).

Environment and Ecology of Iximché

Iximché is located in the Department of Chimaltenango, close to the Pan American highway, and about 2.5 km south of the town of Tecpán. It is quite near the continental divide (McBryde 1947: map 5); its closest stream, forming the northeastern boundary of the site, drains into the Pacific. The site is situated on a promontory set off by two deep canyons; to the northeast, the valley of the Río Tzaragmajya, and to the southwest, an unnamed tributary canyon occupied by an intermittent stream. Topographic relief is pronounced with the site elevated approximately 80 m above the two canyon floors. The flat living surface of Iximché is between 2240 m and 2260 m above sea level ("Sololá," Instituto Geográfico Nacional, 1959, Scale 1:50,000). The climate in the vicinity of Iximché is classified as Mesothermal with dry winters ("Cwg" according to the Köppen classification) by McBryde (1947: map 6), and the natural vegetation is categorized as oak-pine forest, shifting to pine and bunch grass at higher elevations (McBryde 1947: map 7). Physiographically, the region is in the Chiapas-Northern Central American Highlands (West 1964: fig. 3).

Although susceptible to occasional killing frosts and crop failure (Recinos and Goetz 1953: 101; Fox 1987: 186), this area is especially suited for the production of maize, with maize surpluses routinely exported to other regions of Guatemala (McBryde 1947: 75, 125). Feldman (1985: 31) noted that control of this area with its agricultural abundance might have been key to the political ascendancy of Iximché. With easy access to population centers in the broad Chimaltenango uplands as well as the Lake Atitlán basin to the west, Iximché also was well situated to be a regional market. Feldman (1985: 31) reported that there was a "large district market" at Iximché or Tecpán in the sixteenth century, a market which evidently has persisted to the present (cf. McBryde 1947: map 19).

There are other important resources in the vicinity of Tecpán/Iximché which have contributed to the local economy. Lime is widely used to convert dried maize to *masa*, the basic food staple of the Highlands. It also has been and continues to be used widely in building construction, both in mortar and plaster, and was so employed extensively at Iximché (see chap. 4). In the Highlands, where soils and rock are generally volcanic, there are just six lime-producing centers, and one of these is at Santa Apolonia, only 3.5 km northwest of Tecpán (McBryde 1947: 73). Another mineral resource in relatively short supply is clay for making pottery. Santa Apolonia also provided the only important source for pottery clay in the entire region encompassing Lake Atitlán and uplands to the east (McBryde 1947: map 15). Pottery production may have a long history in the Tecpán area, extending at least back to the occupation of Iximché; Reina and Hill (1978) studied the contemporary industry.

2

⊓⊔⊓⊔⊓⊔

Iximché and the Cakchiquels, ca. 1450–1540

An Ethnohistorical Perspective

Archaeological work in the Central Guatemalan Highlands has, until very recently, concentrated on the excavation of major sites or "cities," regional centers like Quiché Utatlán and Cakchiquel Iximché. Systematic archaeological settlement pattern surveys, similar to those carried out decades ago in the Basin of Mexico, have been completed in only some portions of the Central Guatemalan Highlands. Despite the continuing work of many dedicated scholars, much basic archaeological work remains to be completed in the Cakchiquel region. Fortunately, there is a long tradition of ethnohistorical scholarship in Guatemalan studies, which both complements the expanding archaeological record and acts as an independent source of data against which to compare archaeological results.

Ethnohistory has contributed substantially to our understanding of Prehispanic events in the protohistoric period. The documentary sources are rich and varied for Highland Guatemala and include, for example, native chronicles written soon after the Conquest such as the *Annals of the Cakchiquels* and the *Popol Vuh* (the Quiché Maya creation epic); the writings of the first Spanish conquerors, priests, and settlers; early Colonial census documents, maps, and wills; surveyors' maps and notes; and lengthy court cases, which sometimes continued for decades and which often included the testimony of native informants.

The history of Maya scholarship has shown that no center can be understood without reference to its resident urban population, its own rural hinterland, and other neighboring groups. Fortunately, ethnohistory has helped to clarify our understanding of the establishment of Iximché, its relationships to other Cakchiquel and to other ethnolinguistic groups, its military activity before Spanish Contact, and its role in early Colonial history during the first 20 years after the Spanish Conquest of the Quiché Maya (summarized in table 2.1).

The Cakchiquels and the Quichean Confederation, ca. 1450

The Cakchiquel Maya, who built and resided in the city of Iximché, shared with other Highland Maya groups both a two-thousand-year-

Table 2.1. Cakchiquel Chronology

1540s–1550s	Spanish congregate dispersed Cakchiquel communities into towns on the Spanish model. Many Cakchiquel flee to remote areas toward the Motagua River and the vicinity of Mixco Viejo [Jilotepeque Viejo].
1540	The imprisoned Iximché Cakchiquel kings are hanged by the Spanish, because Spanish settlers fear additional native uprisings.
1530s	Cakchiquel revolts against the Spanish continue, at least until 1535 when the last two Iximché Cakchiquel kings are imprisoned. Revolts in outlying areas such as Sacatepéquez may continue after 1535.
Aug. 1524–1530	Iximché Cakchiquels rise in revolt against the cruelty of Alvarado shortly after initially seeking an alliance with him.
Feb. 1524	The Spanish conquer the Quiché Maya. Cakchiquels allow peaceful entry of the Spanish, hoping to enlist them as allies to subdue their traditional enemies.
1523	After the Spanish conquest of Mexico, but before Alvarado's arrival in Guatemala, the Cakchiquel rulers of Iximché-Tzololá send peace envoys to Cortés in Mexico.
1517–1524	Iximché forces finally conquer the rebellious Chajomá Cakchiquel of the Sacatepéquez region. Some Sacatepéquez leaders may be Tukuchés who escaped from Iximché after the unsuccessful 1493 internal revolt.
1517	Iximché conquers the neighboring Cakchiquel center of Tzololá, and the second-ranking ruler of Iximché is sent there as military governor. Military expansion continues toward the Pacific Coast. Ultimately, Iximché forces press from the west and south toward Sacatepéquez.

old cultural tradition stretching back to the Maya Preclassic and more recent "Mexicanizing" influences which political realignments, and possibly even population movements, brought to the entire Maya region after the decline of Classic Maya civilization. The Quichés and Cakchiquels were two of several aggressive ethnolinguistic groups in Highland Guatemala vying for military and cultural ascendancy during the latter centuries of Maya cultural evolution normally referred to as the Late Postclassic period (ca. A.D. 1200–1500).

Between ca. 1350 and 1450 the militaristic Quiché Maya extended their control over much of the Central Guatemalan Highlands, incorporating such neighboring groups as the Rabinal, Mam, Tzutujil, and Cakchiquel, at least some of which they subjected to military control and tribute obligations. Quiché elites traced their descent from Tollan, a mythical place which may also have been an historical place or places at

Table 2.1. Cakchiquel Chronology (*continued*)

May 18 or 20, 1493	The Tukuché branch of the Cakchiquel instigate an unsuccessful internal revolt at Iximché which began as a dispute over land. The event was considered so important that Cakchiquel history, as recorded in the *Annals of the Cakchiquels*, is calculated forward from this date.
ca. 1475–1524	Warfare is continuous between Iximché Cakchiquels and the Quichés. Several attempts by the Quichés to conquer the Iximché fail. Finally the Cakchiquel defeat the Quichés (about 1491) and force them to pay tribute.
ca. 1475?	The Iximché Cakchiquel conquer the Chajomá Cakchiquel of the Jilotepeque region, probably because of important obsidian mines located there, and retain control of this region until the Spanish conquest. Other Chajomás move south into Sacatepéquez and remain independent.
ca. 1475	The Quiché ruler Quicab, who had been a strong ally of the Iximché Cakchiquels, dies. As a result of this event, or possibly even before, other Cakchiquel living near Joyabaj and Zacualpa begin to move south into the Jilotepeque region.
ca. 1463–1470	The Cakchiquel abandon the Quiché confederation on the advice of Quicab, and found their own capital at Iximché. They remain at peace with the Quichés while king Quicab, their mentor and ally, lives.
ca. A.D. 1425–1475	The Quiché kingdom reaches its maximum expansion with the help of at least one group of Cakchiquel confederates, a subordinate but talented warrior cadre, who live at Chiavar near present-day Chichicastenango.

various times in prehistory. Classic Teotihuacán and Postclassic Tula of the Toltecs in Central Mexico, Postclassic Chichén Itzá in northern Yucatán, and others have all been mentioned as possible "Tollans" (great cities) (Schele and Mathews 1998: 200–201, 284). Sharer (1994: 424, 431) suggests that the Tollan described in the Quiché *Popol Vuh*, the "homeland" to which three Quiché princes traveled to receive their authority to rule, was possibly Chichén Itzá, a city far to the north but known to the Quichés within their larger Maya world.

One major group of Cakchiquels originally resided in the vicinity of the modern towns of Zacualpa and Joyabaj north of the Motagua River (Carmack 1979; Borg 1986: 12). Another branch of the Cakchiquel, mentioned by Carmack (1979), those who apparently built and inhabited Iximché, may have come from a region farther west near present-day Chichicastenango. Recruited or conquered by the Quichés sometime before about 1460, the Cakchiquels have been described as a "subordinate cadre" of warriors who comprised one of two lower ranking divisions in a confederacy formed by the Quichés, which included the Tzutujils, Rabinals, and Cakchiquels (Carmack 1981: 72). As part of this alliance the Cakchiquel lived northwest of their later capital of Iximché, at a place called Chiavar near to or synonymous with the town of Chuilá, now called Chichicastenango (Recinos and Goetz 1953: 91; Carmack 1981: 68, 72; see map 2.1 for key localities). During the reigns of the Quiché kings Gucumatz (ca. 1400–1425) and Quicab (ca. 1425–1475) the Cakchiquel distinguished themselves as fearless warriors, and with their assistance the Quiché kingdom reached its maximum expansion (Carmack 1981: 122, 134).

The Founding of Iximché, ca. 1465

The previously intertwined Cakchiquel and Quiché histories began to diverge shortly before 1470 during a period of growing tensions between the Quiché ruler Quicab and an opposing faction led by two of his sons. Resentment against the elevated status Quicab awarded the four Cakchiquel warrior kings, Huntoh and Vukubatz and the lower ranked Chuluc and Xitamal Queh, led some Quiché nobles to pressure Quicab to have them killed. Instead, Quicab warned his loyal Cakchiquel confederates to leave Utatlán immediately and advised them to establish an independent capital some distance away at the site of Iximché ("ramon tree" or "tree of corn") on the mountain called Ratzamut

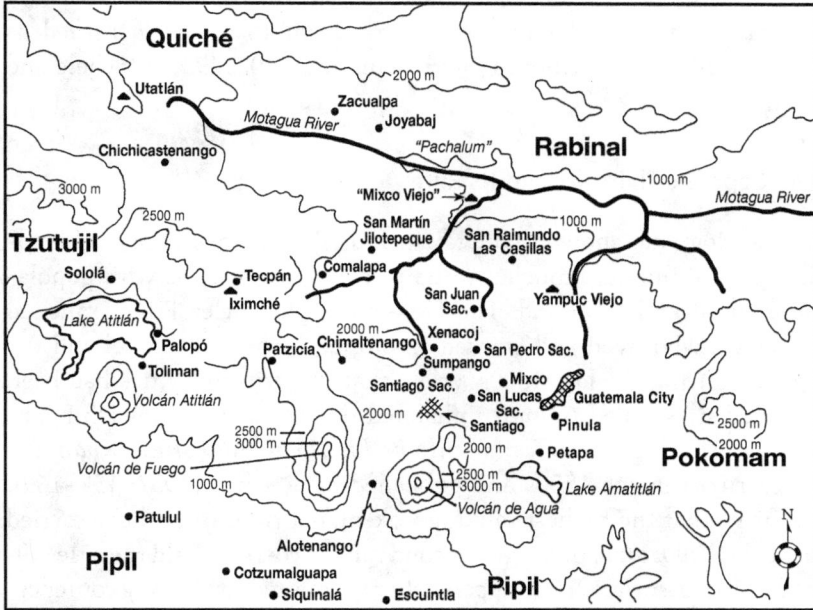

Map 2.1. Map of Cakchiquel Region Surrounded by Other Late Postclassic Ethnolinguistic Groups

(Recinos and Goetz 1953: 94–100). This founding probably occurred about 1463 (Wauchope 1949: 19) or 1470 (Carmack 1981: 136).

The Cakchiquel remained at peace with the Quichés because of their loyalty to Quicab until his death in 1475, but then entered into continuous warfare with their former allies. The Quiché made several attempts to attack Iximché but were never successful (Carmack 1981: 137–138). One particular "destruction of the Quichés," which occurred about 1491, according to the *Annals of the Cakchiquels,* resulted in the Quichés being forced to pay tribute to Iximché (Recinos and Goetz 1953: 103–104). As among the Quiché, internal squabbles and power struggles also plagued the rulers of Iximché who attempted to control an area already inhabited by rival Cakchiquel groups (Swezey 1998: 24-25). In May 1493, within 30 years of the city's establishment and during a period of military expansion, an internal revolt broke out against Iximché's ruling elite over a land dispute between the Akajal and the Tukuché clans. Although the offending Tukuchés were vanquished and the survivors fled Iximché, the incident was considered so significant that for more than 100 years Cakchiquel history, as recounted in the

Annals of the Cakchiquels, was dated from that day, identified as May 18, 1493, by Recinos (1950: 35) and May 20, 1493, by Schele and Mathews (1998: 297).

The Capital of Iximché and Its Elite

Archaeology has shown that Utatlán and other towns in the Highlands such as Cakchiquel Iximché were nucleated urban areas with populations of several thousand. The Dominican chronicler Friar Francisco Ximénez, who lived and worked among both the Cakchiquel and the Quiché during the late 1600s, wrote that the principal cities had been fortified sites called *tinamit,* inhabited by rulers and elites (Ximénez 1929-1931, 1: 75). The *Testamento de los Xpantzay (Título Xpantzay III),* written in the 1550s and published by Recinos (1957: 151–169), confirms that the highest ranking Cakchiquel ruler of Iximché carried the title *Ahpozotzil,* or king. A second ranked co-ruler held the title *Ahpoxahil,* or associate. They apparently represented two strong confederated lineages at Iximché, the Zotzils and the Xahils. Upon the death of a king, the oldest son assumed the title of Ahpozotzil, and the younger son was made Ahpoxahil. Many authors, including Wauchope (1949), have recognized that such a system of dual kingship was characteristic of both the Quichés and the Cakchiquels.

This may have been the ideal, but Wauchope (1949: 16) demonstrated that succession was more flexible, not always passing from father to son. Succession could pass instead to the most qualified royal individual of the appropriate age or generation. An advisory council may have chosen from among several eligible candidates, given the realities of death in war or from disease and that a candidate might be too young or otherwise unsuitable to rule. Indeed, the *Annals of the Cakchiquels* refers to such a procedure in the naming of the last Cakchiquel kings. By this time, however, any normal pattern of succession would have been disrupted, as the last kings were named subsequent to the plague of 1520–1521 which killed many Cakchiquel (Recinos and Goetz 1953: 115–117). On some occasions, or perhaps routinely, the co-ruler, or Ahpoxahil, was designated military ruler of a conquered city (Swezey 1985: 161).

Ximénez also wrote that the position of supreme ruler was viewed as hereditary although the ruler was not all-powerful. His power was balanced by a council of principal lords (probably the heads of confederated lineages) who, acting in concert, could even remove an unacceptable or ineffective king. Among the neighboring Quiché there were 24 such lords who were the most eminent in the domain and who counseled the king on all matters. The Quiché realm was divided among these 24, and each was recognized as lord by all the towns in his district (Ximénez 1929–1931, 1: 103). It is possible that the Iximché Cakchiquels employed a similar administrative structure.

There were also two additional Cakchiquel rulers, the *Ahpotukuché* and the *Ahporaxonihay,* who had considerably less power than the Ahpozotzil and the Ahpoxahil (Recinos 1957: 155–57). They are referred to in the *Annals* and in works describing the Cakchiquel during the Spanish Conquest (Recinos and Goetz 1953: 100; Polo 1977: 36–37). The *Guerras comunes de Quichés y Cakchiqueles (Título Xpantzay II),* written in 1554 (Recinos 1957: 149), refers to four divisions of the Cakchiquel—Zotzils, Cakchiquels, Tukuchés, and Akajals—with which these four ruling titles may correlate. It is impossible to ascertain whether these four divisions, which probably represent confederated lineages, were ever voluntarily unified, especially if they also represent, in part, geographical entities. The *Annals* describes different Cakchiquel groups as allies in some years, enemies in others. Alliances between and among factions appear to have been brittle, engaged in for military advantage, and often short-lived. The Zotzil and Cakchiquel lineages were resident at Iximché, as were apparently at least some of the Akajals and Tukuchés until the great internal revolt of 1493. The Ahpotukuché originally represented those Tukuchés defeated and expelled from Iximché during that incident, whereas the Ahporaxonihay may have headed the Akajals. Other Akajals (who called themselves the Chajomá) also inhabited the region east of Iximché near present-day San Martín Jilotepeque (Recinos and Goetz 1953: 89–90; Recinos 1957: 155–157; Polo 1977: 36–37; Carmack 1979: 140). Apparently, Iximché took control of the Jilotepeque region fairly early; thus, it would seem reasonable that the Akajals would be represented by their elites at Iximché.

Carmack described the Cakchiquels as a group which claimed superiority not so much through their "Toltec" ancestry, which was in any case indirectly derived through their former Quiché overlords, but because of the very military prowess which had made them invaluable as a warrior cadre to the Quiché kings. Carmack (1981: 378–379) noted, however, some fundamental differences between the Quichés and the

Cakchiquels. Cakchiquel rule by lineage confederation and military prowess was probably much simpler than the centralized bureaucracy at Utatlán. Because the relationship between lords and warriors at Iximché was closer, there may have been less formal stratification, with a smaller ruling hierarchy sharing power with the heads of the confederated lineages (especially the Xahils and the Zotzils). The sun cult of the Quichés was much less important to the Cakchiquel than earth deities, "such as the Cakix family (mountains, earthquakes) and the serpent (the plains)" (Carmack 1981: 378–379). The Cakchiquel were a more secular society than the Quiché. Their history included more references to actual events (such as natural disasters) and absolute dates derived from their own Long Count calendar system. Polo (1977: 37–38) adds that, in addition to the higher nobility or ruling class, Cakchiquel society was further divided into the lesser nobility (comprised of the most distinguished families from whom provincial governors, ambassadors, and tribute collectors were chosen), commoners, and slaves. Nonelites and slaves, as well as elites, would have resided at Iximché as they did at other Maya centers.

The Rural Hinterland Surrounding Iximché

The city of Iximché and its surrounding rural hinterland depended upon a subsistence base of Highland dry farming of maize and other typical crops to which were added Lowland coastal products. Living at an elevation 300 m higher than Quiché Utatlán made agriculture more risky for the Iximché Cakchiquel, who were plagued by early frosts and generally less stable agricultural conditions. Outside of the major centers the rest of the Cakchiquel population lived in a dispersed settlement pattern in the surrounding hills and on the plains where they could cultivate their fields. According to the chronicler Ximénez (1929–1931, 1: 130), each family group lived in an area which was more or less extended, depending upon whether the group was large or small. The population was called an *amac*, which was a small town or *aldea* stretched out like the legs of a spider, from whence the name derived.

A principal lord functioned as the head of each town or community and governed with the advice of the other household heads, in a manner similar to the Central Mexican *calpulli*, but called a *chinamit* in the Guatemalan Highlands. If the town paid tribute (or taxes), the household heads collected from each family what was due and presented the total to their lord. He, in turn, remitted the payment to his principal lord who delivered it to the supreme ruler. In cases of offenses, delinquencies, or crimes the *chinamit* heads heard the cases, rendered judgments, and decreed punishments. A high-ranking member from the *chinamit* of an accused person was summoned to act as his defending counsel. Ximénez (1929–1931, 1: 104) was impressed with the fairness of this indigenous legal system through which poor and rich alike could seek justice and which survived into the Colonial period.

Hostile Cakchiquel Populations Resistant to Iximché Control

Tzololá

The Cakchiquel were not unified but were divided into four separate geographical branches, located at or near Iximché, Tzololá, San Martín Jilotepeque, and San Juan Sacatepéquez. Employing primarily documentary rather than archaeological evidence, William Swezey (1985: 155–168) identified the archaeological site of Cakhay, halfway between Patzícia and Tecpán Guatemala (Iximché) in Chimaltenango department, as the probable site of Prehispanic Tzololá, a town mentioned twice in the *Annals of the Cakchiquels*, once as Cakhay and once as Oronic Cakhay. Later archaeological research demonstrated that this site dated instead to the Classic period, and therefore could not have been the Late Postclassic center of Cakhay/Tzololá (Swezey 1998: 7).

Nevertheless, the late-seventeenth-century writings of the chronicler Friar Francisco Vásquez, which Swezey employed, describe Tzololá as a Cakchiquel kingdom which had developed apart from and in opposition to other Cakchiquel and Quiché groups. Tzololá was conquered by Iximché in 1517 during a period when the Cakchiquel were engaged in continuous warfare with the Quichés to the north, while also attempting to gain control of the rich cacao fields along the Pacific coast in the south. The conquered city of Tzololá was ruled by the second ranking Cakchiquel king (the Ahpoxahil), brother of the principal Cakchiquel ruler (the Ahpozotzil) of Iximché. Evidently, Iximché controlled Tzololá for a number of years because around 1523, after the Conquest of Mexico but before the invasion of Guatemala by Alvarado, the governing brothers of Iximché and Tzololá sent ambassadors to Cortés, offering peace and obedience to Carlos V in exchange for assistance in defeating their enemies, the Quichés (Vásquez 1937–1944, 1: 111). By 1524 the Iximché-Tzololá coalition controlled the lands of Siquinalá, Cotzumalguapa, and Patulul on the Pacific coast and had established settlements in the Escuintla area (Swezey 1985: 154, 160–161).

The Chajomá Cakchiquel of Jilotepeque

If Iximché and Tzololá were Cakchiquel centers at least potentially hostile toward each other, the third and fourth branches of the protohistoric Cakchiquel began as a single population, according to their oral histories. These were Cakchiquel people called Akajal Winak, or simply Akajals, by the Iximché Cakchiquel, but their name for themselves was Chajomá. According to the Cakchiquel origin myth, recounted in the *Annals*, a man called "Chahóm Ahau" was the head of one of the original four branches, or tribes, of the Cakchiquel who went to "Tulán" (Recinos and Goetz 1953: 44–45). "Chahóm" usually is translated as "the burning of the brush, or clearing," referring to clearing the land for planting (Recinos and Goetz 1953: 67).

A native account from 1576, included in a later Colonial land dispute case, stated that the Chajomás came from the area north of the Motagua River near the modern towns of Zacualpa and Joyabaj in the department of El Quiché (Borg 1986: 12). Robert Carmack's (1979) study of land documents and censuses has traced the movements of the Chajomás from Joyabaj, where they at one time had been the subjects of the Quichés and Rabinals, to the region surrounding the modern town of San Martín Jilotepeque. Carmack (1979) also presents a convincing argument that the well-known archaeological site called Mixco Viejo, located northeast of San Martín Jilotepeque just south of the Motagua River and directly on this migration route, is instead Jilotepeque Viejo, a Prehispanic Cakchiquel fortress of the Chajomá. Feldman (1981: 7), however, disagrees.

Robert Carmack's (1979: 139) study of a 1555 land title known as the *Título Chahomá*—or in the published version *Trasunto de un Título de los del Pueblo de San Martín Xilotepeque* (Crespo 1956)—from the community of San Martín Jilotepeque discusses six "Sacatepéquez," or Chajomá, Spanish-congregated towns. These are San Martín Jilotepeque itself, and five others to the south and southeast (San Juan Sacatepéquez, San Pedro Sacatepéquez, Santiago Sacatepéquez, San Lucas Sacatepéquez, and Sumpango) in the present-day Sacatépequez region. According to Carmack, the Chajomás of the old fortress of Jilotepeque Viejo/"Mixco Viejo" (who became the Colonial San Martín Jilotepeque population) had strong kinship ties to both Iximché and Sacatepéquez.

Jilotepeque, however, fell under Iximché domination long before Sacatepéquez, and remained so until the Spanish Conquest. One compelling reason for its early conquest may well have been the important obsidian source at Choatalum in the Jilotepeque region, recently studied and reported by Braswell (1998: 146–147). After conquering Jilotepeque, the Iximché Cakchiquel pressed only as far east as Chimaltenango, which was the wartime boundary with "los Sacatepéquez" (Carmack 1979: 141–142). Thus, the Jilotepeque Chajomá population was a definable entity during the protohistoric period and can be considered the third division of the Cakchiquel.

The Chajomá Cakchiquel of Sacatepéquez

As previously mentioned, some of the Chajomás continued their migration south and east into neighboring Sacatepéquez, possibly to escape Iximché's domination of the Jilotepeque region through which they had passed and in which they probably settled for a time. "Sacatepéquez" is the Aztec Nahuatl place name meaning "hill of straw," which replaced the Cakchiquel "Chajomá" soon after the Spanish Conquest. The first Chajomá migrants into this area established themselves close to present-day San Juan Sacatepéquez, which is recorded in the earliest Spanish documents as San Juan Chajomá (Carmack 1979: 139; Borg 1986: 12–13). From a study of surnames appearing in the native chronicles, Carmack (1979) concluded that the Chajomás who eventually migrated to the Sacatepéquez area were closely allied to the Jilotepeque "Akajals" (Chajomás) even before other Cakchiquel branches had established themselves at Iximché. A sixteenth-century land document revealed that one *parcialidad* (identifiable population segment) in San Juan Sacatepéquez held the lands north of the Motagua River known as Pachalúm (still visible on modern maps) in the territory of present-day Joyabaj through which the Chajomá had migrated on their way south.

Fuentes y Guzmán (1932–1933, 1: 322–328) referred to a Prehispanic population center in the Sacatepéquez area called "Ucubil." Villacorta (1926: 249; 365–366) and Gall (1976 and ms.: 9181) identified Ucubil as ancient San Pedro Sacatepéquez. Although Carmack (1979:

143) also agreed that Ucubil was near San Juan and San Pedro Sacatepéquez, the actual location of the site is unknown. "Ucub" means "seven" in Cakchiquel, and early Spanish documents confirm the existence in the area of a large population consisting of several settlements. At least until 1549, the early Colonial towns called San Juan and San Pedro Sacatepéquez were still referred to by their Prehispanic name, "los Sacatepéquez." Census documents show that the town of San Juan probably represents the Spanish *congregación* of the largest single Chajomá population in the area. In contrast, San Pedro was comprised of at least five smaller population segments (Borg 1986: 13). By 1555, the name "los Sacatepéquez" was no longer in use, replaced by the two separate place names San Juan Sacatepéquez (also known as San Juan Chajomá) and San Pedro Sacatepéquez (Carmack 1979; Crespo 1956).

Slightly later, in 1562, the combined populations of San Juan and San Pedro Sacatepéquez consisted of six *parcialidades*: Chajomá, Tepemiac, Chagüite, Tukuché, Los Uspantecas, and Sinaca [Xenacoj]. The town of San Juan was composed of the *parcialidad* of Chajomá (the largest) and part of the *parcialidad* of Tepemiac (the second largest). San Pedro was also made up of part of Tepemiac plus the remaining four *parcialidades*, of which Chagüite was by far the largest. Tepemiac, mentioned in the census for both towns, was obviously the geographical connecting link between the two (Borg 1986: 31). The guidelines given to Dominican friars for "congregating" the normally more dispersed Cakchiquel into controllable towns during the 1540s specified that the native hierarchy was to be preserved, and *caciques* (elite leaders) were to be given local jurisdiction in their towns as well as extra land (Remesal 1932, 1: 109). Congregated into separate towns sometime between 1549 and 1555, the towns of San Juan and San Pedro may very well have retained considerable civil autonomy, though under the religious guidance of the Dominican Order, until sometime between 1559 and 1562 when Spanish wheat farmers were first encouraged to settle in the region (Sherman 1979: 206; Borg 1986: 31–32).

In Sacatepéquez two rural *calpules* (territorial divisions, or *chinamits*), similar to some 40 such rural *calpules* which Carmack (1981:112) equated with modern hamlets in the Quiché area, have been located within the lands belonging to the town of San Pedro Sacatepéquez. They are specifically named in early Colonial period sources, and there were probably many others. A document from 1644 records the *composición*, or legalization of land title, of the lands called Carrizal belonging to *calpul* Ya-Jonica. From the description of the land measurement, these lands were located in the area of the modern town of El Carrizal, east of San Raimundo Las Casillas, and had been occupied "since ancient times" by people living in "four thatched houses in four separate locations," engaged in maize agriculture on fairly marginal lands. An old stone edifice near a *barranca* (gully) called Ruyalsite was the boundary between their lands and the lands of another San Pedro rural *calpul* called Ji-Chamale (Borg 1986: 32). The Sacatepéquez towns as a group, which retain many Prehispanic place names and clues to their social organization, thus constitute the fourth geographical grouping of protohistoric Cakchiquels.

Maximum Expansion of Iximché Cakchiquel Political Control

The 1565 *título* (land title) of the town of Alotenango, published by Francis Polo (1979), further confirms that the Cakchiquel were ruled by four lords, two of whom had the greatest power, as stated in the *Annals*. This document, as well as the *Annals*, gives us the names of the Iximché lords who governed at the time of Spanish Contact: the Ahpozotzil Cahi Imox (also called Sinacán) and the Ahpoxahil Belehé Cat (also called Sacachul). The título's naming of a third Cakchiquel lord, Potocope, is the only known reference to this individual in the ethnohistorical sources (Polo 1979: 32). But most significant, this document delineates the southernmost boundary of Cakchiquel expansion before the Spanish Conquest. The three Cakchiquel lords mentioned were at war with the Escuintepeq Pipil and other towns in the region of the present-day town of Escuintla over control of the rich south coast cacao fields. To that end the Iximché forces had established military garrisons south of a river called Xoxoycapa (the ancient Pipil boundary) in lands called Xeococo in Cakchiquel and Zilohuixil in Nahuatl. Along this border were many Cakchiquel houses and two sacrificial stones which had been placed there as markers (Polo 1979: 32). In wartime the Cakchiquel placed arrows with bloodied flint points on the sacrificial stones as a warning; when they were at peace the arrows were replaced with little balls of wax (Polo 1979: 37). Nearby, in a place called Los Chiagüites (significant in Iximché's later conquest of the Sacatepéquez Chajomá), there was a large Cakchiquel population, and fields of corn, beans, and chile (Polo 1979: 33). After warfare with the Pipil ended, the Iximché Cakchiquel moved north and established their town near Alotenango (Polo 1979: 34).

The título also records that later, after Spanish Contact and during the six-year Cakchiquel rebellion (1524–1530), the Cakchiquels living in Alotenango took refuge on the slopes of the Agua volcano and, with the permission of the Pipils, in the lands belonging to Escuintepeq. The Iximché Cakchiquel continued to claim as theirs all the lands between the Agua volcano on the north and their Prehispanic wartime boundary with the Pipils in Xeococo/Zilohuixil to the south. This included the site of their old settlement, Los Chiagüites (Polo 1979: 41). This is possibly the same place as the early Spanish Colonial town called San Sebastián Chiagüité located south of Alotenango, referred to in documents but no longer in existence (Polo 1979: 33). The Colonial period towns of Alotenango and Escuintla continued to dispute the ownership of this boundary settlement of Los Chiagüites into the eighteenth century (Polo 1979: 54).

To the southwest, the limit of Iximché's expansion is recorded in a 1587 land dispute document from the town of Patulul (Carmack 1973: 154). The land in question was claimed by both the Cakchiquel and the neighboring Lake Atitlán Tzutujil and was probably a hostile frontier zone similar to the Cakchiquel-Pipil boundary. According to Sandra Orellana, the Cakchiquel fought the Tzutujils for control of this area, which included an important mountain pass to the south coast. The Cakchiquel controlled the eastern edge of Lake Atitlán to Palopó and Tolimán and the piedmont lands as far west as Patulul during the late fifteenth century, including the mountain pass. By Spanish Contact, however, the Tzutujils were once again in control of the pass (Orellana 1984: 18).

The Iximché Cakchiquel confrontations, first with Tzololá and then with the Pipil and Tzutujil, illustrate the instability of internal boundaries within the Cakchiquel region during the era of military expansion characteristic of the protohistoric period. In addition, however, the título of Alotenango provides important information concerning the history of the Sacatepéquez Chajomá. In stating clearly that the protohistoric Iximché/Alotenango Cakchiquel claimed lands as far north as the Agua volcano, the título has, in combination with Ximénez (1929–1931, 1: 77–79) and Carmack (1979: 152), defined the southern boundary of the protohistoric Sacatepéquez Chajomá region. North of Alotenango and the Agua volcano stretched the Valley of Panchoy and the Spanish capital of Santiago, the nucleus of the incipient Spanish colony founded in lands formerly controlled by the Sacatepéquez Chajomá.

Ximénez (1929–1931, 1: 77–79) also tells us that the Cakchiquel had four kings before the Spanish Conquest but states that a united kingdom did not last long. The area called "los Sacatepéquez," the towns of the Sacatepéquez Chajomás (San Lucas, San Santiago, Sumpango, San Pedro, and San Juan Sacatepéquez), rose in revolt against the Iximché Cakchiquel. A lord (possibly a Tukuché) who had previously participated with other Cakchiquel when they split away from the Quiché confederation, later fled Iximché (possibly after the 1493 internal Tukuché rebellion), and eventually arrived in Sacatepéquez, where he joined or led a revolt against Iximché. This may have been the lord called "Achicalel" who Ximénez (1929–1931, 1: 76) describes as a lord with the title of *Achi Kalel* ("the man who is great"), chosen leader by the Sacatepéquez, and who established a new stronghold in the place called Yampuc. In the Colonial period this area near the modern town of San Pedro Ayampuc was on the easternmost fringes of the lands of San Pedro Sacatepéquez and was as far away from Iximché as one could travel and still be in Cakchiquel territory. There are a number of fairly unimpressive Late Postclassic sites in the region built with defense as a high priority, but it is impossible at this time to link any of them to the "Achicalel" mentioned by Ximénez. However, Yampuc Viejo, mentioned by archaeologist John Fox (1977: 95; see below), is one possibility.

The Sacatepéquez Chajomá region appears to have been alternately allied with (or dominated by) and in rebellion against the Iximché Cakchiquel. About 1475 the Cakchiquel of Iximché and Sacatepéquez, acting in concert, countered a Pokomam intrusion into the region northeast of present-day Mixco, a strategic area near the El Chayal obsidian mines on an important trade route north to Verapaz. Although Iximché may have controlled (or at least attempted to control) this key region, it would have been equally important to the Sacatepéquez. The Sacatepéquez Chajomá do not appear to have been in open rebellion against Iximché in 1475, but there was apparently cause for concern, because the Sacatepéquez Chajomá allowed the Pokomam to settle along their eastern borders near Mixco on the condition that they would not ally themselves with the Iximché Cakchiquel (Carmack 1979: 151).

The "no man's land" between Iximché on the west and the often hostile Sacatepéquez Chajomás on the east was near the present-day town of Chimaltenango; before the Conquest it was called Pocob, which means "shield" or "defense" (Carmack 1979: 141–42). Despite tensions and outright hostilities the two factions also established, perhaps by tacit agreement, a neutral zone near Chimaltenango and Comalapa where mutual trading could take place. This inland port-of-trade was called *tianguesillo,* and Ximénez (1929–1931, 1: 77) identified it as the well-known Chimaltenango market still in use during the seventeenth century. Ximénez also wrote that though the frontier between Iximché and Sacatepéquez was near Chimaltenango and Comalapa, the Sacatepéquez had established other strongholds at Sumpango, Santiago Sacatepéquez, and San Lucas Sacatepéquez. These towns were located along the western half of the Sacatepéquez southern frontier. The eastern half of the Sacatepéquez southern frontier had been left relatively unprotected, and it was into this area that the Sacatepéquez moved their Pokomam allies.

Settling the Pokomam along the southeastern Sacatepéquez periphery not only kept them from passing westward through Sacatepéquez and allying themselves with Iximché, but also discouraged them from becoming allies of another equally threatening group, the Iximché Cakchiquel at Alotenango, who were expanding up from the south. Apparently unable to overcome the Sacatepéquez Chajomás directly from the west via Chimaltenango, Iximché positioned its warriors to attack from the south as well, a tactic which eventually proved successful.

Iximché achieved a short-lived military victory over the Sacatepéquez Chajomá sometime between 1517 and the Spanish Conquest in 1524. The assault on the Sacatepéquez Cakchiquel area, which had stubbornly maintained its independence, was a major accomplishment in a single-minded campaign which had begun sometime before 1480, during which Iximché attempted to gain control of the surrounding region. Carmack (1979: 152) cites the Villacorta (1934) edition of the *Annals of the Cakchiquels* which states that the town of Mixco (the Prehispanic Pokomam site of Chinautla Viejo) on Sacatepéquez's southeastern periphery was conquered by Iximché in 1480, and many Mixqueños were taken as slaves. A little more than a decade later the Iximché faced trouble at home, putting down the Tukuché revolt within their own ranks in May 1493 (Recinos 1950: 111). But in December 1497, Iximché attacked Mixco a second time, leaving a strong military force to guard its border against the Sacatepéquez (Recinos 1950: 114). The Iximché conquered two other nearby Pokomam towns, Petapa and Pinula, during this period, but Petapa regained its independence before the Spanish Conquest (Carmack 1979: 152).

Archaeologist John Fox (1977: 95) has identified the Late Postclassic site called Yampuc Viejo near San Pedro Ayampuc as one which shows evidence of having been conquered by Iximché. A distinctive type of "garrison plaza," similar to the elevated (fortified) platforms at Iximché and Quiché Utatlán, has been found there as well as at other sites conquered by Iximché—Jilotepeque Viejo [Mixco Viejo] and Chinautla Viejo [Mixco]. Testimonies from land disputes also clearly indicate that after the Iximché forces conquered Sacatepéquez they assigned a military leader as provincial governor over the town of San Pedro Sacatepéquez (which included the Ayampuc region). This military governor was later given the Christian name of Alfonso and lived after the Spanish Conquest until about 1543. According to the 1562 census, San Pedro's largest *parcialidad* was called "Chagüite" or "Cachigüite." Alfonso and the rest of his garrison probably came to San Pedro Sacatepéquez from the large Iximché military outpost and settlement south of Alotenango and near Escuintla called "Los Chiagüites." It is possible that the military governor assigned to oversee San Pedro, known only by his Spanish name "don Alfonso," might have been Potocope, the third Iximché Cakchiquel lord with the Nahua-sounding name mentioned along with Cahi Imox and Belehé Cat in the *Título de Alotenango* (Borg 1986: 23).

Despite Iximché domination, the Sacatepéquez maintained their separatist identity even after the Spanish Conquest by launching revolts and rebellions independently of those instigated by the Iximché Cakchiquels. J. Daniel Contreras R. (1965: 43) and Polo (1977: 87), citing the chronicler Vásquez, place these post-Conquest Iximché Cakchiquel revolts against the Spaniards between 1531 and 1535.

Conquest and Early Spanish Control, 1524–1540

The Iximché Cakchiquel were to enjoy only briefly the smell of victory. As early as 1510, the Quichés of Utatlán had agreed to pay tribute to the Mexica emperor Moctezuma; thus, by 1512 the Quichés were aware of impending Spanish activity as seen through Mexica eyes (Carmack 1981: 142). The presence of Mexica in Guatemala during this period, and after 1524 as mercenaries with the Spanish forces, resulted in the assignation of many Nahua place names to existing locations. Before the Spaniards ever saw them, the Quiché capital of K'umarcaaj was already known by its Nahua name, Utatlán, and the Cakchiquel fortress of Iximché as Cuauhtemallan (Guatemala). Diseases introduced by the Europeans spread ahead of the conquering armies. As Cortés was beginning his conquest of Mexico, the Indians of the Central Guatemalan Highlands were experiencing terrible epidemics, as recorded in the *Annals of the Cakchiquels* for the years 1520–1521. Elites and commoners alike succumbed, including many in the Iximché Cakchiquel ruling family (Recinos and Goetz 1953: 115–116). According to MacLeod (1973: 19), the pandemics which began to strike Central America about 1520 (and which lasted until 1580) were a combination of smallpox and pulmonary plague which killed one-third to one-half of the Indian population.

In 1520 the Iximché Cakchiquels sent emissaries to Hernán Cortés offering to become his subjects. They also requested Spanish aid to conquer their archenemies, the Quichés. Cortés contacted the Quichés, inviting them to surrender peacefully, but with no success. The Quichés made a valiant effort to unite the Guatemalan peoples, including their enemies the Cakchiquels, against the common foe but were unable to do so. Those who did rally around the Quiché king lost their leader to death shortly before the Spaniards arrived. Pedro de Alvarado, sent by Cortés, left Mexico for Guatemala late in 1523. Passing through the rich cacao producing area of Soconusco, previously under Mexica control, Alvarado made contact with the Cakchiquels.

The Spaniards clashed with Quiché forces in the Valley of Quetzaltenango, and after several defeats Utatlán surrendered on February 20, 1524. A planned ambush of Spanish forces inside the city of Utatlán also failed, and in retaliation Alvarado ordered many lords burned to death on March 7, 1524. He also took many others as hostages and demanded large quantities of gold (Carmack 1981: 143–146; Recinos and Goetz 1953: 119–120). The *Annals of the Cakchiquels* note that Alvarado "concealed a cruel soul behind an agreeable and smiling face. Because of his gallant bearing and blond hair, the Mexicans called him Tonatiuh, the sun" (Recinos and Goetz 1953: 119).

The news of Pedro de Alvarado's conquest of the Quichés of Utatlán traveled quickly to the Cakchiquel court at Iximché. Sinacán (Cahi Imox), the Cakchiquel king, sent ambassadors to Alvarado with gifts of gold and offers of peace. This only reinforced the Spaniard's greed for the precious metal, and Alvarado saw in the Cakchiquels' continued peace offer an open door to the remainder of the province. To test Sinacán's sincerity Alvarado requested two thousand men to clear the rugged, mountainous roads between Utatlán and Iximché. Sinacán sent the men as well as provisions for Alvarado's journey (Ximénez 1929–1931, 1: 126). The Cakchiquels sent assistance twice more to Utatlán, a total of four thousand men, while Alvarado spent an additional seven or eight days subduing the Quichés (Carmack 1981: 146).

Alvarado then traveled to Iximché, where representatives of other Maya groups, threatened with attack and too weak to resist, arrived to make peace. The Cakchiquel were eager for Alvarado to vanquish all the remaining allies of their former enemies the Quichés, including the Tzutujil of Lake Atitlán. And one by one they were attacked and subdued, or surrendered voluntarily (Ximénez 1929–1931, 1: 127–128).

Ximénez described how the king of Iximché, Sinacán, failed to foresee the treatment his people would receive from the Spaniards when he first declared peace with Alvarado. He had anticipated a peaceful, mutually productive alliance, but when he saw his wife appropriated by the conqueror, himself deprived of his kingdom, and the countryside under Alvarado's absolute control, he realized his mistake. The Spaniard's appetite for precious metals was insatiable, and the Cakchiquel were forced to provide large work crews to pan for gold. Alvarado demanded two hundred men every week, and each was assigned a weekly quota. If the quota was not met more men were assigned to gold panning. Unreasonable tribute demands were placed upon a town called Patinamit, where more than four hundred young men and women toiled daily to produce a small container of washed gold the size of a person's little finger, under penalty of slavery if they failed. As the demand for gold grew, treatment of the Indians became increasingly more cruel (Ximénez 1929–1931, 1: 149–150).

Following the advice of a religious leader who promised that the Spaniards would be defeated and Alvarado killed, the Cakchiquel abandoned Iximché. Within 10 days Alvarado had retaliated and war had begun, ending the brief alliance between Cakchiquels and Spaniards. The first twenty years after the Spanish conquest of the Quiché Maya in 1524 were years of chaos, unrest, and military consolidation. Unlike their experience with the unified Mexica empire in Central Mexico, Spaniards in Guatemala were forced to deal with many independent nonallied warring groups. Conquest of this region was more prolonged, and some areas of Guatemala were never brought under effective Spanish control. Cakchiquel guerilla tactics against Alvarado's forces included digging deep holes and setting sharp stakes in the bottom to trap and kill horses. Many Quichés and Tzutujils, enemies of the Cakchiquels forced to fight alongside Spaniards, were also killed (Recinos and Goetz 1953: 123–125).

The Iximché Cakchiquel insurrection began in 1524 and lasted until 1530, when its rulers, Sinacán and Sacachul, surrounded by many loyal lords, finally gave up the fight. The chronicles describe how a surprised Sinacán, expecting death at the hands of Alvarado, was set free after his surrender. Disgruntled because he was required to pay tribute like a commoner he left the Spanish capital of Santiago and returned to Iximché. As Daniel Contreras (1965) hypothesized, Sinacán probably organized other rebellions between 1531 and his final capture in 1535.

During these two decades of upheaval it is evident that there were serious disagreements concerning acceptance of Spanish rule throughout the rest of the Cakchiquel region. Fuentes y Guzmán (1932–1933) is the only chronicler who describes the Spanish Conquest of the Sacatepéquez Chajomá as well as a rebellion in 1526. He writes that some of the population, such as the people near Xenacoj and Sumpango, submitted early to Spanish rule. However, in late 1524 or early 1525 an intractable rebel element among the Sacatepéquez Chajomá began to wage war against these peace-seeking towns, carrying off women and children from the *milpas*, abducting and sacrificing messengers sent between towns, and vowing never to submit to foreign domination. In desperation, the caciques of Xenacoj and Sumpango appealed to Alvarado for protection. After a bloody battle of several days duration an army of Spaniards with the help of Mexican and Tlaxcalan mercenaries defeated the Sacatepéquez at a place called Ucubil (Fuentes y Guzmán 1932–1933, 1: 313–330). As noted above, Ucubil was probably located near the Colonial and modern towns of San Pedro and San Juan Sacatepéquez. This battle obviously did not end the unrest, however, since Spanish fears concerning Cakchiquel uprisings continued. Later, because the Spanish citizens of the capital of Santiago feared that Sinacán and Sacachul would escape from jail to lead another Indian uprising, the two leaders—the last kings of Prehispanic Iximché—were finally ordered hanged by Alvarado in 1540 (Vásquez 1937–1944, 1: 39; Recinos and Goetz 1953: 132).

Conclusion

This summary is only a sketch providing the basic outline of Cakchiquel protohistory and early Colonial history derived from native and Spanish documentary sources. Those written records are even richer in detail which cannot be included here. Through these sources, selected aspects of Cakchiquel culture have been summarized, especially the military struggles between the Iximché elites and other groups both inside and immediately adjacent to the Cakchiquel region. Clearly, Iximché's ability to expand militarily during the last 50 years before Spanish Contact was curtailed by strong warlike neighbors to the north (Quichés and Rabinals), west (Tzutujils), and south (Pipils), with whom they continuously fought. In attempting to control crucial resources such as mountain passes and the cacao fields on the Pacific coast, and important obsidian mines in Jilotepeque and at El Chayal, the Iximché rulers were often victorious and probably did control many of these resources, at least periodically.

Within the Cakchiquel region, Iximché comprised the Cakchiquel "heartland" in terms of power relations, and Tzololá, Jilotepeque, and Sacatepéquez were an often defensively hostile Cakchiquel "hinterland," where being Cakchiquel did not mean being on good terms with Iximché. Iximché's elites brought both Jilotepeque and Tzololá under control soon after their capital was founded. On the eve of the Spanish Conquest the Sacatepéquez Chajomás appear to have been the last thorn in the side of Iximché's ruling elite, and every attempt was made to subdue this stubbornly independent Cakchiquel group and its Pokomam allies to the east. Despite considerable resistance and the concentration of strongholds along their western and southern peripheries, the Sacatepéquez Chajomás, who probably made their last stand in the easternmost part of their territory known as Ayampuc, were overcome sometime between 1517 and the arrival of the Spaniards in 1524.

Iximché's rulers clearly dominated the Cakchiquel region at Spanish Contact but lost control immediately thereafter when they broke their short-lived alliance with Alvarado and went to war. Old pockets of resistance revived, and the Spaniards were forced to subdue native populations one at a time across the entire Guatemalan Highland area, including outside the Cakchiquel region.

As has been demonstrated, ethnohistorical research is an important tool in our understanding of the protohistoric period, especially when much basic archaeological work still remains to be carried out in the Cakchiquel region. The two approaches complement each other as separate data sets which can be used as important comparative cross-checks. Each approach obviously contributes the most when utilized in conjunction with the other. In general, historical archaeology in Latin

America has lagged far behind that in North America. As the utility of this approach gains in popularity, great strides will be made in the Cakchiquel region and elsewhere.

For example, Prehispanic Tzololá and Ucubil cannot be currently located using documentary sources alone; however, archaeology may yet do so. Iximché was excavated by Guillemin, who wrote extensively about the site but who took few field notes and failed to complete the analysis of many artifacts. Ethnohistory cannot fill all the lacunae, but nevertheless it has contributed significantly to our knowledge of Iximché and the Cakchiquels. In the Quiché region, a growing number of sites, in addition to the capital of Utatlán, have been excavated, complementing ethnohistorian Robert Carmack's decades of effort. The recent addition of Braswell's archaeological survey of Jilotepeque makes the Quiché-Jilotepeque area one of the best studied from both perspectives.

Scholarship of this kind, although significant in its own right, is also important to the modern inhabitants of the Cakchiquel region. The courage with which the Cakchiquel people, including the last rulers and lords of Iximché, resisted Spanish domination is reflected in the persistence of traditional customs, beliefs, and lifeways across the region today. Indeed, the site of Iximché has become a focus of modern Cakchiquel life as a sacred place, and because of a revived interest in teaching Cakchiquel language and culture to the young. Linda Schele described being one of very few non-Cakchiquel in a gathering of thousands of Maya at Iximché in 1990. Increasing numbers of Cakchiquel from all over the region return to Iximché to pray, burn incense and candles, dance, and celebrate their identities as Maya (Schele and Mathews 1998: 311–317). It is thus incumbent upon us as scholars interested in Guatemalan studies to continue to reconstruct, using all the means at our disposal, the history of a vibrant, living Cakchiquel culture, including their Prehispanic ancestors and the focus of their Late Postclassic civilization, the capital city of Iximché.

3

ⲛⲛⲛⲛⲛ

Cakchiquel Ethnohistory

An Archaeological Perspective

In the archaeological study which follows, reference will be made to the kings of Iximché, to the high priest of the same community, to palaces, to temples, and to evidence of human sacrifice. Ceramics will be examined for evidence of ceremonialism and sculpted clay human and animal effigies for the belief systems they represent. Because Iximché was occupied at the threshold of modern recorded history, beginning around 1470 and continuing until the arrival of the Spanish in 1524, it is important to examine the ethnohistorical record. What can perusal of sixteenth-century accounts, both Spanish and indigenous, tell us about these people which might inform this archaeological enterprise?

The following sketch is based primarily on the sixteenth-century account of Bartolomé de Las Casas (1958) and several other early Spanish sources. Las Casas refers to the indigenous people of Guatemala and specifically to the Quiché Maya and the people of Verapaz, probably the Pokomam Maya, but it is not clear that any of his descriptions pertain directly to the Cakchiquel. For most of his information, Las Casas relied on accounts by survivors of the Conquest instead of on first-hand observation. He arrived in Guatemala in the 1530s (Miles 1957: 736), and he remains the best early source for material which can be used at least inferentially to understand early Cakchiquel customs and social institutions. His work has been explored more fully by Miles (1957) and Carmack (1973: 100–105). This chapter also draws from the work of modern ethnohistorians and their research on early documents pertaining to the Cakchiquel as well as the Quiché and Pokomam, located immediately west and east of Cakchiquel territory, respectively. Finally, we refer to several Maya documents which were written at the beginning of the Colonial era but which long since have been translated and published. Most important of these is the *Annals of the Cakchiquels* (Recinos and Goetz, 1953), a history of Iximché written by two Cakchiquels who survived the Spanish invasion of that city and who had learned to write in Cakchiquel using the Spanish alphabet.

Geography

Iximché was the capital of an independent state which at the time of the Conquest covered roughly 2800 to 3000 km² (Feldman 1985: fig. 1). Of the kingdom of Guatemala, Las Casas (1958, 3: 157) wrote that while the kings and lords lived in towns most of the population was scattered through the mountains in houses numbering "10,000 to 15,000 or more." The towns, which Las Casas (1958, 3: 157) described as having 200 to 1000 houses, were both political and religious centers "where there were temples, and where the gods were worshiped . . . royal houses of the kings and lords were located near other houses of important people." He attributed this dispersed settlement pattern to the rugged terrain and the poverty of the citizens. People needed to live close to their sources of drinking water, agricultural fields, and the mountains which supplied their firewood. In a second estimate, Las Casas (1958, 3: 158) saw populations of "10,000 houses or inhabitants" spread over a distance of three to five leagues, and this may refer to more intensively occupied regions surrounding capital towns. Feldman (1985: 1, fig. 1) found early sixteenth-century documents which suggested an area of high population in the vicinity of Iximché, about 30 km across and within the larger Iximché territory; correspondingly, the three to five leagues of Las Casas would have covered between 16 and 28 km. Hill (1996) used archaeological site distributions and early Colonial documents to estimate the size and population of the Chajomá, an independent Cakchiquel polity in the Late Postclassic. The territory of the Chajomá was east of Iximché, reaching the vicinity of present-day Guatemala City. It may have covered about 900 km² and been inhabited by 10,000 to 20,000 people (Hill 1996: 82, 85). All of this suggests that the neighboring Iximché state, or *vinak* (see below), covered between 2800 and 3000 km² and was occupied by between 10,000 and 30,000 people.

Political Organization

Cakchiquel sociopolitical organization at the time of the Conquest is poorly understood. No doubt the society was highly stratified with commoners separated from an aristocracy above and a slave class below. Perhaps Quiché sociopolitical organization will serve as an analogue for the Cakchiquel system. Las Casas described the government of the Quiché capital, Utatlán, as controlled by a supreme king and principal men of the council, including a king-elect and a greater and a lesser captain. The four were related, "descended from the supreme lord or king" (Las Casas 1958, 4: 342) and were set apart from others by trappings of rank. The king was sheltered by four superposed canopies ("of very rich feathers, one on top of the other; the water from each fell on the other" (Las Casas 1958, 4: 343)), while the king-elect employed three canopies and the other two, two each. These national leaders were in charge of the legal system as well as taxation. Taxed goods were divided between the king and needs of the state (Las Casas 1958, 4: 342).

How the various communities were linked together in alliances may have varied from region to region and fluctuated with the strength of individual leaders and towns. According to Las Casas, influence from the Quiché capital of Utatlán extended through officials who resided in other towns of the kingdom. These constituent towns, Las Casas wrote, were not obligated to pay taxes but recognized the authority of Utatlán and provided military support in time of warfare. Evidently, the Utatlán legal system extended to these towns where local lords decided cases "of little substance" (Las Casas 1958, 4: 343). Serious crimes or disputes were adjudicated by supreme lords in the capital. That subsidiary towns were not required to pay taxes is affirmed by another early source on the Quiché, a letter by Friar Pedro de Betanzos to the king of Spain (written in 1559 and published in Carrasco 1967: 255–259): "no particular Indian gave tribute nor had a bill with Utatlán or was forced [to pay], but only to his own lords to whom they were subjects in each of the towns, and these lords had no other recognition of obligation to the said town of Utatlán more than the adoration of idols as in the so-named pantheon of Rome, save that as they had recourse to that adoration, they always respected those lords from there as relatives and friends to which they gave their presents, and the lords from Utatlán did the same thing for these from each one of the above-mentioned towns; they sent them their messengers with their presents and offerings by way of friendship and relationship" (Betanzos in Carrasco 1967: 257).

In his reconstruction of Quichean sociopolitical organization, Carmack (1977: 15–17) characterized Las Casas's portrayal as that of a centralized political system which was both a kingdom and a monarchy. Carmack contrasted this to the aforementioned description by Betanzos. Carmack (1977: 14) wrote that Betanzos saw the same political system as highly decentralized with the lords of four principal lineages sharing power at Utatlán. Each of these four men was elected to office by members of his lineage at Utatlán and at other Quichean communities, and ultimately the four were controlled by the lords of towns making up a Quichean confederacy. Carmack attempted to reconcile these differences by suggesting that all four of the major officers mentioned by Las Casas came from the same lineage, a possibility supported by the Título of Totonicapán (Chonay and Goetz 1953), and that these were not the lineage lords described by Betanzos.

Some of the same ambiguity regarding political organization can be found in the *Annals of the Cakchiquels*. Throughout its history, Iximché was led by two co-ruling monarchs, the Ahpozotzil and the Ahpoxahil (Recinos and Goetz 1953: 74). Evidently, each of these positions was passed down from father to son, but there is also mention of the election of kings in the *Annals* (Recinos and Goetz 1953: 117), and it seems likely that there was a measure of popular participation in the selection of rulers, possibly through electing one from a pool of eligible princes (cf. Carrasco 1961: 490). One passage of the *Annals* states that, "The four clans unanimously consented to the rule of the king Hunyg" (Recinos and Goetz 1953: 112). Another statement describing post-Conquest events leaves little doubt about the traditional importance of the electoral process or at least public consent in leadership changes. "Immediately after the death of the king [September 24, 1532], Tunatiuh [Pedro Alvarado] came here to choose a successor to the king. Then the lord Don Jorge was installed in the government by order of Tunatiuh alone. There was no election by the people to name him. Afterwards, Tunatiuh talked to the lords and his orders were obeyed by the chiefs for in truth they feared Tunatiuh" (Recinos and Goetz 1953: 129). Las Casas (1958, 4: 343; 348–349) also mentioned elections in the political process at Utatlán, and speaking generally of the selection of government officials among the Maya, wrote of elections by all the town or principal people of the town (also see Zorita, 1963: 272, on the election of the Utatlán king). Finally, Las Casas (1958, 4: 348) indicated that elections corrupted by bribes were still known "even after the entrance of our friars into the province of Verapaz."

According to Hill (1996: 64), the Cakchiquel nation (*vinak*) based at Iximché included three groups (*amaq*): the Cakchiquel proper, the Zotzil, and the Tukuché, but only two after the Tukuché revolt in 1493. Still allied, the two amaqs comprised a total of eight to ten politico-territorial units known as chinamits. The nature of the chinamit among the Cakchiquel and the chinamit-amaq relationship remains poorly understood, and this is the case as well for the Quiché, who are better documented ethnohistorically.

Carmack (1977: 12) wrote that the chinamit has been confused with the lineage, and that for the Quiché, each chinamit was headed by an aristocratic lineage. Both vassals and nobility residing within a chinamit took the name of the leading lineage, but since chinamits evidently admitted unrelated people they cannot be regarded as patrilineal descent groups in the strict sense of the term. Hill (Hill and Monaghan 1987: 24–42) revisited this problem and concluded that there probably was a core aristocratic lineage or exogamous family unit in charge, but that other members of the territorial-based group formed a generally endogamous unit.

It seems likely that the Iximché state consisted of amaqs coexisting in loose, unstable relationships. From an archaeological perspective, the monumental architecture at Iximché with its pyramids, paved public areas, and religious and political structures served to enhance the city's prestige and, hence, its position of leadership in this unstable political environment.

Descent

We now consider social organization and the question of form of descent for the protohistoric Cakchiquel. Again, the evidence is not clear, although patrilineal descent seems likely. Miles (1957: 759, 765) saw evidence for patrilineal descent in the sixteenth- and seventeenth-century sources for the Highland Maya and concluded that patrilineal clans existed for the Pokomam, serving as a basis for both territorial and political organization. Carmack (1977: 10) also saw the patrilineage as integral to Quiché political organization. Las Casas (1958, 4: 355), in a discussion of Guatemalan Indian marriage customs, seemed to be dealing with rules of exogamy required by patrilineal descent. On the other hand, Hill (1992: 31–35) could not find convincing evidence for patrilineal descent in Cakchiquel terms employed in Colonial times and recorded in early Spanish-Cakchiquel dictionaries. Carrasco (1964), in a study of early Colonial documents, seemed convinced of the existence of both patriclans and lineages among the Quiché and Cakchiquel, but did not find evidence in intergenerational names among related individuals to establish this point.

Warfare

Warfare was an important activity in the Highlands, and Las Casas provided some detail for the province of Verapaz. He wrote that raids were often held before important festivals in order to obtain slaves for human sacrifice (Las Casas 1958, 4: 353). He also spoke of military specialists occupying different ranks, captains, "jack" captains (*sota capitanes*), and sergeants, with people organized both as combatants and support personnel: "standard bearers and other officials that had charge of distributing meals and drinks to the soldiers" (Las Casas 1958, 4: 352). Preparations for war were organized by a council of experienced warriors. Operating in secret, they determined the time and place of attack, the number of people involved, and the types of arms required. Warriors learned of these plans only when they assembled at the king's palace and were issued their weapons: "without anyone suspecting a thing of that, nor did he know through indications, until the hour that the people were ordered to meet at the doors of the house and palaces of the king where they were given and provided their bows and arrows, lances and shields with their standard of very beautiful plumes and their flags" (Las Casas 1958, 4: 352). Carmack (1981: 152-153) reported that military prowess was a means of social mobility among the Quiché, with vassals acquiring titles and competing for position with established nobility.

The bellicose behavior of the citizens of Iximché is well-demonstrated in the *Annals* and reflected in the defensive position of the site, surrounded on three sides by precipitous ravines and fronted on the fourth by a man-made moat, 25 feet deep, as Guillemin (1965a; 1967) determined through his excavations (see chap. 4). The *Annals* (Recinos and Goetz 1953: 108) records one attack on Iximché with the battle beginning at one end of the bridge over this moat.

Economy

Economic activity included the organization of production and exchange of goods, both private and through state-controlled taxation.

State-controlled wealth gathered from the populace in late prehistoric Mesoamerica is often referred to in English as tribute, but in some cases this is likely a misnomer, and discussion of this point seems in order. Tribute is the English cognate for the Spanish *tributo*, but tributo can mean either tribute or tax (*Cassell's Spanish-English Dictionary* 1978: 578). For example, the Spanish word *impuesto*, a common word for tax, is defined in the *Diccionario manual e ilustrado de la lengua español* (1950: 853) as "Tributo, carga." In English, tribute and tax, of course, have different meanings. Tribute can designate wealth "paid from one nation to another" (*Webster's Third International Dictionary* 1966: 2441) or an excessive extralegal, or coercive tax. When Las Casas writes of tributo which is intra-national and when he does not specify that it is either coercive or excessive, the term is probably best translated as tax (which does not necessarily have to take a monetary form). Zorita (1963: 188–189) reported that taxes were relatively low in Prehispanic times, and that the Spanish increased them to six times pre-Conquest levels. If Zorita was correct, it would seem realistic in most cases to refer to taxes before and tribute after the advent of Spanish rule.

Forms of taxation include excise taxes (that is, taxes on production), which, Las Casas reported, were paid by hunters, those who raised poultry, and farmers. "When they harvested the corn and fruit of the land, they carried part of the first harvest to the lord, not as a tax but as a voluntary present" (Las Casas 1958, 4: 352). There was also an import tax imposed on goods of both indigenous and foreign merchants, and an inheritance tax, with the whole estate often falling to the government (lord) if there were no heirs. Additionally, the Maya of Guatemala paid a marriage tax to the state both on the marriage of their own children and on that of a lord's son or daughter (Las Casas 1958, 4: 349–351). A tax was also paid on the birth of a child (Las Casas 1958, 4: 156). Wealth so accumulated consisted not only of agricultural produce and meat but also of luxury goods such as gold, plumes, and cacao, and of manufactured items, including pottery. Las Casas (1958, 4: 349) related that on inaugural day, when festivities had concluded and the people and vassals had returned home, the new king met with his aristocratic cohorts to plan the collection and distribution of these taxes. At times, this taxation did take the form of tribute, which was coerced from towns refusing to accept the rule of a conquering polity (Zorita 1963: 188).

In addition to providing support for governing families, taxed wealth served various other functions. Las Casas mentioned that taxes supported people when they attended major religious festivals and important foreigners visiting royal towns; taxed wealth also was employed as tribute, gifts to foreign rulers to establish or maintain alliances. Portions also went to pay dowries of lords' sons, and since these brides were often daughters of foreign aristocrats (Las Casas 1958, 4: 354; see also Carrasco 1964: 329 and Betanzos in Carrasco 1967: 257), this is another example of taxes expended to secure foreign relations. Taxes were used as well to support military raids and campaigns (Las Casas 1958, 4: 352; Zorita 1963: 182). Towns suffering from crop failure would be excused from tax levies, and, in extreme situations, such towns would be provided food from royal store houses and seed for the next year's planting (Zorita 1963: 194).

Agricultural land and production were generally organized at the chinamit level, under control of the ruling aristocratic family or lineage (Hill 1992: 39). The lords leased farmland to the poor for "very little rent," and, on other holdings, slave families produced food, and their taxes were based on the amount of land sown and the quantity of firewood and pieces of pitch pine (for torches) collected (Las Casas 1958, 4: 351).

There were markets where goods were exchanged by the rich as well as the poor. Las Casas (1958, 4: 353) described these for Verapaz, where they were located in towns near temples. Trade was in staples and luxury items: maize, beans, salt as well as fruit and game; manufactured items, such as cotton blankets and copper and gold axes; and other luxury items, including emeralds, turquoise, and feathers. Long-distance trade of gold took place from the Pacific coast of Mexico and Guatemala (the Soconusco) to Verapaz. The Cakchiquel and Tzutujil obtained cacao from territory they controlled in the Piedmont (Feldman 1985: 86, citing Vasquez 1937). Among the Quiché, wealthy merchants, occupying an intermediate social position between vassals and aristocrats, transacted long-distance trade (Carmack 1977: 8).

According to Las Casas, public inspectors policed the markets, setting prices and settling disputes. Markets were also populated by artisans trading their wares: "silver smiths, painters, feather workers, who [produced] very artistic and subtle work; smelters of small copper axes (Las Casas 1958, 4: 353). Women brought fabric and clothes they made at home for trade. Others visited the market to offer their skills and labor, and Las Casas (1958, 4: 353) mentioned house-builders and doctors, "great herbalists and perhaps greater sorcerers." One is certainly reminded of Bernal Díaz del Castillo (1927: 176–177) and his observations on the Aztec market at Tenochtitlan, as well as *relaciones* describing the protohistoric Tarascan economy (summarized by Gorenstein and Pollard, 1983). Feldman (1985) studied the trading system for eastern Guatemala, as reconstructed from early Colonial documents.

At Iximché, an extensive trading network is indicated by archaeological evidence. For example, achiote seeds which Guillemin (1977; see chap. 4) recovered from Iximché are from fruit probably grown in the province of Verapaz and the middle Motagua Valley (Feldman 1985: 46). Shell ornaments from Iximché (Guillemin 1965a) are of Pacific coast marine shell, possibly imported from Oaxaca, Mexico (Feldman 1985: 83). Clearly, knowledge of Late Postclassic subsistence and trade would be expanded and refined with an augmentation of archaeological research.

Religious Ritual

Las Casas devoted more attention to religion than to other aspects of Maya culture in Guatemala, not so much to belief systems as to rituals performed in public and private ceremonies. The goals of religion, he wrote, were four: to achieve long life, health, human procreation, and economic well-being, that is, to obtain the means for long life (Las Casas 1958, 4: 155). And, while most people pursued their personal goals through private rituals and petitions to priests, the kings, other lords, and priests practiced penance and directed public ceremonies on behalf of the community.

Turning first to private aspects of religion, Las Casas describes rituals surrounding the home, the harvest and other economic activities, illness, and human fertility. Newly built houses were consecrated to an individual god of the home, who protected its inhabitants in exchange for sacrifices of birds and incense. Such offerings were made at a square altar in the patio of the house or at the front door. The blood of eaten animals was placed on the threshold.

Rituals were not confined to the vicinity of the house. The Maya also maintained shrines in the forests, ideally near springs surrounded by densely wooded areas. At these places auto-sacrifice was performed: "they tortured themselves, taking blood from their ears and fleshy parts and thighs and from other parts" (Las Casas 1958, 4: 153). Similar sacrifices were made in caves, at crossroads, and on hilltops. At roadside shrines on the outskirts of towns, travelers left offerings of whatever they transported: "cotton, cacao, or their pepper or salt" (Las Casas 1958, 4: 154).

Sacrifice or offerings preceded all economic activities, the burning of incense before the hunt, for example, or sacrificing a bird and spilling its blood on the ground before planting. At harvest, for certain plants, they burned incense "at the four corners of the planting" (Las Casas 1958, 4: 154).

Illness was treated with the sacrifice of birds and ultimately the assistance of a priest or doctor. A priest might sacrifice on behalf of the ill person's family. Doctors treated the sick with herbs but could resort to castigating the patient for his sins and seeking confession in order to remove the affliction. In extreme circumstances, especially for a lord near death, a slave might be sacrificed or even a son or daughter (Las Casas 1958, 4: 155, 361). Divination was part of the process. Las Casas (1958, 4: 155) mentioned that doctors cast lots to determine the appropriate sacrifice; that lots were cast to determine the reason for a couple's infertility; and in another instance, that the casting of lots decided the day the umbilical cord would be cut away from the newborn (Las Casas 1958, 4: 156).

Births were celebrated with sacrifices and feasts for relatives and friends. The newborn was washed in a river or spring, while "they offered sacrifice of incense and parrots." Pottery in use on the birthday was sacrificed to the river. Many of these activities were repeated when the infant began to crawl, at weaning, "and when he began to speak, they made major feasts and festivals and more sacrifices of incense and birds of diverse colors" (Las Casas 1958, 4: 157). The pleasures of parenthood were accompanied by deep concern for the childless couple. Doctors confessed the couple to determine the sins that dissuaded the gods from giving them children. Doctors also prescribed sexual abstinence for 40 or 50 days, fasting, and other ritual prohibitions (Las Casas 1958, 4: 156).

If commoners found these ritual demands both painful and expensive, such burdens apparently were even more onerous for the Maya king, priests, and other lords. Las Casas (1958, 4: 149) related that "in times of great necessity" such a man spent up to eight or nine months a year living in a small hut, "a miserable little hovel, very small and covered with green leaves," that he would not enter his regular abode nor speak to anyone, and that his diet was restricted to dried maize and fruit. Las Casas added that "offerings were made of all things except men," and that sacrificed items included "all types of birds, animals, vegetables, meats, incense, all the rest, and they themselves spilled their own blood daily for many hours: sometimes from their ears, others from their tongues, [other times] from the fleshy parts of the arms, others from their thighs, others from their genitals" (Las Casas 1958, 4: 149). This penance was offered for all the town to the gods, "as a good prelate that loaded upon himself all the community sins."

There are clear archaeological correlates for Iximché: hundreds of broken incense burners have been found. Of identifiable ceramic effigies, birds outnumber other life forms except humans (see chap. 5). Also, a drawing preserved on the wall of an Iximché temple depicts a man perforating his tongue in auto-sacrifice (Guillemin 1965a: 28, 45). Altars are certainly common in the ceremonial complex at Iximché, both in patios and in front of doors, and tend to be square. The importance of the quadrilateral form in traditional Maya ritual persists to the present day, where the four sides of a table, for example, are oriented to the cardinal directions (see, e.g., Vogt 1990: 127–130). The account by Las Casas, however, points to what is probably a major gap in the archaeology of ritual at Iximché. A systematic survey of the surrounding hills and streams, along roads, and especially at crossroads very likely would locate isolated shrines in the vicinity.

Priests

Las Casas (1958, 4: 149) wrote that in some provinces the king took the role of high priest, but generally he differentiated between the two, describing the distinct role of each, as, for example, in the sacrificial ceremony referred to below. For Verapaz, Las Casas recounted that the principal priest was one of the lords and always "the most respected and esteemed person for the king and supreme lord and for the lesser persons and all the rest" (Las Casas 1958, 4: 351). He also alluded to a hierarchy of priests and to the election of the leading priest in a manner similar to that for kings. In general, Carrasco (1961: 485) saw the priesthood as one of several avenues for social mobility among societies in Prehispanic Mesoamerica, others existing for those in the military and merchants in international trade.

Public Ceremonies—Human Sacrifice

Of all the information provided by Las Casas, his description of major religious ceremonies seems most germane to this archaeological study. Some of the ceramics from excavations in the very center of the ceremonial complex at Iximché must have been used in such public rituals. All lines of evidence (see chaps. 9 and 10; Guillemin 1965b; 1967) indicate that the bulk of the human skeletal remains are of sacrificial victims who were probably dispatched during the course of ceremonies to some extent resembling those recounted by Las Casas (see below).

Five or six major festivals were held regularly each year, with their dates determined by an astrologer. Las Casas described several of these, in whole or part, and, from what he wrote, the following events may have been typical. Before each, men of the community spent several nights in the temples, sometimes smudging themselves with smoke and practicing auto-sacrifice. In one case, Las Casas mentioned they burned themselves with firebrands. Temples and plazas were swept clean and idols refurbished and decorated with gold, paint, and cloth. Green branches and pine boughs were spread on the ground, "as we in Spain throw Cyprus" (Las Casas 1958, 4: 151). Then sons of aristocrats, under priestly supervision, brought idols from their customary repositories to the town center, proceeding to the sound of trumpets, drums, and other instruments, and moving, Las Casas (1958, 4: 149) wrote, "with inestimable devotion." Ball courts figured in these festivals, since the idols were taken to them as well as to the temples. Las Casas remarked that lords and chiefs played ball games during the ceremonies; in the *Popol Vuh*, gods of the underworld contended through ball games with creator gods for supremacy. Such confrontations may have been acted out by elite during festivals at Iximché.

During what Las Casas called their festival of Lent, slaves to be sacrificed were allowed to roam the town for several days before they were executed. Yoked and guarded by three or four men, they visited any houses they chose, eating and drinking what they wished, although they were prohibited from leaving the town (Las Casas 1958, 4: 150).

The night before beginning the ceremony and the day of sacrifice, the idols were in place or were brought to the temples; the gods were said to be arriving. There were "many sacrifices of birds and parrots, quails and other birds of diverse species and colors . . . the musical instruments began to sound and [there were] songs and dances and farcical inventions and as many other kinds of games and delights as they were able to invent and they were caught up in this, and on this the dawn broke" (Las Casas 1958, 4: 151). Las Casas described the various performances as the hour of human sacrifice approached. "Gathered there were the ministers and musicians and singers and dancers with their exercises never ceasing . . . and those that were playing did not obstruct those that were singing, nor the buffoons, nor the others represented; they were in agreement on the material which was well organized and coordinated" (Las Casas 1958, 4: 151–152).

The slaves slated for sacrifice probably were dragged forward by the hair, each by a lord, with the supreme lord praying in a loud voice: "God remember us, that we are yours. Give us health; give us children and prosperity for your people that promote and serve you. Give water and good weather to maintain us so that we can live. Hear our petitions; receive our prayers; help us against our enemies; give us leisure and rest" (Las Casas 1958, 4: 152). At the sacrificial altar, each victim was delivered to the priest-executioner and his ministers. They removed the victim's heart with a knife and offered it to an idol. The priest then smeared blood on idols at the various altars, "because each [idol] had its dedicated altar, and the sun had its own and the moon its own and the East and the West and the part of the North and of the South" (Las Casas 1958, 4: 152). The heads were then severed from the corpses and placed on poles at a "certain altar dedicated to this," and when some time had passed, the skulls were buried. Among reasons Las Casas gave for this display was that of putting fear in their enemies.

The remaining meat was cooked and eaten "as a very sacred thing, consecrated to the gods, and he was happy who received at least a bite. The hands and feet and other delicate parts were presented to the grand priest and the king as things most delicious and esteemed. All the rest was distributed to the other priests and ministers of the altar, because not one piece was distributed to the people of the town, and that was done for religion, and not for any other reason" (Las Casas 1958, 4: 152).

Fifty decapitated skulls provide convincing evidence for human sacrifice at Iximché (see chap. 10). The skulls were found next to two low platforms (see chaps. 4 and 9), probably the altars where, according to Las Casas, these skulls were displayed on poles before their interment. Guillemin did not encounter much of the postcranial skeletons of these individuals, evidence, albeit negative, that the meat was cooked and eaten. The bones may have been discarded as food refuse or buried ceremonially. Certainly this is a controversial issue, but one amenable to archaeological investigation. The ravine slopes next to the ceremonial center at Iximché should be examined and any bone from midden dumps there analyzed.

4

⎍⎍⎍⎍⎍

Iximché and Details of the Excavations

In this chapter we provide a general orientation to the site of Iximché and to Guillemin's work there. This is not an exhaustive summary of his findings or interpretations, and the careful student will consult Guillemin's publications, especially items dated 1959, 1965a, 1965b, 1967, and 1977. At his death, Guillemin left unpublished certain information in the form of notes and manuscripts as well as captioned photographs of his discoveries at Iximché, and much of that information is summarized here. To our knowledge, all of the photographs included in this chapter were taken and printed by George Guillemin or his associates, and most are published here for the first time.

The extent of greater Iximché, including outlying communities, neighborhoods, and individual homesteads, remains poorly understood. The site's ceremonial center, however, is better known. It is laid out along a narrow point of land as a series of five contiguous plazas (designated by Guillemin as A to E) surrounded by building platforms. We will proceed from west to east and discuss the four plazas investigated by Guillemin (A to D), beginning with the area west of Plaza A. The chapter will conclude with general discussions of the site settlement plan and details of construction.

Burials which Guillemin excavated are described separately in chapter 9. For ease of cross reference, these data are also organized by plaza, again proceeding from west to east (Plaza A to Plaza C).

The Protective Trench (Area West of Plaza A)

Iximché is on a point of land isolated by deep gorges to the north and south. The point is formed by the juncture of these gorges at the site's southeastern end. On the west, the natural defenses of the locale were augmented by a man-made ditch cutting across the peninsula from gorge to gorge. Although mostly filled in at the time of Guillemin's investigations, this moat still had considerable depth when visited by Fuentes y Guzmán (Sáenz de Santa María 1969, 1: 333) at the end of the seventeenth century and even later when described by Stephens in the 1840s. In 1963, Guillemin trenched through the filled-in moat and determined its original cross section and depth of 8 m. Figures 4.1 and 4.2 show this work in progress and the cross sectional outline.

The moat is 60–70 m northwest of Plaza A, its location depicted in site maps (Guillemin 1965a, 1967). The effect of the ditch was heightened by the construction of two building platforms along its interior, or eastern, border, probably the associated "breastwork" mentioned by Fuentes y Guzmán (Sáenz de Santa María 1969, 1: 333). The gap between these platforms forms the present-day entrance into the ceremonial center of Iximché. Evidently, Guillemin did not investigate any of the 12 platform structures he mapped south and west of Plaza A.

Plaza A

Plaza A is dominated by two pyramids, or elevated temple bases, facing each other across the Plaza from east to west (see fig. 1.1). They were designated as Structures 2 and 3 by Guillemin, and in this and every case we will follow his numerical assignments for structures.

Temple (Structure) 2

Figure 4.3 shows Temple 2 from the southeast in 1959, before excavation; the low remnants of Structures 17 and 18 are in the foreground. Temple 2 is ca. 8 m high. Figure 4.4 depicts Temple 2 with excavations in progress, the angle of view now more from the south. Another view of Temple 2 is shown in figure 4.5 with restorations complete and from essentially the same perspective. Remnants of the two latest phases of construction were stabilized and are visible in this photograph. At the base are remnants of the latest, or Phase III, mostly removed, Guillemin (1965b) believed, since the Conquest to be used as building stones. Most

Fig. 4.1. Moat, Excavation in Progress

Fig. 4.2. Cross Section of Excavated Moat

of the exposed facade of the Temple 2 pyramid, then, is of Phase II. The remnant of the adobe-wall temple on top of the structure is also of Phase II, the walls having been truncated and buried during Phase III construction. Remnants of the earliest phase, Phase I, were found through an exploration tunnel from the front base into Temple 2: "80 cm inside the pyramidal base 2 there is another construction of the same kind (that is, graduated terraces)" (Guillemin 1965b: 29). Figure 4.6 shows the entrance to the tunnel and the two most recent phases of construction. In figure 4.5, what Guillemin interpreted to be a sacrificial block can be seen in front of the temple doors with an associated altar just below it. Inside the temple, Guillemin (1967: 29) found traces of ten polychrome wall murals, all of human figures. Because the outlines had been incised into the clay base, he was able to record several of these figures accurately, and he reproduced three of these as line drawings (Guillemin 1965a: 44–45; 1967: 30). A description and plan-view drawing of this temple are included in Guillemin's 1967 (pp. 28–29) article. According to the 1960–1961 field notes, walls and benches of this structure on Temple 2 were constructed of adobe blocks covered with stucco.

Fig. 4.3. Temple 2, Before Excavation

Structure 74

Adjoining Temple 2 on its south corner, Structure 74 is a small platform probably associated with human sacrifice. Two decapitated skulls were found deposited behind this structure (Guillemin 1969: 27; see chap. 9).

Temple (Structure) 3

This pyramidal temple base is approximately 7 m high and situated in the eastern corner of Plaza A. Guillemin excavated a large quantity of cylindrical *incensario* fragments from its deposits, and wrote that "more than a dozen of these incensarios were in use in this temple" (Guillemin 1965a: 25). Stone artifacts of note were found in the vicinity of Temple 3 as well, including a small carved pendant(?), 6.5 cm × 5.5 cm, of white crystallized material (fig. 4.7). In the ground outside of Temple 3, near the east-southeast corner, Guillemin encountered and

Fig. 4.4. Temple 2, Viewed from Southeast, Excavation in Progress

Fig. 4.5. Temple 2, Restoration Complete (previously published in Guillemin 1968: 70; © *Archéologia* No. 23, 1968)

Fig. 4.6. Temple 2, Entrance to Exploratory Tunnel

recorded a crudely sculpted human effigy (fig. 4.8). The outside dimensions of the figure are ca. 36 cm × 24 cm. Near these two objects, in the Plaza between Structures 3 and 79, excavators found a stone vessel interpreted to be a brazier (*quemador*). Sketched in the 1960 field notes, this is probably the artifact photographed in Guillemin (1965a: 48).

Figure 4.9 shows Temple 3 before excavation, photographed from Temple 2. Figure 4.10 was taken from the same locale but after restoration of the facade (Great Palace I and Plaza B are in the background). Finally, in figure 4.11, excavation is just beginning on the northeast side

Fig. 4.7. Temple 3, Pendant

Fig. 4.8. Temple 3, Sculpted Human Effigy (front)

Fig. 4.9. Temple 3, Before Excavation

of Temple 3; Structures 23 and 22, with restoration in progress, extend from the left foreground back toward Temple 3.

Structures 22 and 23

Figures 4.12 and 4.13 show these platforms before and after restoration, respectively. On the back of the original photograph for figure 4.12, Guillemin noted that these structures had been partially excavated by J. de Szecsy in 1956. According to the 1963 field notes, Structure 22 evidenced three phases of construction.

Structure 27

This platform (fig. 4.14), located behind Temple 2 on the western perimeter of Plaza A, contained a dug-out crypt with the remains of four skeletons. Grave goods with the principal burial (27-A/IV) included a gold headband, ten small gold jaguar heads thought to be collar ornaments, and a bracelet possibly fashioned from a human occiput carved with bird and star motifs in a "Mexican style" (Guillemin 1961; 1965a: 33; see chap. 9).

Fig. 4.10. Temple 3, Front Facade Restored

Fig. 4.11. Temple 3, Excavation of Northeast Side

Fig. 4.12. Structures 22 and 23, Before Excavation

Fig. 4.13. Structures 22 and 23, Restoration Complete

Fig. 4.14. Structure 27 (published previously in Guillemin 1961: 90; republished by permission of the Sociedad de Geografía e Historia de Guatemala)

Structure 8 (Ball Court)

The Plaza A ball court has enclosed end zones with a playing field measuring 30 m × 6 m (Guillemin 1965a: 27). Figure 4.15 shows this ball court during excavation in 1960.

Plaza B

The front facade of Great Palace I was reconstructed and Plaza B cleared during the 1959 field season. Figures 4.16 and 4.17 are photographs of work in progress. The front wall of the Great Palace I platform can be seen in figure 4.17 to the left. Figure 4.18 shows the work almost completed.

Great Palace I

This massive elevated platform covers ca. 2500 m², and through extensive excavation Guillemin identified three different superposed periods of construction and occupation. The three stucco floors of Great Palace I are visible in figure 4.19. Guillemin (n.d.a) wrote that the uppermost and lowest structural phases could be comprehended more clearly than

Fig. 4.15. Ball court (Structure 8), Excavation in Progress

Fig. 4.16. Plaza B, Excavation in Progress

Fig. 4.17. Great Palace I and Plaza B, Excavation in Progress

Fig. 4.18. Plaza B, Restoration Complete (in Guillemin 1969: fig. 20; republished by permission of the Société Suisse des Américanistes)

Fig. 4.19. Great Palace I, Excavation in Progress (Stratigraphy)

those of middle deposits because of more disturbance there by subsequent construction.

Figure 4.20 shows the beginning of Guillemin's work, from west to east across Great Palace I with Temple 4 in the background. Prepared floors which appear somewhat weathered may have been cleared by Janos de Szecsy in 1956. ("The southwest side had been exposed by Janos Szecsy and restored by the undersigned in 1959" [Guillemin n.d.a].) In figure 4.21, excavations are underway, and a hearth/basin complex has been exposed in the southwest quadrant of the structure, not far beneath the surface. See figure 4.22 for a closeup of the hearth/basin complex. Guillemin's hand-written notation for figure 4.22 indicates that it was from the structure's intermediate phase.

Guillemin wrote that the lowest level was well preserved and that it "consisted of four house units looking onto a square court with an altar in its center. This altar is of the same type as those of the two later phases of construction. Of three altars, only the bases survive. They vary slightly in shape and size but have in common a small basin without drain let into the cemented floor on the side of each. The altar on the

Fig. 4.20. Great Palace I, Beginning Stage of Excavation

Fig. 4.21. Great Palace I, Excavation in Progress

Fig. 4.22. Great Palace I, Hearth

lowest level is the only one to show the traces of four posts" (Guillemin n.d.a; translated from French). An isometric drawing of this early phase of Great Palace I is included in Guillemin's 1965a (p. 23) publication. The basin of this central altar is that exposed in the foreground of figure 4.19 (viewed from the south). Figure 4.23 is of the same feature but from an elevated perspective. A posthole and the two far corners of the hearth platform are visible. On the back of this photo Guillemin wrote, "Great Palace Phase I (early) Altar with Basin and Postholes 1963."

Another altar (fig. 4.24) is more difficult to locate. It is from the "first phase" (earliest) and a "southern" patio. The altar is relatively small; a trowel left for scale in another photo suggests that the upper surface is about 85 cm². Guillemin identified another altarlike feature as from the first phase of construction and located "in front of a house" (fig. 4.25). This is the same block protruding over the step in figure 4.26 and depicted in an apparently heretofore unpublished plan view of rooms and other features of the first phase (fig. 4.27).

One other detail can be documented photographically. Figure 4.28 is of an exposed storm drain in Great Palace I. Evidently, locations of storm drains in this structure were not recorded in detail as they were

Fig. 4.23. Great Palace I, Central Altar-Basin Complex, Phase 1

Fig. 4.24. Great Palace I, Phase 1, Altar from "Southern" Patio

Fig. 4.25. Great Palace I, Phase I, Altar in Front of Room

for Great Palace II (discussed below), possibly because they were poorly preserved.

Temple (Structure) 1

This pyramidal temple base had been severely eroded but had a remaining elevation of ca. 5 m (fig. 4.29). The temple platform of the final construction phase was estimated to have been 6 m above the Plaza surface. Guillemin (1959: 28) found evidence for an earlier construction phase, a substructure about 1 m inside the other. He (1959 field notes) recorded the remains of a square altar (fig. 4.30) centered at the base of the stairs rising from Plaza B. Guillemin (1959 field notes) mentioned finding important incensario fragments near the summit of this structure. Also, an aboriginal copper bell and three forged iron crossbow darts were found next to or within the southwest corner of this structure (1959 field notes). The crossbow darts are illustrated elsewhere (Guillemin 1965a: 34). During excavation, Guillemin also reported finding adobe and stucco wall fragments painted yellow, dark blue, and red: "The walls

Fig. 4.26. Great Palace I, Phase 1, Steps and Altar in Front of Room

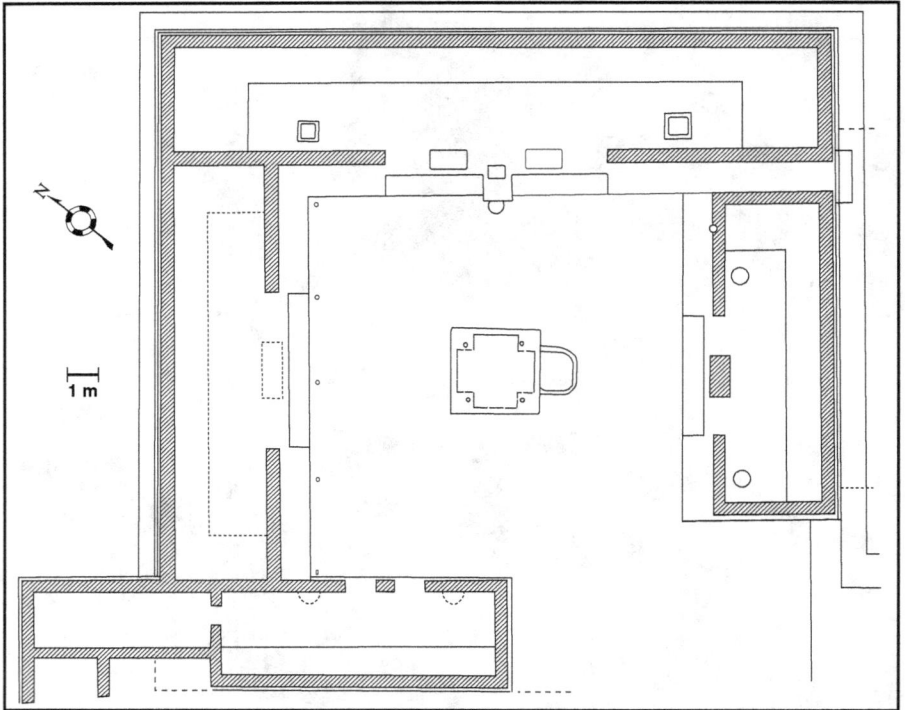

Fig. 4.27. Plan of Great Palace I, Phase 1

of the corner [southwest] have the color of yellow ochre on the stucco, the neighboring corner, that striking west, has the color dark blue . . . I found the color red on adobe near the highest point (*"cuspide"*); they are probably the remains of the superstructure" (1959 field notes). Finally for Temple 1, Guillemin (1959 field notes) sketched two ceramic incensario effigies which could be linked to photographs. For the specimen in figure 4.31, about one-third of the vessel had been restored; it had an overall height of 48 cm and manifested spikes and vertical flanges (see chap. 6, ceramic type Beaker Incensario). The partial remains of this vessel were found upon (*"sobre"*) Temple 1. Excavators found the other incensario fragment at the base of Temple 1 (fig. 4.32; maximum vertical dimension = 32 cm). Figure 4.33 shows Guillemin surrounded by his crew in 1959. They were working here in the gap between Structures 1 (left) and 13, which was the passageway between Plazas A and B.

Fig. 4.28. Great Palace I, Storm Drain

Fig. 4.29. Temple 1, Restoration in Progress

Structure 9

Directly across Plaza B from Temple 1, the building remnant on this platform was well-enough preserved that Guillemin (1965b: 30) could define a bench along the back and lateral walls interrupted by a square altarlike construction near the rear-center. This was finely made of pumice blocks and covered with stucco. In figure 4.34 the altar is visible on the back wall of the edifice. It appears to resemble that in figure 4.24 from Great Palace I. In the floor of this structure was a circular hearth (fig. 4.35), 1 m in diameter, with a concave cross section, and a floor of pumice blocks (Guillemin 1965b: 30). Guillemin believed it was used for burning incense (see Guillemin 1959 for a photograph of the Structure 9 bench, altar, and hearth). Details on three excavated burials are included in chapter 9.

Great Palace II (Plaza C)

Guillemin (n.d.b) reported on excavations of this complex in a typed manuscript, titled, "Excavations 1971–72," which appears to be a portion

Fig. 4.30. Temple 1, Remains of Altar at Base of Stairs

Fig. 4.31. Temple 1, Ceramic beaker incensario with Human Effigy (published previously in Guillemin 1965a: 49; republished by permission of the Instituto de Antropología e Historia de Guatemala)

Fig. 4.32. Temple 1, Ceramic Human Effigy from Base of Structure

Fig. 4.33. Temple 1, Excavation in Progress; George Guillemin and Crew, 1959

Fig. 4.34. Structure 9, Excavation in Progress

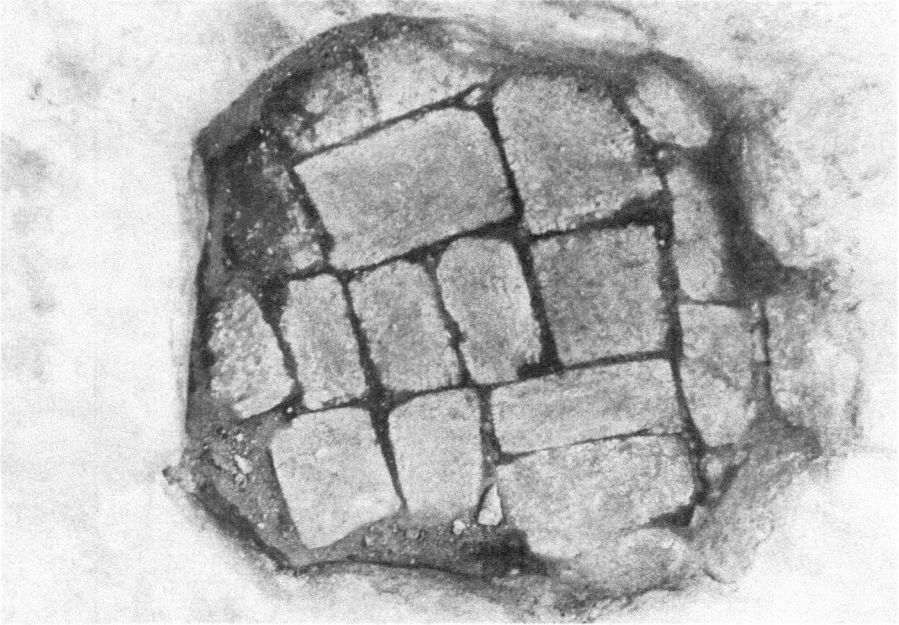

Fig. 4.35. Structure 9, Hearth Lined with Pumice Blocks

of a research proposal. Additional information is from his 1977 article, a detailed plan of Great Palace II (fig. 4.36), and a few photographs. Surviving photographs were taken from the top of Temple 5, looking south. In figure 4.37, the Central Patio (Patio A in fig. 4.36) and Patio B (foreground) are shown in an early stage of excavation. (For patio and structure (room) designations, see fig. 4.36.) The same stage of excavation is revealed in figure 4.38, which includes Patio C, room 114, Patio B, and the eastern corner of the Central Patio (A). The photographs in figures 4.39 and 4.40 were taken from the same location, but excavations are more complete. The former is of Patio B with the Central Patio (A) and Structure 110 (left background), and the latter is of Structure 114 with Patios B and C to either side.

Central Patio

Guillemin wrote (n.d.b) that the Central Patio (A) was more elevated than adjoining buildings and had been subjected to more erosion.

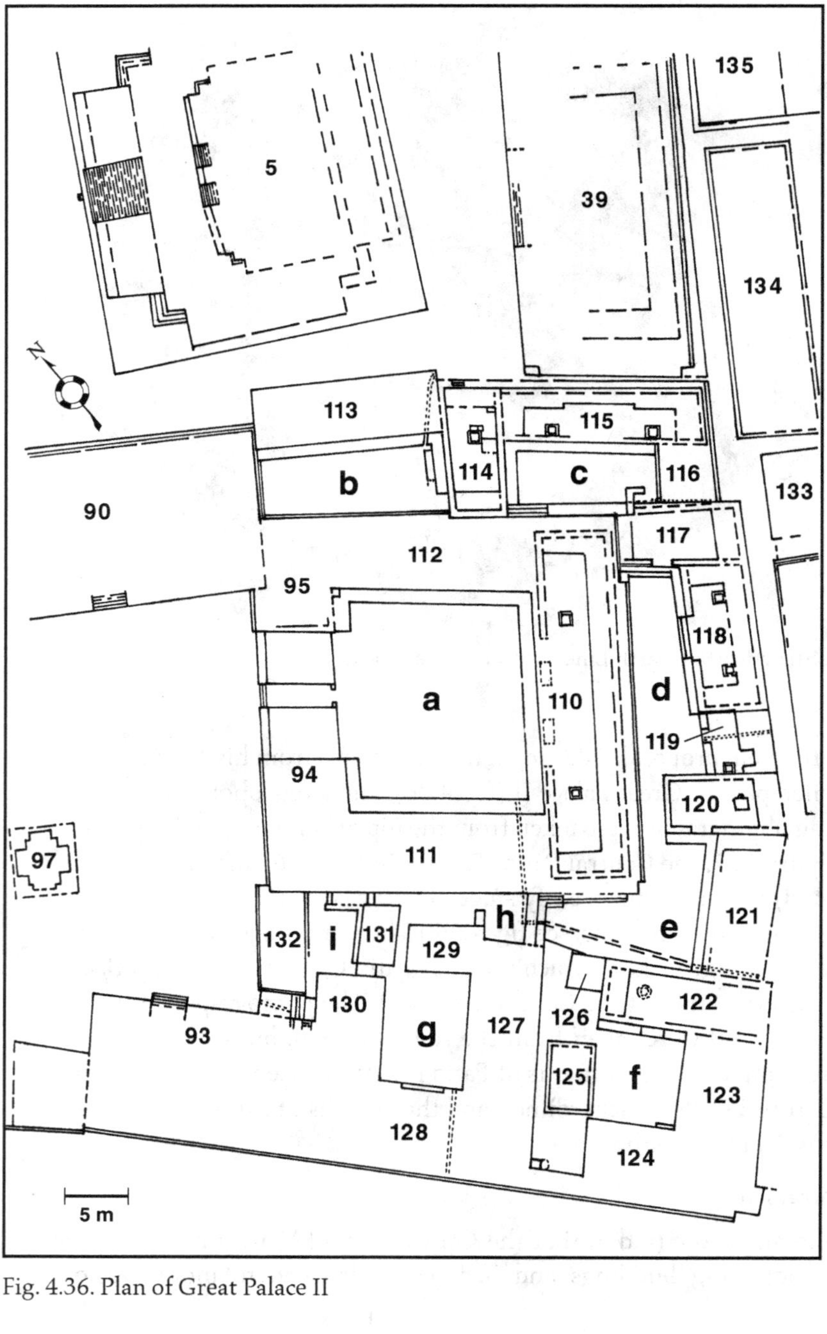

Fig. 4.36. Plan of Great Palace II

Because of this, he believed that "there was no hope of finding details of structures around the Central Patio."

Structure 110

Situated on the southeastern side of the Central Patio (A), Structure 110 was, for Guillemin, the "principal house of the palace." It was slightly elevated through two broad risers a few centimeters above the floor of Central Patio (A). Guillemin found traces of a stone, adobe, and stucco masonry bench which extended 22.93 m along the back wall. Two square hearths were dug into the structure floor. Finally, Guillemin (n.d.b) wrote that "facing the Central Patio (A), there were certainly three doors separated by two columns, but there are not sufficient elements to reconstruct the plan with precision" (cf. Guillemin 1977: 240).

Structures 111 and 112

Given the eroded condition of the floors, Guillemin found few useful details through excavating Structures 111 and 112 on the northeast and southwest sides of the Central Patio. There was some evidence, however, of two fireplaces in each and a bench in Structure 112 (Guillemin 1977: 241; n.d.b). Test excavation to a lower depth in Structure 111 revealed no evidence of an earlier phase of construction (Guillemin n.d.b).

Structures 94 and 95

Structures 94 and 95 are small edifices at either side of the Palace main entrance. Guillemin noted that they may have served as "bastions for defense," and that they might have housed palace guards (Guillemin 1977: 240; n.d.b).

He wrote that "the limit between Structure 95 and 112 is not visible" and that Structure 90 was contemporaneous with them (Guillemin n.d.b). At the time of writing, Structure 113 had not been excavated.

Structure 114

Because he found no trace of a door opening onto either Patio B or Patio C, Structure 114 posed a problem for Guillemin. He thought it likely that a door once existed to Patio B because of broad steps against its east wall. The small steps from the north end of structure 114 were poorly preserved and may not have been used during final occupation of the palace, an interpretation supported by a partially preserved bench across the northern end of Structure 114. Another bench across the

Fig. 4.37. Great Palace II, Central Patio (A) and Patio B, Excavation in Progress

Fig. 4.38. Great Palace II, Patio C, Structure 114, Patio B, Excavation in Progress

Fig. 4.39. Great Palace II, Patio B, Central Patio (A), Structure 110, Excavation in Progress (published previously in Guillemin 1977: fig. 4; republished by permission of Academic Press Ltd.)

southern end and a central fire hearth render Structure 114 a unique edifice in Great Palace II. Guillemin suggested that it might have functioned as "the quarters of a guard or possibly a steam bath." From the floor of the structure excavators recovered the remains of straw and carbonized wood and corn, and "among numerous ordinary sherds . . . one piece painted red on cream with the effigy of a frog" (not found in the ceramic collection; Guillemin n.d.b).

Structure 115

Two hearths were preserved in Structure 115 as well as several benches. The rear bench was set back slightly and was more than 5 m long. Guillemin (n.d.b) described Structure 115 as a "house unit"; it faces Patio C to the south.

Patio D; Structures 117, 118, and 119

Behind Structure 110, this narrow patio served three rooms opening onto it from the north and east. Structure 117, Guillemin wrote, was

Fig. 4.40. Great Palace II, Patio B, Structure 114, Patio C, Excavation in Progress (published previously in Guillemin 1977: fig. 4; republished by permission of Academic Press Ltd.)

similar to Structure 114, although it had not been completely excavated at the time of writing. He (n.d.b) described Structure 118 as a "house-base with two hearths and a bench on three sides" and with "access by a stairway of three steps." Structure 119 apparently had been a house-sized room which later was reduced in size by construction of Structure 120. Entry was by a narrow door; a single hearth was situated next to a wall. On the floor of this room, excavators found "fragments of two 'comales' . . . a small entire bowl [and] a miniature jug (height 10.5 cm) containing carbonized achiote seeds" (Guillemin n.d.b; fig. 4.41).

Patio E, Structures 120 and 121

Structure 120 was elevated one step above the floor of Patio E. The room had a bench at its eastern end and on the floor, a hearth with two cemented basins (possibly the hearth/basin complex in fig. 4.42). Guillemin believed that Structure 121 was similar to Structure 118, although erosion had removed all but the extreme northern end of the bench.

Fig. 4.41. Great Palace II, Structure 119, Carbonized Achiote Seeds

Fig. 4.42. Great Palace II, Structure 120(?), Hearth and Basin Complex

Patio F, Structures 122–125

The only features found in these structures were the western bench and hearth of Structure 122. Other details were lost because of extensive erosion.

Structure 126

This "small, square base" was annexed to the west end of Structure 122. A quantity of carbonized corn cobs (fig. 4.43) was found in the alcove formed by Structures 122 and 126; Guillemin (n.d.b) suggested that Structure 126 "could have been a granary."

Patio G, Structures 127–130

The floor surfaces of Structures 127 and 128 had been eroded away. Investigation of Structures 129 and 130 had not been concluded at the time of writing.

Patio I, Structures 131 and 132

No information survives regarding Structures 131 and 132, but Guillemin (n.d.b) described a stairway originally accessing Patio I from out-

Fig. 4.43. Great Palace II, Structure 126, Carbonized Corn Cob

side the palace, although later the stairway was blocked by a 2-m-thick wall. Fragments of ladle incense burners had been deposited on the stairway, and fragments of a cylindrical incense burner were found in front of the first step, its effigy attributed by Guillemin (1977: 256–257, fig. 8) to the Maya god Gucumatz. Guillemin (n.d.b) described one other building alteration. Sometime after initial construction, the narrow passageway from Patios I to G (between Structures 131 and 132) was walled-off and traffic between the patios routed through the two-stepped passageway north of Structure 131.

Drains

Rainwater falling on roofs and patios was channeled out of the palace through drains. These conduits were square in section and constructed of flat pieces of dressed stone. Foundation slabs supported both lateral walls and covering elements where drains passed beneath structures (Guillemin 1977: 241). Locations of these storm drains, issuing out of most patios, are depicted in figure 4.36. Guillemin (n.d.b) noted that the stucco floor of Patio B had been inclined slightly to the east in order to direct water to the drain-opening in its northeast corner.

Other Structures in Plaza C

Structure 39

Guillemin mentioned "clearing the posterior facade of this house platform" but provides little detail and an incomplete drawing of the structure base (see fig. 1.1). The structure was built on an "elevated cornice" or large terrace.

Three burials recovered from the vicinity of this platform are described in chapter 9. Excavators found one of these near fragments of a large stone ball-game yoke, probably that depicted in figure 4.44, leaning against the rear facade of the structure and 8.9 m from its southern end. The burial probably was situated between Structures 39 and 134. Beneath the skeleton were the remains of a gold necklace (Guillemin 1977: 242–243) comprised of 15 bells and 87 small spherical beads (see fig. 9.18).

In the vicinity of the yoke and Burial 39-A, excavators also recovered fragments of a carved stone cylinder as well as remains of a stone ball. Guillemin described the stone cylinder as having a "simplified human

Fig. 4.44. Structure 39, Stone Yoke

head wearing a slightly conical cap" and regarded it as a "phallic ab-
straction [which] could be planted in the ground and certainly was a cult
object" (Guillemin 1977: 243; probably the artifact in fig. 4.45).

Associated with one of two burials found near Burial 39-A was a carved
jade pendant, 27 mm × 41 mm (fig. 4.46; Guillemin 1977: 243; n.d.b).

Structure 38

This 68-m-long platform on the northeast side of Plaza C served as an
elevated base for three separate houses. Guillemin (1967; 1969) excavated here intensively and identified three superposed phases of construction, which are visible in figure 4.47. The houses, each with its
own staircase, were reported by Guillemin to have had walls and pil-
lars of adobe. Because of the destructive agencies of weather and
agriculture, surficial features consisted only of traces of hearths and
masonry benches. For the ceramic study reported here, no pottery
from Structure 38 survived (with provenience intact). Nevertheless,
although Guillemin reported mostly domestic pottery from the
platform, he did mention a fragment of an incensario (fig. 4.48), the
effigy of which he identified as the Mexican god Tlaloc (Guillemin
1977: 252).

Fig. 4.45. Structure 39, Stone Phallus

Structures 36 and 37

These platforms, on the west side of Plaza C, were in a deteriorated state, and Guillemin investigated them superficially. The two were separated by a 1-m-wide passage providing the only discernible access to Plaza C from the west, as, according to Guillemin (1969: 26), secondary walls had been constructed to block other entrances. On the floor of this passage Guillemin (1969: 26) found the remains of carbonized straw,

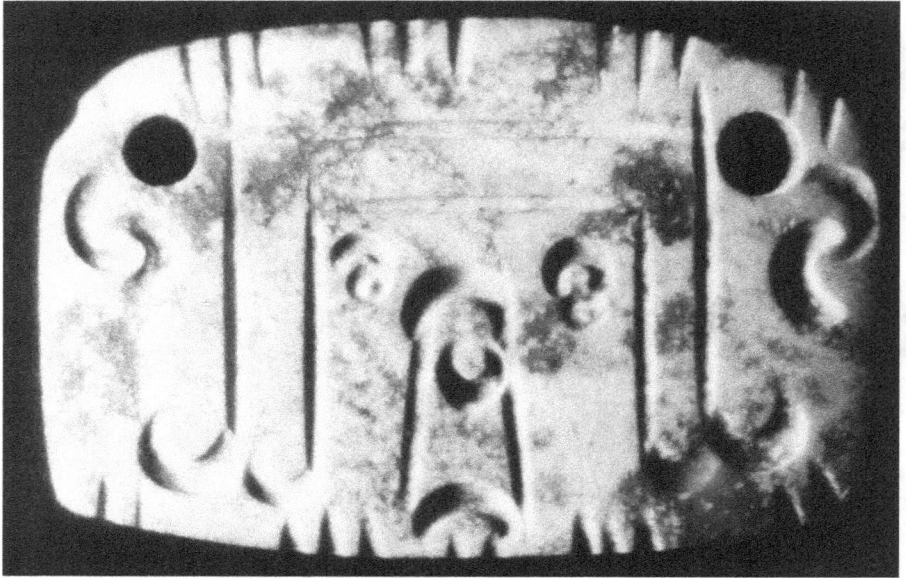

Fig. 4.46. Structure 39, Jade Pendant

Fig. 4.47. Structure 38, Excavation in Progress (Published previously in Guillemin 1969: Fig. 5; republished by permission of the Société Suisse des Américanistes)

Fig. 4.48. Structure 38, Ceramic Effigy Fragment

and he commented, "this seems to confirm that most of the roofing of the houses was probably of straw." Later, he seems to have reversed himself on the existence of a passageway between Plazas B and C, by stating simply that, "Group C is isolated from Group B by a wall" (Guillemin 1977: 235).

Temple (Structure) 4

Guillemin (1963 field notes) found evidence for two phases of construction in this temple base which rises 7 m above Plaza C on its western edge and which abuts Great Palace I to the east. A small annex, Structure 104, is situated on the south corner of Structure 4. Adjacent to it, buried in the plaza floor, were 48 human skulls, the scattered bones of other body parts, and associated obsidian blades. (See chap. 9. Structure 104 is designated as such on the final map [see fig. 1.1] but is referred to as Structure 98 in Guillemin's 1969 publication and as the Structure 4 Annex in his 1963 field notes.)

Temple (Structure) 5

The Temple 5 pyramid faces its counterpart, Temple 4, from the east. Nine meters high and 27 m across at the base, its sloping sides are interrupted by four corniced terraces. The 4.35-m-wide staircase becomes a double staircase between the final terrace and the summit (temple) platform. Two construction phases were identified through excavation.

Plaza C Ball Court (Structure 7)

In terms of restoration, this ball court received little attention compared with that in Plaza A, although Guillemin related that the proportions of the two structures are similar. Architectural differences are described elsewhere (Guillemin 1969).

Placita C, Temple (Structure) 6, and Structure 97

Five meters high, Temple 6 is just east of the ball court but faces onto Placita C, the small plaza just west of Great Palace II. It was in a state of poor preservation when investigated by Guillemin (1965b: 29). Structure 97, in the center of Placita C, was "a small altar in the form of a cross" (Guillemin 1969).

Structures in Plaza D

In his unpublished report, "Excavations, 1971–72," Guillemin provided a few details regarding Structure 40, the long base for three aligned edifices, from west to east, Structures 136, 137, and 138. Structure 136 is the longest at 20.35 m. A short wall section connects the backs of Structures 136 and 137. Guillemin suggests that it might have been constructed as a shield against the wind, but its primary purpose also might have been to limit access. Guillemin (n.d.b) wrote that "a drain passed beneath this wall." In Structure 137, Guillemin found evidence for two phases of construction. Structure 69 is an elevated platform, 3 m high, behind Great Palace II. Although stairs link it to Plaza D, "with a large stairway of 4.95 m facing east, between the posterior facade and the Great Palace II (Structures 118, 119, 120) there is a narrow and deep passage."

Palace III occupies the southern side of Plaza D. It contained two small interior patios surrounded by house platforms and a main patio without an altar (like Great Palace II and in contradistinction to Great Palace I; Guillemin 1977: 244). It also resembles Great Palace II in not being elevated. Palace III is smaller than the two Great Palaces, covering about 800 m^2 (Guillemin 1977: 244).

Structures 43 and 45

Two structures for which there is no descriptive information were mentioned. Notes with some human skeletal remains identified them as coming from Structure 45, which may be located on the western periphery of Plaza E (that is, just east of Plaza D; see fig. 1.1). Structure 43 produced a sample of potsherds but is otherwise unknown.

Settlement Plan at Iximché

Discussion is limited to the plaza areas investigated by Guillemin, especially Plazas A, B, and C, and Placita C. As Guillemin (1977) points out, strong parallels are evident when Plazas A and B are compared to Plaza C and Placita C. In each of these two-plaza complexes, there is a large ceremonial plaza to the west with two large facing temple pyramids aligned roughly east to west. There is a ball court in the southwest corner of each of these western plazas (A and C) and lower building platforms along the western and northern borders. Of the facing temple pyramids, those to the west (Structures 2 and 4) are associated with human sacrifice, each having a small southwestern annex with skulls of those sacrificed within or in close proximity. The eastern temple mounds (Structures 3 and 5) are those most closely aligned with the cardinal directions (see fig. 1.1); altars or small structures were arrayed on the plaza floors across the fronts of these buildings.

The two smaller plazas to the east (Plaza B and Placita C) also have similarities: each has a smaller temple pyramidal base in its southwest corner (Structures 1 and 6), a single central altar, and a very large structure facing onto it (one of the two Great Palaces).

The *Annals of the Cakchiquels* (Recinos and Goetz 1953) indicates that Iximché was ruled by a dual monarchy, and Guillemin (1977: 235) suggested that the symmetry offered by Plazas A and B on the one hand and Plaza C and Placita C on the other was because each two-plaza complex was occupied by one of the Iximché kings. Each resided in a Great Palace with its own immediate courtyard, and each had control over his own ceremonial complex just to the west. The layout of the site, as described above, certainly supports this idea.

Plaza D seems to follow the format of the two complexes just discussed, Plazas A and B and Plaza C and Placita C, but on a diminished scale. Two elevated structures face each other from east to west across the plaza (Structure 69, 3 m high, and Structure 42, "less than 4 m high" [Guillemin 1959: 35]). There is a single altar and the remains of another low structure between them (Structures 141 and 142; see fig, 1.1). No ball court is associated with Plaza D, but Palace III does have a small (unnamed) placita with a single altar, analogous to Plaza B and Placita C. The altars in the unnamed placita (Structure 143) and Placita C (Structure 97) are cruciform (Guillemin 1977: 245; Guillemin 1969: 24–25, map), but that in Plaza B (Structure 14) is round. On the southwest corner of the placita, Structure 73 compares in location and outline with Structures 1 and 6 (see fig. 1.1). Finally, long one-room structures aligned on a single low platform constitute the northern boundary of Plaza D, recalling the northern perimeters of Plazas A and C.

Construction at Iximché: Methods and Materials

Fill for the platform cores consists of dirt, rock, and, occasionally, large boulders. Facing walls were built of dressed stone set in mortar and covered with thick layers of plaster (Guillemin n.d.c). As mentioned in chapter 1, the abundant use of cement was made possible by the nearby lime-producing center at Santa Apolonia. Plaster also was employed to surface the floors of structures, patios, and plazas and sometimes was found two and three layers thick on buildings. Guillemin (n.d.c) wrote of open areas that "these large paved areas were drained by a slight slope in the plaza floors" and that "cement-lined gutters were built at certain spots along their peripheries." Cut pumice blocks were also employed in construction, sometimes around cornices, although there are no clear details of this in Guillemin's writings. As far as can be determined, superstructures were made of sun-dried adobe blocks set in ce-

Fig. 4.49. Structure 27, Construction Detail of Plaster on Adobe Blocks

ment mortar and then plastered on interior and exterior surfaces. A corner of Structure 27 shows evidence of this type of construction (fig. 4.49). Piers between doorways were constructed similarly, as were interior benches. Guillemin believed that roofs were thatched, based on his findings of burned grass at several localities. In addition, he thought that many structures were painted or covered with polychrome murals, "sometimes on stucco but otherwise on a fine clay facing applied to the mud-brick adobe walls" (Guillemin n.d.c).

5

ꓽꓹꓹꓹꓹꓹꓹꓹ

Ceramic Variables and Attributes

In chapters 5 and 6 contrasting views of Iximché ceramics are presented. The more traditional approach is in chapter 6, where Iximché pottery is described in terms of 43 different types. The reader can obtain an impression of the whole by reading "the sum" of the individual type descriptions. Chapter 5 contains a cross-cutting assessment of the same collection, which is intended to increase both the reader's understanding of and access to what is a large and diverse group of potsherds. Here, the pottery is described by variable. For example, if one wishes to assess the importance of painted decoration in the collection, then chapter 5 can be consulted, under the variables EXTPAINT (paint, exterior surface) and INTPAINT (paint, interior surface). For the EXTPAINT variable, the reader will find that 711 sherds, all types combined, evidenced some form of painted decoration, or, ca. 7% of the 9508 sherds in the data set. If more detailed information is required, this section of the chapter also lists those types with highest frequencies of paint-decorated sherds as well as all types with any painted sherds at all. Finally, the same section lists 64 different forms (attributes) of painted decorations which were identified and recorded across the whole collection. One value of chapter 5 is that in some cases it can lead the reader quickly to types and type descriptions of specific interest.

All potsherds studied were recorded by type and other selected variables. A few variables were recorded for all sherds. These are type designation, maximum thickness, and whether or not a specimen is a rim sherd. Nance examined most sherds twice, first during the initial sorting by type and second when he recorded variables by individual sherd number. He examined sherds of the Unpolished Utility type only once, however, during initial sorting. For this type, an assistant recorded variables by sherd number. The assistant worked on these sherds while Nance was not in Guatemala. In part because this assistant had limited training in archaeology, but mostly because as a second observer, trained or not, he would record sherds differently from Nance, the assistant recorded only those few variables (along with PROVNO, BAGNO, and CATNO) which could be described most objectively. These included COLORLD, HANDLET, HANDLEW, RIMBOD, and THICK (variables described below). Owing to a lack of time, the variables COLORLD and HANDLET were recorded only for this Unpolished Utility type. In sum, the range of variables used to describe sherds of the Unpolished Utility type is more limited than the range applied to all other types.

Some variables pertain to just one or a small number of types, but sherds of each type were recorded consistently with only a few exceptions. For example, if some sherds in a type were found to be slipped, then the variable SLIP was recorded for each sherd as present or absent on interior and/or exterior surfaces.

A few words on the mechanics of recording variables are in order. Sherd maximum thicknesses and maximum handle widths were recorded using calipers to the nearest millimeter. Using a low-power microscope, Nance examined a small sample of sherds in each type collection for paste characteristics, describing paste color and temper. In all cases, temper appeared to be ground-up volcanic tuft or ash; no consistent differences by type could be discerned (appendix B).

Variables are described below in terms of their alternative attributes, with each attribute listed by its numerical code as represented in the SAS data set.

TYPE

1. Unpolished utility
2. Black slipped and polished
3. Gray slipped and polished
4. Orange on gray-buff
5. Black and red on white
6. White on red

7. Gray on red
8. Red bands on white
9. Red on orange
10. Red slipped and polished
11. Cacao pod effigy vessel
12. Brown slipped and polished incised
13. Brown-black on buff
14. Reed punctate
15. Other punctate
16. Unique black slipped and polished incised
17. Polished brown-black incised
18. Fine-incised beaker
19. Zoned crosshatched incised
20. Ladle incensario
21. Brown slipped and polished
22. White streaky slipped (combined with type no. 8)
23. Buff slipped and polished
24. Gray-brown slipped and polished
25. Orange polished
26. Micaceous paste
27. Thick, white-painted
28. Nonslipped, nonpolished fine ware
29. Micaceous slip
30. Black on red
31. Gray-green on red (combined with type no. 7)
32. Eroded fine ware (combined with type no. 43)
33. Unique (deleted)
34. Orange, matte-finish
35. Unique bichrome and polychrome
36. Red slipped incised
37. Brown polished punctate
38. Brown polished utility
39. Small micaceous-slip dish
40. Micaceous paste utility
41. Red polished utility
42. Black polished utility
43. Eroded fine ware
44. Thick black and white painted
45. Thick beaker incensario

46. Unique polychrome (combined with type no. 35)
47. Carinated, Late Preclassic

This variable was recorded for all sherds in the study collection.

APPLIQUÉ

1. Node
2. Ridge parallel to exterior rim
3. Aligned nodes
4. Strips, slabs, straps
5. Spike
6. Nondescript
7. Exterior ridge
8. Exterior notched ridge
9. Exterior appliquéd notched rim
10. Notched fillet
11. Lug handle
12. Vertical flange
13. Vertical flange and spike
14. Spike (no. 5) plus nondescript (no. 6)

The appliqué variable was systematically recorded where present for all types except no. 1 on a total of 239 sherds. The variable was most frequently recorded for type nos. 11 (18 sherds), 27 (20 sherds), 38 (15 sherds), and 45 (161 sherds). It was infrequently recorded (1–5 sherds) for type nos. 1, 2, 10, 20, 21, 23, 28, 29, 37, 41, 42, 43, and 44. For frequently recorded types, appliqué attributes most commonly identified are for type no. 11, nodes (100% of the appliquéd sherds for the type); for type no. 27, nondescript (85%); for type no. 38, exterior notched ridge (87%); and for type 45, nondescript (47%), spike (27%; see fig. 6.30), and flange (23%; see fig. 6.30).

AREA

This variable is summarized through the NEWPROV variable. It refers to general areas of site, Plaza A, Plaza B, et cetera.

BAGNO

(This variable identifies plastic bags of sherds found inside larger bags; 1 = A, 2 = B, et cetera.)

CATNO

This is the individual sherd identification number within a bag. For example, if bag (PROVNO) 300 contained 6 sherds, they would have been labeled individually 300-1, 300-2, 300-3, 300-4, 300-5, and 300-6.

DATE

Date of Excavation; given as DDMMYY8, SAS format. This variable was recorded for just a minority of PROVNOs, where the date of excavation was recorded on a bag label.

COLORLD

Paste color, light or dark.
1. dark (value of 4 or less, p. 5YR, *Munsell Soil Color Chart*)
2. light (value of 5 or greater, p. 5YR, *Munsell Soil Color Chart*)
This variable was described just for type no. 1.

EXTINC (exterior surface incising)

1. Engraved line around rim
2. Incised node
3. Preslipped exterior groove, incised
4. Preslipped grooved ridge(s)
5. Grooved/incised around rim
6. Preslipped groove around body
7. Reed punctate
8. Rectilinear or square punctations
9. Curvilinear designs, incised
10. Rectilinear designs, incised
11. Nested triangles, incised
12. Parallel lines below rim, incised
13. Engraved parallel lines around vessel
14. Zoned crosshatched incised
15. Punctated around rim
16. Grooved and perforated lug handle
17. Incised
18. Shallow preslipped groove around vessel
19. Incised, modeled object

20. Net impressed
21. Groove(s) and ridge(s), smoothed
22. Punctated
36. (Error)

Where represented the variable was recorded systematically for all types, except no. 1, for a total of 428 sherds. It was most frequently recorded for type nos. 17 (20 sherds), 18 (12 sherds), 21 (13 sherds), 38 (160 sherds), 40 (28 sherds), 41 (122 sherds), 42 (19 sherds), and 43 (10 sherds). It was recorded infrequently (1–8 sherds) for type nos. 1, 2, 8, 10, 12, 14, 15, 16, 19, 24, 27, 33, 36, 37, 44, and 45. On the eight most frequently recorded types, 87% of the exterior-incised sherds exhibit attribute 21, groove(s) and ridge(s) smoothed (see fig. 6.11B).

INTINC (interior surface incising)

(See EXTINC for attribute codes and descriptions.) This variable was recorded systematically for all types except no. 1. A total of four sherds was recorded for this variable for type nos. 2, 21, and 33.

EXTPAINT (paint, exterior surface)

1. Whole surface red
2. Red paint on black slip
3. Red paint, trace
4. Black paint, trace
5. Orange rectilinear design
6. Orange cross-hatching
7. Orange cross-hatching plus/or zoned parallel dots
8. Orange paint near rim
9. Orange paint, band around rim
10. Orange paint, lines parallel to rim
11. Orange paint, eroded
12. Orange paint, parallel lines
13. Orange paint, one line
14. Red paint, rectilinear design
15. Red paint, parallel lines
16. White paint, lines parallel to rim
17. White paint, curvilinear design

18. White painted lines
19. Red and white painted rectilinear design
20. White parallel lines and dots
21. White lines parallel to rim and parallel lines and dots
22. White rectilinear design
23. White bands in grooves
24. White lines parallel to rim and curvilinear design
25. Gray line and aligned dots
26. Red line(s)
27. Red line(s) parallel to rim
28. Black paint
29. Trace, blue-green paint
30. Red and green paint
31. Green paint
32. Black-brown parallel lines and dots
33. Black-brown parallel lines
34. Black-brown paint, rectilinear design
35. Black-brown paint
36. White paint
37. Gray paint
38. White and black stripes
39. Black stripes
40. Red paint
41. White stripes
42. Green stripes
43. White and green paint
44. White and red paint
45. White and orange paint
46. White stripe
47. Red stripe vertical to rim
48. Red stripes
49. Metallic/white paint/wash surface
50. Metallic surface
51. Orange paint
52. Parallel black lines in triangular pattern
53. Black parallel lines with zoned dots parallel to rim
54. Brown and orange bichrome
55. Brown, black, and orange on gray

56. Highly micaceous surface
57. Solid black paint
58. Traces of white and black paint
59. Black band parallel to rim on white surface
60. Black band(s) parallel to rim
61. Black band (stripe) on white
62. White and black stripes (bands)
63. Trace, white paint
64. Stucco

This variable was recorded systematically for all types except no. 1 for a total of 711 sherds. It was most frequently recorded for type nos. 4 (55 sherds), 6 (19 sherds), 8 (86 sherds), 20 (97 sherds), 27 (32 sherds), 40 (124 sherds), 44 (39 sherds), and 45 (191 sherds). It was recorded infrequently (1–11 sherds) for type nos. 1, 2, 3, 5, 7, 10, 11, 13, 23, 28, 29, 31, 33, 35, 38, and 43.

Most commonly recorded attributes were: for type no. 4, orange rectilinear design (69%); for type no. 8, white paint (83%); for type no. 20, white paint (52%); for type no. 27, white paint (81%); for type no. 44, solid black paint (33%); for type 45, stucco (29%) and white paint (29%).

INTPAINT (paint, interior surface)

(See EXTPAINT for attribute codes and descriptions.)

This variable was recorded systematically for all types if present except for type no. 1. Paint was recorded as present on vessel interior surfaces for 392 sherds, most frequently for type nos. 4 (82 sherds), 8 (62 sherds), 20 (94 sherds), 44 (15 sherds), and 45 (105 sherds). Types less frequently recorded for the variable (1–9 sherds) are nos. 2, 3, 5, 6, 9, 13, 23, 27, 30, and 40.

Most commonly recorded attributes are for type no. 4, orange crosshatching (67%); for type no. 8, white paint (92%); for type no. 20, white paint (49%); for type no. 44, solid black paint (40%) and black band(s) parallel to rim (33%); and for type no. 45, stucco (23%) and white paint (70%).

HANDLET (strap handle thickness in millimeters)

Handle thickness was recorded, using calipers, to the nearest millimeter for type no. 1, only.

HANDLEW (strap handle width in millimeters)

This variable, measured using calipers to the nearest millimeter, was systematically recorded for all types with strap handles for a total of 1406 sherds. Those with the most strap handles are type nos. 1 (983 sherds), 27 (17 sherds), 38 (66 sherds), 40 (301 sherds), and 41 (29 sherds). Other types with 1–4 sherds recorded are nos. 8, 10, 42, 43, and 44.

Average handle widths for types with many strap handles are type no. 1, 32.37 mm; type no. 27, 32.82 mm; type no. 38, 30.89 mm; type no. 40, 34.33 mm; and type no. 41, 30.31 mm.

LOCALE (summarized through the NEWPROV variable.)

LOTNO (This variable specifies unique sherd lots, that is, each BAGNO-PROVNO combination has a unique lot number.)

MODELED

1. Human effigy face
2. Bird effigy
3. Human figure
4. Human limb
5. Fish effigy
6. Animal effigy
7. Plant effigy
8. Nondescript
9. Horn
10. Cylinder
11. Ceramic ball
12. Monster effigy
13. Eye

Systematically recorded for all types, the modeled variable is listed for a total of 139 sherds. Types with high frequencies of modeled sherds are nos. 1 (52 sherds), 2 (10 sherds), 21 (12 sherds), 27 (37 sherds), and 45 (14 sherds). Other types represented (1–7 sherds) are nos. 8, 10, 20, 23, 29, 40, 41, and 42.

For the five relatively high frequency types, 42% of modeling is recorded as nondescript. Aside from nondescript, the most characteristic forms of modeling by type are: for type no. 1, human limb (13%); for type no. 2, bird effigy (30%); for type 21, bird effigy and human limb (17% each); for type no. 27, plant effigy (13%); for type 45, human effigy face and human limb (43% each).

MOLDED

1. Molded decoration-base (or molded decoration)
2. Molded body
3. Molded base
4. Plant effigy
5. Molded vessel support
6. Handle fragment

This variable was recorded for all types where present, except for type no. 1, for a total of 95 sherds: 1 sherd for type no. 4 and the remaining 94 sherds for type no. 20. For type no. 4, a mold-made vessel support was recorded; attributes listed for type no. 20 include molded base (26%), molded body (2%), and molded decoration-base or molded decoration (72%).

NEWPROV (summarized proveniences)

1. Great Palace II, Patio E Centro
2. Great Palace II, Patio S-E
3. Great Palace II, Patio N-E
4. Great Palace II, Patio N
5. Great Palace II, Patio S/S-E
6. Great Palace II, Patio E/S-E
7. Great Palace II, Patio Centro E
8. Other Great Palace II
9. No provenience, 1972
10. No provenience
11. Great Palace I
12. No provenience, pre-1972
13. Extreme E surface
14. Great Palace II/Structure 5, western corner
15. Structure 49
16. Great Palace I/Structure 4

17. Structure 2
18. Structure 3/Structure 79
19. Structure 27 (near burials 27-A and 27-B)
20. Structure 4
21. Great Palace II/Structure 45
22. Structure 43
23. Structure 78/Structure 79 E (No. 24. Not assigned.)
25. Structure 49/Structure 4
26. Great Palace II, Passageway from Patio E Centro to Patio E- SE
27. Great Palace II/Structure 39

In keeping with the organization of chapters 4 and 10, NEWPROV attributes are discussed by Plaza, moving from Plaza A to C.

For Plaza A, NEWPROV 17 identifies potsherds from Structure (Temple) 2. Structure 79 abuts Temple (Structure) 3 on its northeast corner. Structure 79 was not labeled as such on Guillemin's map as published in 1977. The identity of Structure 79 was determined from an unpublished 1969 map by Guillemin (NEWPROV 18). Structure 27 is on the northwest side of Plaza A and just northwest of Temple 2 (NEWPROV 19; see fig. 1.1). Structure 78 is just east of Structure 22 and west of Structure 79; its location was also determined from Guillemin's unpublished 1969 map (see fig. 1.1; NEWPROV 23).

For Plaza B, sherd lots could be summarized either as from Great Palace I (NEWPROV 11; see fig. 1.1) or Great Palace I and/or Structure 4; the latter is just southeast of Great Palace I (NEWPROV 16).

The greatest number of known proveniences for ceramic lots are from Great Palace II in Plaza C. NEWPROVs 1 through 7 refer to patios within Great Palace II; see figure 4.36 and the discussion linking NEWPROV designations to patios labeled "a" through "i" in chapter 8. NEWPROV 8 covers sherd lots with a general Great Palace II provenience. For NEWPROV 14, Temple 5 is almost contiguous to Great Palace II (Room 113) on its northern corner (indicated in fig. 1.1). NEWPROV 21 probably refers to a provenience adjacent to Great Palace II, but on the 1977 map (see fig. 1.1) Structure 45 is on the far side of Plaza D from the palace. The Great Palace II passageway referred to for NEWPROV 26 is between Patios "e" and "d" in figure 4.36. Structure 39 is just northeast of Room 115, Great Palace II (see fig. 1.1; NEWPROV 27).

Several ceramic proveniences fall outside Great Palace II, but still within Plaza C. Structure 49 is at the northern corner of Plaza C (NEWPROV 15; see fig. 1.1). Temple (Structure) 4 is on the northwest side of

Plaza C (NEWPROV 20; see fig. 1.1), whereas for NEWPROV 25, Structure 49 is just northeast of Temple (Structure) 4 (see fig. 1.1).

"Extreme E surface" may refer to a surface collection from the unexcavated portion of Iximché east of Plazas E and F (not shown in fig. 1.1; NEWPROV 13). The location of Structure 43 is unknown.

Several proveniences are associated with no structure number. NEWPROV 9 encompasses fragmentary labels with only 1972 dates surviving or labels which contain only a 1972 date. Guillemin clearly intended to determine provenience from his field notes for these date-only labels. However, most daily field notes for 1972 are missing. Bags with no labels are assigned to NEWPROV 10. NEWPROV 12 was assigned to all bags lacking proveniences except for dates before 1972. Some of these were determined from the dates on newspapers in which artifacts were wrapped.

The NEWPROV variable is listed for all sherds in the data set. In chapter 6, individual type provenience data were summarized by grouping NEWPROV data together as follows:

Great Palace II	NEWPROV = 1–8, 14, 21, 26, 27
Plaza C	NEWPROV = 15, 20, 25
Great Palace I	NEWPROV = 11, 16
Plaza A	NEWPROV = 17–19, 23
Other	NEWPROV = 13, 22
Unknown	NEWPROV = 9, 10, 12

POLISH

1. Neither surface polished
2. Exterior surface polished
3. Interior surface polished
4. Both surfaces polished

This variable was recorded systematically for all types except nos. 1, 27, 38, 39, 40, 41, 42, 43, 44, and 45.

PROVNO provenience number (i.e., original bag number)

Proveniences summarized through the NEWPROV variable.

RIMBOD (rim vs. body sherd)

1. Rim sherd
2. Body sherd

This variable was recorded for all sherds in the study collection. This collection consists of all rim sherds from bags studied and some body sherds, the latter selected because of their uniquely finished surfaces or because they exhibit decoration or evidence of vessel form. This selection of some body sherds biases the proportions of types as they existed in the areas of Iximché excavated by Guillemin. To approach these true proportions, the frequencies and percentages of types are listed below for rim sherds only.

Rim Sherd Frequencies and Percentages by Type

1. Unpolished utility 1325 (26.3%)
2. Black slipped and polished 123 (2.4%)
3. Gray slipped and polished 50 (1.0%)
4. Orange on gray-buff 61 (1.2%)
5. Black and red on white 1 (0%)
6. White on red 7 (.1%)
7. Gray on red 1 (0%)
8. Red bands on white 68 (1.4%)
9. Red on orange 1 (0%)
10. Red slipped and polished 113 (2.2%)
11. Cacao pod effigy vessel 6 (.1%)
12. Brown slipped and polished incised 1 (0%)
13. Brown-black on buff 1 (0%)
14. Reed punctate 1 (0%)
15. Other punctate 0 (0%)
16. Unique black slipped and polished incised 0 (0%)
17. Polished brown-black incised 1 (0%)
18. Fine-incised beaker 0 (0%)
19. Zoned crosshatched incised 0 (0%)
20. Ladle incensario 82 (1.6%)
21. Brown slipped and polished 225 (4.5%)
22. White streaky slipped (combined with type no. 8)
23. Buff slipped and polished 63 (1.3%)
24. Gray-brown slipped and polished 54 (1.1%)
25. Orange polished 5 (.1%)
26. Micaceous paste 9 (.2%)
27. Thick, white-painted 75 (1.5%)
28. Nonslipped, nonpolished fine ware 12 (.2%)
29. Micaceous slip 4 (.1%)
30. Black on red 3 (.1%)

31. Gray-green on red (combined with type no. 7)
32. Eroded fine ware (combined with type no. 43)
33. Unique (deleted)
34. Orange, matte-finish 4 (.1%)
35. Unique bichrome and polychrome 3 (.1%)
36. Red slipped incised 0 (0%)
37. Brown polished punctate 4 (.1%)
38. Brown polished utility 819 (16.3%)
39. Small micaceous-slip dish 219 (4.3%)
40. Micaceous slip utility 900 (17.9%)
41. Red polished utility 425 (8.4%)
42. Black polished utility 94 (1.9%)
43. Eroded fine ware 180 (3.6%)
44. Thick black and white painted 19 (.4%)
45. Thick beaker incensario 75 (1.5%)
46. Unique polychrome (combined with type no. 35)
47. Carinated, Late Preclassic 1 (0%)

RIMMORPH (rim morphology)

1. Flange rim
2. Straight
3. Incurved
4. Outcurved
5. *Tecomate*
6. Unique
7. Carinated

This variable was recorded for all types except no. 1.

SHDMORPH (sherd morphology)

1. Rim
2. Body
3. Strap handle
4. Base
5. Rim with handle
6. Other

7. Shoulder
8. Ring base
9. Hollow leg with rattle, plain
10. Hollow leg fragment, plain
11. Dog effigy leg, rattle
12. Disk
13. Mammiform vessel leg
14. Solid vessel leg
15. Flat base
16. Base, footed vessel
17. Lug handle
18. Pedestal base
19. Stem/body fragment (ladle incensario)
20. Stem end (ladle incensario)
21. Stem midsection (ladle incensario)
22. Body (cup of ladle incensario)
23. Stem end with handle (ladle incensario)
24. Stem midsection with handle (ladle incensario)
25. Stem/body with handle (ladle incensario)
26. Lid
27. Hollow fish-head vessel support
28. Vessel support
29. Whole vessel
30. Appendage (appliqué fragment)
31. Base with handle fragment
32. Perforated sherd
33. Ceramic ball
34. Human-foot-shaped vessel foot
35. Loop handle
36. Unique handle
37. Ceramic square
38. Curved base
39. Concave base
40. Rounded base
41. Tube; spoutlike small hollow tube
42. Beaker base
43. Sherd from vessel with interior wall or compartment (e.g., incensario)

This variable was recorded for all types except no. 1.

SLIP

1. Neither surface slipped
2. Exterior surface slipped
3. Interior surface slipped
4. Both surfaces slipped

The variable was not systematically recorded for type nos. 1, 27, 38, 40, 43, 44, and 45.

STEMDIA (diameter of ladle incensario handles)

Measured in millimeters, using calipers, the variable was recorded for type no. 20 only.

THICK (sherd thickness)

The variable was recorded in millimeters, using calipers, for all types and for all sherds manifesting a complete body cross section.

VESMORPH (vessel morphology)

1. Tecomate
2. Miniature tecomate
3. Shallow bowl
4. Necked jar
5. Miniature effigy pot
6. Flat-based beaker
7. Flat-based dish
8. Flat-based; footed
9. Small necked jar
10. Open bowl/dish
11. Bowl
12. Small bowl
13. Beaker
14. Ladle incensario
15. Large bowl
16. Small flat-based dish
17. Thick amorphous vessel
18. Small shallow bowl

19. Pod shaped plant effigy vessel
20. Small open bowl
21. Miniature necked jar
22. Comal
23. Bird effigy bowl

The VESMORPH variable was recorded for all sherds diagnostic of vessel form for all types except no. 1.

WEAR

1. Pitted interior
2. Battered rim
3. Pitted exterior
4. Charcoal on interior
5. Eroded interior
6. Eroded interior and exterior
7. Drilled hole through sherd
8. Burned interior
9. Burned interior and exterior

Sherd surfaces were inspected for wear for all types but no. 1. Identified for a total of 55 sherds, the variable was recorded in low frequencies (1–3 sherds) for types 3, 8, 10, 23, 24, 38, 40, 42, and 46. Types with 5–7 sherds include nos. 21 (80% pitted interior), 39 (100% drilled hole through sherd), and 41 (86% eroded interior). Type 45 has 25 sherds listed: burned interior for 96% and burned interior and exterior for 4%.

6

ᒍᒪᒪᒪᒪᒪ

Typological Descriptions and
Extra-Site Relationships

Ceramic Typology

The ceramic typology for this study is based upon seven underlying considerations or processes. These encompass the typological methodology.

1. Chronological Assumptions

The classification developed without benefit of clear chronological controls, given the lack of stratigraphic excavations by George Guillemin. We were forced to assume that all types were on the same time level, the Late Postclassic, with the exception of a single large sherd identified to be from a Late Preclassic vessel. This assumption was based on ethnohistorical documentation in the *Annals*, the clear affiliation of diagnostic sherds with the Late Postclassic horizon, and the absence in the study collection of any other demonstrably earlier material, including Plumbate pottery (see below). This does mean, however, that the typology must be regarded as preliminary and subject to refinement when stratigraphic excavations are conducted at Iximché.

2. Surficial Appearance

Owing to time constraints, all sherds could not be examined on a fresh break surface for paste color, paste characteristics, or temper. These observations did not figure in the development of the classification, which was based on surficial examination of the washed sherds.

3. Comparative Exercise

The typology developed through the physical sorting of study collection sherds into type groupings. The assignment of a particular sherd to a type did not just depend on whether or not a sherd manifested defining characteristics for a type, but also on its similarity to other sherds in the assigned type and its dissimilarities to sherds in comparable type groupings.

4. A Two-Stage Process

A preliminary classification was conducted during a one-month period in 1990. During the summer of 1992, with the exception of sherds assigned to the Unpolished Utility type, the typological affiliations of all sherds were reassessed and some sherds reassigned to other types. With this exception, then, all final typological assessments were made after each sherd in the study collection had been examined at least twice.

5. Holistic Assessments

Sherd surfaces are not absolutely uniform in color and surface finish, each varying somewhat across a surface and from exterior to interior. Typological assignments then, often involved a generalized assessment.

6. Types as Conventional Categorizations

In order to benefit as much as possible from earlier research and to the degree possible, types were formulated using conventional distinctions already employed in Postclassic Highland archaeology. For example, micaceous-paste types have already been proposed for other contemporary sites, and two other types defined earlier, Chinautla Polychrome and Fortress White on Red, are incorporated into this study (see below).

7. Type as Variable

In this study ceramic type can be conceptualized as one of several variables recorded for each sherd. For a given sherd, the attribute."5 cm" might be assigned for the variable THICK and the attribute "Black Slipped and Polished" for the variable TYPE. An implication here is that each variable was recorded independently, so that a typological assessment once determined would not be altered by an assessment for any other variable. In other words, in this study the typology never was conceptualized as dependent upon or as developing out of an attribute analysis. Because of this, TYPE data can be contrasted to or used in conjunction with data generated for other variables.

Some discussion is in order, however, because the process did lead to some apparent contradictions. By way of example, this can be seen for the variables TYPE and SLIP. For the 231 sherds assigned to the TYPE Black Slipped and Polished, 38 were found to be slipped on neither surface when assessed for the SLIP variable. The question naturally arises, how can an unslipped sherd remain assigned to this type? The answer relates to the fact that the determination of SLIP and the determination of TYPE were independent assessments for two different variables. For TYPE, as indicated above, the determination was surficial, holistic, macroscopic, and comparative. For the SLIP variable, the determination was made on a small fresh break surface, using a low-power binocular microscope. Here, an effort was made to distinguish a crust or thin layer of slip on one or both surfaces in cross sectional view. The presence of a slip may be obvious and easily identified in this manner. On the other hand, it can prove very difficult to identify, and a judgment of "no slip" cannot absolutely mean that a slip was not applied to the vessel. It does mean that evidence for a slip was not identified by this observer looking at a randomly positioned (created) small break surface on the periphery of the sherd. Although this approach did generate some apparent inconsistencies, it maintained the independence of all variables so they could be applied collectively in the analysis, which is described below.

Design of the Typology

The typology utilized in this study is based on several criteria which can be listed by level of precedence: (1) chronology, (2) function, and (3) surface finish, surface color, decoration and vessel form. The general classes of types are listed below. The term "ware" is sometimes used to refer to these groupings of types at Iximché when it is used in an etic sense. When the same term is employed occasionally in an emic sense or context, it then refers to functional categories which might have been recognized by the inhabitants of Iximché.

Utility Ware

These types generally encompass sherds from large thick-walled vessels which appear to be from ollas, necked jars, or bowls. Rim forms are

TYPE CLASSES (WARES)

I. Chronology
Late Postclassic (42 types)
Late Preclassic (1 type)

II. Functional
Utility Ware (5 types)
Nonceremonial Fine Ware
   Monochrome (6 types)
   Bichrome (8 types)
   Polychrome (2 types)
Other Decorated (12 types)
Ceremonial Ware (3 types)
Other Minority (5 types)
Residual (2 types)

simple, decoration is rare to absent, and, with the exception of one type, slipped surfaces are not in evidence. (Slipped surfaces were detected on 23% of the sherds of the Red Polished Utility type.) Polishing, when present, was to a low luster. This portion of the collection was judged most likely to have been used for the mundane tasks of food cooking and storage and water storage and transportation. The taxonomy for these utility types is depicted in figure 6.1. Each type numeric code is in parentheses.

Nonceremonial Fine Ware

All Nonceremonial Fine Ware types tend to be represented by thin sherds from small vessels. Vessel forms are more varied than for utility types, and surfaces tend to be slipped, well-polished, and/or decorated.

Monochrome Slipped and Polished
Included types are of well-finished sherds, most of them slipped on one or both surfaces and/or polished. Types were distinguished on the basis of surface color.

Bichrome
With one exception, all sherds of these types display paint of one color decorating a contrasting-colored background. The Red Bands on White type is the exception because plain white sherds have been included, owing to their distinctive, chalky white surfaces which link them to the bichrome sherds in this type collection.

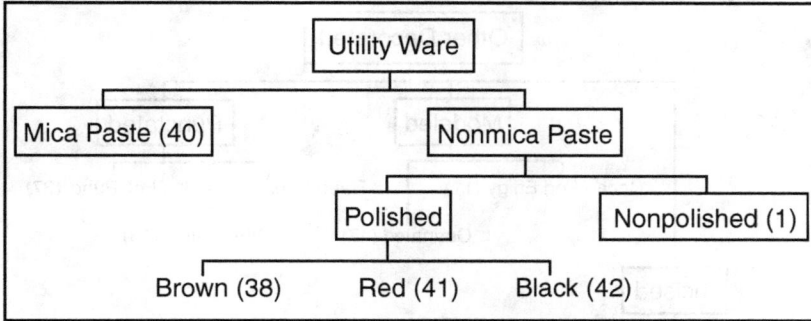

Fig. 6.1. Taxonomy for Utility Ware

Monochrome Slipped and Polished Types

Name	Code
Black slipped and polished	2
Brown slipped and polished	21
Red slipped and polished	10
Gray slipped and polished	3
Buff slipped and polished	23
Gray-brown slipped and polished	24

Bichrome Types

Name	Code
Orange on gray/buff	4
White on red	6
Gray on red	7
Red bands on white	8
Red on orange	9
Brown-black on buff	13
Black on red	30
Thick black and white painted	44

Polychrome Types

Name	Code
Black and red on white	5
Unique bichrome and polychrome	35

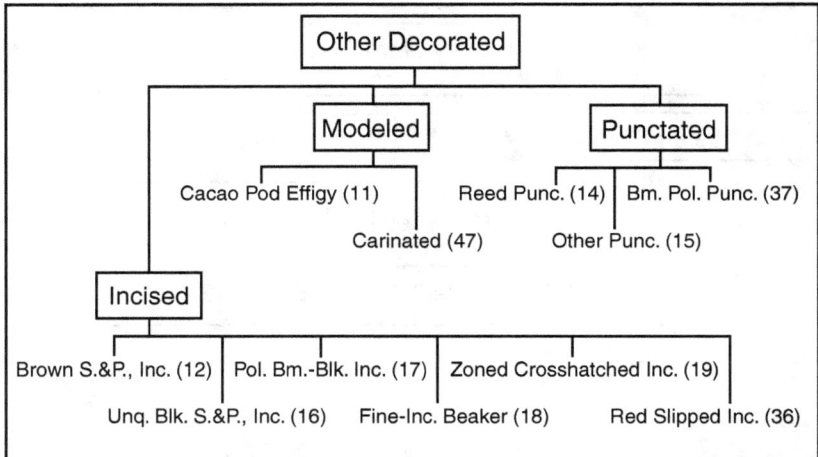

Fig. 6.2. Taxonomy for Other Decorated Types

Polychrome
Included here is one distinctive polychrome type and a second category which includes a few unique well-finished bichrome and polychrome sherds. There is little internal consistency in the latter grouping.
Other Decorated Types
Types included here are decorated through incising, modeling, or punctation. For each type, design motif and technique vary with differences in surface appearance and general sherd thickness. Figure 6.2 displays a taxonomy for these types with type numerical codes in parentheses.

Ceremonial Ware

Three distinct vessel forms comprise the basis for defining three types, the sherds of which are believed to be the remains of incense burners.

Other Minority Types

Sherds from these type collections are all from relatively small thin-walled pots which were well finished. They lack decoration and differ from sherds of monochrome slipped and polished types in color and finish.

Residual Types

Two large categories of sherds resulting from the classification process could not be subsumed under any major type heading. Most included sherds appear eroded.

Ceremonial Types

Name	Code
Ladle incensario	20
Small micaceous-slip dish	39
Thick beaker incensario	45

Other Minority Types

Name	Code
Orange polished	25
Nonslipped, nonpolished	28
Micaceous slip	29
Micaceous paste	26
Orange matte finish	34

Residual Types

Name	Code
Thick white painted	27
Eroded fine ware	43

Utility Ware

Provenience and frequency of type distributions are given in tables 6.1–6.40.

Unpolished Utility

This large group consists of plain sherds with smooth, nonpolished surfaces (table 6.1). Some sherds may have slightly eroded surfaces and without this surface deterioration might have been typed differently. Other sherds are clearly noneroded, and most of these appear to be fragmentary remains of (a) plain utility ware(s). The rim morphology and vessel morphology variables were not recorded for this type, but many sherds (33.6%) exhibit the remains of strap handles, suggesting that many vessels were necked jars with handles. A small thick-walled jar of this type is illustrated (fig. 6.3). Generally, represented vessels were probably large, as the sherd average thickness is 9.03 mm.

One variable recorded just for this type concerns paste color. For 3018 sherds (97.4%) a fresh break surface was examined and recorded

Table 6.1. Unpolished Utility Type Distribution

Provenience	Frequency	% by Type	% by Prov.
Great Palace II	1759	56.80	35.29
Other Plaza C	126	4.07	31.74
Great Palace I	184	5.94	33.45
Plaza A	82	2.65	32.93
Other	123	3.97	24.26
Unknown	823	26.57	29.18
Total	3097	100.00	

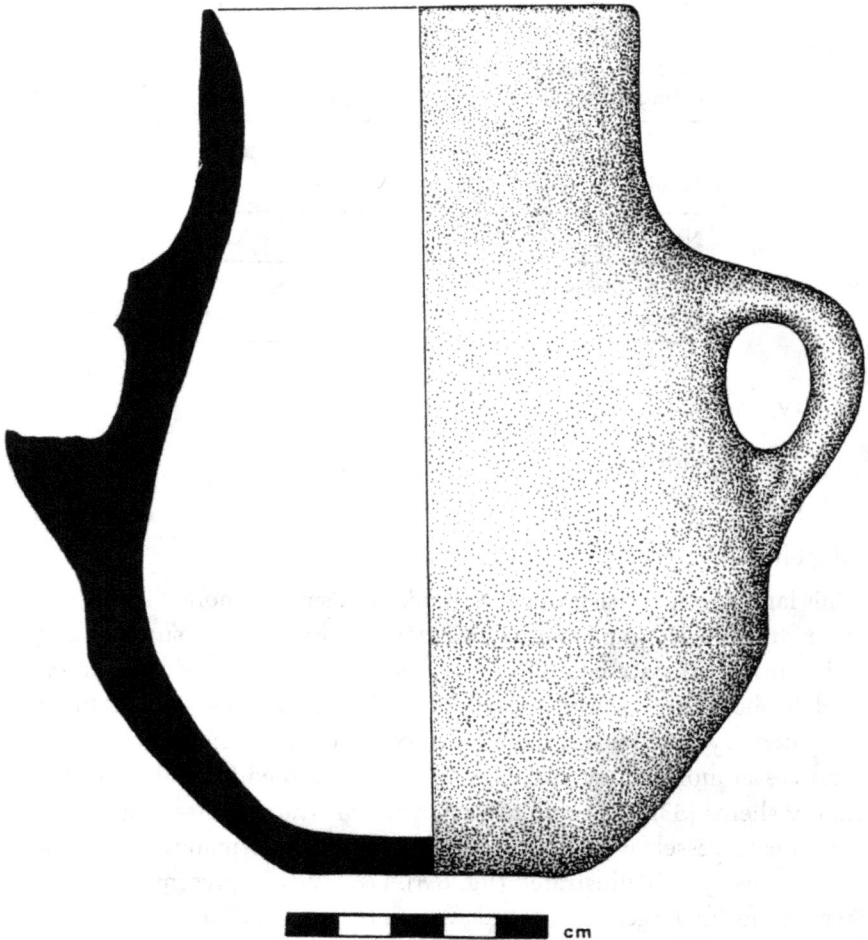

Fig. 6.3. Potsherds: Unpolished Utility. Provenience: unknown

as "light" or "dark" through reference to a *Munsell Soil Color Chart.* One finding is that thicker sherds and larger strap handles tend to have darker paste colors.

Of 980 strap handles observed for paste color, 715 had dark paste. Of these, 355 were in the thin category (T < 33 mm) and 360 (50.35%) in the thick category (T >= 33 mm). By contrast, of the 265 sherds with light paste color, 163 are thin, and 102 (38.49%) are thick. A similar difference can be seen for 2554 sherds which are not handles. Of 1657 sherds with dark paste, 717 are relatively thin (T < 9 mm), and 940 (56.73%) are thick (T >= 9 mm). This compares to 897 sherds with light paste, where 476 are thin, and 421 (46.93%) are thick.

These findings indicate different manufacturing technologies for different sized vessels within the type. Larger vessels might have been fired for shorter periods, been fired in more reduced atmospheres, or been manufactured from clay containing more organic material. This is potentially important, since traditional potters used different technologies to manufacture vessels of different intended functions. If this paste-color variable is employed more systematically in future research, it may be possible to develop a more refined classification based on technology of manufacture as well as on vessel morphology. Better informed estimates of type function should then be possible. Nance (1988) pursued this approach more fully in a study of ceramics from a late prehistoric village site in Alabama.

John Weeks (1983: 154–190) recognized the importance of paste color in his study of ceramics from Chisalín, a Late Postclassic Quiché site near Utatlán. He defined four ceramic groupings of types, two with types manifesting light-colored paste and two with dark-colored sherds interpreted to be incompletely oxidized.

Several vessels of this type were decorated with modeled appendages representing birds (fig. 6.4A–C), snakes (figs. 6.4D; 6.5A), and other animals (fig. 6.5B). Figure 6.5C depicts a modeled plant pod vessel. Other elaborations include a few vessels with ring bases and a hollow fish-head vessel support. Some of these sherds suggest nonutilitarian functions for part of the type collection. Five small ceramic balls presumably were originally rattles in hollow vessel feet.

Brown Polished Utility

This large sherd collection is from well-made utility vessels, brown to reddish-brown in color (table 6.2). The pots were smoothed and polished, at least on exterior surfaces. Evidence of slip is rare. The sherds

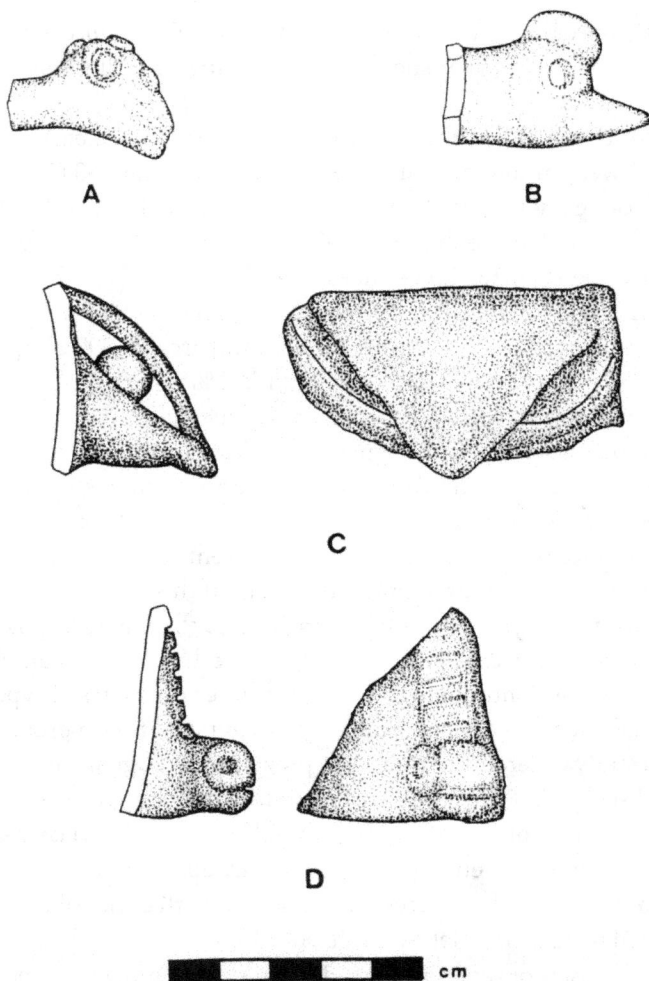

Fig. 6.4. Potsherds: A–D, Unpolished Utility. Provenience: A, Great Palace II, Patio NE; B, unknown; C, unknown; D, Great Palace II, Patio N

range in thickness from 5 mm to 26 mm and average 9.80 mm. Regarding vessel shape, 110 sherds are indicative of form, and represented are the bowl (.9%), tecomate (40.9%), and necked jar (58.2%). Vessels were almost entirely plain except for low ridges and shallow grooves modeled into exterior vessel walls, below and encircling many rims. These simple but well-executed decorations occurred on tecomates and necked jars; in some cases, they may have functioned to secure

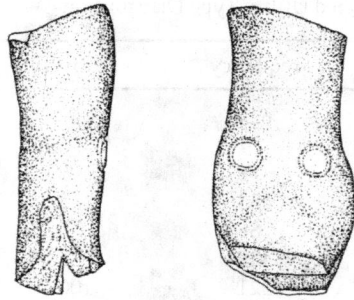

A

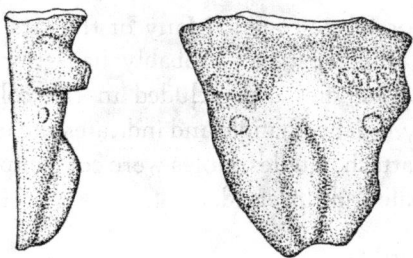

B

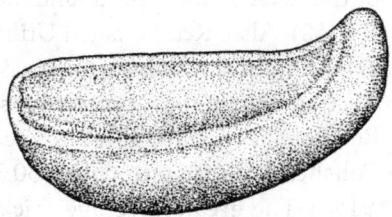

C

cm

Fig. 6.5. Potsherds: A–C, Unpolished Utility. Provenience: A, unknown; B, Great Palace II/Structure 39; C, Great Palace II/Structure 39

Table 6.2. Brown Polished Utility Type Distribution

Provenience	Frequency	% by Type	% by Prov.
Great Palace II	624	47.24	12.52
Other Plaza C	71	5.37	17.88
Great Palace I	78	5.90	14.18
Plaza A	33	2.50	13.25
Other	86	6.51	16.96
Unknown	429	32.48	15.21
Total	1321	100.00	

"tie-downs" for fabric covers. Many of the jars had out-angled rims (fig. 6.6A, B), and most jars probably had strap handles (fig. 6.6C). Sixty-six strap handles are included in the collection. Figure 6.7A shows a poorly finished handle and indicates the method used by Iximché potters to attach handles. Holes were cut completely through vessel walls, and handle ends inserted.

Red Polished Utility

Sherds of the Red Polished Utility type (table 6.3) closely resemble the Brown Polished Utility type. Outstanding differences are the red to dark red surface colors for the Red Polished sherds and the presence of slipped surfaces on some (23.4%). Also, Red Polished Utility sherds tend to be thinner, averaging 9.09 mm in thickness, compared to 9.80 mm for the Brown Polished collection. Vessel form proportions are comparable for the two types. For Red Polished Utility, these are necked jars (64.9% vs. 58.2% for Brown Polished Utility), tecomates (30.5% vs. 40.9%), and bowls (4.63% vs. .91%). The greater average thickness of Brown Polished Utility sherds may, in part, be because of the larger percentage of tecomates for that type. In a comparison of vessel form by thickness for the Red Polished Utility type, sherds indicative of the tecomate vessel form were thicker than those of other forms: 35 (76.08%) of 46 sherds indicative of the tecomate form fall into the thick category ($T >= 10$ mm) vs. 42 (39.62%) of 106 sherds from bowls or jars. Illustrations depict a strap handle on a jar (fig. 6.7B), jar rim forms with slight ridges or ridge-groove decoration (fig. 6.8A–C), and a tecomate rim sherd (fig. 6.9A).

Black Polished Utility

Black Polished Utility sherds (table 6.4) are much like those of the previous two utility types and are mainly distinguished from those on the

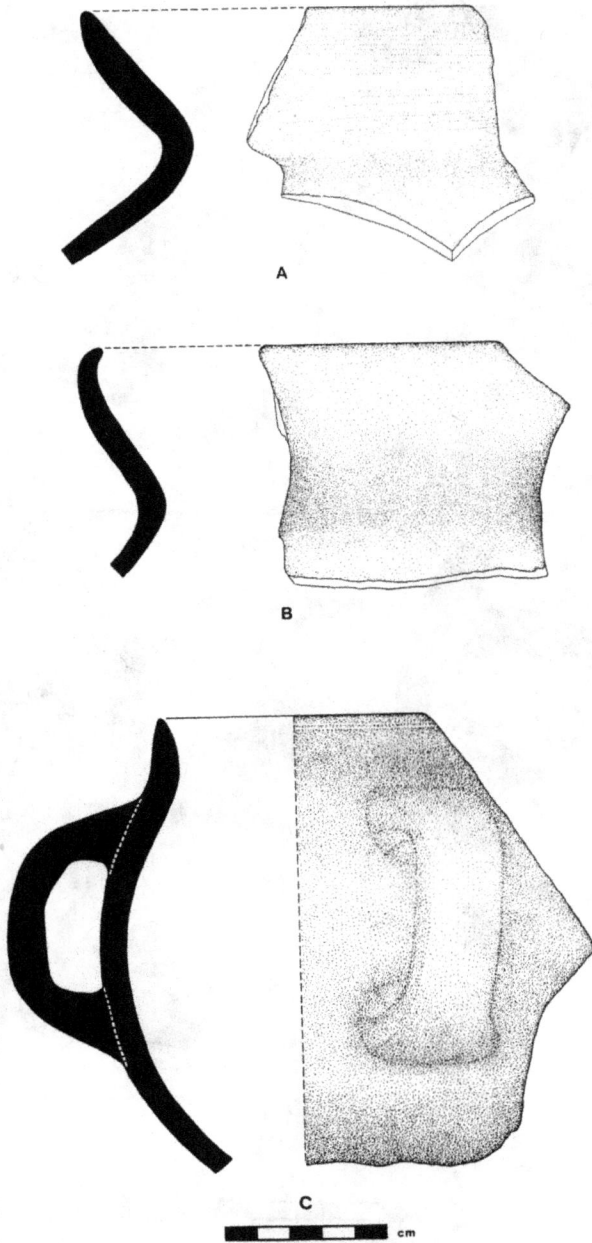

Fig. 6.6. Potsherds: A–C, Brown Polished Utility. Provenience: A, Great Palace I; B, unknown, 1972; C, unknown

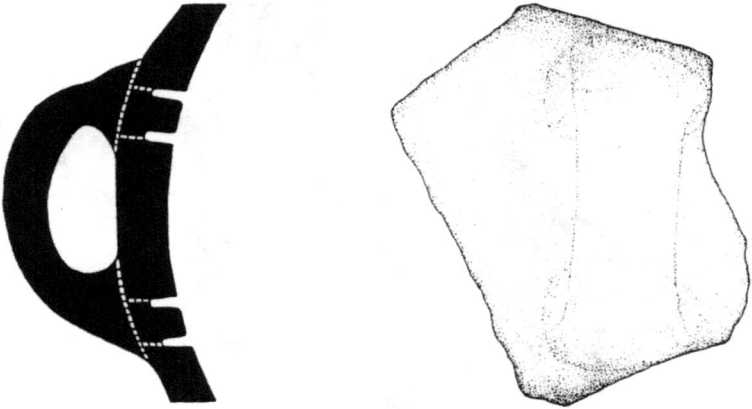

A

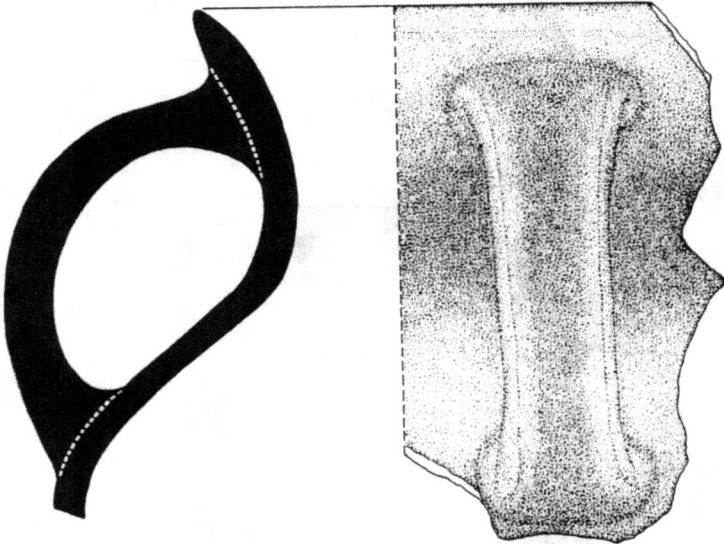

B

Fig. 6.7. Potsherds: A, Brown Polished Utility; B, Red Polished Utility. Provenience: A, unknown; B, Extreme E Surface

Table 6.3. Red Polished Utility Type Distribution

Provenience	Frequency	% by Type	% by Prov.
Great Palace II	397	53.36	7.96
Other Plaza C	30	4.03	7.56
Great Palace I	41	5.51	7.45
Plaza A	16	2.15	6.43
Other	41	5.51	8.09
Unknown	219	29.44	7.77
Total	744	100.00	

basis of surface color. Similar to the Red Polished Utility type, some of these sherds (18.5%) are slipped on one or both surfaces. Sherd average thickness is 8.19 mm. Represented vessel forms include the tecomate (41.9%), necked jar (38.7%), and bowl (19.4%).

Micaceous Paste Utility

These sherds were typed together on the basis of their highly micaceous paste (table 6.5). Apparently, all are from large jars, most, if not all, with handles. Of 151 sherds indicative of vessel shape, all were classified as representing necked jars. Strap handles are evidenced on 322 sherds, or 23.5% of the sample. Handles were attached either at the neck (figs. 6.9B; 6.10A) or lower on the body (fig. 6.10B), and vessel rims were either straight or outcurved (fig. 6.11A). Sherd average thickness is 9.28 mm.

A minority of sherds (123, or 9.0%) have very distinctive exterior surfaces, gold or copper-colored and with a metallic sheen. These surfaces seem to have been produced through slipping or painting. A few vessels were encircled on the body wall or at the rim by low ridges or several low ridges separated by shallow grooves (fig. 6.11B). A much higher percentage of the metallic-painted sherds manifest these carefully modeled ridges than do nonpainted sherds in the collection. Of the 1369 sherd total, 123 evidence metallic paint, and of these, 22 (17.89%) also show ridge/grooved decoration. This contrasts to the nonpainted sample of 1246 sherds, of which just 6 (.48%) were decorated in this manner. On this basis, it is suggested that this group be distinguished as a separate type in future research.

Extra-Site Comparisons

Robert Wauchope (1970: 116–117) reported mica ware in ample quantities in his study of mostly surface ceramics from Late Postclassic sites in

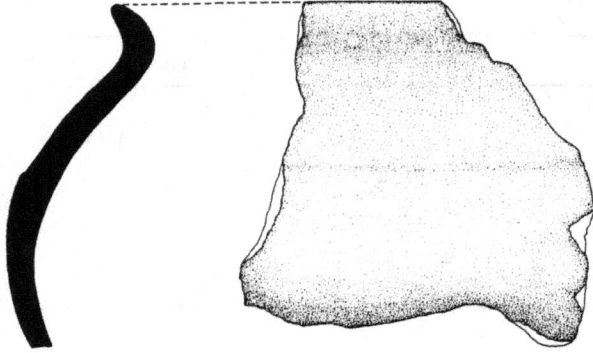

A

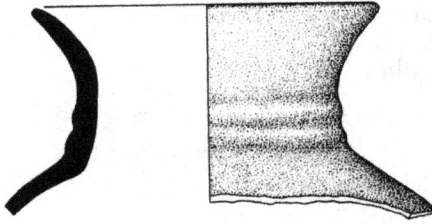

B

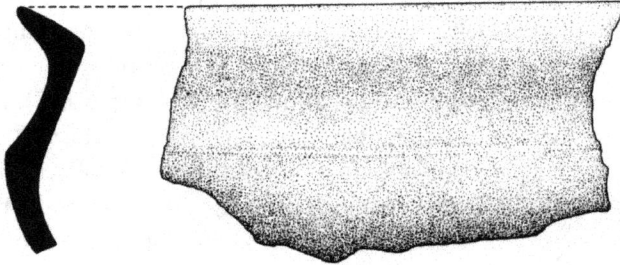

C

Fig. 6.8. Potsherds: A–C, Red Polished Utility. Provenience: A, Great Palace II, Patio NE; B, unknown; C, Structure 4

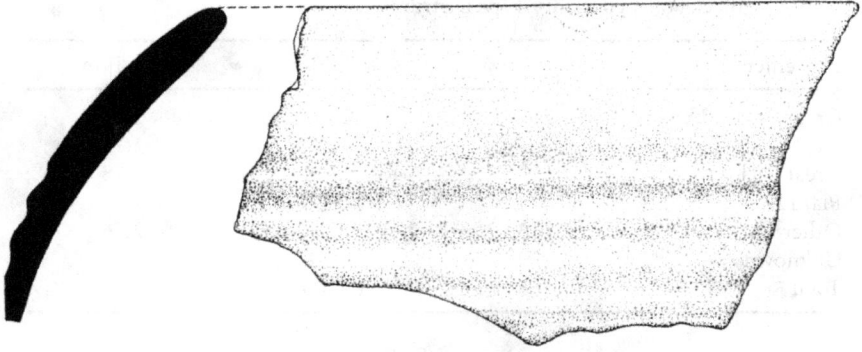

A

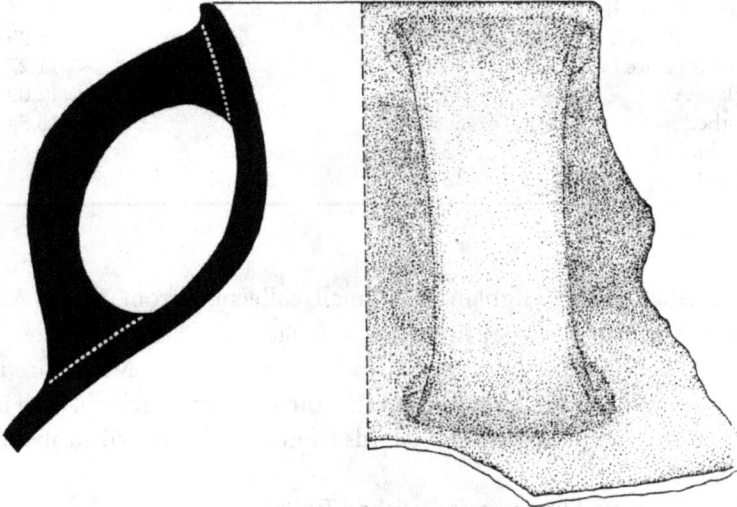

B

Fig. 6.9. Potsherds: A, Red Polished Utility; B, Micaceous Paste Utility. Provenience: A, Great Palace II, Patio NE; B, unknown, pre-1972

Table 6.4. Black Polished Utility Type Distribution

Provenience	Frequency	% by Type	% by Prov.
Great Palace II	103	61.31	2.07
Other Plaza C	7	4.17	1.76
Great Palace I	12	7.14	2.18
Plaza A	4	2.38	1.61
Other	13	7.74	2.56
Unknown	29	17.26	1.03
Total	168	100.00	

Table 6.5. Micaceous Paste Utility Type Distribution

Provenience	Frequency	% by Type	% by Prov.
Great Palace II	725	52.96	14.54
Other Plaza C	73	5.33	18.39
Great Palace I	62	4.53	11.27
Plaza A	30	2.19	12.09
Other	94	6.87	18.54
Unknown	385	28.12	13.65
Total	1369	100.00	

the Guatemalan Highlands. A small collection from Mixco Viejo is stored in the National Museum in Guatemala City, a sample from a larger collection studied by Carlos Navarette (1961). Mica ware in this museum collection, examined in the course of this research, is all identical to the "metallic-painted" sherds from Iximché described above.

Monochrome Slipped and Polished Types

Black Slipped and Polished

Clearly representing an important ware at Iximché, these Black Slipped and Polished sherds are very well finished (table 6.6). They manifest a variety of small vessel forms and modeled decorative appendages. The sherds are very dark brown to black in surface color. Both surfaces were slipped on 57% of the sample, and 69% of the sherds evidence polishing on one or both surfaces. Several sherds bear traces of white, black, or red paint on one surface. A few sherds exhibit a single preslip groove or incised line which probably encircled the rim

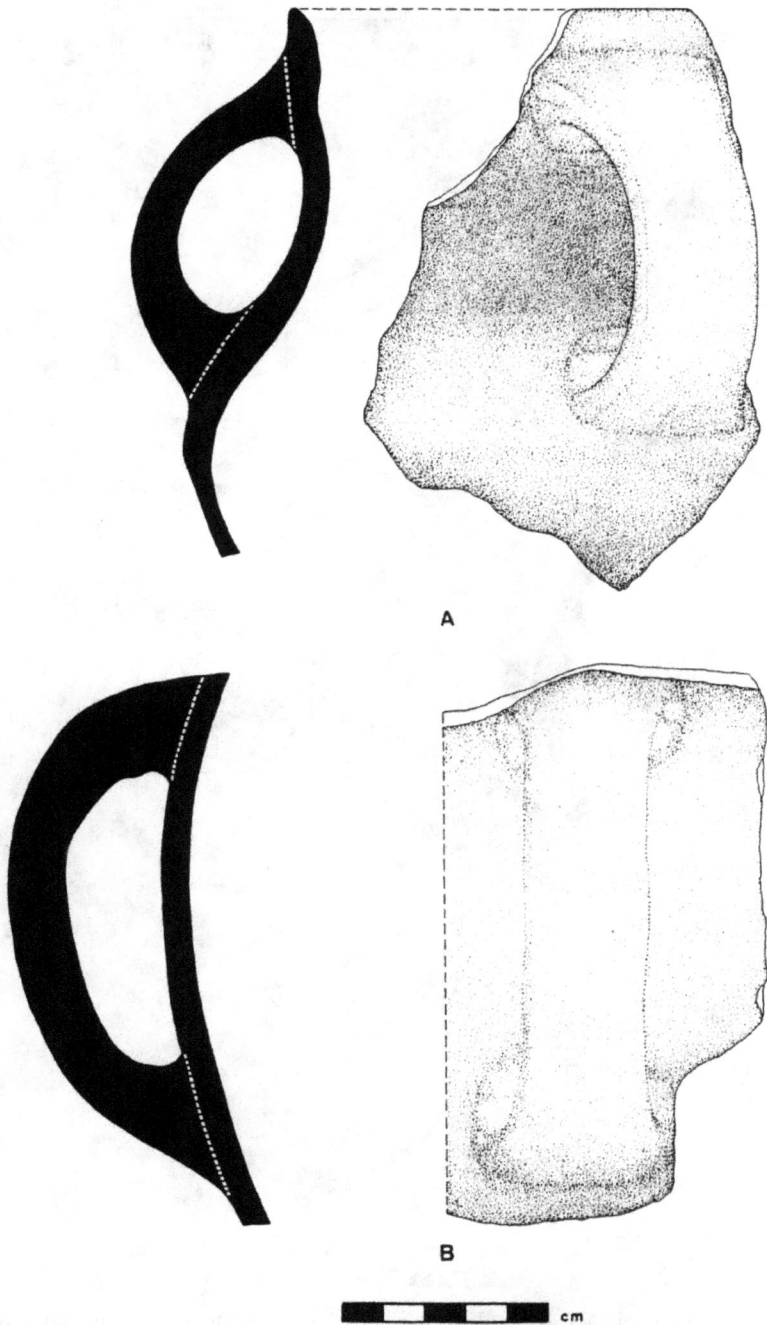

Fig. 6.10. Potsherds: A, B, Micaceous Paste Utility. Provenience: A, unknown, 1972; B, unknown

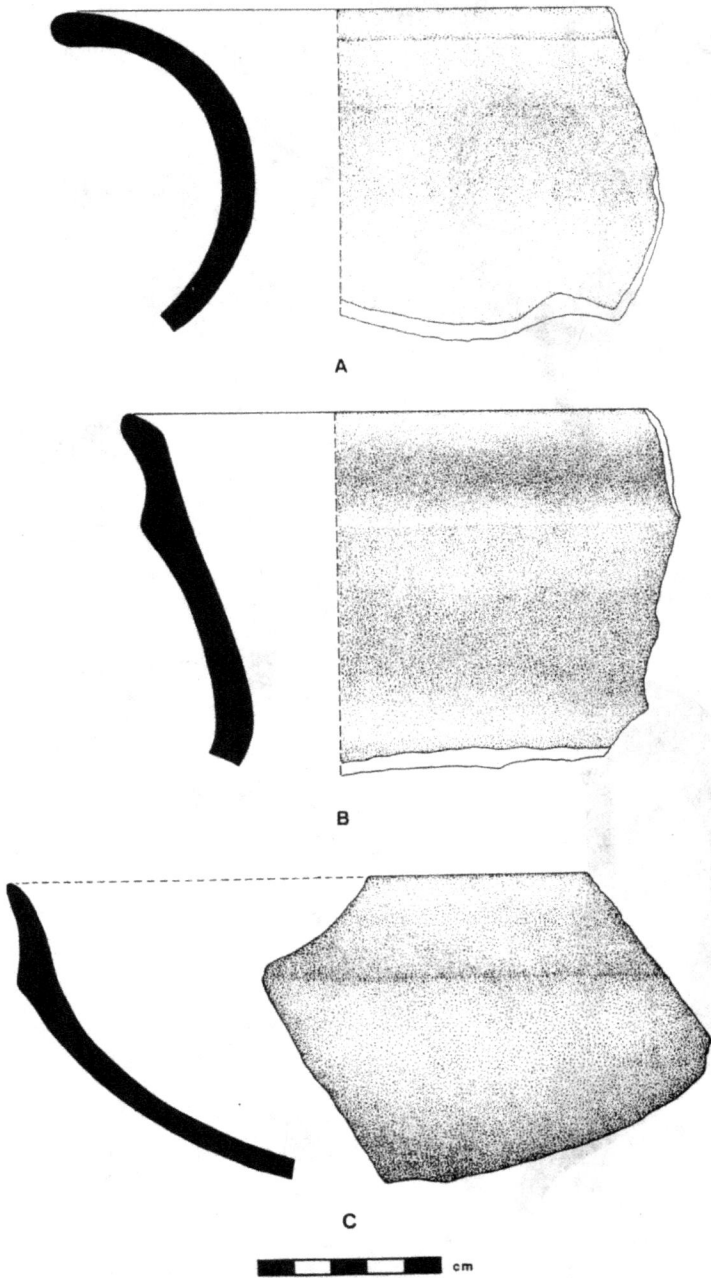

Fig. 6.11. Potsherds: A, B, Micaceous Paste Utility; C, Black Slipped and Polished. Provenience: A, Other Great Palace II; 1972; B, unknown; C, Great Palace II, Patio E CN

Table 6.6. Black Slipped and Polished Type Distribution

Provenience	Frequency	% by Type	% by Prov.
Great Palace II	116	50.22	2.33
Other Plaza C	6	2.60	1.51
Great Palace I	10	4.33	1.82
Plaza A	10	4.33	4.02
Other	5	2.16	0.99
Unknown	84	36.36	2.98
Total	231	100.00	

in most cases, whereas other vessels had a slight ridge or shoulder below the rim (figs. 6.11C; 6.12A).

One sherd is the fragment of a miniature tecomate. Most vessels, however, probably were small bowls, some with flat bases, and some of the latter had podal supports. Most rims were straight or outcurved. Figures 6.11C and 6.12B illustrate round-based bowls; figure 6.12C depicts a flat-based beakerlike bowl with missing podal supports. Podal supports are hollow, and some contain clay rattles. Those recovered are either plain (figs. 6.12D; 6.13A), modeled to form animal head effigies (fig. 6.13B–D), or mammiform (fig. 6.14A). One solid modeled vessel support is in the shape of a human foot. Several other bases were supported by ring-shaped pedestals (fig. 6.14B). Other examples of decorative appliqué include bird head effigies (fig. 6.14C), (one on a miniature jar [fig. 6.14D]) and incised nodes (fig. 6.14E). Several sherds display modeled fragments of human limbs, indicating that human figures, modeled in semirelief, decorated a few of these vessels.

Brown Slipped and Polished

Brown to dark brown in surface color, these sherds are from well-finished small to medium vessels, mostly bowls and shallow bowls (table 6.7). Other vessel forms represented are the necked jar and tecomate. Illustrated are a small dish (fig. 6.15A), a bird effigy bowl (fig. 6.15B), what is believed to be the lid to a small vessel (fig. 6.15C), and an effigy cup or handled bowl (fig. 6.15D). Some of these vessels have a slightly built-up encircling ridge (figs. 6.15E; 6.16A); others manifest a shallow, encircling, preslip groove; and a few others display several ridges separated by groove(s). Altogether, however, only 10 sherds show one of these forms of exterior surface treatment. Four sherds were

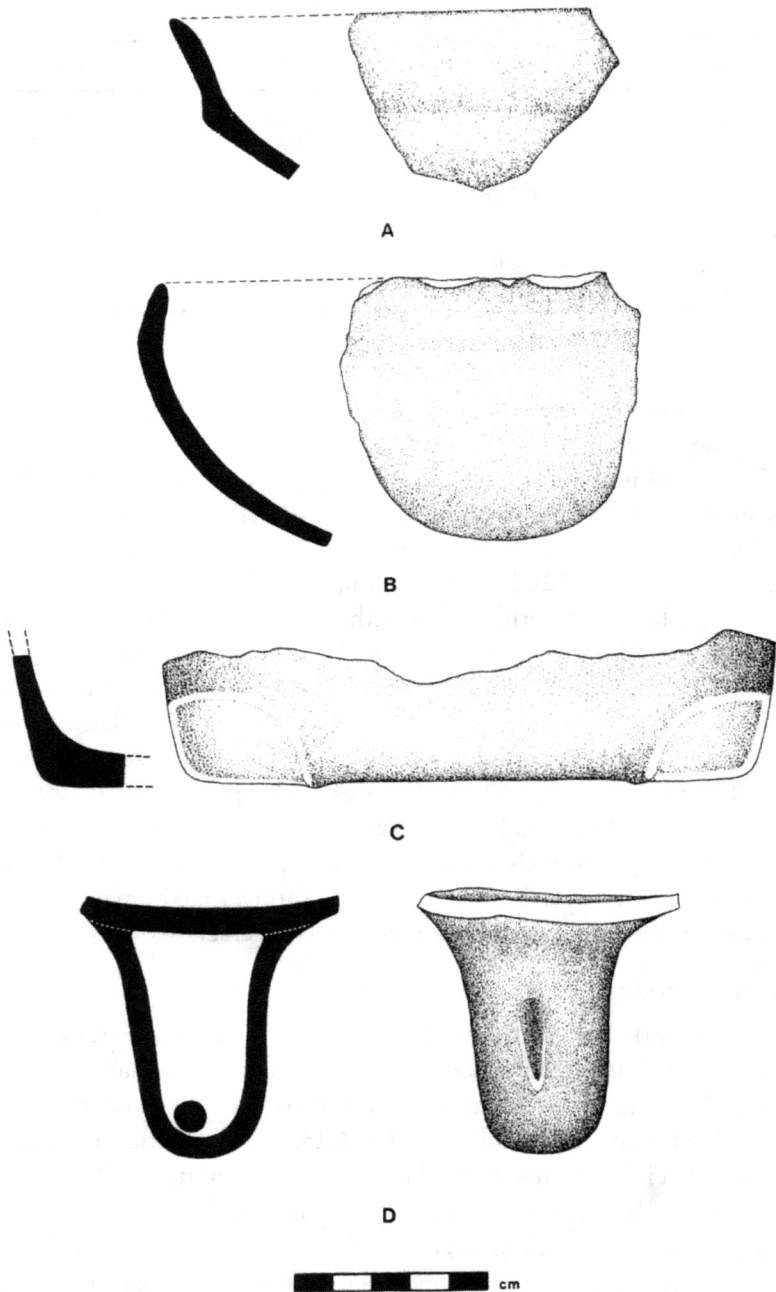

Fig. 6.12. Potsherds: A–D, Black Slipped and Polished. Provenience: A, unknown; B, Great Palace I; C, unknown, pre-1972; D, Great Palace II/Structure 45

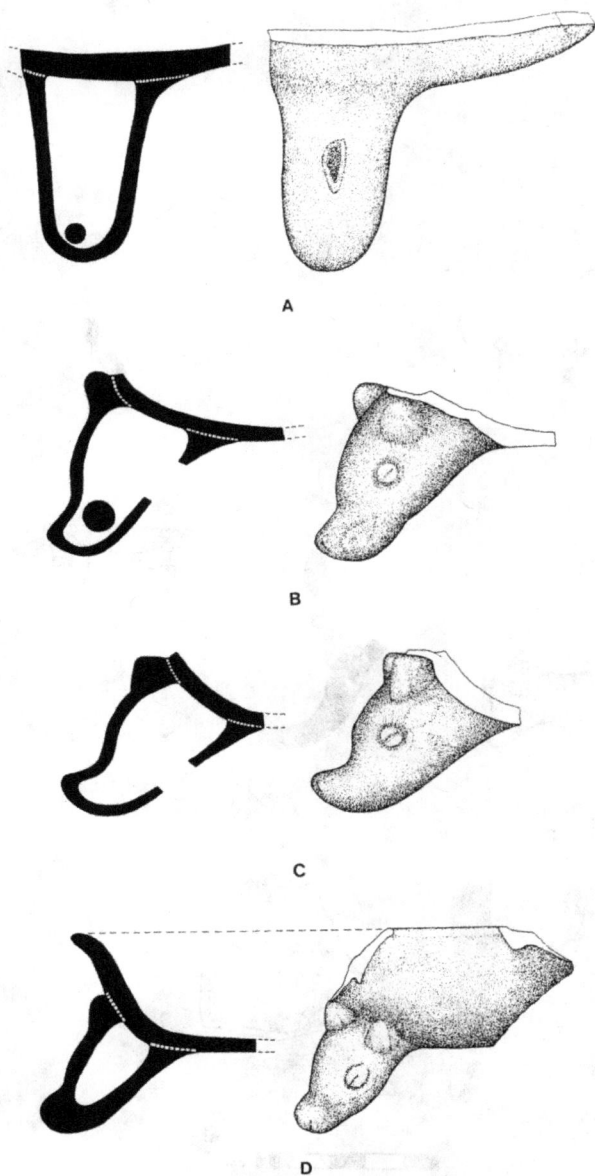

Fig. 6.13. Potsherds: A–D, Black Slipped and Polished. Provenience: A, Great Palace II/Structure 45; B, Great Palace II, Patio NE; C, unknown; D, Great Palace II, Patio S/SE

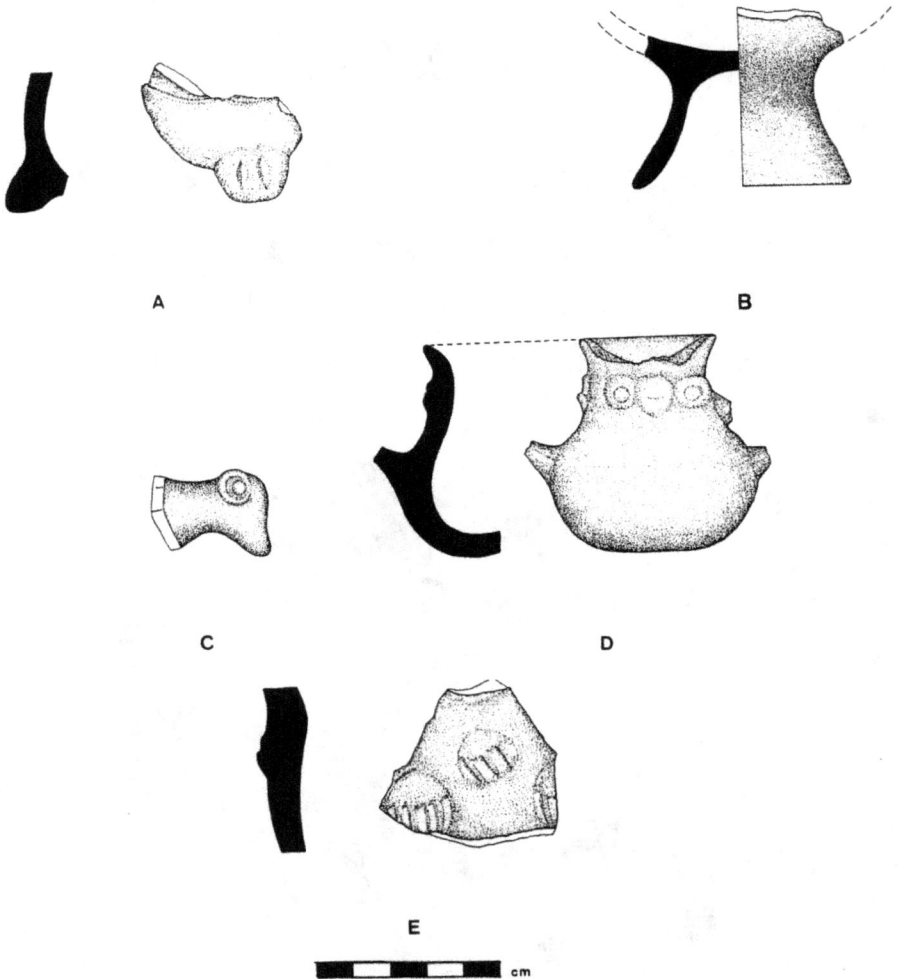

Fig. 6.14. Potsherds: A–E, Black Slipped and Polished. Provenience: A, Great Palace II, Patio NE; B, unknown, 1972; C, Other Great Palace II; D, unknown, 1972; E, Other Great Palace II

Table 6.7. Brown Slipped and Polished Type Distribution

Provenience	Frequency	% by Type	% by Prov.
Great Palace II	168	47.06	3.37
Other Plaza C	12	3.36	3.02
Great Palace I	25	7.00	4.55
Plaza A	10	2.80	4.02
Other	18	5.04	3.55
Unknown	124	34.73	4.40
Total	357	100.00	

punctated on one surface. Both surfaces were slipped and polished on a majority (57.48%) of sherds; 77.87% were slipped on one or both surfaces; and 87.68% were polished on one or both surfaces. Sherd average thickness is 6.37 mm. A study of 31 sherds which are indicative of vessel shape revealed that simple bowls tended to be better finished in terms of slipping and polishing than vessels of other forms.

Red Slipped and Polished

Sherds of this monochrome fine-ware type are thin (average thickness = 6.60 mm) and well finished (table 6.8). Both surfaces of the Red Slipped and Polished type were slipped for 31% of the sherds, and an additional 53% were slipped on just one surface. Polishing was identified for one or both surfaces for 65% of the sherds. Similar to several types discussed above, sherds showing interior slipping tend to be thinner than those with just exterior slip. Compared to Black Slipped and Polished, more sherds of this red ware derive from jars with strap handles (fig. 6.16B, C): 6.1% of the red ware sherds are strap handles compared to 1.3% for Black Slipped and Polished. Several of the strap handles in the Red Slipped and Polished collection bear modeled effigies; one is a hollow human head with rattle (fig. 6.17A, B). Other vessel forms include small flat-based bowls (fig. 6.17C, D) and bowls with plain podal supports. Other decorative elements are a human-foot-shaped vessel support and a human limb fragment. One vessel, a deep, straight-sided bowl or beaker was decorated with nodes. A common decorative technique described above and represented here on larger jars consists of low ridges separated by shallow grooves which were modeled into vessel walls before slipping. For this type, these encircle

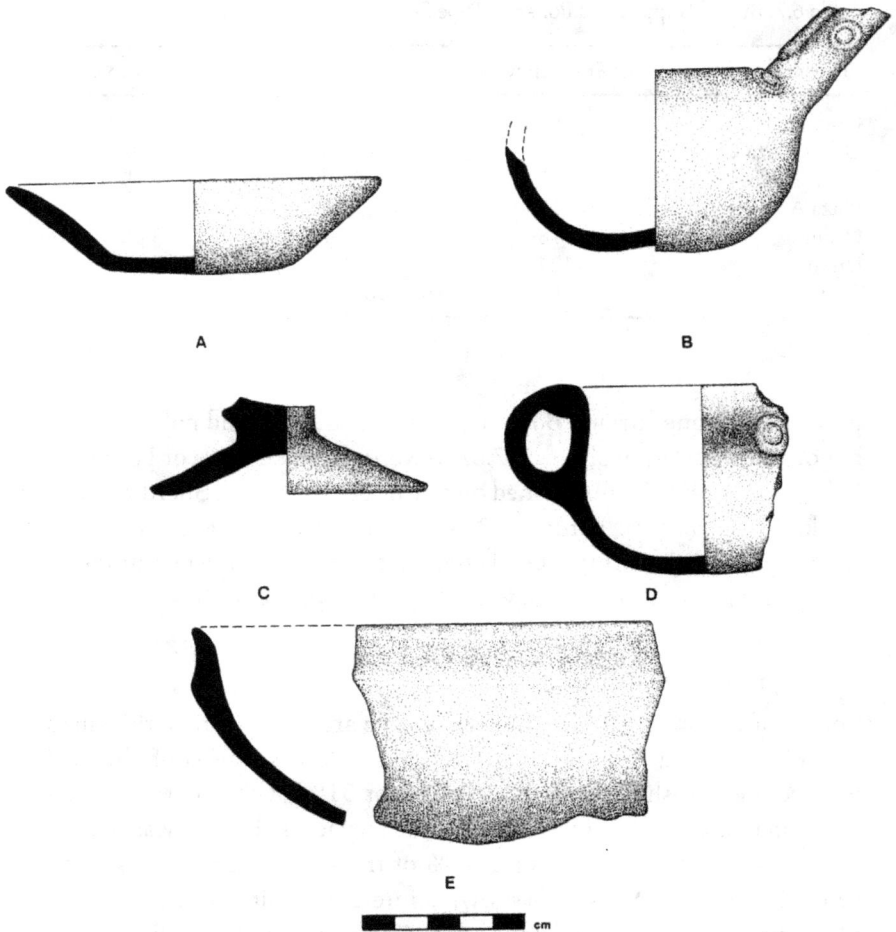

Fig. 6.15. Potsherds: A–E, Brown Slipped and Polished. Provenience: A, unknown; B, Great Palace II/Structure 45; C, unknown; D, unknown, 1972; E, Extreme E Surface

the vessel at the point of maximum diameter (fig. 6.16B, C). One sherd evidences interior wear in the form of pitting.

Gray Slipped and Polished

The Gray Slipped and Polished category consists of monochrome gray sherds from well-finished vessels (table 6.9). The sherds are relatively thin (average thickness = 6.99 mm), and most are probably from small straight-rimmed bowls. One sherd diagnostic of vessel form is from a medium-sized hemispherical bowl with a slightly constricted rim. This

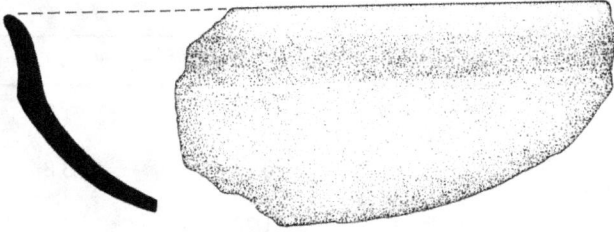

A

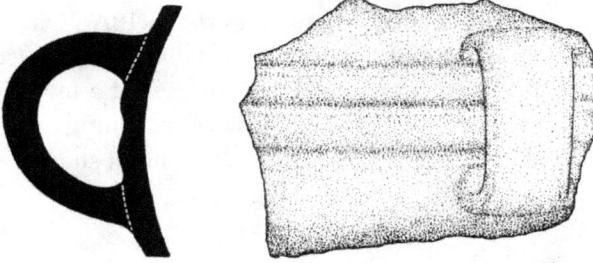

B

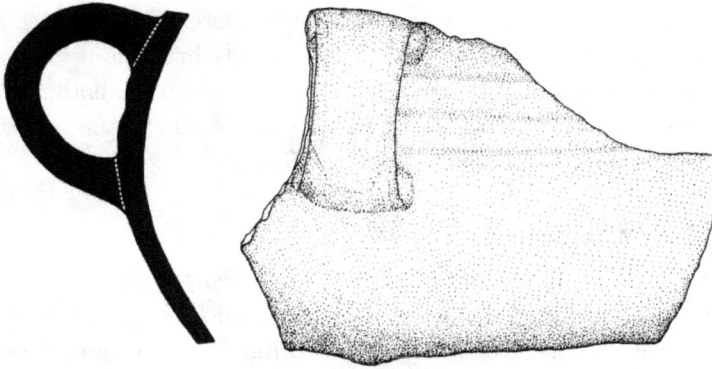

C

Fig. 6.16. Potsherds: A, Brown Slipped and Polished; B, C, Red Slipped and Polished. Provenience: A, Great Palace I; B, unknown; C, unknown, 1972

Table 6.8. Red Slipped and Polished Type Distribution

Provenience	Frequency	% by Type	% by Prov.
Great Palace II	85	43.59	1.71
Other Plaza C	10	5.13	2.52
Great Palace I	21	10.77	3.82
Other	18	9.23	3.55
Unknown	61	31.28	2.16
Total	195	100.00	

sherd and one other exhibit small lug handles (fig. 6.18A). One other sherd seems to be a fragment of a flat-bottomed dish. Traces of red or black paint occur on the exterior or interior surfaces of a few sherds. Most sherds (62%) were slipped on both surfaces; polishing on one or both surfaces was identified for 41%. Finally, one sherd showed wear on the interior surface in the form of pitting.

Buff Slipped and Polished

Most vessel forms represented in the Buff Slipped and Polished type are bowls, some of these, shallow bowls or dishes; a neck fragment of a medium-sized jar is also present (table 6.10). These sherds are buff in surface color, and sherds that are not slipped were very well fired in an oxidizing atmosphere. They are buff-colored throughout the paste. Most are slipped (71.8%) or polished (61.2%) on one or both surfaces. Evidence of decoration is very limited; a single bird effigy is illustrated (fig. 6.18B). Sherd average thickness is 5.99 mm.

Gray-Brown Slipped and Polished

Surface color for Gray-Brown Slipped and Polished sherds (table 6.11) is variegated, although in surface finish and thickness (average = 6.64 mm) these sherds resemble those of other monochrome fine-ware types. Most vessels of this type evidently were bowls, some small and shallow. A few jars also are represented. Most sherds were slipped (64.5%) and/or polished (86.8%) on one or both surfaces. Similar to the Buff Slipped and Polished type, evidence for decoration is almost absent. Exterior surfaces of two sherds, however, are incised.

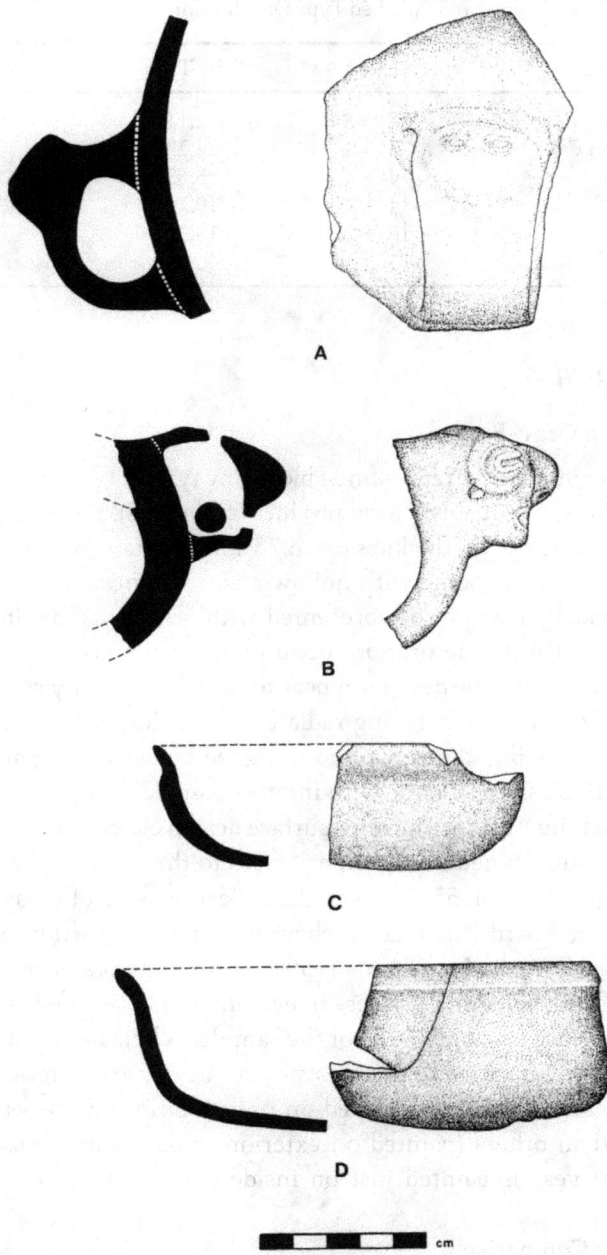

Fig. 6.17. Potsherds: A–D, Red Slipped and Polished. Provenience: A, unknown; B, unknown, 1972; C, Great Palace II/Structure 45; D, Great Palace I/Structure 4

Table 6.9. Gray Slipped and Polished Type Distribution

Provenience	Frequency	% by Type	% by Prov.
Great Palace II	37	52.11	0.74
Other Plaza C	3	4.23	0.76
Plaza A	4	5.63	1.61
Other	14	19.72	2.76
Unknown	13	18.31	0.46
Total	71	100.00	

Bichrome Types

Orange on Gray-Buff

The most abundantly represented bichrome type at Iximché, Orange on Gray/Buff was probably a local product (table 6.12). The sherds are relatively thin (average thickness = 6.73 mm). Pots were mostly bowls with straight rims, some with hollow podal supports (fig. 6.18C). One small necked jar was also represented with a strap handle in evidence (fig. 6.19A). Painted decorations occur on interior and exterior surfaces. On bowl interiors, the designs appear to have been highly standardized: bands of zoned cross-hatching radiate from a ring encircling the base, the ring consisting of a row of dots aligned between two parallel lines (fig. 6.19B, C). Of 83 sherds with interior painted designs, 68% display cross-hatching. Another interior surface design element consists of parallel lines and aligned dots at right angles to the rim (fig. 6.20A). Exterior designs occur on 55 sherds in the collection, and, of these, 69% exhibit checkerboard (fig. 6.20B), chevrons, or some portion of another rectilinear design. Most sherds (73%) appear to have been slipped on both surfaces; polishing was less in evidence and was identified for one or both surfaces for only 34% of the sample. When sherd thickness for the type was compared to the presence of interior and exterior painting it was found that sherds painted on only interior surfaces tend to be thinner than others (painted on exterior or both surfaces). This suggests that vessels painted just on inside surfaces tended to be small bowls.

Extra-Site Comparison

Wauchope (1970: 196, fig. 87b) describes a Red on Tan type for Utatlán. The type is represented by only two sherds, both from the same bowl, and, as illustrated, they display the same standard design described

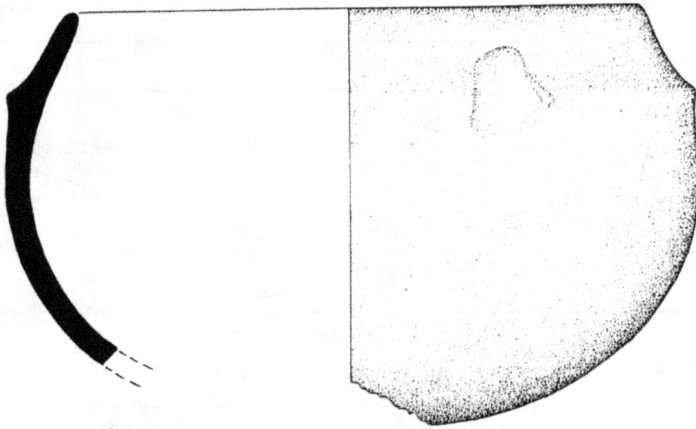

A

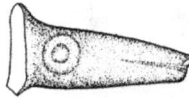

B

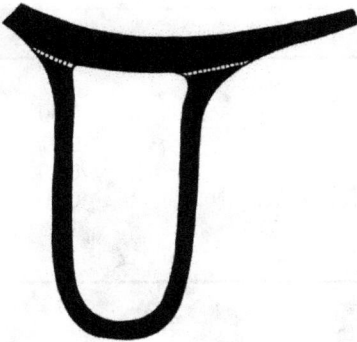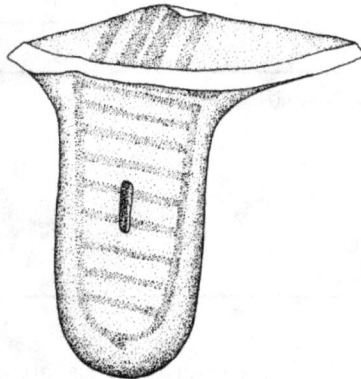

C

cm

Fig. 6.18. Potsherds: A, Gray Slipped and Polished; B, Buff Slipped and Polished; C, Orange on Gray-Buff. Provenience: A, Extreme E Surface; B, Great Palace II/Structure 45; C, Great Palace I

Table 6.10. Buff Slipped and Polished Type Distribution

Provenience	Frequency	% by Type	% by Prov.
Great Palace II	36	42.35	0.72
Other Plaza C	5	5.88	1.26
Great Palace I	9	10.59	1.64
Plaza A	1	1.18	0.40
Other	3	3.53	0.59
Unknown	31	36.47	1.10
Total	85	100.00	

Table 6.11. Gray-Brown Slipped and Polished Type Distribution

Provenience	Frequency	% by Type	% by Prov.
Great Palace II	34	44.74	0.68
Other Plaza C	3	3.95	0.76
Great Palace I	1	1.32	0.18
Plaza A	1	1.32	0.40
Other	2	2.63	0.39
Unknown	35	46.05	1.24
Total	76	100.00	

Table 6.12. Orange on Gray-Buff Type Distribution

Provenience	Frequency	% by Type	% by Prov.
Great Palace II	88	69.84	1.77
Other Plaza C	2	1.59	0.50
Great Palace I	5	3.97	0.91
Plaza A	1	0.79	0.40
Other	1	0.79	0.20
Unknown	29	23.02	1.03
Total	126	100.00	

above. On the interior, crosshatched bands seem to radiate outward from double lines encircling the base of the bowl.

White on Red

Sherds in this fine wear category have white painted designs on a red slipped/painted background (table 6.13). Most sherds painted just on the exterior may be from necked jars, since interior surfaces show no interior slip. Polishing is limited to exterior surfaces (9 of 22).

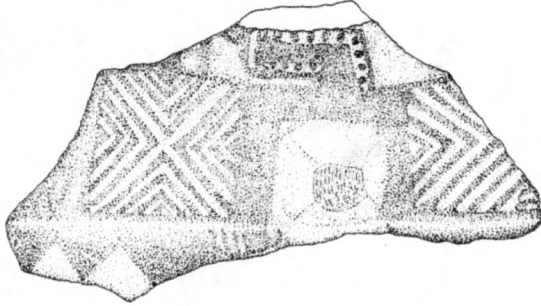

A

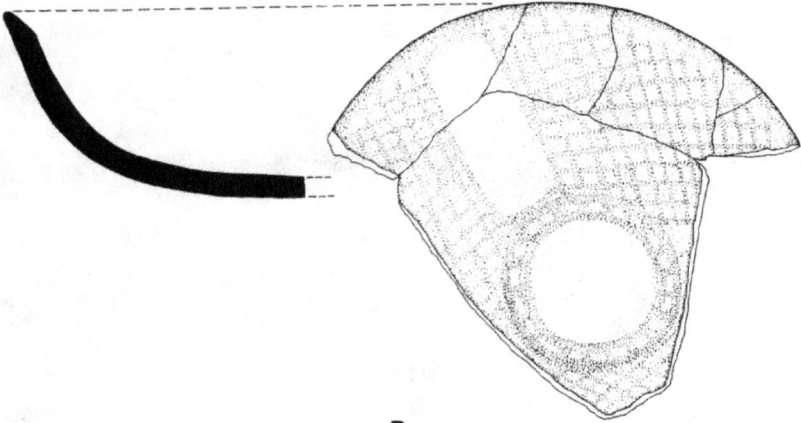

B

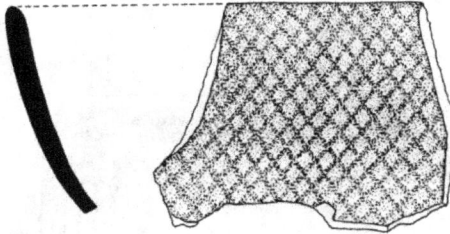

C

Fig. 6.19. Potsherds: A–C, Orange on Gray-Buff. Provenience: A, Great Palace I; B, Great Palace II/Structure 45; C, Great Palace II, Patio S/SE

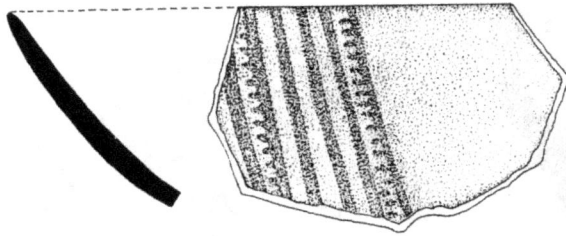

A

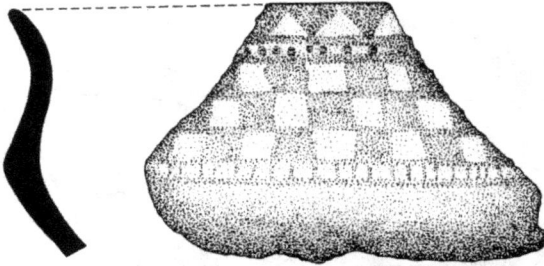

B

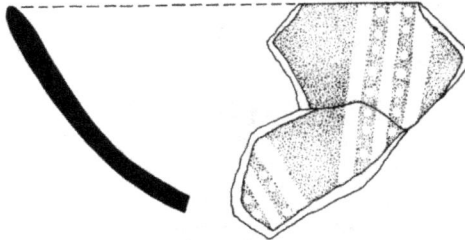

C

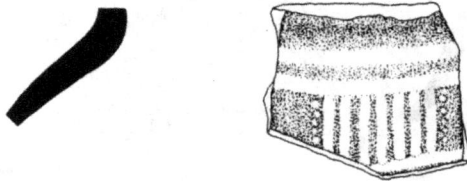

D

Fig. 6.20. Potsherds: A, B, Orange on Gray-Buff; C, D, White on Red. Provenience: A, Great Palace II, Patio NE; B, Great Palace II, Patio NE; C, unknown, 1972; D, Great Palace I/Structure 4

Table 6.13. White on Red Type Distribution

Provenience	Frequency	% by Type	% by Prov.
Great Palace II	5	22.73	0.10
Great Palace I	3	13.64	0.55
Other	4	18.18	0.79
Unknown	10	45.45	0.35
Total	22	100.00	

Both the bowl (fig. 6.20C) and necked jar (fig. 6.20D) forms are represented in the collection as are strap handles (fig. 6.21A) from large vessels. Bowls tend to be smaller than jars, as evidenced by comparing sherd thickness to surface painted. Based on data for 22 sherds, those painted on interior surfaces (bowls) are thinner than those painted on the exterior, and sherds painted on both surfaces fall between the two extremes.

Interior decorations consist of lines painted parallel to the rim and blocks of straight parallel lines and dots radiating from bowl centers (fig. 6.20C). Exterior decorations show more variability with straight parallel dots and lines but also curvilinear motifs (fig. 6.21B, C).

Extra-Site Comparisons

Wauchope believed that Fortress White on Red has some legitimacy as a Late Postclassic Highland type. White on Red is numerically dominant among bichrome and polychrome types at Chisalín (Weeks 1980: 602) and, on the basis of test excavations by Wauchope (1970: 100–103, 182), at nearby Utatlán as well.

Gray on Red

The several sherds in the Gray on Red category resemble those of White on Red, except that the designs are executed in gray or gray-green paint (table 6.14). The sherd with unknown provenience is slipped and polished on the exterior; the painted design is a single straight line paralleled by a row of dots. The two Great Palace II sherds, from the same provenience (PROVNO) and bowl, are decorated by two parallel lines separated by a row of dots encircling the rim on the exterior surface. The latter two sherds are coated with a red slip on both surfaces. Sherd average thickness is 8.33 mm.

Red Bands on White

Sherds of the Red Bands on White type (table 6.15) have in common white chalky slip applied as a solid coating, as a thin wash, or unevenly to

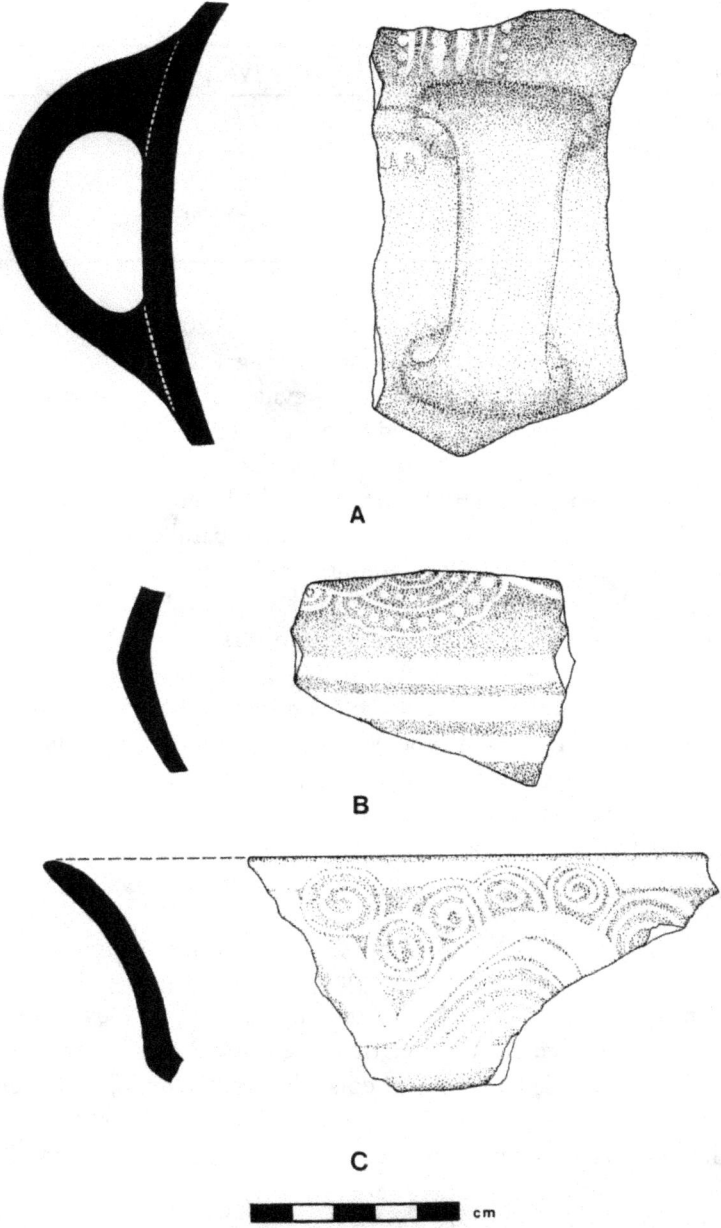

Fig. 6.21. Potsherds: A–C, White on Red. Provenience: A, C, unknown; B, Structure 43

Table 6.14. Gray on Red Type Distribution

Provenience	Frequency	% by Type	% by Prov.
Great Palace II	2	66.67	0.04
Unknown	1	33.33	0.04
Total	3	100.00	

Table 6.15. Red Bands on White Type Distribution

Provenience	Frequency	% by Type	% by Prov.
Great Palace II	72	62.07	1.44
Other Plaza C	2	1.72	0.50
Great Palace I	2	1.72	0.36
Plaza A	3	2.59	1.20
Other	2	1.72	0.39
Unknown	35	30.17	1.24
Total	116	99.99	

form streaky surfaces. This finish covers both surfaces (62.4%) or one surface (19.7%). On other sherds, the white material was applied as paint, incompletely covering the sherd surface. Only 4% of the sherds show any surface polishing. Most vessels were probably large; sherd average thickness is 8.89 mm. Vessel forms represented are the tecomate, the necked jar, and the bowl, with the tecomate possibly being most common. With only two strap handles (3.4%) in the collection, it seems that few large jars are represented. Two effigy sherds were assigned to the type, one of a plant, the other, a portion of a human face (fig. 6.22A). A few sherds are painted either on the exterior or interior surfaces with red stripes: on two, a single red band encircles the interior rim. A few other sherds bear traces of red or black paint on the white-slipped exterior surfaces. Wear was recorded for three sherds as exterior surface pitting.

Red on Orange (fine paste)

This large Red on Orange sherd (table 6.16) is from a beaker or steep-sided jar. There is no slip, but the interior surface is polished and bears a single red band encircling the rim. The sherd is notable for its very fine paste and may be an import. It is 5-mm thick.

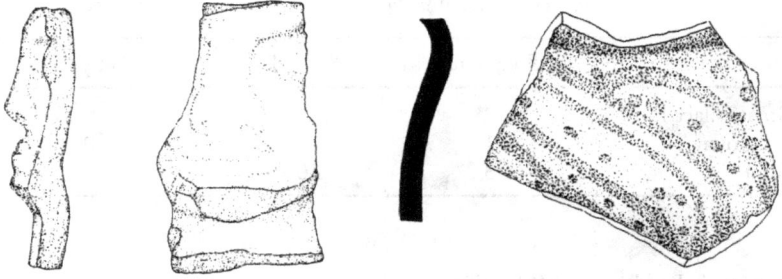

A   B

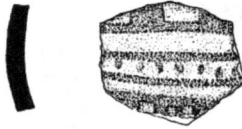

C

D

Fig. 6.22. Potsherds: A, Red Bands on White; B–D, Brown-Black on Buff. Provenience: A, Great Palace II, Patio NE; B, Great Palace I/Structure 4; C, Great Palace II, Patio NE; D, Great Palace II/Structure 45

Table 6.16. Red on Orange (Fine Paste) Type Distribution

Provenience	Frequency	% by Type	% by Prov.
Great Palace II	1	100.00	0.02
Total	1	100.00	

Table 6.17. Brown-Black on Buff Type Distribution

Provenience	Frequency	% by Type	% by Prov.
Great Palace II	5	71.43	0.01
Great Palace I	2	28.57	0.36
Total	7	100.00	

Brown-Black on Buff

On all but one of these Brown-Black on Buff type sherds (table 6.17), painted designs are crudely formed on exterior slipped surfaces. One sherd bears unique decoration, possibly white paint on a black background. Most designs are parallel lines and dots (fig. 6.22B, C) and crude, line-filled triangles (fig. 6.22D). A broad strap handle is attached to one sherd. Sherd average thickness is 6.43 mm.

Black on Red

All from the same provenience (bag), these uniquely decorated Black on Red type sherds are probably from the same vessel (table 6.18). On the interior of a flat-based bowl and above a solid black base, the red wall is decorated with regularly spaced, painted black lines forming contiguous triangles (fig. 6.23A). The sherds are slipped but not polished on both surfaces. Sherd average thickness is 5.22 mm.

Thick Black and White Painted

These sherds (table 6.19) are from large thick-walled vessels (average thickness = 13.7 mm) which were painted with broad black or black and white bands around the rim or black bands on a white wash or white-painted background. Rim sherds are either straight (63%) or out-curved. No sherd in the group is indicative of vessel form, but one sherd consists of a strap handle, another, a loop handle, and a third, a vessel support.

Table 6.18. Black on Red Type Distribution

Provenience	Frequency	% by Type	% by Prov.
Great Palace II	9	100.00	0.18
Total	9	100.00	

Polychrome Types

Black and Red on White (Chinautla Polychrome)

These sherds are clearly affiliated with the established type, Chinautla Polychrome (table 6.20). One sherd (fig. 6.23B) is well finished (slipped and polished) on both surfaces and manifests a well-executed polychrome design on the exterior surface. The others (figs. 6.23C; 6.24A) are slipped on the exterior surfaces only, and designs are more crudely delineated. If the former is from a vessel imported to the site, the latter may represent local copies. Sherd average thickness is 8.45 mm.

Unique Bichrome and Polychrome

Resembling no other potsherds from the site, these four unique sherds may not even be contemporaneous with the Iximché occupation (table 6.21). The three specimens from Great Palace I are thin (average thickness = 5.66 mm), slipped and polished on both surfaces, and very well fired. Two are brown on orange bichrome, the third is brown, black, and orange on gray polychrome. The thin polychrome sherd from Great Palace II may be from a Classic Petén site.

Other Decorated Types

Cacao Pod Effigy Vessel

From plant effigy vessels believed to represent cacao pods (fig. 6.24B, C), these sherds all manifest modeled ridges and aligned nodes (table 6.22). On one fragment the point of stem attachment is clearly indicated. They lack slipping and polishing, but half bear traces of green paint, and one shows traces of red and green paint. These vessels were small and boat- or pod-shaped. Sherd average thickness is 6.11 mm.

Ethnohistorical Note

Cacao was an item of high prestige in late prehistoric times (Feldman 1985: 86). It is noteworthy that 12 of the 13 sherds of known provenience

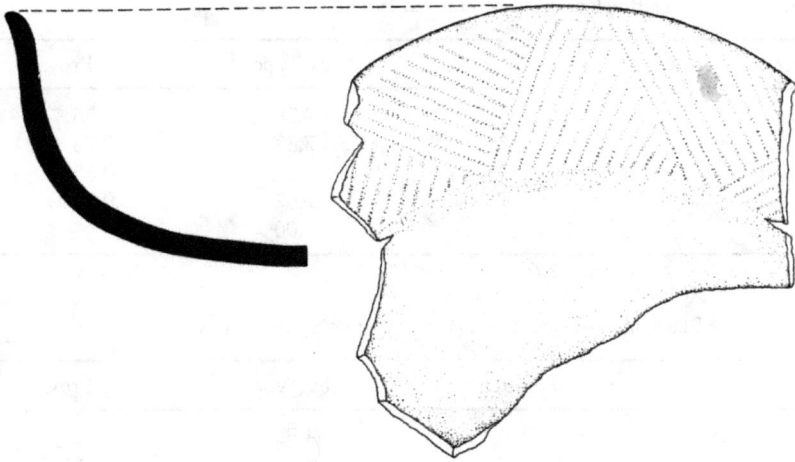

A

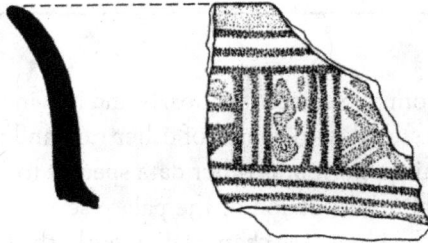

B

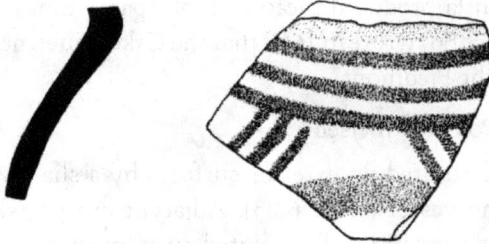

C

cm

Fig. 6.23. Potsherds: A, Black on Red; B, C, Black and Red on White. Provenience: A, Other Great Palace II; B, unknown, 1972; C, unknown

Table 6.19. Thick Black and White Painted Type Distribution

Provenience	Frequency	% by Type	% by Prov.
Great Palace II	28	68.29	0.56
Other Plaza C	3	7.32	0.76
Great Palace I	3	7.32	0.55
Unknown	7	17.07	0.25
Total	41	100.00	

Table 6.20. Black and White on Red (Chinautla Polychrome) Type Distribution

Provenience	Frequency	% by Type	% by Prov.
Great Palace II	6	54.55	0.12
Great Palace I	2	18.18	0.36
Unknown	3	27.27	0.11
Total	11	100.00	

for this type came from two adjacent patios, N and NE, in Great Palace II, where they were clustered with sherds of other rare and possibly exotic types. Altogether, this pattern plus other data specific to Patio NE led to the interpretation that this portion of the palace served as domicile for one of the two Iximché kings (see chap. 8). Evidently the Cakchiquel had access to tropical land where cacao was grown. Orellana (1995: 30–31) reports that the Cakchiquel conquered Esquintla in the late fifteenth century and that Esquintla produced cacao in Prehispanic times. Vásques (cited in Feldman 1985: 86) wrote in 1689 that the Cakchiquel maintained cacao plantations in the Piedmont.

Brown Slipped and Polished Incised

These sherds were decorated on exterior surfaces by a shallow preslip groove encircling the vessel (table 6.23). Adjacent are postslip, fine-incised, parallel lines forming well-executed curvilinear or rectilinear designs (figs. 6.24D; 6.25A). Exterior surfaces were well polished after incising. Exterior surface colors vary from dark brown to dark red; interior surfaces are black. Sherd average thickness is 7.00 mm.

Reed Punctate

Three sherds, all from very large pots (average thickness = 14.44 mm), evidence aligned reed- or bone-punctate decorations (table 6.24). The sherds are neither slipped nor polished.

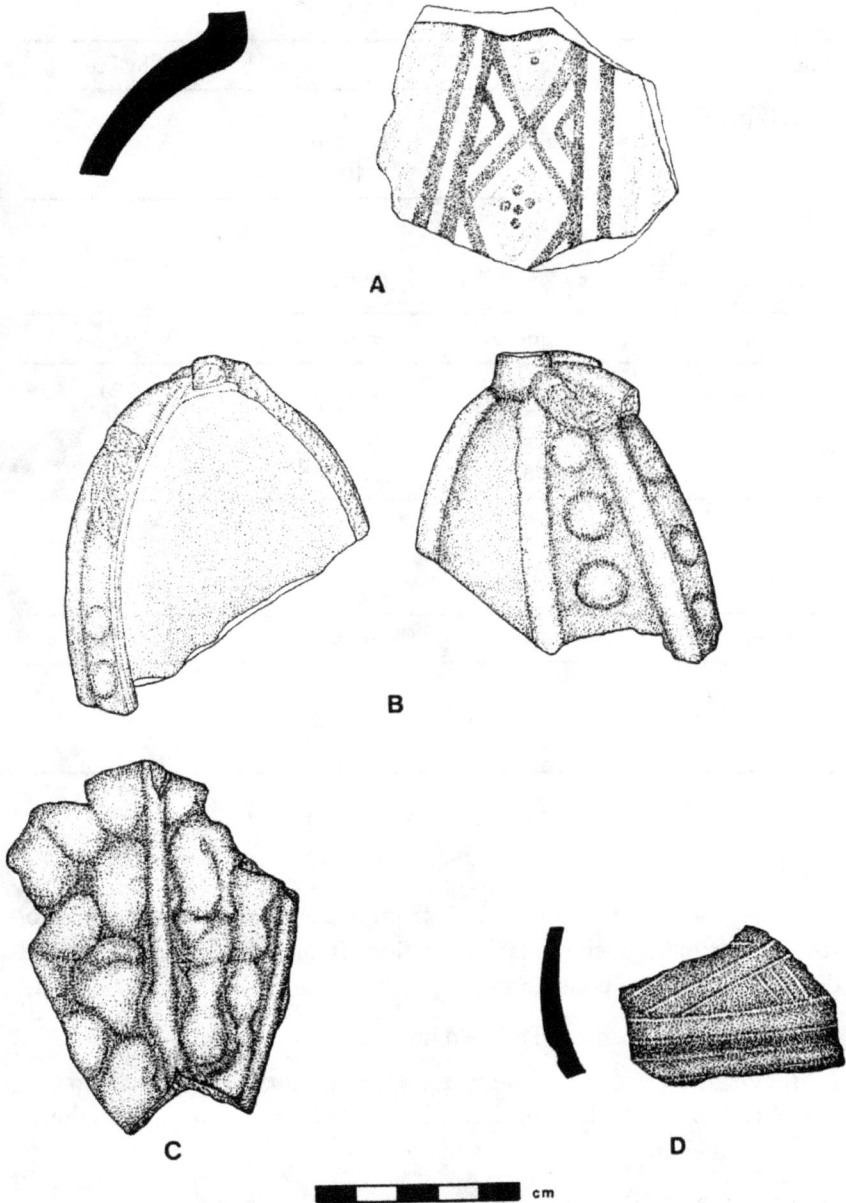

Fig. 6.24. Potsherds: A, Black and Red on White; B, C, Cacao Pod Effigy Vessel; D, Brown Slipped and Polished, Incised. Provenience: A, Great Palace II, Patio S/SE; B, unknown; C, Great Palace II, Patio N; D, Great Palace II, Patio NE

Table 6.21. Unique Bichrome and Polychrome Type Distribution

Provenience	Frequency	% by Type	% by Prov.
Great Palace II	1	25.00	0.02
Great Palace I	3	75.00	0.55
Total	4	100.00	

Table 6.22. Cacao Pod Effigy Vessel Type Distribution

Provenience	Frequency	% by Type	% by Prov.
Great Palace II	12	66.67	0.24
Plaza A	1	5.56	0.40
Unknown	5	27.78	0.18
Total	18	100.01	

Table 6.23. Brown Slipped and Polished Incised Type Distribution

Provenience	Frequency	% by Type	% by Prov.
Great Palace II	2	66.67	0.04
Unknown	1	33.33	0.04
Total	3	100.00	

Other Punctate

This single sherd, 11-mm thick, is from a large vessel which had two rows of encircling rectangular punctations (table 6.25). There is no evidence of slipping or polishing.

Unique Black Slipped and Polished Incised

A unique, finely executed design sets this sherd apart from others in the larger collection (table 6.26; fig. 6.25B). This vessel was small (sherd thickness = 5 mm) and slipped and polished on the exterior.

Polished Brown-Black Incised

These sherds are all from large vessels and show relatively crude parallel-line incising on the exterior surfaces (table 6.27). The only vessel form suggested is the large slightly necked jar with thick strap handles. The most typical design is a series of two crude nested triangles

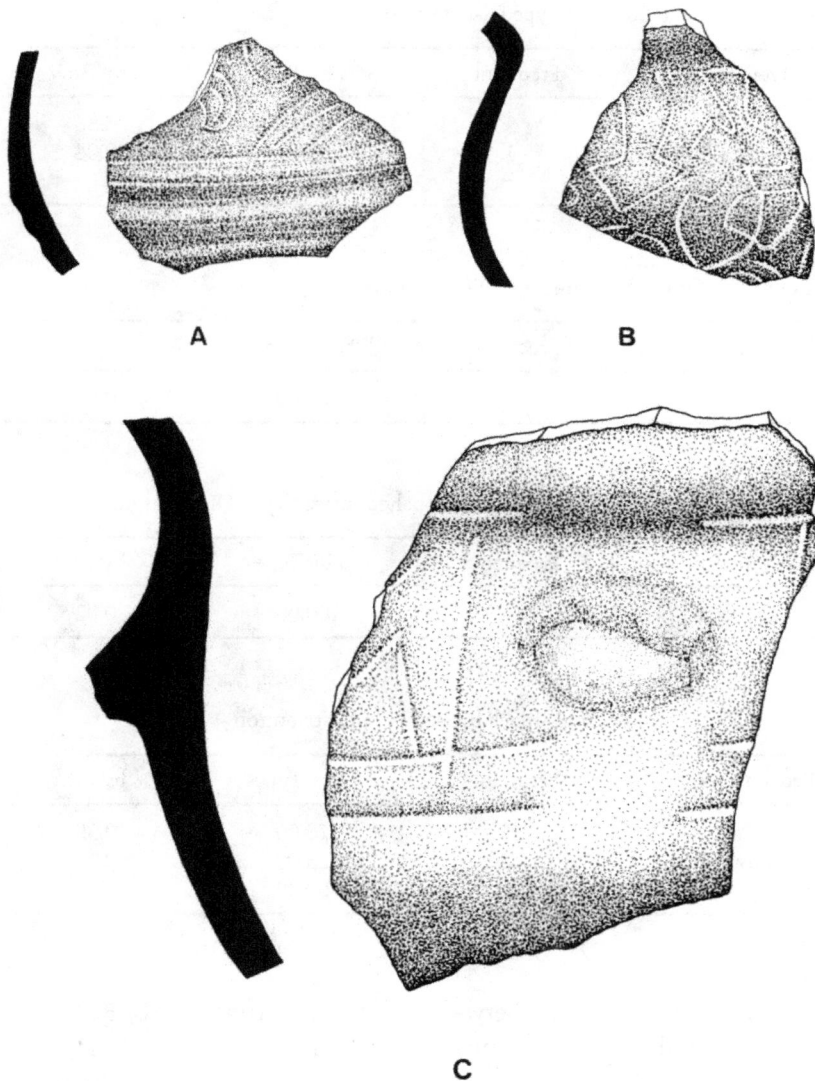

Fig. 6.25. Potsherds: A, Brown Slipped and Polished Incised; B, Unique Black Slipped and Polished, Incised; C, Polished Brown-Black Incised. Provenience: A, unknown, 1972; B, Great Palace II/Structure 45; C, unknown

Table 6.24. Reed Punctate Type Distribution

Provenience	Frequency	% by Type	% by Prov.
Great Palace I	2	66.67	0.36
Unknown	1	33.33	0.04
Total	3	100.00	

Table 6.25. Other Punctate Type Distribution

Provenience	Frequency	% by Type	% by Prov.
Unknown	1	100.00	0.04

Table 6.26. Unique Black Slipped and Polished Incised Type Distribution

Provenience	Frequency	% by Type	% by Prov.
Great Palace II	1	100.00	0.02

Table 6.27. Polished Brown-Black Incised Type Distribution

Provenience	Frequency	% by Type	% by Prov.
Great Palace II	15	75.00	0.30
Unknown	5	25.00	0.18
Total	20	100.00	

repeated around the rim between incised lines (figs. 6.25C; 6.26A, B). Two sherds show parallel-line curvilinear designs (fig. 6.26C, D). Several appear to be rim sherds, except the rims apparently have been battered repeatedly, and the lip surface is no longer extant. Interior surfaces of these utility vessels have been wiped smooth but otherwise are poorly finished. An exterior slip was identified for three sherds and exterior polishing for five. Sherd average thickness is 8.40 mm.

Fine-Incised Beaker

Most Fine-Incised Beaker sherds probably are the remains of a single vessel: eleven came from the same bag and derive from Patio N (table

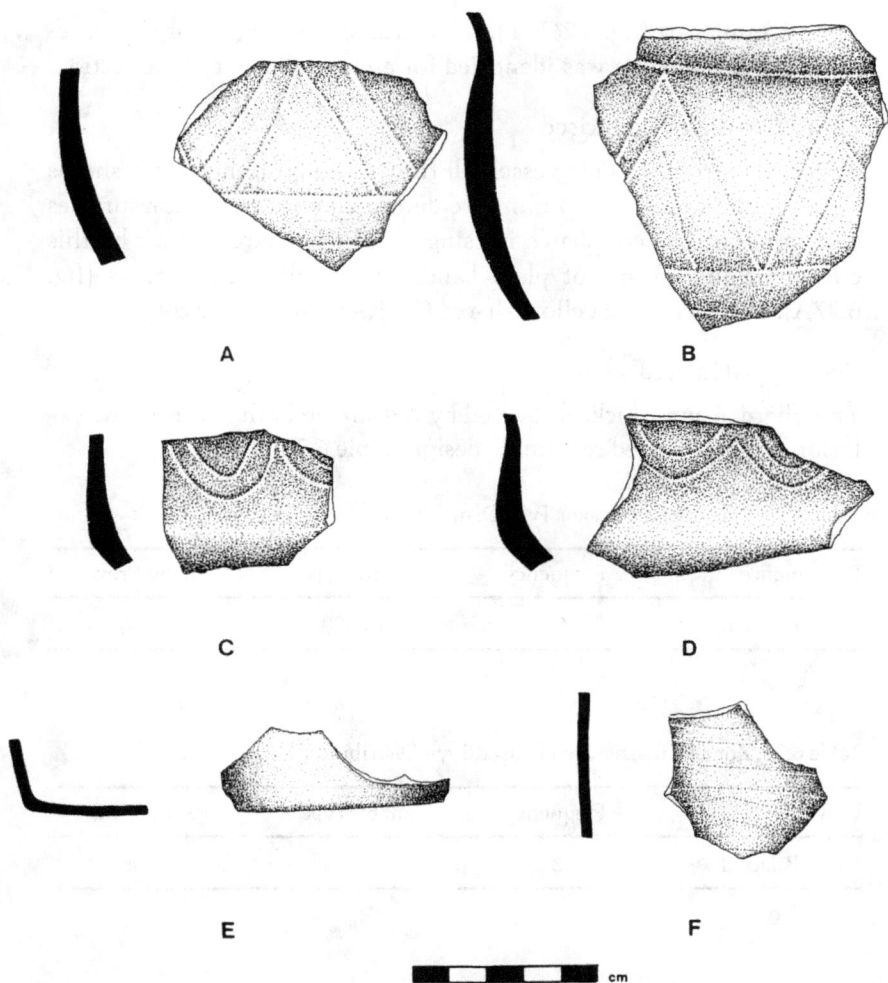

Fig. 6.26. Potsherds: A–D, Polished Brown-Black Incised; E, F, Fine-Incised Beaker. Provenience: A, Great Palace II, Passageway from Patio E CN to Patio E/SE; B, unknown, 1972; C, Great Palace II, Patio S/SE; D, Great Palace II, Patio S/SE; E, Great Palace II, Patio NE; F, Great Palace II, Patio N

6.28). The two other sherds, however, were recovered from different patios (Patio S/SE and Patio NE). The sherds seem to represent small beaker-shaped vessels with flat bases and very thin walls (sherd average thickness = 3.92 mm). Decoration consists of a preslip ridge encircling at least one pot as well as preslip fine incised lines parallel to the ridge and rim and spaced about 5 mm apart (fig. 6.26E, F). All sherds show an exterior slip; exterior surface polishing was identified for about half the type collection.

Zoned Crosshatched Incised

Apparently from a single vessel (all from Patio NE), these thin sherds (average thickness = 4.33 mm) are decorated on the interior surfaces with zones of fine crosshatch incising (table 6.29). Areas offset by this cross-hatching consist of plain bands and small circular areas (fig. 6.27A). The sherds are yellowish-red (5 YR 4/6) in surface color.

Red Slipped Incised

This sherd, 6-mm thick, is covered by red slip on both surfaces; the exterior bears an incised rectilinear design (table 6.30).

Table 6.28. Fine-Incised Beaker Type Distribution

Provenience	Frequency	% by Type	% by Prov.
Great Palace II	13	100.00	0.26

Table 6.29. Zoned Crosshatched Incised Type Distribution

Provenience	Frequency	% by Type	% by Prov.
Great Palace II	3	100.00	0.06

Table 6.30. Red Slipped Incised Type Distribution

Provenience	Frequency	% by Type	% by Prov.
Great Palace II	1	100.00	0.02

Table 6.31. Brown Polished Punctate Type Distribution

Provenience	Frequency	% by Type	% by Prov.
Unknown	8	100.00	0.28

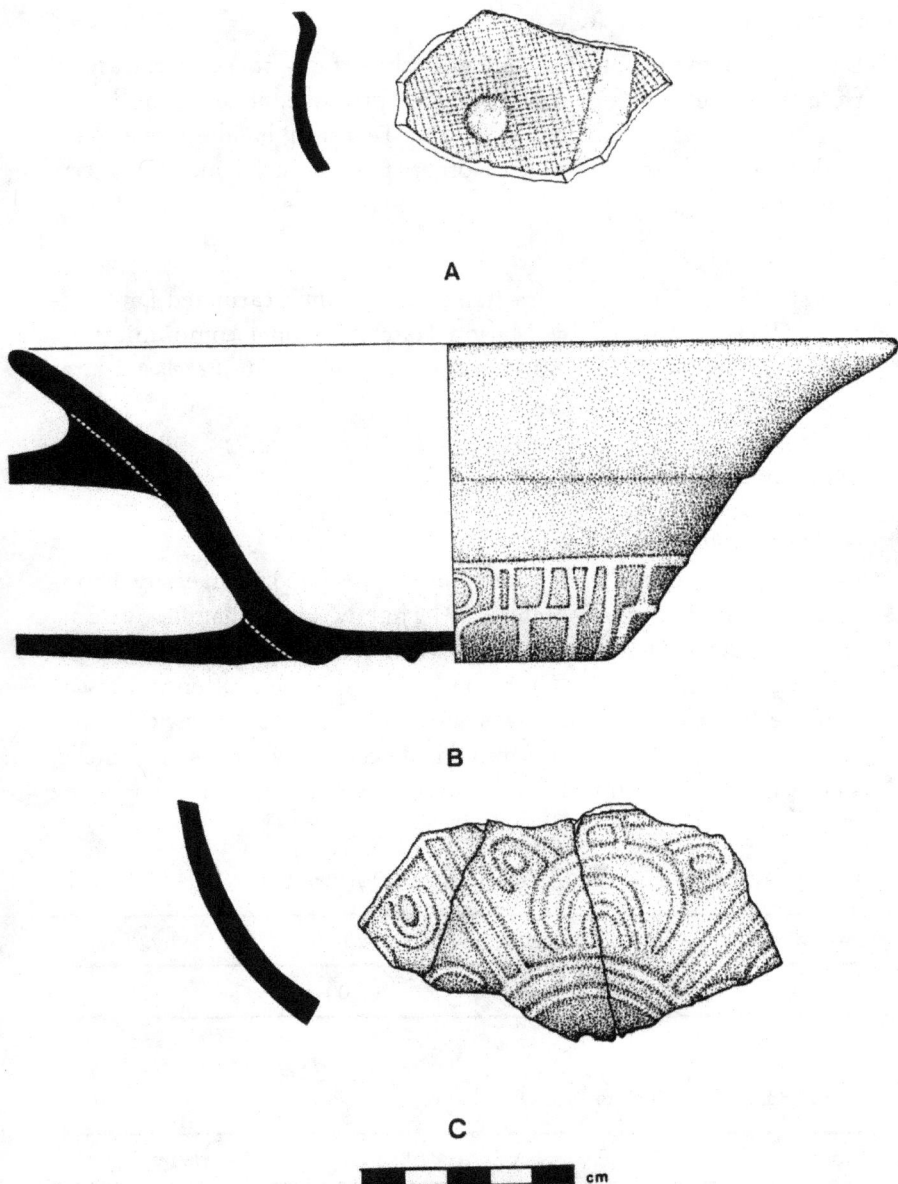

Fig. 6.27. Potsherds: A, Zoned Crosshatched Incised; B, C, Ladle Incensario. Provenience: A, Great Palace II, Patio NE; B, unknown; C, Great Palace II, Patio S/SE

Brown Polished Punctate

Dark brown and polished on one or both surfaces, these sherds are all from the same bag (table 6.31). They are punctated in single or double rows around vessel exteriors at the rim. Two strap handles are also included. These sherds resemble no others from Iximché and almost certainly are foreign in origin. Sherd average thickness is 7.85 mm.

Carinated Late Preclassic

The specimen is a large sherd (table 6.32) from a carinated Late Preclassic bowl (identified by Marion Hatch, personal communication, 1990). Guillemin (1965a: 30) mentions finding a Late Preclassic stratum at Iximché.

Ceremonial Types

Ladle Incensario

Ladle incense burners from Iximché are represented by an easily distinguished class of potsherds (table 6.33). Hollow tubular handles were attached to small flat-bottomed bowls which had rounded or straight, expanding sides (fig. 6.27B, C). Elaborate designs were often impressed into the bottoms of these bowls by means of molds (figs. 6.27B, C; 6.28A–C). These are the only moldmade ceramic artifacts at Iximché, and there may be both a functional as well as an aesthetic reason for the

Table 6.32. Carinated Late Preclassic Sherd Type Distribution

Provenience	Frequency	% by Type	% by Prov.
Unknown	1	100.00	0.28

Table 6.33. Ladle Incensario Type Distribution

Provenience	Frequency	% by Type	% by Prov.
Great Palace II	112	42.26	2.25
Other Plaza C	4	1.51	1.01
Great Palace I	21	7.92	3.82
Plaza A	7	2.64	2.81
Other	13	4.91	2.56
Unknown	108	40.75	3.83
Total	265	99.99	

application of this technique. Some of the bases are particularly thin (figs. 6.27B; 6.28A), and the raised patterns may have strengthened these very thin flat bases sufficiently to keep them from breaking. Such thin bases probably served to dissipate heat, so the handles could continue to be held during the burning of incense.

Many of the bowl fragments evidence exterior (97) or interior (94) surface painting. Typically, this took the form of broad white or black stripes radiating outward (and expanding) from the base. Occasionally the stripes were alternating white and black. Traces of red, green, and gray paint were also found on a few of these sherds. On one bowl the entire exterior surface had been painted or slipped red. The color and extent of painted decorations were often difficult to discern, given the extensive burning of the bowl surfaces. Hollow handles (figs. 6.28D; 6.29A–C) often had a solid loop handle extending above their non-bowl ends as well as human faces modeled into their extremities.

Extra-Site Comparisons
Ladle incensarios with mold-impressed decorations on bowl bases are common for Late Postclassic Highland Guatemala (Wauchope 1970: 117–118).

Small Micaceous-Slip Dish

This distinctive type collection consists of sherds from small, relatively thick dishes, each covered with what appears to be a micaceous slip on the upper surface (table 6.34). Sherd average thickness is 7.78 mm. Bottom surfaces are poorly finished. The dishes are either flat or have slightly raised rims. A few sherds evidence carinated rims with holes drilled through the expanded rim portions. These vessels may have been either comales or incensarios. If the latter, string handles may have been connected through these holes in expanded-rim (carinated) areas on opposite sides of some of the vessels.

Extra-Site Comparisons
Wauchope described mica-ware dishes which he collected from Iximché and Utatlán and from Cahyup in Baja Verapaz. Only for specimens from Iximché, however, did he mention that "the under surface of the base is rough" (Wauchope 1970: 195, 208–209, 228).

Thick Beaker Incensario

Sherds in this category generally represent large thick-walled beakers which probably functioned as incensarios or braziers (table 6.35). Some sherds (7.6%) show pronounced burning on interior surfaces. Sherd

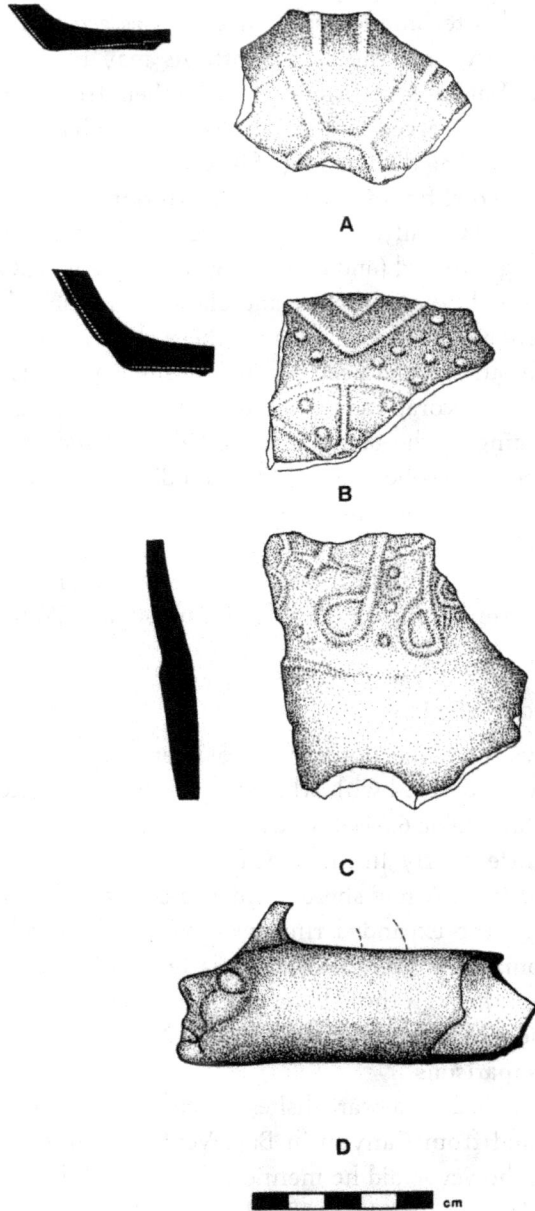

Fig. 6.28. Potsherds: A–D, Ladle Incensario. Provenience: A, unknown; B, Great Palace I; C, Great Palace I/Structure 4; D, Great Palace II, Passageway from Patio E CN to Patio E/SE

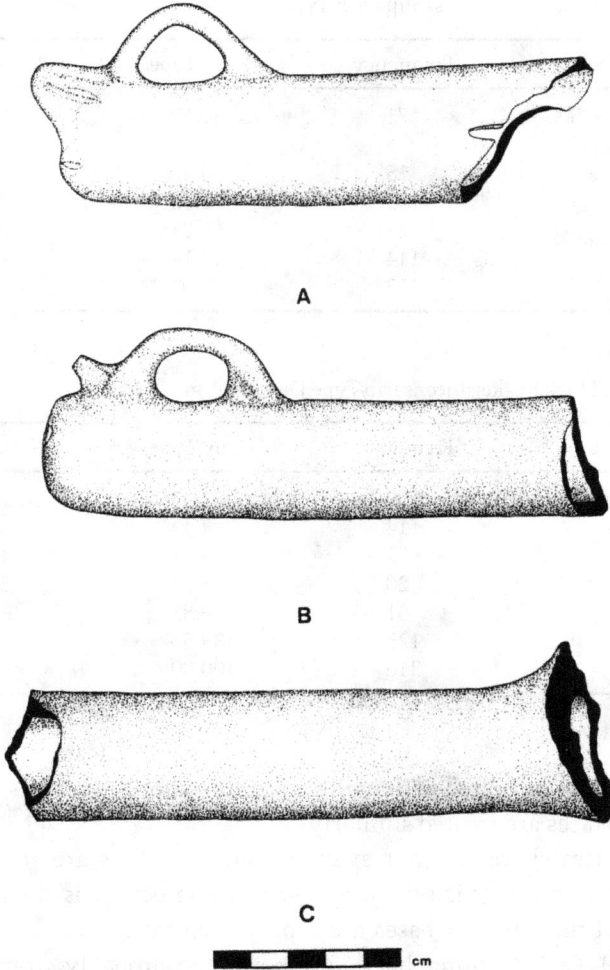

Fig. 6.29. Potsherds: A–C, Ladle Incensario. Provenience: A, Great Palace II, Patio E CN; B, unknown, 1972; C, unknown, 1972

average thickness is 13.5 mm. Beaker bases are flat, and straight-sided walls often are appliquéd with conical spikes and vertical flanges (fig. 6.30A, B). These spikes and flanges are characteristic of the type, occurring on 14.8% and 12.3% of the sherds, respectively. Fewer sherds bear more elaborate appliquéd decoration in the forms of modeled human heads (fig. 6.31A–C), human limbs (figs. 6.31D; 6.32A), or animals (fig. 6.32B). Many other sherds (24.7%) exhibit fragmentary and indescribable appliquéd decorations (fig. 6.32C). Most sherds (58.2%) are

Table 6.34. Small Micaceous-Slip Dish Type Distribution

Provenience	Frequency	% by Type	% by Prov.
Great Palace II	71	30.60	1.42
Other Plaza C	6	2.59	1.51
Great Palace I	15	6.47	2.73
Plaza A	5	2.16	2.01
Other	21	9.05	4.14
Unknown	114	49.14	4.04
Total	232	100.01	

Table 6.35. Thick Beaker Incensario Type Distribution

Provenience	Frequency	% by Type	% by Prov.
Great Palace II	99	31.33	1.99
Other Plaza C	14	4.43	3.53
Great Palace I	27	8.54	4.91
Plaza A	20	6.33	8.03
Other	31	9.81	6.11
Unknown	125	39.56	4.43
Total	316	100.00	

painted white or coated with white stucco on exterior surfaces; some interior surfaces are treated similarly.

Some rim sherds exhibit exterior flanges; others are straight; but the greatest number is outcurved (48%). The beaker is the dominant form, and thick beaker bases are represented by 46 sherds (14.5% of the total). On the other hand, 38 sherds are probably from double-chambered incensarios.

Extra-Site Comparisons and Iconography

Wauchope (1970: 118) reports vertical-flanged censers from Iximché and Utatlán and spiked censers from Zaculeu, Chutinamit, and Utatlán.

Marqusee (1980: 67, 250–251) believed that the Maya creator god, Itzam Na, or a closely allied deity, might have been part of the Cakchiquel Late Postclassic pantheon and saw possible evidence for this in a ceramic monster effigy from Iximché. This assessment evidently was based on a photograph published by Guillemin (1965a: 47) of a ceramic monster with a human head emerging from its jaws. The monster has reptilian characteristics and bone-shaped nostril stoppers. The latter

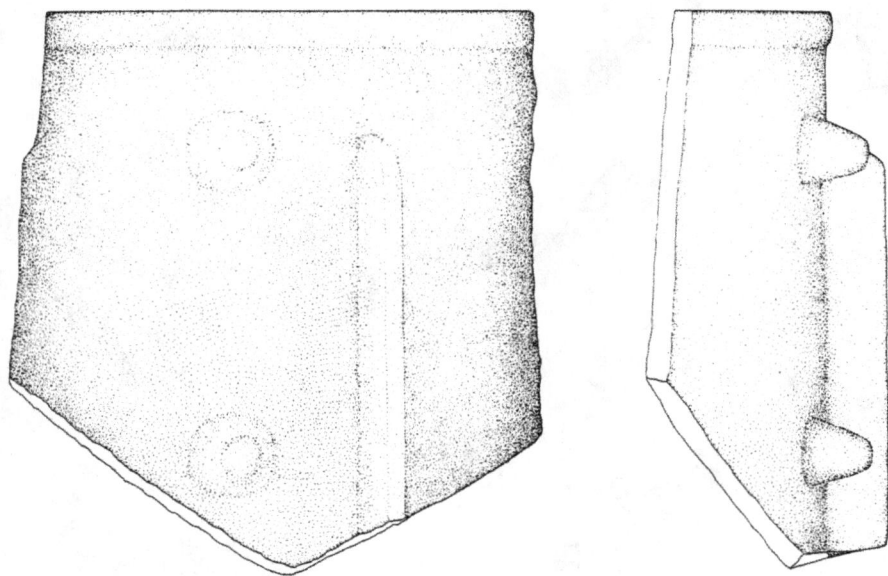

A

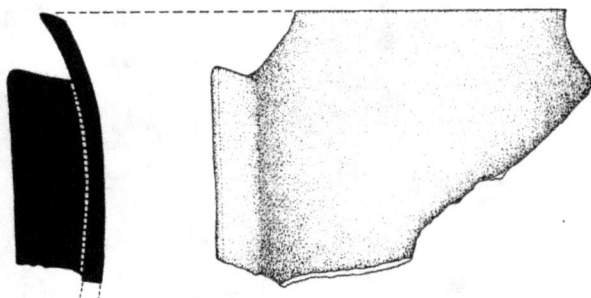

B

Fig. 6.30. Potsherds: A, B, Thick Beaker Incensario. Provenience: A, unknown; B, Extreme E Surface

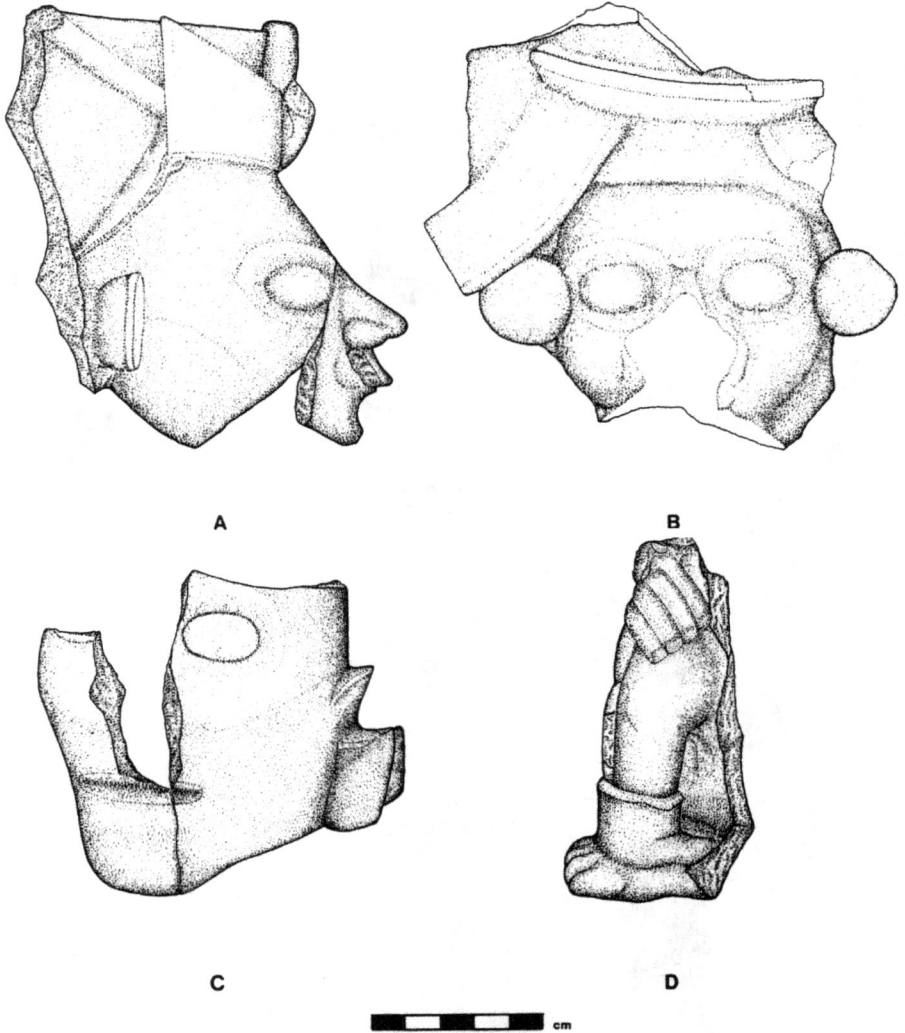

Fig. 6.31. Potsherds: A–D, Thick Beaker Incensario. Provenience: A, B, D, unknown; C, unknown, 1972

were not clearly visible as photographed in the 1965a publication, but they can be seen in another photograph taken by Guillemin from a different perspective (published here as fig. 6.33). Tubular stoppers and reptilian characteristics are both traits which can be manifested by Itzam Na. Also, artisans occasionally portrayed Itzam Na with a human head fixed between its open jaws (Thompson 1970: 209–233). It is also possible that the same creature is represented in the artifact illustrated here

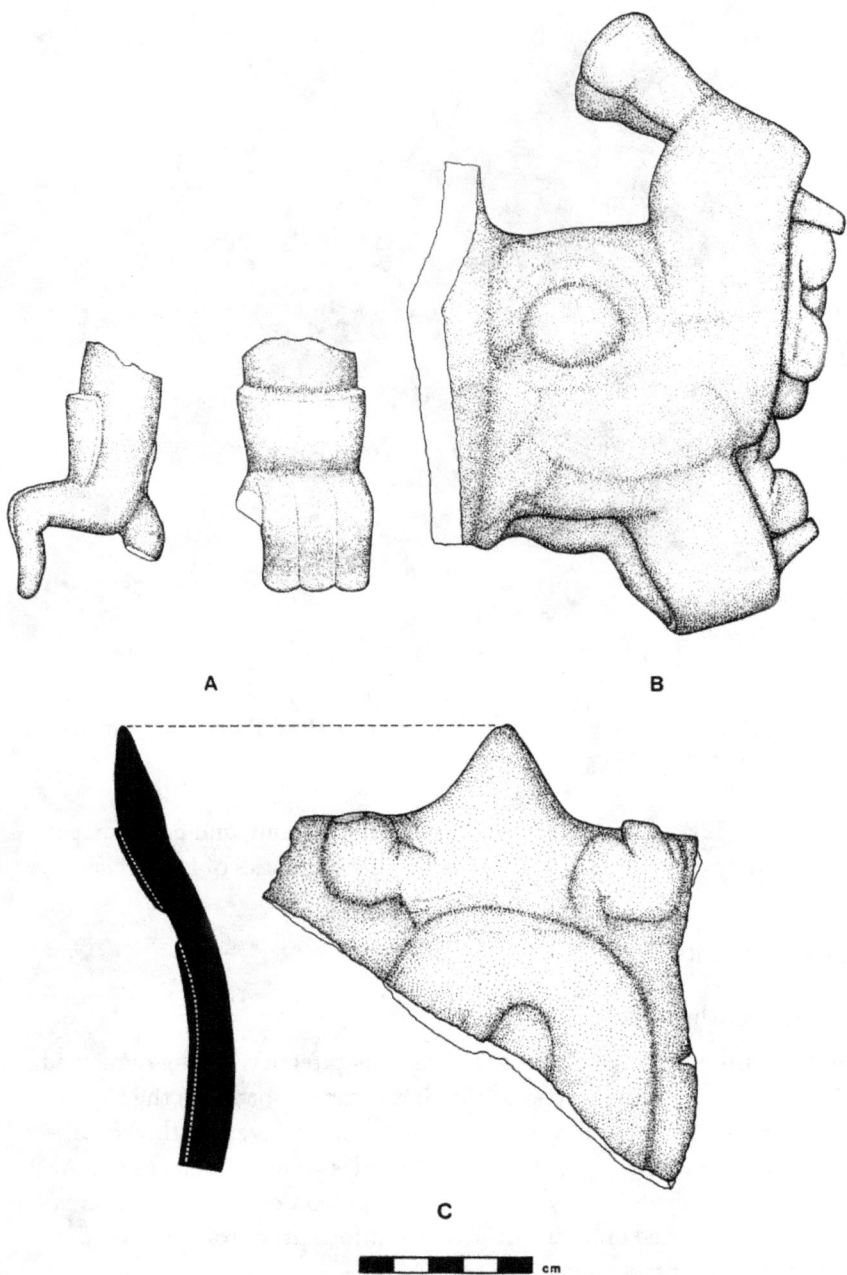

Fig. 6.32. Potsherds: A–C, Thick Beaker Incensario. Provenience: A–C, unknown

Fig. 6.33. Ceramic Effigy, Monster with Human Head Emerging from Jaws (Itzam Na?)

in figure 6.32B. Its reptilian features, extended snout, and bone-shaped stoppers are all, according to Thompson, characteristics of Itzam Na.

Other Minority Types

Orange Polished

Although there are very few sherds in this category, Orange Polished seems to be a legitimate type, as the sherds can be sorted on the basis of their orange surface color, their relative thinness (average thickness = 5.55 mm), and their polished, nonslipped surfaces (table 6.36). Although well finished, only 33.3% are slipped on one surface, whereas 66.7% are polished on both surfaces. No information was recovered on vessel shape or decoration.

Well Finished, Nonslipped, Nonpolished

These few sherds are nonslipped and most have matte nonpolished surfaces (table 6.37). Nevertheless, the sherds are all well finished

Table 6.36. Orange Polished Type Distribution

Provenience	Frequency	% by Type	% by Prov.
Great Palace II	3	33.33	0.06
Other Plaza C	3	33.33	0.76
Plaza A	1	11.11	0.40
Unknown	2	22.22	0.07
Total	9	99.99	

Table 6.37. Well-Finished, Nonslipped, Nonpolished Type Distribution

Provenience	Frequency	% by Type	% by Prov.
Great Palace II	4	26.67	0.08
Other Plaza C	1	6.67	0.25
Great Palace I	1	6.67	0.18
Unknown	9	60.00	0.32
Total	15	100.01	

(smooth). All may be from miniature jars (fig. 6.34A); six sherds suggest the jar or miniature jar form, and five strap handles are included. Eight of the sherds have what appears to be a metallic wash on the exterior surface. Sherd average thickness is 5.66 mm.

Micaceous Slip

These sherds resemble those of the Well Finished, Nonslipped, Nonpolished type except exterior surfaces are covered with a definite micaceous slip instead of a wash (table 6.38). A majority (60%) of these sherds are slipped on one or both surfaces. The only vessel form indicated is the necked jar. Sherd average thickness is 6.38 mm. Illustrated is a fragment of a small animal effigy (fig. 6.34B).

Micaceous Paste

These are well-finished sherds which lack both slip and polishing (table 6.39). They can further be distinguished by their thinness (average thickness = 6.69 mm) and their highly micaceous paste. There is no evidence regarding vessel shape or decoration.

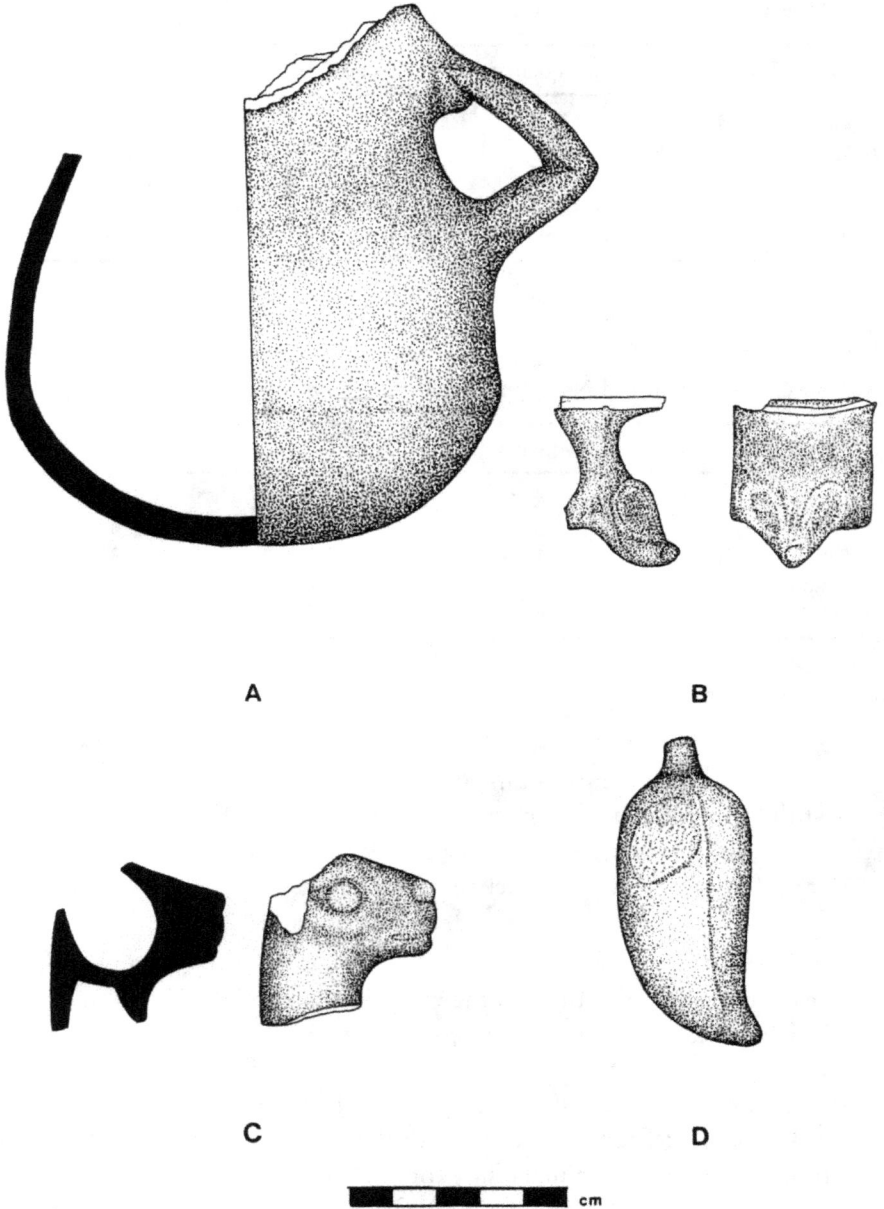

Fig. 6.34. Potsherds: A, Well Finished, Nonslipped, Nonpolished; B, Micaceous Slip; C, D, Thick, White-Painted. Provenience: A, unknown, 1972; B, Great Palace II, Patio S/SE; C, Great Palace II/Structure 45; D, Great Palace II, Patio N

Table 6.38. Micaceous Slip Type Distribution

Provenience	Frequency	% by Type	% by Prov.
Great Palace II	2	20.00	0.04
Other Plaza C	1	10.00	0.25
Great Palace I	1	10.00	0.18
Unknown	6	60.00	0.21
Total	10	100.00	

Table 6.39. Micaceous Paste Type Distribution

Provenience	Frequency	% by Type	% by Prov.
Great Palace II	2	15.38	0.04
Plaza A	11	84.62	4.42
Total	13	100.00	

Table 6.40. Orange, Matte-Finish Type Distribution

Provenience	Frequency	% by Type	% by Prov.
Unknown	4	100.00	0.14

Orange, Matte-Finish

From a single bag, these four sherds are likely from the same pot (table 6.40). They are unique for their bright orange exterior color, and the vessel, possibly a large tecomate, may have been imported. Sherd surfaces are neither slipped nor polished. Sherd average thickness is 9.25 mm.

Residual Types

Thick White Painted

Thick White Painted is a residual category containing what are probably eroded sherds of White Slipped as well as sherds of larger vessels showing traces of white paint and/or wash on one or both surfaces (table 6.41). Large strap handles suggest large pots or jars. Evidence of appliqué decorations suggests that some of these sherds are from large painted incensarios. Unique sherds include one with a ceramic hook (for storage?)

Table 6.41. Thick White Painted Type Distribution

Provenience	Frequency	% by Type	% by Prov.
Great Palace II	108	57.45	2.17
Other Plaza C	6	3.19	1.51
Great Palace I	8	4.26	1.45
Plaza A	9	4.79	3.61
Other	9	4.79	1.78
Unknown	48	25.53	1.70
Total	188	100.01	

and a sherd with faint impressions of a net. A third is a small square ceramic plaque. Illustrated are a hollow animal effigy (fig. 6.34C) and a solid plant pod effigy (fig. 6.34D). Sherd average thickness is 10.79 mm.

Eroded Fine Ware

This is a residual class, containing sherds believed to be members of fine ware types described above, but unassignable owing to their eroded surfaces (table 6.42). The sherds are thin, averaging 6.15 mm in thickness. Some sherds (32) are indicative of vessel form, including the tecomate (15.6%), necked jar (37.5%), and bowl (46.9%).

Extra-Site Relationships

A Comparative Discussion of the Ceramics

In the Guatemalan Highlands the only comprehensive analysis of Late Postclassic ceramics from a single site is that by Weeks (1983: 154–190) for Chisalín. There are a few general similarities with Iximché: brown and red wares tend to predominate at both sites; polychrome decoration is all but absent, and bichrome types constitute a small minority of sherds. Striking contrasts, however, tend to outweigh these parallels. There seems to be much more micaceous paste pottery at Iximché (compare Weeks's Caca Micaceous to Micaceous Paste Utility). And, the same is true of Black Slipped and Polished or Black Polished Utility and solid white painted or slipped types. Bichrome designs at Chisalín are much bolder, involving broad painted stripes. At Chisalín, the most important bichrome type is Fortress White on Red. (Similar boldly executed designs are present on Fortress White on Red sherds from Zac-

Table 6.42. Eroded Fine Ware Type Distribution

Provenience	Frequency	% by Type	% by Prov.
Great Palace II	235	71.43	4.71
Other Plaza C	9	2.74	2.27
Great Palace I	12	3.65	2.18
Other	9	2.74	1.78
Unknown	64	19.45	2.27
Total	329	100.01	

uleu, a site farther to the west of Iximché than Chisalín, in the Department of Huehuetenango (Woodbury and Trik 1953, 1: 173; 2: 247–248).) Another contrast is that the most frequent bichrome type at Iximché is not White on Red, but Orange on Gray-Buff. Also, Weeks describes comales for a variety of types. At Iximché, the flat dish form is limited to the Small Micaceous-Slip Dish type. Ladle Incensarios have human faces modeled into handle ends at Iximché. At Chisalín, similarly placed faces were rendered through stamping.

It is possible the bichrome and polychrome types will prove important in defining cultural and/or linguistic territories for the Highland Late Postclassic (cf. Rands and Smith 1965: 139–142). For the two Quiché collections studied thus far, from Chisalín and Wauchope's Utatlán test excavations, Chinautla Polychrome is rare and the only numerically significant bichrome type is Fortress White on Red. Feldman (1985: 68) remarks that "Fortress White-on-Red, perhaps better called Jocopilas White-on-Red—for it is most common in that area . . . fades as one goes south and east." Jocopilas is in the Department of El Quiché. For Iximché, Chinautla Polychrome is again scarce, and the only bichrome type present in any quantity is Orange on Gray-Buff. To the east, however, Chinautla Polychrome predominates over bichrome types. This is indicated for Mixco Viejo (Navarette 1961: 9) as well as in Wetherington's (1978: 173–184) summary of ceramics from Beleh (Chinautla Viejo) in the vicinity of Guatemala City.

All comparative data indicate that the Iximché collection, with the exception of a few sherds, is Late Postclassic in age. The almost complete absence of Tohil Plumbate pottery, diagnostic of the Early Postclassic, may be significant here, although Rands and Smith (1965: 134) reported that Tohil Plumbate was rare in their Central Zone of the Highlands, which includes Iximché. Plumbate ware was neither encountered in initial sorting and washing of Iximché ceramics nor later in the study. Guillemin (1965a: 29) regarded as an heirloom the only example of Plumbate he found at Iximché, the remains of a single vessel. A similar, isolated find was made during excavations at Utatlán (Carmack 1981: 292).

1

ᴨᴨᴨᴨᴨ

Ceramic Type Distributions

Type distributions for most of the ceramic collection from Iximché were studied through correspondence analysis and through a contingency table, comparing proportions of ceramic wares from the two Great Palaces. In part, the focus is on these two structures because they produced the most sherds of known provenience from the site. Based on ceramic contrasts and other factors, we propose that one of these edifices was not a king's residence at all, but the main religious structure, or temple, at Iximché.

Correspondence Analysis

Correspondence analysis (CA) is a form of multivariate statistics which allows one to explore the relationships among variables and the different collections or samples in a data set. It is not meant to test specific hypotheses (Blasius 1994: 23) but instead projects both samples and variables as points on a two-dimensional grid. One can infer relationships or lack thereof from relative positions on the grid. Some applications of CA in archaeology have been made previously (e.g., Bølviken et al. 1982; Clouse 1999). Professor Jan de Leeuw of the UCLA Statistics Department conducted the CA of Iximché ceramics and describes this type of analysis as follows:

> Correspondence analysis starts with the cross-table of variables (types) and samples (sites). Each cell of the table gives the frequency with which a type occurs at a site. The rows of the table correspond with sites, the

columns with types. As a first step, we use the type distribution to quantify in how far two sites are alike. Thus we compare rows of the table, and we define a distance between the rows using type frequencies. Because we deal with frequency data, we should compute our distance in such a way that it takes the statistical precision of the frequency counts into account. For that reason, we use the chi-square distance between the rows. Thus the distance between rows is basically the chi-square test statistic for testing the hypothesis that the two rows are equal. In this way we can compute distances between all pairs of rows.

The second step is to make a picture or map of the rows. Each site will become a point in the picture, and we will make the picture in such a way that the Euclidian distance between the points in the plot is approximately equal to the chi-square distance between the rows of the table. Thus, similar sites will be close in the map and dissimilar sites, with very different type profiles will be far apart. Observe that no spatial or other information about the sites is used while making the map, only the type profiles.

The third step is to put points corresponding with types into the picture as well. There will be two sets of points, for types and sites, and a type point will tend to be close to a site point if that site contains a relatively large number of sherds of that type. The easiest way to get the type points is to repeat the analysis on the type profiles, which are the columns of the table. We define chi-square distances between columns, construct a map which approximates these distances and overlay the two maps we have. (de Leeuw, personal communication, March 2002)

In the research reported here, the variables are ceramic types and the samples are the original lots or bags; that is, the analysis deals with type frequency proportions on a bag-by-bag basis. In order to maintain an unbiased approach in this analysis, all types in the greater collection with frequencies of 125 or greater were included, as were all lots containing a sample of at least 50 typed sherds, whether or not the provenience of the lot was known. The resulting subset contains data on the 14 most frequent types and involves 90 lots and a total of 6208 potsherds. Types included are in the table on page 183.

This analysis is based on the idea that potsherds bagged together by Guillemin and his crew would have been in close proximity in the ground. Certainly they would be from the same structure. From the analysis, then, it was hoped that type relationships would emerge and that from these one could infer common functions or use in common tasks or events. From here, the potential existed for exploring functions of rooms and structures and even social settings, all based on contrasting ceramic type distributions. More specifically, it seemed likely that

Type No.	Name
1	Unpolished Utility
2	Black Slipped and Polished
4	Orange on Gray-Buff
10	Red Slipped and Polished
20	Ladle Incensario
21	Brown Slipped and Polished
27	Thick White Painted
38	Brown Polished Utility
39	Small Micaceous-Slip Dish
40	Micaceous Slip Utility
41	Red Polished Utility
42	Black Polished Utility
43	Eroded Fine Ware
45	Thick Beaker Incensario

CA would shed light on the nature of ceramic similarities and differences between Great Palaces I and II. Of 9508 sherds in the larger data set described above, 6688 are of known provenience, and, of these, 5335 sherds (83%) are from these two structures.

Distribution of the Types

Figure 7.1 shows the distribution of types resulting from the analysis. Although types and lots both were projected onto a single grid, it is preferable to consider each separately because of differences in scale between the two. Here, six of the types are clustered together in an area located approximately between 0 and –1.00 on axis 1 and 0 and –1.00 on axis 2. It is the remaining eight types, however, which show a definite pattern. The types appear to be aligned along a curve. Beginning with Type 39, the curve dips toward the intersection of the axes, then curves upward at the location of Type 2, continuing to the position of Type 4.

The depiction of such curvilinear relationships among variables is not uncommon in CA. "The curve is called a 'horseshoe.' One way to think about it is that the ordering induced by the first dimension of correspondence analysis (the seriation) is so dominant that the second dimension is not an independent alternative ordering but an uncorrelated nonlinear transformation of the first ordering. Generally, the horseshoe indicates a dominant first order ordinal effect, in other words an unambiguous seriation of types and sites along the curved dimension" (de Leeuw).

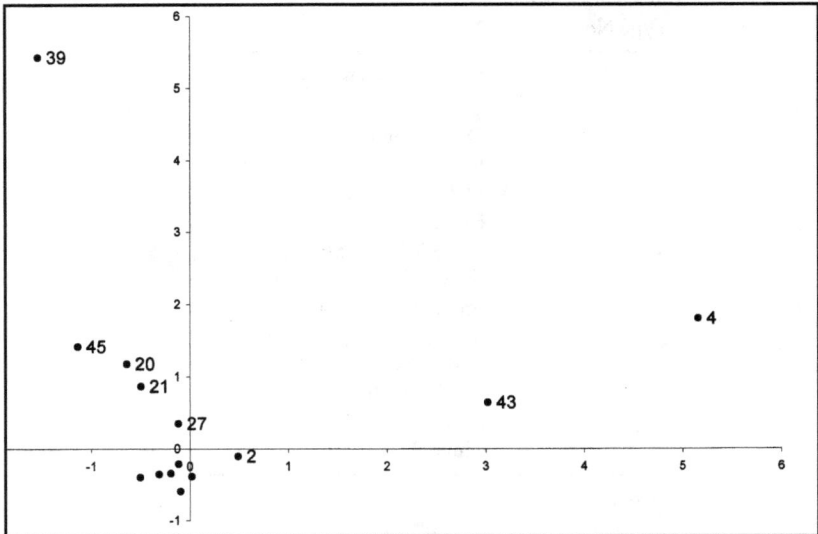

Fig. 7.1. Correspondence Analysis Map of Ceramic Types

This alignment of types can be understood by considering the proportions of sherds for these eight types as they occur for Great Palaces I and II (table 7.1). Proportions tend to decrease regularly from the Type 4 end of the curve to the other, so that ratios correlate highly with type order on the curve (R = .927; p <.001). We also found that sherds for types at the Type 4 end of the curve tend to be more concentrated in distribution. For example, for Type 4, 95% of sherds occurred in Great Palace II, and none in the Other category for all other lots represented in the 6208-sherd subset. At the other end of the curve, by contrast, 48% of Type 39 sherds are from Great Palace II, and 42% are from lots in the Other category. The one exception to the trend is Type 43, but this unique type is a residual one, consisting of eroded fine ware sherds. It is not a category which could have had significance to the prehistoric inhabitants of Iximché but is a product of postoccupational processes. That the "type" would be prevalent in Great Palace II is not surprising given the shallow deposits of the structure relative to Great Palace I and the poor state of preservation which Guillemin encountered there (see chap. 4).

Distribution of Lots

A second chart (fig. 7.2) shows lot locations from the same CA but drawn to a scale different from that employed in figure 7.1. Data are in-

Table 7.1. Type Order along Curve and Type Frequencies by Great Palace and Other

Type No.	Great Palace II	Great Palace I	Other	Ratio, II/I	Order
4	88	5	0	17.6	8
43	235	12	49	19.6	7
2	116	10	16	11.6	6
27	108	8	7	13.5	5
21	168	25	53	6.7	4
20	112	21	31	5.3	3
45	99	27	27	3.7	2
39	71	15	62	4.7	1

cluded only for lots from Great Palaces I and II; also, lot data are averaged by the NEWPROV variable (described in chap. 5), that is, general provenience within each Great Palace. For example, the CA generated locations on the grid for eight different lots of pottery from Great Palace II, Patio E. Centro (NEWPROV = 1), and these points are summarized as one (by averaging axis scores) in figure 7.2. Altogether, 54 of the 90 lots included in the CA are represented, summarized in terms of nine general proveniences for Great Palaces I and II. A key finding from figure 7.2 is that the two points for Great Palace I occur in proximity to one another and are isolated from the seven points for Great Palace II. There is, then, clear evidence for ceramic differences between the two structures.

An Interpretive View of Great Palace Ceramics

As mentioned in chapter 4, Great Palace I and Great Palace II were so-named because Guillemin considered them to be the residences of Iximché's co-ruling kings. Table 7.2 is a summary of ceramics by Great Palace for four major ceramic categories. It shows that the percentage of slipped monochrome fine ware is higher in Great Palace I. Another class of fine-ware types, bichrome ware, is more plentiful in Great Palace II. It also can be seen that painted fine ware compared with monochrome fine ware represents a much smaller fraction of the whole sample. Moreover, the fraction is actually much smaller than suggested by this table. All sherds with painted designs were selected to be catalogued, so,

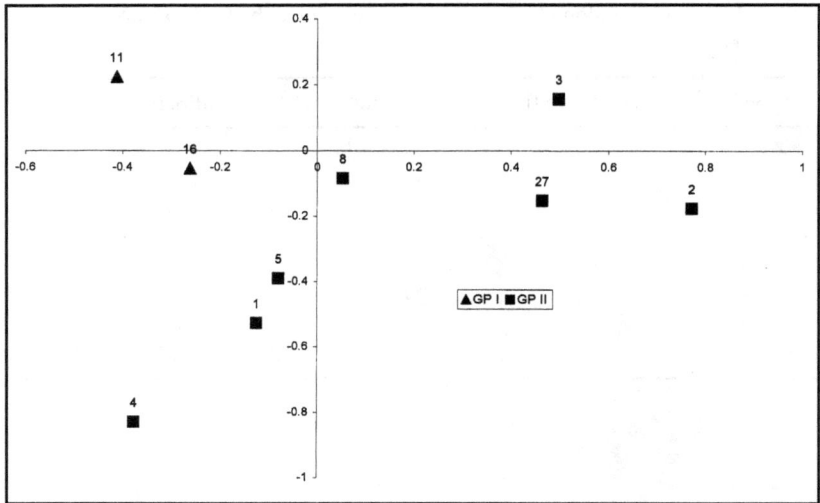

Fig. 7.2. Correspondence Analysis Map of Mean NEWPROV Scores, Great Palaces I and II

for example, the ratio of paint-decorated to all (catalogued and uncatalogued) plain sherds from Great Palace II is less than 1%. Guillemin (1977: 239) commented on this striking lack of painted pottery at Iximché, comparing his ceramics from the site to a surface collection reported by Wauchope (1970).

Iximché ceramics are technically excellent, and decorating pottery with painted designs was certainly within the capabilities of Iximché potters. We suggest, then, that this dearth was intentional, that the production of painted pottery was controlled by the elite of Iximché, and that this pottery was reserved for their exclusive use. In the CA discussed above, the bichrome type Orange on Gray-Buff is at the extreme end of the curve in figure 7.1, is a high-proportion Great Palace II type, and tends to be concentrated in that structure (table 7.1). Bypassing the type Eroded Fine Ware for reasons discussed above, the next type (fig. 7.1) is Black Slipped and Polished. This type is the most elaborate monochrome type from the site, very well finished, and with skillfully modeled effigy vessel feet. In contradistinction to other monochrome fine ware types, it also is a high-proportion Great Palace II type (table 7.1).

Hypothetically, these types represent vessels which once served as indicators of superior status. Wobst (1977) might call this a boundary-

Table 7.2. Partial Ceramic Summary by Great Palace

	Utility Ware	Monochrome Slip, Pol.	Bichrome Fine Ware	Ceremonial Ware	Total
GP II					
freq.	3609	476	180	282	4547
exp. freq.	3578.35	486.57	172.36	309.72	
cell chi²	0.263	0.23	0.339	2.481	
GP I					
freq.	377	66	12	63	518
exp. freq.	407.65	55.43	19.64	35.28	
cell chi²	2.304	2.016	2.972	21.78	
Total	3986	542	192	345	5065

Note. Chi-Square = 32.385, 3 DF, p<.001

maintaining mechanism but one having to do with social class rather than geography (cf. Neitzel 1995: 396–397).

If Great Palaces I and II were homes of Iximché's co-rulers, according to Guillemin's interpretation, then ceramic signatures (that is, proportions of functionally diagnostic types) should be similar. However, as table 7.2 illustrates, there are statistically significant differences. For example, the proportion of utility ware is higher at Great Palace II, suggesting more domestic activity there.

Ceremonial types for the purposes of this research include ladle and thick beaker incensarios and small micaceous-slipped dishes. The last-mentioned form warrants some discussion. Often termed comales and thought to be griddles for cooking tortillas, small plates have been described for a variety of wares in late prehistoric to protohistoric Highland contexts (e.g., Weeks 1980; Wauchope 1970). Borhegyi (1959: 57), however, hypothesized that these Highland plates were incensarios and not comales. He illustrated Classic Lowland composite incensarios consisting of small unattached plates supported by ceramic stands. Gonzales and Wetherington (1978: 285–286) considered this alternative but favored "a secular or domiciliary function for these dishes." The upper surfaces of the small plates in question from Iximché are coated with a micaceous slip. Arnold (1978) described this same technology in the manufacture of contemporary comales in Mixco, where ground up soft rock is applied to prevent tortillas from sticking while cooking. Contemporary comales, however, average around 50 cm in diameter at Mixco and are larger than Iximché counterparts, which probably averaged less than 20 cm. (The average diameter estimated in this research is less than that by Wauchope [1970: 117] for his Iximché surface collection.)

In the CA plot of figure 7.1, the type Small Micaceous-Slip Dish stands at the end of the curved line opposite that anchored by Orange on Gray-Buff. Adjacent to it are the types Thick Beaker Incensario followed by Ladle Incensario, so that the Small Micaceous-Slip Dish type is directly associated with two ceremonial types and none other. Based on these findings, all three types were included as ceremonial ware in table 7.2. As indicated there, the clearest point of contrast in the ceramics of these two structures is the higher proportion of ceremonial ware for Great Palace I.

What table 7.2 as well as the CA suggest, then, is not two royal palaces, but one, Great Palace II, with Great Palace I probably a major ceremonial edifice with some residential activity.

This interpretation is supported by the recovery of much more pottery from Great Palace II than from Great Palace I: 4986 vs. 550 sherds in the study collection, or approximately 23,500 vs. 2400 in the larger samples of catalogued and uncatalogued sherds. This does suggest the multifarious activities of a cultural and political center at Great Palace II.

Guillemin, however, attributes this difference in ceramic abundance, in part, to differential preservation: "Great Palace I, in its third phase, consists of one general raised level; it has been thoroughly eroded by four and a half centuries of alternative agriculture and forest growth. It was practically bare of middens or artifacts. In contrast, Great Palace II, with its high nucleus and its surrounding units separated by patios and passages, presented a more accidented configuration. Those patios and passages have been filled and covered by debris from the demolition of superstructures, thick adobe walls and columns; thus the archaeological deposits on the floors are in part protected by that thick layer of debris. Quantities of sherds from domestic and ceremonial ceramics were found" (Guillemin 1977: 236).

A deep midden deposit at Great Palace I (see fig. 4.19) and earlier, well-buried phases of construction do suggest that large quantities of sherds, if they existed, would have survived destruction in post-Conquest times. However, close comparisons with Great Palace II remain impossible, because some bags of artifacts from Great Palace I deposits might have lost their provenience labels or been lost entirely. The distribution of Eroded Fine Ware (table 7.1), though, does suggest more not less erosion at Great Palace II.

Guillemin also explained the large quantities of cultural debris at Great Palace II as the result of a very late occupation at the site. Guillemin (1977: 236) found "traces of fire almost everywhere in the palace." He couples that to "the fact that most of the sherds and other deposits are found directly on the floors and immediately covered by debris with adobe (which) is an indication that the fire was shortly followed by demolition of the buildings" (Guillemin 1977: 238). This led him to conclude that the fire was probably that of 7 February 1526, the day Iximché was burned by the Spanish, as recorded in the *Annals of the Cakchiquels* (Recinos and Goetz 1953: 126). Furthermore, Guillemin believed that the "presence of important middens in most patios of Great Palace II tends to indicate that there was a dense domestic occupancy between the abandonment on 28 August 1524 and the fire of 7 February 1526" (Guillemin 1977: 238). Of the included artifacts, Guillemin (1977: 239) wrote that, "most of the sherds are utilitarian ceramics and the quantity is such that it cannot possibly belong to one occupation only, that of a reigning dynastic family."

Although Guillemin had an intimate knowledge of the site, it seems more likely to us that Great Palace II stood unoccupied from its sudden abandonment in late August 1524 until the fire of early February 1526. It was probably this fire which caused ceramic debris left on patio floors to be sealed under the rubble of collapsed walls and ceilings. Guillemin cites no direct evidence of a Cakchiquel refugee population at Iximché during this 1524–1526 interval, and the *Annals of the Cakchiquels* indicate the contrary: "Six months had passed of the second year of our flight from the city, or [from the time] when we abandoned it and departed when Tunatiuh came to it in passing and burned it" (Recinos and Goetz 1953: 126). Cakchiquel occupation of Iximché then in any form also seems improbable because warfare with the Spanish began in 1524 and continued during 1525. The Spanish had built a settlement at Iximché from which Pedro de Alvarado (Tunatiuh to the Cakchiquel) wrote his second letter to Cortés in July 1524 (Recinos and Goetz 1953: 125; Alvarado 1969).

Also, our analysis of the recovered pottery from Great Palace II does show an assemblage which can be construed to be refuse of a royal household, at least, more so than ceramics recovered from Great Palace I. This is based on the higher percentage of the elaborate type Black Slipped and Polished. This assessment is also based on the higher percentage of bichrome types, especially the important Orange on Gray-Buff type. The CA revealed the more exclusive or limited distribution of important Great Palace II types, compared to their counterparts for Great Palace I. There is a higher percentage of utility types, and a much lower percentage of ceremonial types, again, compared to Great Palace I. The idea is also supported by the distribution of pottery among the patios of Great Palace II, which is discussed in chapter 8.

A much simpler explanation than Guillemin's leaves out differential preservation and mid-Conquest occupation of the Palace: Great Palace II produced more pottery because it was occupied more intensively over its life span. The pottery excavated by Guillemin represents the remnant debris of this intensive occupation which was left in place because of the sudden abandonment of the entire community.

8

ЛЛЛЛЛЛ

Ceramic Attribute Analysis

The results of the attribute analysis are considered here. The process of recording these sherd attributes is described in chapter 5, which also includes a list of variables and the constituent attributes (with numerical codes) for each. An important issue, of course, is whether such a mass of descriptive data can add anything of value to the typological analysis presented in the previous chapter.

Attribute Distributions between the Great Palaces

The major hypothesis considered in chapter 7 is that Great Palace II was primarily residential, while Great Palace I functioned on a religious level, with residential activity of secondary importance. All sherds in the study collection with a complete cross-section portion of the vessel wall were recorded for maximum thickness; each sherd was measured with calipers to the nearest millimeter. Sherd average thickness should relate to vessel function which in turn may correlate with the functions of structures from which the sherds were excavated. Residential activities would have involved utility vessels, and utility types tend to be represented by sherds of above-average thickness (see chap. 6). We assume that utility vessels were larger and had thicker walls to withstand daily use. Table 8.1 is a summary of sherd thickness for all types for the two palaces. Sherds from Great Palace II are considerably thicker than those

Table 8.1. Sherd Thickness by Great Palace

	T < 9 mm	T >= 9 mm	Total
G.P. II	2321	2261	4582
	50.65%	49.35%	
G.P. I	281	222	503
	55.86%	44.14%	
Total	2602	2483	5085

Note. Chi-Square = 4.924, 1 DF, p < .026

from Great Palace I. This could be random variation, but that seems un-likely when utility types are examined individually.

Table 8.2 shows the percent of thick sherds (T $\geq$ = 9 mm) for each of the four major utility types, again comparing collections from the two Great Palaces. These data exhibit real differences between ceramic collections from the two palaces much more clearly than the proportional difference for utility types presented in chapter 7 (see table 7.2).

Another variable indicating a difference between the two palaces is that of POLISH. The Polish variable was recorded for many types in terms of four attributes: neither surface polished, interior polished, exterior polished, and both surfaces polished. In table 8.3 and subsequent tables, the inclusion of types was determined by whether a type was rep-resented in one or both of the palace collections and whether the vari-able was recorded for the type in question. (See appendix A and chap. 5.) Table 8.3 indicates that relatively more Great Palace I sherds were pol-ished on one or both surfaces. This is consistent with the use of more and thicker-walled utility vessels in Great Palace II. Table 8.4 for the SLIP variable shows a parallel trend, but it is statistically nonsignificant.

The HANDLEW variable records strap handle maximum width. Strap handles tend to be wider for Great Palace II than for Great Palace I: 53.3% vs. 45.8%, respectively, of measured handles are in the wide category, where HW $>=$ 33 mm. This also suggests the use of larger vessels in Great Palace II, although for the small samples of measured handles (738 from Great Palace II, 91 from Great Palace I), the differ-ence is not statistically significant.

Another contrasting variable is paste color as viewed on a sherd fresh break surface (COLORLD). This was measured for all sherds of the Un-polished Utility type. Control in recording this variable was maintained through reference to a *Munsell Soil Color Chart*, as discussed in chap-

Table 8.2. Thick sherds (T $\geq$ = 9 mm): Major Utility Types by Great Palace

	Unpol. Utility	Brown Polished	Red Polished	Mica Paste
G.P. II	837	410	228	412
	56.82%[1]	65.81%	57.87%	60.95%
G.P. I	69	52	18	28
	46.00%	66.67%	45.00%	50.00%

1. E.g., 56.82% of Unpolished Utility Sherds from G.P. II are thick

Table 8.3. Polished Surface by Great Palace

	No Pol.	Ext. Pol.	Int. Pol.	E + I Pol.	Total
G.P. II	410	147	45	224	826
	49.64%	17.80%	5.45%	27.12%	
G.P. I	42	23	2	41	108
	38.89%	21.30%	1.85%	37.96%	
Total	452	170	47	265	934

Notes. Chi-Square = 9.336, 3 DF, p < .025; (types not included: 1, 7, 27, 32, 34, 37, 38, 39, 40, 41, 42, 43, 44, 45, 47)

Table 8.4. Slipped Surface by Great Palace

	No Slp.	Ext. Slp.	Int. Slp.	E+I Slp.	Total
G.P. II	647	220	149	375	1391
	46.51%	15.82%	10.71%	26.96%	
G.P. I	77	27	19	53	176
	42.75%	15.34%	10.80%	30.11%	
Total	724	247	168	428	1567

Notes. Chi-Square = .851, 3 DF, p < .837; (types not included: 1, 7, 27, 32, 34, 37, 38, 40, 43, 44, 45, 47)

ter 5. Data in table 8.5 point to darker paste colors for Unpolished Utility sherds from Great Palace II. As described in chapter 6, thicker sherds of this type tend to have darker interior core or paste colors. This may indicate that thicker-walled utility vessels were not as thoroughly fired at Iximché as thinner-walled vessels, and, therefore, that these vessels did not become as completely oxidized in the firing process. It is also possible that dark-colored clays with high humus content were employed in the manufacture of utility wares (see Rice 1978: 431–432).

Table 8.6 includes data for sherds indicative of vessel form. Thick Beaker Incensario sherd data were not incorporated into this table, as

Table 8.5. Paste Color by Great Palace

	Dark[1]	Light	Total
G.P. II	1176	536	1712
	68.69%	31.31%	
G.P. I	113	63	176
	64.20%	35.80%	
Total	1289	599	1888

Notes. Chi-Square = 1.483, 1 DF, p < .223; (included sherds only of type 1)
1. "Dark" = value of 4 or less; "Light" = value of 5 or greater.
Source: *Munsell Soil Color Chart* (Baltimore: Munsell Color, 1975), p. 5YR.

vessel form was not as obvious for this type as for the included sherds of other types. Tecomates and necked jars were relatively more common in Great Palace II, and the Ladle Incensario and the Small Micaceous-Slip Dish forms were more plentiful, by percentage, in Great Palace I.

The rim morphology variable showed little variation between the two structures (table 8.7).

Altogether, although not compelling statistically, attribute data tend to support interpretations offered in chapter 7 regarding functional differences between the two Great Palaces. Ceramic vessels from Great Palace II generally tended to be larger (thicker-walled; wider handles) and less well finished than those from Great Palace I. Incensario forms were relatively more common in Great Palace I, and tecomates and necked jars were more plentiful in Great Palace II. These differences could be expected given the domiciliary activities of a palace compared to the ceremonialism of a religious structure.

Attribute Distributions among the Patios of Great Palace II

With the above contrasting variables in mind, we can now address Great Palace II exclusively. A majority of sherds in the study collection are from this structure. Great Palace II is also the only locality for which detailed information on provenience survived. Most pottery was excavated from interior patios within the palace, and Guillemin provided

Table 8.6. Vessel Morphology by Great Palace

	Tecomate	Bowl	Dish Bk.	Neck Jar	Ldl. Inc.	Mic. Dish	Total
G.P. II	64	49	13	191	109	70	496
	12.90%	9.88%	2.62%	38.51%	21.98%	14.11%	
G.P. I	5	6	0	24	21	15	71
	7.04%	8.45%	0.00%	33.80%	29.58%	21.13%	
Total	69	55	13	215	130	85	567

Notes. Chi-Square = 7.711, 5 DF, p < .173; (included types: 1, 2, 3, 4, 6, 8, 9, 10, 18, 20, 21, 23, 24, 28, 38, 39, 40, 41, 42, 43)

Table 8.7. Rim Morphology by Great Palace

	Flanged	Straight	Incurve	Outcurve	Tecomate	Unique	Total
G.P. II	11	785	62	379	60	2	1299
	0.85%	60.43%	4.77%	29.18%	4.62%	0.15%	
G.P. I	1	91	6	45	5	0	148
	0.68%	61.49%	4.05%	30.41%	3.38%	0.00%	
Total	12	876	68	424	65	2	1447

Notes. Chi-Square = .969, 5 DF, p < .965; (included types: 2, 3, 4, 8, 10, 20, 21, 24, 25, 38, 39, 40, 41, 42, 43, 44, 45)

these individual identities on bag provenience labels. These bag labels, each tied to a specific NEWPROV, are listed in table 8.8. Also, Guillemin produced a detailed map of Great Palace II (see fig. 4.36). Here, these patios are clearly indicated and labeled "a" through "i." Unfortunately, most of Guillemin's field notes for 1972, the year he excavated Great Palace II, have not survived, nor have any other documents which would allow unequivocal linkage of bag labels to the patios as mapped. In table 8.8, patio map labels are paired with patio designations from bag labels with possible matches based on compass headings. These matchings are probably accurate concerning patios "b" through "e" because one of Guillemin's bag labels reads "Great Palace II, Passageway from Patio E Centro to Patio E-SE." This must refer to the passageway between Patios "d" and "e," the only passageway linking patios in the palace. This, in turn, means that Patio "c" was the provenience for bags labeled "Patio N-E," and that Patio "b" produced the bags of sherds labeled "Patio N." Linkages for the other patio collections are not as certain because there are four patios south and west of Patio E/SE and only two bag designations, "Patio S-E" and "Patio S/S-E." Also, we cannot know for certain whether Patios Centro E and E Centro are different patios or the same with bags having slightly different labels.

Table 8.8 also indicates the number of bags of sherds (PROVNO's) and the total number of sherds in the study collection for each patio (NEWPROV).

Regardless of ambiguities involved, these patio collections can still be examined, especially in view of the type and variable contrasts between the two great palaces.

Our approach has been to generate hypotheses which might scale these seven collections from that representing the greatest proportions of commoner/utilitarian activities (such as pottery used in cooking or food or water storage by domestic support personnel or ceramics used by administrative functionaries) to that patio collection at the other end of the scale most reflecting elite/nonutilitarian activities (such as vessels used by the monarch, his family, and guests on a daily or ceremonial basis). We assume that the identification of Great Palace II as a king's residence is correct and that the ceramic remains are those of a prehistoric royal occupation. Each scaling variable will be discussed.

Table 8.8. Patio Potsherd Summaries, Great Palace II

NEW PROV	Bag Labels	Map Designations	Bag Freq.	Sherd Freq.
1	Patio E Centro	d^1	17	792
2	Patio SE	f	9	534
3	Patio NE	c	20	1332
4	Patio N	b	7	318
5	Patio S/SE	g	8	407
6	Patio E/SE	e	2	93
7	Patio Centro E	a	3	118

1. Affiliations of map designations to bag labels are probable to possible.

Thickness

The seven patio collections can be scaled according to the relative thickness of their sherds, with thick sherds indicating commoner/utilitarian activities. Thickness data for the seven patios are included in table 8.9.

Paste Color

Paste color is considered similarly to the Thickness variable, with a high percentage of dark paste sherds indicating (hypothetically) relatively poorly fired utilitarian pottery. Data are included in table 8.10.

Both Surfaces Slipped

The percentage of sherds with both surfaces slipped was employed as an indicator of surface finish. The lowest patio percentage would rank at the utilitarian/commoner end of the scale (table 8.11).

Both Surfaces Polished

The POLISH variable was treated similarly to the Both Surfaces Slipped variable. The percentage of sherds with both surfaces polished

Table 8.9. Sherd Thickness by Patio, Great Palace II

	Pat. E CN	Pat. SE	Pat. NE	Pat. N	Pat. S/SE	Pat. E/SE	Pat. CN E	Total
T < 9 mm	346	247	704	142	196	28	59	1722
	47.14%	51.46%	57.19%	50.53%	50.65%	33.73%	53.64%	
T >= 9 mm	388	233	527	139	191	55	51	1584
	52.86%	48.54%	42.81%	49.47%	49.35%	66.27%	46.36%	
Total	734	480	1231	281	387	83	110	3306

Notes. Chi-Square = 32.019, 6 DF, P < .001; (types not included: 7, 15, 16, 22, 30, 34, 35, 36, 37, 47)

Table 8.10. Paste Color by Patio, Great Palace II

	Pat. E CN	Pat. SE	Pat. NE	Pat. N	Pat. S/SE	Pat. E/SE	Pat. CN E	Total
Dark[1]	197	156	260	62	102	24	20	821
	62.34%	75.73%	62.50%	73.81%	72.86%	72.73%	71.43%	
Light	119	50	156	22	38	9	8	402
	37.66%	24.27%	37.50%	26.19%	27.14%	27.27%	28.57%	
Total	316	206	416	84	140	33	28	1223

Notes. Chi-Square = 18.709, 6 DF, p < .005; (included only sherds of type 1)
1. "Dark" = value of 4 or less; "Light" = value of 5 or greater.
Source: *Munsell Soil Color Chart* (Baltimore: Munsell Color, 1975), p. 5YR.

Table 8.11. Slipped Sherds (Both Surfaces) by Patio, Great Palace II

	Pat. E CN	Pat. SE	Pat. NE	Pat. N	Pat. S/SE	Pat. E/SE	Pat. CN E	Total
No. Slp.	105	37	174	51	83	21	19	490
	53.57%	32.46%	42.54%	46.36%	63.36%	84.00%	55.88%	
Ext. Slp.	40	15	63	36	10	1	4	169
	20.41%	13.16%	15.40%	32.73%	7.63%	4.00%	11.76%	
Int. Slp.	16	14	51	8	17	2	3	111
	8.16%	12.28%	12.47%	7.27%	12.98%	8.00%	8.82%	
E + I Slp.	35	48	121	15	21	1	8	249
	17.86%	42.11%	29.58%	13.64%	16.03%	4.00%	23.53%	
Total	196	114	409	110	131	25	34	1019

Notes. Chi-Square = 92.986, 18 DF, p < .001; (types excluded: 1, 27, 38, 40, 43, 44, 45)

Table 8.12. Polished Sherds (Both Surfaces) by Patio, Great Palace II

	Pat. E CN	Pat. SE	Pat. NE	Pat. N	Pat. S/SE	Pat. E/SE	Pat. CN E	Total
No. Pol.	29	39	152	34	31	6	2	293
	35.80%	49.37%	58.24%	43.59%	47.69%	50.00%	10.53%	
Ext. Pol.	19	13	45	24	10	1	3	115
	23.46%	16.46%	17.24%	30.77%	15.38%	8.33%	15.79%	
Int. Pol.	4	5	14	4	3	1	1	32
	4.94%	6.33%	5.36%	5.13%	4.62%	8.33%	5.26%	
E+I Pol.	29	22	50	16	21	4	13	155
	35.80%	27.85%	19.16%	20.15%	32.31%	33.33%	68.42%	
Total	81	79	261	78	65	12	19	595

Notes. Chi-Square = 45.388, 18 DF, p < .001; (types excluded: 1, 27, 38, 39, 40, 41, 42, 43, 44, 45)

served as another indicator of surface finish quality. Again, the lowest patio percentage was fixed to the utilitarian/commoner end of the scale (table 8.12).

Handle Width

This variable was recorded for all types with strap handles. Widest handles are considered to represent large pots and commoner/utilitarian tasks (table 8.13).

Utility Types

In table 8.14, types are clustered according to presumed function and general technological-decorative affinities. Utility types include Unpol-

Table 8.13. Handle Width by Patio, Great Palace II

	Pat. E CN	Pat. SE	Pat. NE	Pat. N	Pat. S/SE	Pat. E/SE	Pat. CN E	Total
HW < 33mm	58	52	78	23	26	4	5	246
	42.65%	52.00%	50.00%	52.27%	52.00%	21.05%	26.32%	
HW >= 33mm	78	48	78	21	24	15	14	278
	57.35%	48.00%	50.00%	47.73%	48.00%	78.95%	73.68%	
Total	136	100	156	44	50	19	19	524

Notes. Chi-Square = 11.994, 6 DF, P < .062; (contributing types: 1, 27, 38, 40, 41, 42, 43, 44)

Table 8.14. Type Summaries by Patio, Great Palace II

	Pat. E CN	Pat. SE	Pat. NE	Pat. N	Pat. S/SE	Pat. E/SE	Pat. CN E	Total
Utility	665	367	893	217	309	78	97	2626
	83.96%	68.73%	67.04%	68.24%	75.92%	83.87%	82.20%	
Mono. SP	71	58	138	38	21	5	18	349
	8.96%	10.86%	10.36%	11.95%	5.16%	5.38%	15.25%	
Bichrome	12	21	76	9	18	0	2	138
	1.52%	3.93%	5.71%	2.83%	4.42%	0.00%	1.69%	
Ceremonl.	19	16	78	11	36	7	1	168
	2.40%	3.00%	5.86%	3.46%	8.85%	7.53%	0.85%	
Other	25	72	147	43	23	3	0	313
	3.16%	13.48%	11.04%	13.52%	5.65%	3.23%	0.00%	
Total	792	534	1332	318	407	93	118	3594

Notes. Chi-Square = 186.255, 24 DF, p < .001; (types not contributing: 7, 14, 15, 16, 30, 34, 35, 36, 37, 47)

ished Utility; Micaceous Paste Utility; and Brown, Red, and Black Polished Utility. Patios are ranked from the commoner/utilitarian end of the scale by decreasing percentages.

Ceremonial Types

This scaling variable consists of the combined percentages of the three ceremonial types: Small Micaceous-Slip Dishes, Ladle Incensarios, and Thick Beaker Incensarios. Patios are ranked with percentages for this variable increasing from the commoner/utilitarian end of the continuum (table 8.14).

Monochrome Slipped and Polished Types

The combined percentages are for the Slipped and Polished types Black, Gray, Red, Brown, Buff, and Gray-Brown. Ranking is based on the idea that these types reflect nonutilitarian, elite activities (data from table 8.14).

Bichrome Types

Ranked in the same way as ceremonial and monochrome slipped and polished types, bichrome types consist of Orange on Gray-Buff, White on Red, Gray on Red, Red Bands on White, Red on Orange, Brown-Black on Buff, Black on Red, and Thick Black and White Painted (data from table 8.14).

Table 8.15 shows the patios ranked for each of the above variables. The variability observed in comparing these rank orderings in this table was not unexpected. Sherd data from different proveniences tend to be somewhat erratic, given the vagaries of discard and cleaning of living surfaces and also given fluctuations caused by the differential effects of pot breakage. A pot of any one type can produce few or many sherds upon breaking. Also, keep in mind that some of the variables employed are not of the most objective sort in the first place (for example, type designation and whether a sherd surface is slipped or polished).

It was hoped, then, that a more stable or overall more accurate rank ordering of patios could be achieved by combining data from all scaling variables to produce a composite rank ordering. For example, Patio E/SE ranks number one for the Thick variable. By adding the relative rank positions for Patio E/SE (1+4+1+5+1+2+6+2+1), a composite score of 23 is obtained. Table 8.16 lists all such patio scores and a final composite ranking of patios. It also ranks the patios by the frequency of study collection sherds recovered from each (data from table 8.8). Two observa-

Table 8.15. Patios Ranked to Reflect Commoner (1) to Elite (7) Activities, Great Palace II

RANK	Thick	Dark Color	Both S. Slipped	Both S. Polished	Wide Handle	Util. Types	Cere. Types	Mono. S.P.	Bichrome
1	E/SE	SE	E/SE	N	E/SE	E CN	CN E	S/SE	E/SE
2	E CN	N	N	NE	CN E	E/SE	E CN	E/SE	E CN
3	N	S/SE	S/SE	SE	E CN	CN E	SE	E CN	CN E
4	S/SE	E/SE	E CN	S/SE	NE	S/SE	N	NE	N
5	SE	CN E	CN E	E/SE	SE	SE	NE	SE	SE
6	CN E	NE	NE	E CN	S/SE	N	E/SE	N	S/SE
7	NE	E CN	SE	CN E	N	NE	S/SE	CN E	NE

tions are readily apparent. First, the composite patio ranking (table 8.16) is identical to that for Thickness (table 8.15). Keep in mind that Patios SE and CN E are interchangeable, since they have identical composite scores. Notwithstanding this, the finding is noteworthy because the THICK variable is the least subjective of all those employed in the Iximché ceramic research. (Maximum thickness was measured with calipers for each sherd possible.) Second, the composite ranking correlates roughly with ranking by patio sherd frequency (table 8.16); that is, patios with elite ranking tend to be those with large collections of potsherds.

This latter finding adds to evidence that Patio NE was the center of elite activity in Great Palace II and was probably the living quarters of one of the Iximché kings. Inspection of Guillemin's map of Great Palace II (see fig. 4.36), reveals two small patios within the northern wing of the palace. Of these, the eastern patio, designated "c," is most likely the one indicated by bags labeled "Patio N-E." The composite score for Patio NE is not simply the highest among the patios; at 48, it stands well above those of six patios with scores ranging from 30 to 39, and far above the last with a score of 23. The sherd frequency for Patio NE is 1332, almost 1.7 times that of the second largest patio collection and 2.4 times that of the entire collection from Great Palace I. If sherd frequency is any indication of human activity, and, based on evidence at hand, Great Palace II was a center of activity in the ceremonial precinct at Iximché, then Patio NE was clearly such a center within Great Palace II.

Table 8.16. Patio Composite Ranking and Ranking by Patio Sherd Collection Size, Great Palace II

Composite Score	Composite Patio Ranking	Sherd Frequency	Rank Order by Increasing Freq.
23	E/SE[1]	93	E/SE
30	E CN	118	CN E
35	N	318	N
38	S/SE	407	S/SE
39	SE	534	SE
39	CN E	792	E CN
48	NE[2]	1332	NE

Notes. 1. Commoner/utilitarian end of scale
2. Elite/nonutilitarian end of scale

In terms of the architecture of Great Palace II, Patio NE and surrounding rooms were well-positioned to serve as a royal apartment—close to the central patio, yet secluded.

The elite status of Patio NE can be assessed in another way, although the data are not entirely independent of those presented above. The ceramic research defined some minority types which, owing to decorative technique, color, or paste characteristics, were unique in the overall collection. These types stood out morphologically, and because they are represented by such small samples of sherds, they may be exotic. One would expect such types to cluster in elite environments. The ruling elite of Iximché certainly controlled foreign trade and diplomatic contacts. Appendix A contains the distribution of all sherds by TYPE and NEWPROV (for the patios, NEWPROV = 1–7). Table 8.17 lists types regarded as potentially exotic. Next to each are listed those two patios with the highest and second highest percentages among the seven patios for the type in question.

Table 8.17. Rare or Potentially Exotic Types and Patios of Greatest Occurrence, Great Palace II

Type	Patio with Highest %	Patio with 2nd Highest %
Orange on Gray-Buff	NE	S/SE
Black and Red on White	S/SE	NE
White on Red	S/SE	SE
Red Bands on White	SE	NE
Red on Orange	N	—[1]
Cacao Pod Vessel	N	NE
Brown Slipped Incised	E/SE	NE
Brown-Black on Buff	SE	NE
Pol. Brown Black Inc.	E/SE	N
Fine-Incised Beaker	N	S/SE
Zoned Crosshatched Inc.	NE	—
Orange Polished	N	NE
Micaceous Paste	NE	—
Nonslp. Nonpol. F.W.	N	NE
Micaceous Slip	N	S/SE
Thk. Blk. Wht. Painted	E CN	NE
Polychrome	NE	—

1. Sherds of type found in one patio, only

The seven patios can now be scaled by using data in table 8.17. A value of "2" was assigned each time a patio is listed in the highest percent column and a value of "1" for each listing in the second highest percent column. When these values were added for each patio, Patios NE and N had scores of 16 and 13, respectively. All other patios produced scores of 7 or less. In all probability, Patio N is patio "b" in figure 4.36. Only one room (Structure 114), then, separates Patio NE from Patio N. These data, therefore, support the hypothesis that Patio NE was the center of elite activity in Great Palace II and the likely center of the royal living quarters. These quarters may have extended, on the basis of data from table 8.17, into Patio N and its several surrounding rooms.

Thickness and Type Reconsidered

Of nontypological variables considered, that of sherd thickness seems to hold the most promise. Given the results reported above, we decided to explore further the matter of sherd thickness by type within the Iximché ceramic-collection data set, specifically for the three ceremonial types, Thick Beaker Incensarios, Ladle Incensarios, and Small Micaceous-Slip Dishes. This discussion centers on the idea that nonutilitarian ceramic vessels involved in public ceremonies or other convocations would have been larger than those of the same wares employed in household activities. If Great Palace I were actually a temple, one would expect that larger (and thicker) ceremonial vessels were employed there. Relatively more public ceremonies would have transpired there than in the more residential complex of Great Palace II. Vessels of the Thick Beaker Incensario type were massive and from this perspective well-suited for public ceremonies. It is not surprising, therefore, that the type is almost 2.5 times more plentiful in Great Palace I than in Great Palace II (4.91% vs. 1.99%). This is a greater difference than found for the other ceremonial types: Ladle Incensarios (3.82% vs. 2.25%) and Small Micaceous-Slip Dishes (2.73% vs. 1.42%).

Also, if Beaker Incensarios sherds found in Great Palace I are from vessels employed more in public ceremonies, one would expect these sherds to be significantly thicker than those of the same type found in Great Palace II. This hypothesis is supported by data in table 8.18. Samples of the other ceremonial types show the same trend: sherds of Small Mica-Slip Dishes and Ladle Incensarios from Great Palace I tend to be thicker, although differences for these two other types are not statistically significant (see tables 8.19 and 8.20). Unless a statistical accident, these differences in the thickness of ceremonial types across the two Great Palaces seem especially noteworthy because they are in contradistinction to the overall sherd thickness differences between these same structures. All pottery is thicker for Great Palace II (table 8.1); utility types are thicker for Great Palace II (table 8.2); but ceremonial types are thicker for Great Palace I (tables 8.18–8.20).

Table 8.18. Thick Beaker Incensario: Sherd Thickness by Great Palace

	T < 13mm[1]	T >= 13mm	Total
G.P. II	51	40	91
	56.04%	43.96%	
G.P. I	6	20	26
	23.08%	76.92%	
Total	57	60	117

Note. Chi-Square = 8.797, 1 DF, $p < .003$.
1. 13mm chosen to avoid small cell frequencies.

Table 8.19. Small Micaceous-Slip Dish: Sherd Thickness by Great Palace

	T < 8mm	T >= 8mm	Total
G.P. II	32	39	71
	45.07%	54.93%	
G.P. I	6	9	15
	40.00%	60.00%	
Total	38	48	86

Note. Chi-Square = .129, 1 DF, $p < .719$

Table 8.20. Ladle Incensario: Sherd Thickness by Great Palace

	T < 8mm	T >= 8mm	Total
G.P. II	61	50	111
	54.95%	45.05%	
G.P. I	10	11	21
	47.62%	52.38%	
Total	71	61	132

Note. Chi-Square = .382, 1 DF, $p < .536$

9

Descriptions of Human Remains and Burial Structures

In his field notes, photographs, and drawings, Guillemin described or otherwise recorded 68 complete or partial burials at Iximché (fig. 9.1), as well as a flute and a musical rasper made from human femurs, an isolated human femur, and unspecified human bones. Recovered skeletal remains which he placed in storage apparently included 65 or 66 crania. Among the burials were 3 child skeletons, 12 adult skeletons (1 described as an adolescent, 1 as incomplete, and 2 as lacking calvaria), 1 skeleton of unknown age, and 50 decapitated crania. In addition, a note in a bag with some bones stated: *"Entierro simple fuera de muros. Julio 1960. Esupal pos.—en campo abierto del lado plebeyo."* [Simple burial outside of walls. July 1960. Supine position(?)—in open field of the plebeian side.] This is the only reference to a burial located beyond the defensive ditch outside of the ceremonial precinct.

Some inconsistencies occur in the archived notes, photographs, and drawings related to Guillemin's excavations of human remains and burial structures. In the following synthesis, assessments concerning the correct interpretation of data are based on the entire quantity of published and unpublished information.

Burial data are organized by Plaza and Structure and are described from west to east across the central precinct, from Plaza A to C. Burials whose bones have been identified subsequently are marked with "IX"

Fig. 9.1. George Guillemin Excavating Decapitated Crania behind Structure 104, Plaza C

numbers (to designate crania) or other two-letter designations (for postcranial material).

Plaza A

Temple (Structure) 2

Excavations exposed a superstructure with walls preserved under the rubble of a later phase of construction (see chap. 4). Here, Guillemin took samples of the dark traces of a liquid that formed a crust more than 1 mm thick. He suspected that it was dried blood, but apparently never tested it. A complete "pentatonic flute" carved from a child's femur was found in addition to the crust of dried liquid (Guillemin 1960 field notes; 1965a: 31; 1966: 11; 1967: 33; 1977: 241, 259).

A pit had been cut into the earlier of two floors in the room on top of Temple 2. It was apparently intended for a burial, but something intervened. It had been refilled and the floor resurfaced. Guillemin believed this might have been related to the epidemic of 1521 (cf., chapter 2, Guillemin 1965a: 28; 1966: 9; 1967: 29).

According to one of Guillemin's associates, a family named Galindo lived on top of Temple 2 for years. They removed five thousand stones to sell to the municipality of Pazticía to build a street. In their house a narrow hole led into the center of the mound, which apparently contained ceramic urns with skeletons inside (Guillemin 1960 field notes).

Temple (Structure) 3

At the eastern end of the rear wall were "signs" of human bones near a pavement over a lower floor. At the southern corner, at the northeastern end of the structure, a human femur was found on top of the floor (Guillemin 1960 field notes; 1961 field notes; 1965a: 30; 1966: 11; 1977: 259).

Structure 27

Structure 27 is a platform bordering Plaza A to the northwest of Temple 2. It has three phases of construction represented by facades facing Plaza A and running from northeast to southwest. Farthest east, the first phase is represented by a vertical facade with a parapet (see fig. 4.14). Within it were two cists with burials (Guillemin 1959: 33).

Burial 27-A

The tomb, located behind the first (rear) facade, was originally opened about 1956, but the interior was not explored at that time (fig. 9.2).

Guillemin estimated that the facade was built around the time Iximché was founded. The lid of the cist was constructed of carved stones covered with a layer of plaster. It was 90 cm long × 90 cm wide × 28 cm high. Part of the lid had collapsed into the tomb owing to decay of the contents. Beneath the cover was fill of mixed earth, including small fragments of Postclassic ceramics and charcoal which probably had been extracted from the hole when the tomb was dug. The bottom of the tomb was concave. Four individuals were crammed into an area of about 2 square yards, and the presence of three "attendants" suggests sacrifice. The series of identification numbers of the individuals (I–IV) is opposite the sequence in which they were placed in the ground (Guillemin 1959 field notes; n.d.d: 13; 1959: 33; 1961; 1965a: 32; 1966: 11; 1967: 33; 1968; fig. 9.3). The cranium of Individual I (IX-9), an adult, was dislocated and leaning against the wall of the tomb in a vertical position. Guillemin believed the dislocation was caused by the sunken cover. The body was parallel to the building with the chest downward and the arms partly raised. The head lay to the east looking up and had a small amount of artificial fronto-occipital deformation, probably unintentional, according to Guillemin. It was crushed in back, and Guillemin believed that the positions of the head and arms indicated that the person had been buried alive. In the pelvic region, a 2-cm-diameter disk with a mineral core and a thin veneer of copper or low quality gold was found 1.5 cm from the end of the vertebral column. Guillemin consolidated the skull with alvar and glued the pieces together. The rest of the bones were removed "by portion," annotated, and stored without being consolidated (Guillemin 1959 field notes; 1961; 1968).

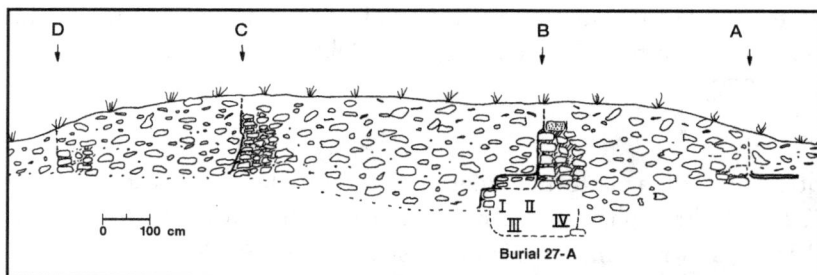

Fig. 9.2. Cross Section of Structure 27 with Location of Burial 27–A, Individuals I–IV. A: front facade; B: first posterior facade; C: second posterior facade; D: third posterior facade. (Redrawn from original in Guillemin 1961: 89; republished with permission of the Sociedad de Geografía e Historia de Guatemala)

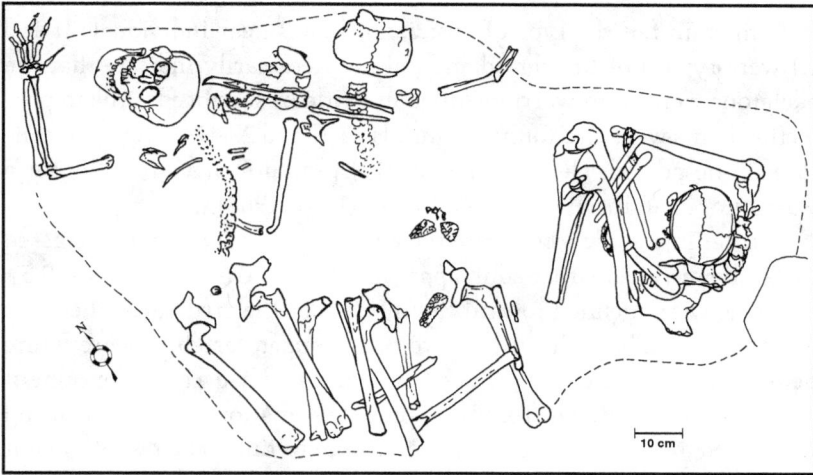

Fig. 9.3. Plan Drawing of Burial 27–A. From left, skeletons are Individuals I, III, II, and IV. Individual IV was principal interment, while Individuals I-III were apparently sacrificed retainers (earlier versions in Guillemin 1961: 91; 1967: 33; 1968: 72; republished with permission of the Sociedad de Geografía e Historia de Guatemala)

Individual II lay face down and parallel to but farther inside the tomb than Individual I. The cranium of Individual II, an adult, according to Guillemin, looked to the northeast and was crushed into the wall of the tomb. It exhibited a small amount of what Guillemin assessed to be probably unintentional artificial fronto-occipital deformation. Only the upper vertebrae were preserved. The femurs and pelvis were still located together. In the center of the pelvis was an obsidian projectile point without its tip. Another obsidian point in two fragments was beneath the kidney region. A small prismatic blade, which Guillemin felt might have been dropped accidentally when filling the tomb, lay in the chest near the vertebrae (Guillemin 1959 field notes; 1961; 1968).

In the center, underneath and parallel to the first two skeletons, was Individual III, an adult, who also lay face down. The cranium, facing northwest, consisted of small crushed fragments. Below the apex of the cranium was a small complete obsidian point. A small fragment of another obsidian biface above it may have come from the tipless point found with Individual II. The lower limbs of Individual III were mixed up with those of Individual II because the bodies had been piled into the tomb (Guillemin 1959 field notes; 1961; 1968).

Guillemin felt the type of obsidian artifacts near Individuals II and III were typical of the period and did not necessarily indicate that the skeletons were from warriors killed in battle or sacrificed. Broken projectile points were also found in Burials 27-C and 27-D, which each contained one person. Neither individual appeared to have been either a warrior or a sacrificial victim (Guillemin 1961; 1968).

Farther inside the tomb were the bent legs of Individual IV, assessed by Guillemin as a mature adult approximately 1.70 m tall (figs. 9.4; 9.5). The legs were inclined toward the interior of the structure. The arms were crossed behind the knees. Two of the upper vertebrae were found below the knees. The skull, which Guillemin said had a small amount of probably unintentional fronto-occipital deformation, was crushed, and he applied alvar to it in hopes of being able to find evidence of violent death. The damage on the left occipital seemed to him to be the result of impact with a sharp object. The edge of the fracture, which was in the center of the bone and not near a suture, was sharp (Guillemin 1959 field notes; n.d.c: 2; 1961; 1968).

Fig. 9.4. Burial 27–A/IV Showing Gold Diadem over Possibly Mutilated Skull (similar plate published in Guillemin 1961: 94)

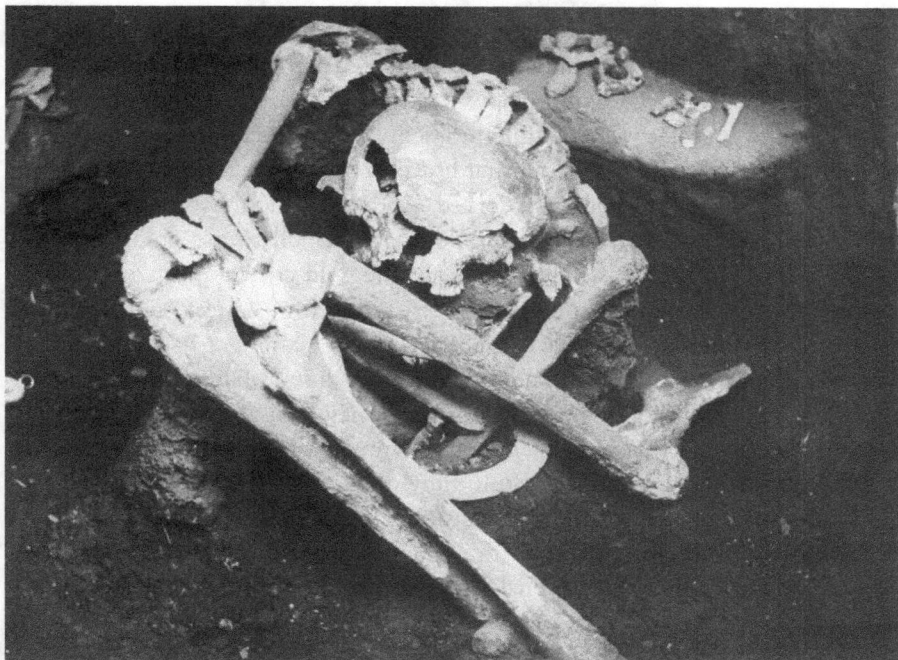

Fig. 9.5. Burial 27–A/IV with Gold Strip Removed from Cranium and Well-Preserved Bone Bracelet Visible between Bones of Left Leg (previously published in Guillemin 1961: 94; republished with permission of the Sociedad de Geografía e Historia de Guatemala)

A gold sheet, 47 cm long × 6 cm wide, with holes in the ends for strings to pass through, encircled the cranium. The sheet had not shifted position, confirming for Guillemin that the damage to the occipital had occurred before burial and that the injury very likely was the cause of death. A copper nose pendant was near the right side of the skull, and a very thin copper earring 1 cm in diameter was near its left side. Nose perforation may have been an exclusive sign of royalty (see Las Casas 1958, 4: 343), although Guillemin expected a king to possess a nose ornament of better quality than copper. A fine 2.5 cm × 1.9 cm rectangular piece of jade in the shape of a human head in profile was lying in soil excavated about 10 cm in front of the skull (fig. 9.6). Guillemin thought it might be from an earlier period and might originally have been placed in the mouth of the deceased (see Las Casas 1958, 4: 361). Slightly below the mandible was a jade bead, and another was near the left side of the mandible. Both beads had good color and polish. In the soil in front of the skeleton were fragile white shell fragments and tiny fragments of turquoise from a mosaic which may have been applied to a perishable substance and originally may have constituted some form of ornamentation. A little above the left elbow were two pieces of a well-preserved sculptured bracelet which Guillemin believed was made from part of a human cranium (fig. 9.7). A similar bracelet was on the right arm, but it was incomplete and badly preserved. Above the floor were 10 small jaguar head beads covered with gold and 40 small round gold beads. Guillemin wrote in his field notes that the gold crown and jade were taken to the Tecpán town hall for greater nighttime safety (Guillemin 1959 field notes; n.d.e: 2; 1961; 1968).

Guillemin believed that Individual IV was a member of the Xahilá family of Oxlahuh Tzíi, heir of Vukubatz, one of the founders of Iximché. Possibly he was either Chopená Tohín or Chopená Tziquín Uqá, who were sons of Vukubatz. Both individuals died in battle while trying to enlarge the kingdom during the reign of Oxlahuh Tzíi and Lahuh Ah. Guillemin felt that Individual IV was more likely Chopená Tziquín Uqá. Depictions of birds were carved on the bracelets, and the

Fig. 9.6. Carved Jade Bead and Reconstructed Gold Necklace from Burial 27–A/IV (similar plate published in Guillemin 1965a: 51)

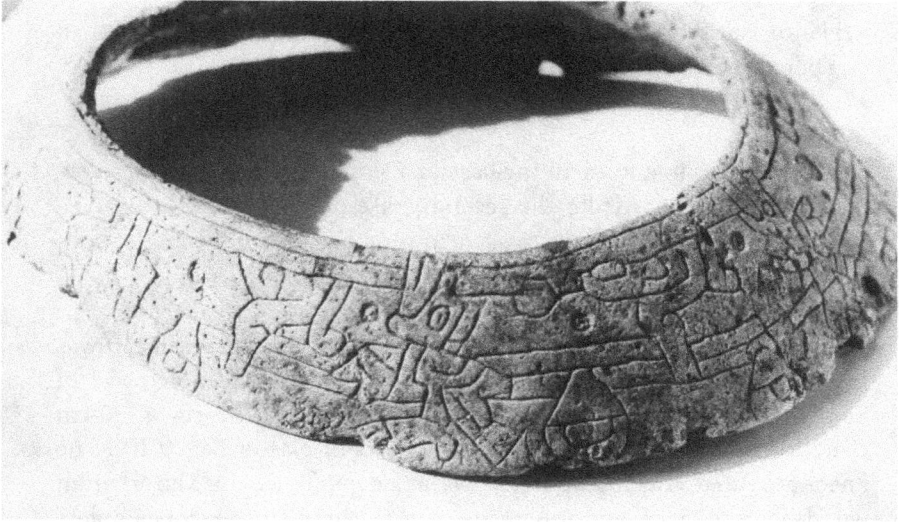

Fig. 9.7. Bracelet Made from Incised Bone, Possibly a Human Occipital, and Found around Left Elbow of Burial 27–A/IV (previously published in Guillemin 1961: 99; re-published by permission of the Sociedad de Geografía e Historia de Guatemala)

Cakchiquel word for "bird" is "tziquín," which was also a day of the calendar (Guillemin 1959 field notes; n.d.d: 8; 1961; 1965a: 21–22, 32–33; 1966: 7, 11–12; 1967: 33; 1968; 1977: 234). For an alternative interpretation of this burial, see chapter 11.

Burial 27-B

Another cist, 1.6 m northeast of Burial 27-A, was also behind the first facade and dates to the earliest phase of construction. The cist was partially emptied by an unknown person, but, according to information given to Guillemin, there were no ceramics in it. There were still some long bones in the hole at the beginning of the excavation project. Therefore, Guillemin felt it did not seem to have been a secondary burial of the type most common in the Late Postclassic, which would have consisted of cremated skeletal remains in an urn (Guillemin 1959: 33).

The incomplete but partially undisturbed bones showed that the seated body was oriented west-southwest. Associated with the bones, which Guillemin identified as being from a woman, were a light green worked jade piece, polished on one side and with a bi-conical hole, and soot-covered cooking vessels: a small black utilitarian vessel with one handle, two fragmentary utilitarian vessels, and a complete red vessel. The fill of Structure 27 was compact adjacent to the burial. There was no evidence that the tomb continued inside or that it contained more than one person (Guillemin 1960 field notes; n.d.d: 13; n.d.f; 1965a: 32; 1966: 11; 1967: 33).

Burial 27-C

This burial was in a tomb in the base of a sloping facade that had a cornice. The facade was from the second phase of construction (fig. 9.8). Inside the tomb (fig. 9.9) were skeletal remains and an incomplete obsidian projectile point (Guillemin 1960 field notes).

Burial 27-D (IX-34)

This was a "lateral" burial adjacent to the structure near the edge. It was just north of the northeast corner of Structure 27 and northwest of Structure 24. The skeleton was inside a 10-cm-high, 50-cm × 80-cm cist, which had been covered with two coats of plaster (fig. 9.10). The knees appeared, sticking up (fig. 9.11), at a depth of 62 cm. The cranium was deeper, at 75 cm, and situated west of the legs. The almost complete but fragile skull was oriented to 160 degrees magnetic. The mandible had only five front teeth; one incisor was lost postmortem and the rest of the teeth were missing antemortem, since the bone was healed, ac-

Fig. 9.8. Burial 27–C Showing Cover of Cist Adjacent to Rear Wall of Structure; Built during Second Phase of Construction

Fig. 9.9. Burial 27–C, Secondary Burial; Obsidian Point Lies below Bones which Cross in front of Cranium

cording to Guillemin. He referred to the individual as an old man. An incised stone from the cist had sunk into the burial and moved the bones somewhat. An obsidian projectile point, broken into three pieces, was at the level of the cranium. A small light green jade bead was near the mandible and another, longer one was southeast of the right femur. The floor of the cist was 120 cm below the top. Guillemin identified what he believed was a pine and oak charcoal deposit associated with the burial; it was 70 cm beneath the level of the plaster plaza floor and extended 40 cm from the northwestern side of the cist (Guillemin 1960 field notes; n.d.d: 13; n.d.f; 1965a: 32; 1966: 11; 1967: 33).

Structure 74

This small structure lies adjacent to the southern corner of Temple 2. Near its northeastern corner, 1 m behind the rear facade, was a plastered hole, 28 cm in diameter. At 10 cm below the level of the floor was a cranium (IX-10) oriented to 110–120 degrees magnetic (fig. 9.12). Obsidian

Fig. 9.10. Burial 27–D, Showing Remains of Cist Cover

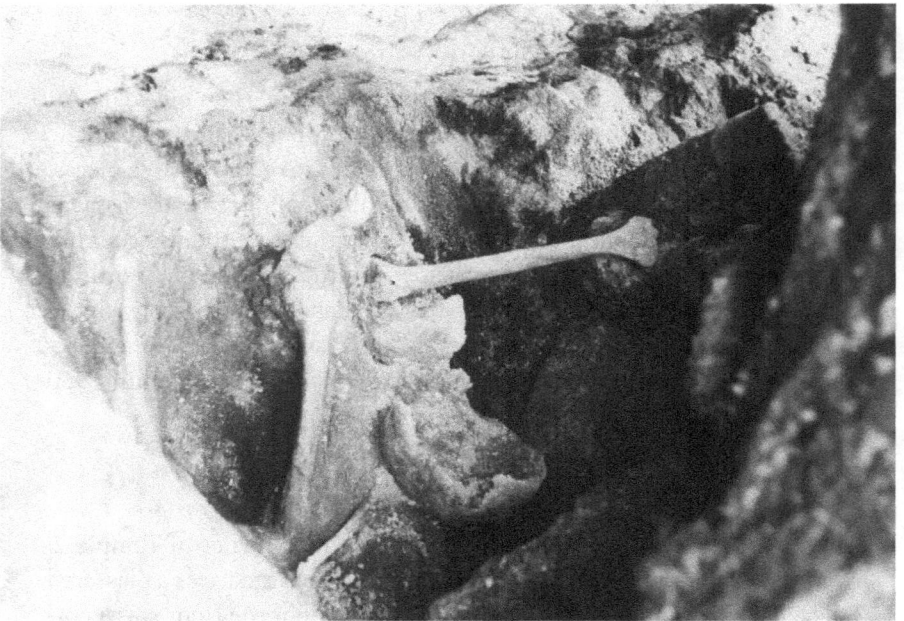

Fig. 9.11. Bones of Burial 27–D, Excavation in Progress

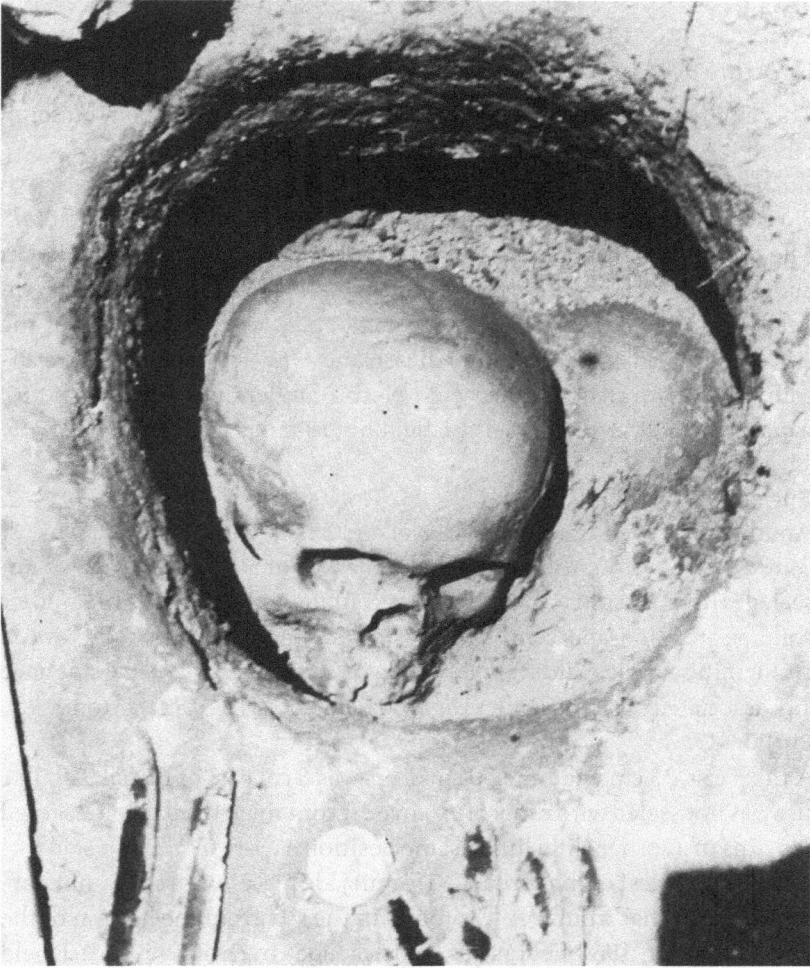

Fig. 9.12. Offering of Two Crania Associated with Structure 74; Probable Skull Rack

blades were scattered about. At a depth of 24 cm was another cranium oriented to 120 degrees, also with scattered obsidian blades. The first cranium was in good condition, but the second was crushed. The cervical vertebrae were in place for both skulls. The second skull was somehow associated with a stone at a depth of 40 cm, under which were two more obsidian blades. The hole was 57 cm deep. Above, the structure was decorated with polychrome murals with stylized skull and crossbones motifs, suggesting it may have been a skull rack (Guillemin 1960 field notes; 1967: 33; 1969: 27).

Plaza B

Structure 9

This elongated platform was at one time topped by a one-room building which faced the center of Plaza B from the southeast.

Burial 9-A

A cist behind Structure 9 contained the remains of a child's skeleton. The top of the cist, which was sealed with a masonry cover, was 16 cm above the level of the surrounding floor, and the bottom was 54 cm below floor level (fig. 9.13). The skeleton, placed on the bottom of the cist, was seated facing east-northeast and was accompanied by a biconically perforated polished jade piece (Guillemin 1960 field notes; paper inside cover of 1960–1961 field notes; n.d.d: 13; 1965a: 32; 1966: 11; 1967: 33).

Burial 9-B

Another cist, 55 cm below floor level and 33 cm wide, lay 45 cm east of Burial 9-A. It was in front of and under the wall of Structure 9 and was not sealed with a masonry cover. The cist contained the remains of another child, seated and apparently facing toward the center of Structure 9. Guillemin said the child was older than the child in 9-A and did not have any associated objects (Guillemin 1960 field notes; fig. 9.14, bottom).

Burial 9-C

A third cist, 33 cm wide and 50 cm deep, was 8 cm east of Burial 9-B. The cist was not sealed with a masonry cover. It contained the badly preserved remains of another child in the same position as 9-B. Guillemin said this was the youngest of the three. A "15-mm jade piece" with the same characteristics as that from 9-A was found in the soil from the bottom of the cist (Guillemin 1960 field notes; paper inside cover of 1960–1961 field notes; n.d.d: 13; 1965a: 32; 1966: 11; 1967: 33; fig. 9.14, top).

Structure 11 (Great Palace I)

The northeastern side of Plaza B is delimited by Great Palace I. In 1959, however, the Palace had been only partially excavated, and Guillemin (1959) referred to it as Structures 11 and 12, with Structure 11 situated in the southeast corner of the larger Palace, as later defined. According to Guillemin, Szecsy discovered during his 1956 excavations a burial in the "lower zone" alongside the eastern half of the northeastern bench and left it unexcavated and protected by surrounding stones in a

Fig. 9.13. Burial 9–A Showing Masonry Cist Cover Adjacent to Rear Wall of Structure with Skeleton Exposed in Profile

Fig. 9.14. Burials 9–B *(bottom)* and 9–C, Children

40-cm × 1.30-m pedestal of earth, 20 cm over the floor. Guillemin excavated this "Structure 11" burial in 1959, finding the incomplete remains of an individual whose bones were decalcified and fragile. Three
vertebrae, the pelvis, and the femurs lay in the bottom of a 15-cm-deep,
65-cm × 45-cm pit dug into the floor of the room alongside the bench.
The lower legs lay outside of the pit on the floor and extended 50 cm toward the eastern corner. Some cranial fragments lay on top of the
pelvis, leading Guillemin to conclude that the skeleton had been flexed
within the pit, a conclusion which is not supported by a sketch in his
notes and photos of the burial (fig. 9.15). A single tooth and some dispersed fragments were also recovered. Guillemin believed the individual was an adult, but he could not accurately determine age and sex.
Only one femur of this burial was kept. The remaining bones were rein-
terred *in situ* (Guillemin 1959 field notes).

Plaza C

Temple (Structure) 5

A fragment of a musical rasper made from a human femur was found
with fragments of a censer on the floor of the plaza near Temple 5

Fig. 9.15. Burial from Structure 11, Adjacent to Northeastern Bench

(Guillemin 1964 field notes; n.d.d: 12; 1965a: 31; 1966: 11; 1967: 33; 1977: 241).

Structure 38

An elongated platform on the northeastern side of Plaza C, this structure has a rear facade consisting of a retaining and defensive wall (Guillemin 1959: 35).

Burial 38-A/I (GO)

Associated with the intermediate phase of construction, a burial of what Guillemin described incorrectly as an adolescent was in a seated position in a hole under the base of Structure 38 (fig. 9.16, right). The hole was sealed with a masonry block which abutted the intermediate phase facade. The poorly preserved skeleton with crossed arms, facing the west-northwest, was in the northwest portion of the cavity and was covered with debris and fallen stones. Guillemin said the cranium was thin and the mandible lacked the front teeth, whose sockets were resorbed. The burial was accompanied by 11 gold beads, several sizes of shell beads with double perforations, two small perforated jade pieces, and two soft tiny green stones under the cranium and in front of the pelvis. A chipped obsidian projectile point was between the knees, and two copper ear ornaments were near the right knee and under the neck of the femur (Guillemin 1966 field notes; 1967 field notes; 1969: 23, 27). Two additional gold beads from this burial were recovered in 1992, when the block of soil which still encased the ribs was finally washed away 25 years after excavation.

Burial 38-A/II (GQ)

More toward the center of the same 1.20-m-diameter pit that held Burial 38-A/I (GO) was another poorly preserved skeleton, represented by femurs, apparently interred in a seated position with arms extended north-south (fig. 9.16, left). Two crude obsidian bifaces were associated with the skeleton. On the north, near the left hand, were the remains of a canine jaw. Also inside the pit and associated were part of a shell, a black tripod bowl with animal effigy feet (in the south), and a red-slipped ceramic vessel in fragments (in the east) (Guillemin 1967 field notes; n.d.h).

Structure 39

Situated on the eastern periphery of Plaza C, the building on top of this platform faced the back of Temple 5, immediately to the west.

Burial 39-A

Adjacent the rear facade of this structure, between Structures 39 and

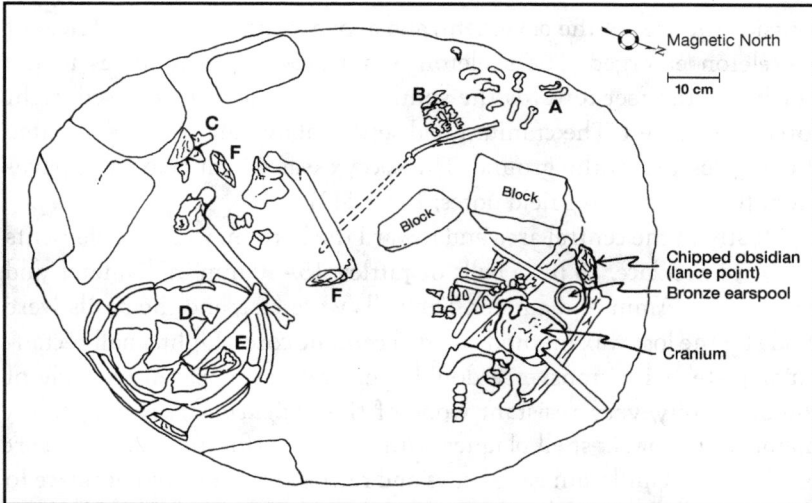

Fig. 9.16. Plan Drawing of Burial 38–A Located inside Second Phase of Construction of Structure 38. Individual I is on right; Individual II is on left. *A:* bones of forearm and hand; *B:* dog teeth; *C:* black-coffee-colored triple vase; *D:* vase destroyed by collapse of burial; *E:* fragment of shell inside destroyed vessel; *F:* obsidian points.

134, is a pavement 57 cm wide and 35 cm high; 8.90 m north of the south corner of this slanting rear facade, a 58-cm-wide intrusion was made into the pavement. This had not been sealed, but rather was overlaid by an entire Late Classic ball-game yoke of smooth stone, broken into five pieces and covering a 1-m area (see fig. 4.44). Nearby, but farther to the northeast, were three fragments of a cylindrical phallic stone (see fig. 4.45). The phallus was 25 cm in diameter and ended in a simplified human head with a conical headdress. Both the phallus stone and the yoke had been exposed to fire before being broken. A fragmentary stone ball approximately 30 cm in diameter was also found nearby among the scattered stones of Structure 39. Guillemin considered the possibility that the burial occurred after the arrival of the Spanish, when the materials and workers needed to seal the tomb were not available. However, that the yoke had been set above the burial and exposed to fire ultimately led him to conclude that the burial antedated the fire set by the Spanish on February 7, 1526. Guillemin believed that this fire destroyed Great Palace II, which was adjacent to Structure 39 (Guillemin 1971 field notes; n.d.b; 1977: 243).

A small quarried stone was found 43 cm below the level of the pavement. When it was lifted, the top of the cranium was revealed (fig. 9.17).

Outside the area of the pavement, and above its level, two bent knees of a skeleton emerged. The skeleton was seated with the knees to the northeast, the feet towards the southeast, and the arms crossed, right forearm over left. The cranium had settled above the pelvis, dislocated due to pressure in the ground. The coccyx was 64 cm below the pavement (Guillemin 1971 field notes; 1977: 242).

Mostly in the central area and toward the bottom, were the elements of a gold necklace, 15 little bells or rattles, 15–40 mm in diameter, and 87 beads, 4–7 mm in diameter. The bells were cast, and the beads were made by the lost wax method and had ceramic cores. Eight small rectangular plates with transverse double perforations, apparently made of the black, oily, very resistant wood of the *guayacan* tree, and the remains of five or six shell plaques with double perforations formed part of a bracelet. Guillemin gave beads and rattles from the gold necklace to the Instituto de Antropología e Historia (Guillemin 1971 field notes, 1972 field notes; n.d.b; 1977: 242; fig. 9.18).

Burial 39-B
South of Burial 39-A were two other burials (fig. 9.19). Burial 39-B was adjacent to and intrusive upon Burial 39-A. The skeleton faced east and

Fig. 9.17. Burial 39–A

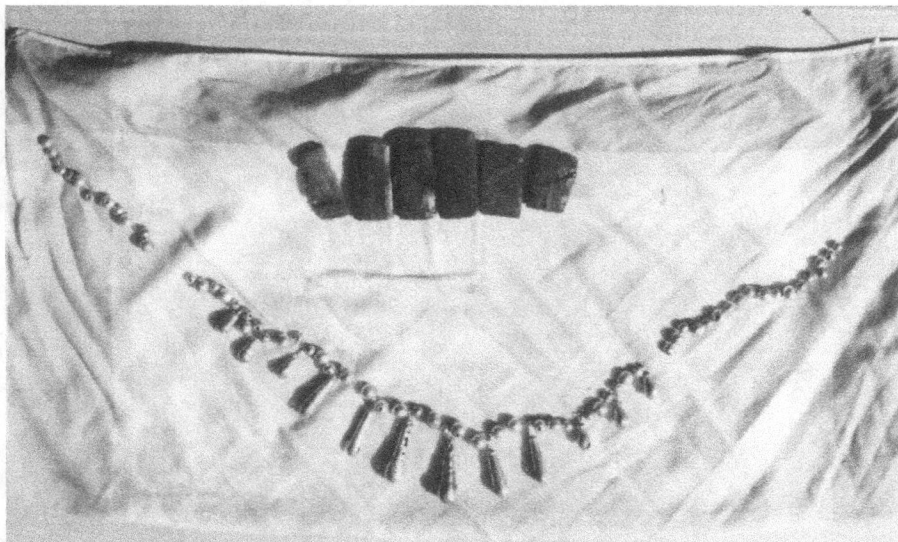

Fig. 9.18. Wooden Plaques from Bracelet and Reconstructed Gold Necklace Found with Burial 39–A

was squatting. The burial was disturbed, and although the mandible was present, the calvarium was not (Guillemin n.d.b; 1977: 243).

Burial 39-C (IX-1)

Farther to the south was another skeleton in a squatting position accompanied by a small jade pendant. The missing part of the stone ball found near the yoke and cylinder of Burial 39-A was discovered north of Burial 39-C (Guillemin n.d.b; 1977: 243; fig. 9.20).

Structures 91 and 92

These structures form the northern corner of the small Placita C at the southern corner of Plaza C. Structure 91 is adjacent to Structure 90 (to the east), and Structure 92 is adjacent to Temple 6 (to the southwest).

A 1.10-m-deep pit with a diameter of 64 cm at the top and 80 cm at the bottom had been cut through the plaza floor at the northwestern corner formed by Structures 91 and 92. In the pit was an offering of a carefully placed calvarium and randomly scattered postcranial bones, a mandible, and parts of a broken *incensario* (fig. 9.21). The bone and ceramic fragments decreased in frequency with increasing depth (Guillemin n.d.g).

Burial 91-A

It is unclear whether Burial 91-A is the same interment as the one in the pit described above for Structures 91 and 92, but it seems not to be.

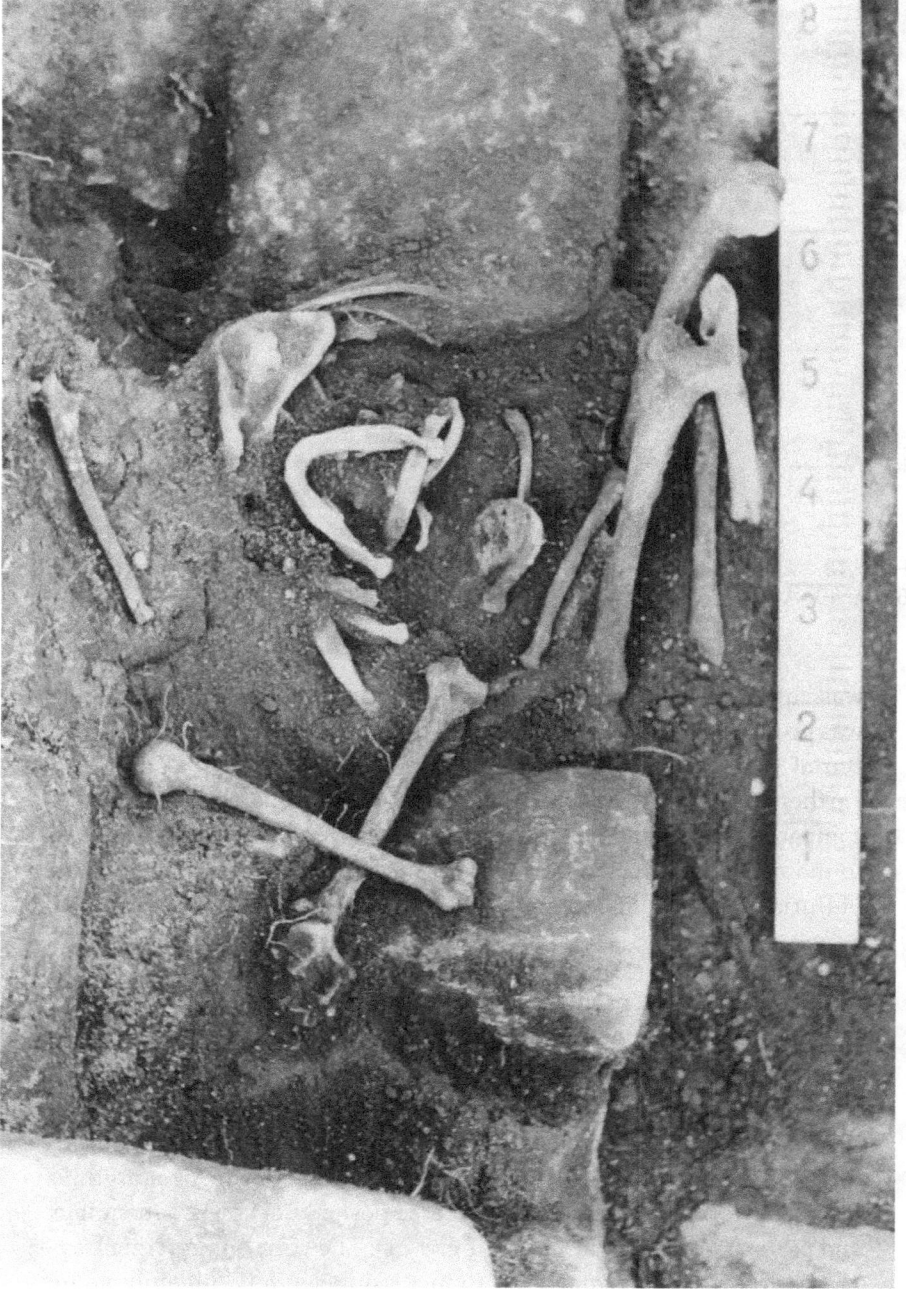

Fig. 9.19. Burial 39–B

Fig. 9.20. Burial 39–C

Burial 91-A was a very incomplete secondary burial, lacking long bones, and found on one side of Structure 91, under the level of the plaza of the southeastern complex. The burial was accompanied by 30 gold beads with ceramic nuclei, 50 small bone elements with double perforations in the front surface, 3 small tubular jade beads, and 2 perforated pumice beads (Guillemin 1966 field notes).

Structure 104

Adjoining the south corner of Temple 4 is the small Structure 104, a skull rack. It was badly preserved and lacked any feature demonstrating its function, but its location in relation to Temple 4 is identical to that of Structure 74 in relation to Temple 2 in Plaza A. The discovery of many decapitations next to the structure supports this identification (Guillemin 1969: 26–27; 1977: 258).

Immediately west of Temple 4 about 10 square yards were paved with human skulls (table 9.1). Guillemin felt that the presence of cervical vertebrae indicated decapitation; that is, that skulls had not become separated from the postcranial skeleton after disintegration of the soft tissue but had been severed through the neck and buried with one or more cervical vertebrae articulated with them. Most of the 48 skulls were accompanied by obsidian blades found under the crania. Some of the skulls were buried in small lots, but the rest had been set

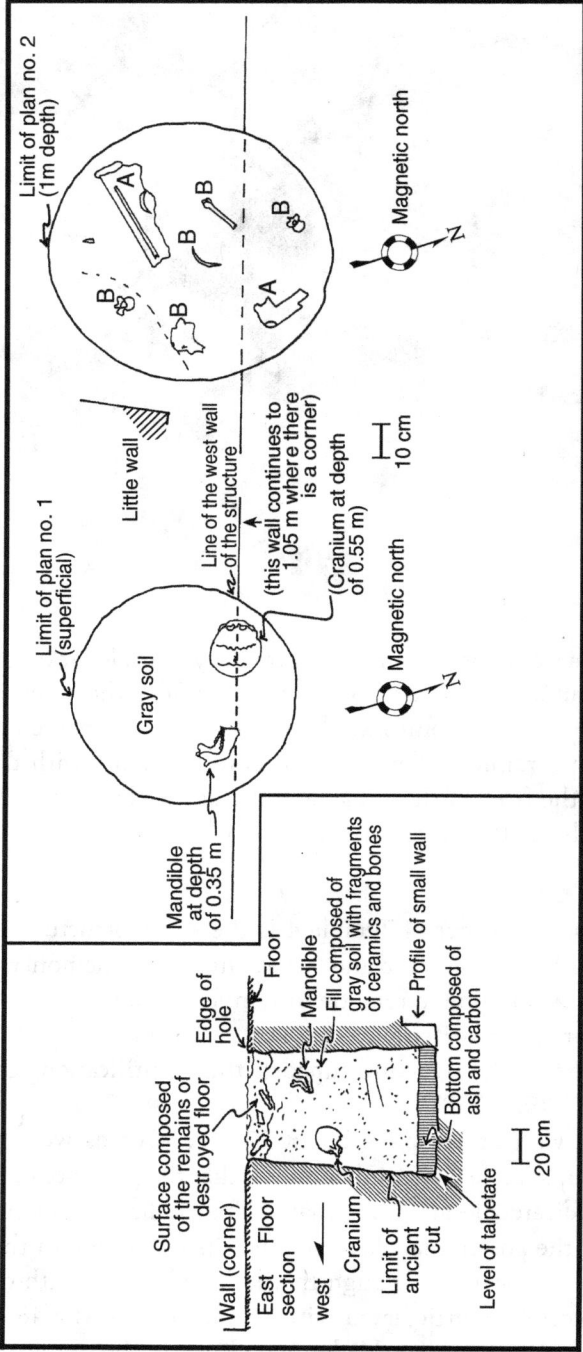

Fig. 9.21. Cross Section and Plan Drawings of Offering on South Side, Northwestern Corner of Structures 91 and 92. *A*: fragments of censer found in this level and disseminated from surface to bottom; *B*: fragments of human bones (vertebrae, ribs, scapula, tibia) which also appear from surface to bottom

individually in pits cut into the plaza floor. Long bones, skeletonized hands and feet, and various loose vertebrae were found among the crania, which were also mixed with quarried pumice stones belonging to the wall of Structure 104, fragments of debris, and some charcoal. Temple 4 was adjoined by a pavement which extended to within approximately 1.5 m of the crania. Two floors were identified near the edge of the pavement, but their precise locations and characteristics cannot be determined from Guillemin's notes. Structure 104 was built on top of one floor. The skulls apparently had been placed in pits intrusive into the other; the floor had been broken and fragments of it were found in the burials (Guillemin 1964 field notes; 1965b: 26; 1967: 33).

It is clear from photographs of the crania (figs. 9.22–9.32) that they were not deposited in a single event, since the state of preservation varies

Table 9.1. Characteristics of Structure 104 Decapitations Based on 1964 Field Notes

Cranium No.	Depth (cm)	Obsidian Blades *in situ*	Cerv. Vert.	Figure	ID	Data from Field Notes
# 1				9.18		
# 2				9.18		
# 3				9.18		
# 4				9.18		
# 5				9.18		
# 6				9.18		
# 7				9.18		
# 8				9.18		
# 9	27	1		9.19		
#10	15		no	9.20	IX-12	#10–#13 form group
#11	15	3	yes	9.20	IX-33	Copper earring
#12	15			9.20	IX-11	
#13	15			9.20		
#14		8		9.21		
#15	24	several	yes	9.19	IX-20	#15–#18 form group
#16	26	several	no	9.19		
#17	22	several	yes	9.19	IX-7	
#18	26	1	yes?	9.19		
#19	25	1	no	9.19		
#20	30	2	no	9.19	IX-46	
#21	18	4	no	9.19	IX-21	Deformation
#22	20		yes	9.19		
#23		4-½	yes	9.21	IX-22	Censer frag.; temporal holes
#24	13	1	no			
#25	15	1	?	9.22		

(continued)

Table 9.1. (*continued*)

Cranium No.	Depth (cm)	Obsidian Blades *in situ*	Cerv. Vert.	Figure	ID	Data from Field Notes
#26			yes	9.22		
#27						Brachiocephalic
#28	19	5	yes		IX-4	
#29		1	yes		IX-13	
#30	33	1	yes	9.23		
#31	40	4	yes	9.23		
#32	30	9		9.23, 9.24	IX-16	
#33		2		9.22		Under long bones; hip frag.
#34		3?	yes?	9.25	1X-53	Adolescent?
#35	15		yes			
#36		3	yes	9.26, 9.27	IX-2	Plagiocephaly
#37				9.26	IX-41	Fragmentary
#38		1-½	yes	9.26	IX-19	
#39				9.26		Fragmentary
#40			yes	9.26		Destroyed face
#41		1	yes	9.26		
#42		2-½	yes			Loose tooth
#43			yes	9.28		Stone on top
#44	22			9.28		
#45	33	1	yes	9.28		Face destroyed
#46			yes		IX-68?	
#47		2-½			IX-5	
#48	36?		yes			

considerably from excellent to poor. In addition, it seems likely that some were buried immediately after decapitation, whereas others were buried only after having been exposed to the elements for extended periods, during which various bones, such as vertebrae and mandibles, were lost. Las Casas (1958, 4: 152) wrote that "they put the heads of the sacrificed on some poles on a certain altar dedicated only to this, where they had these for some time," and that, "when this time passed they buried them." This custom probably explains the varied states of preservation. Las Casas (1958, 4: 152) added that this was done, among other reasons, "because the enemies would have fear of offending them, because if not, they would be certain that they would thus be sacrificed."

Fig. 9.22. Crania Nos. 1–8 in Ceremonial Deposit Adjacent to Temple 4 and Structure 104; Identified as Skull Rack (crania Nos. 1–4, *bottom*)

Fig. 9.23. Crania No. 9 and Nos. 15–22 with Unidentified Worker (crania No. 9 and Nos. 15–20 are closer group; wall to right is rear of Structure 104)

Fig. 9.24. Crania Nos. 10–13 with Associated Stones, Mandibles, Lumbar Vertebra, Hands, and Feet

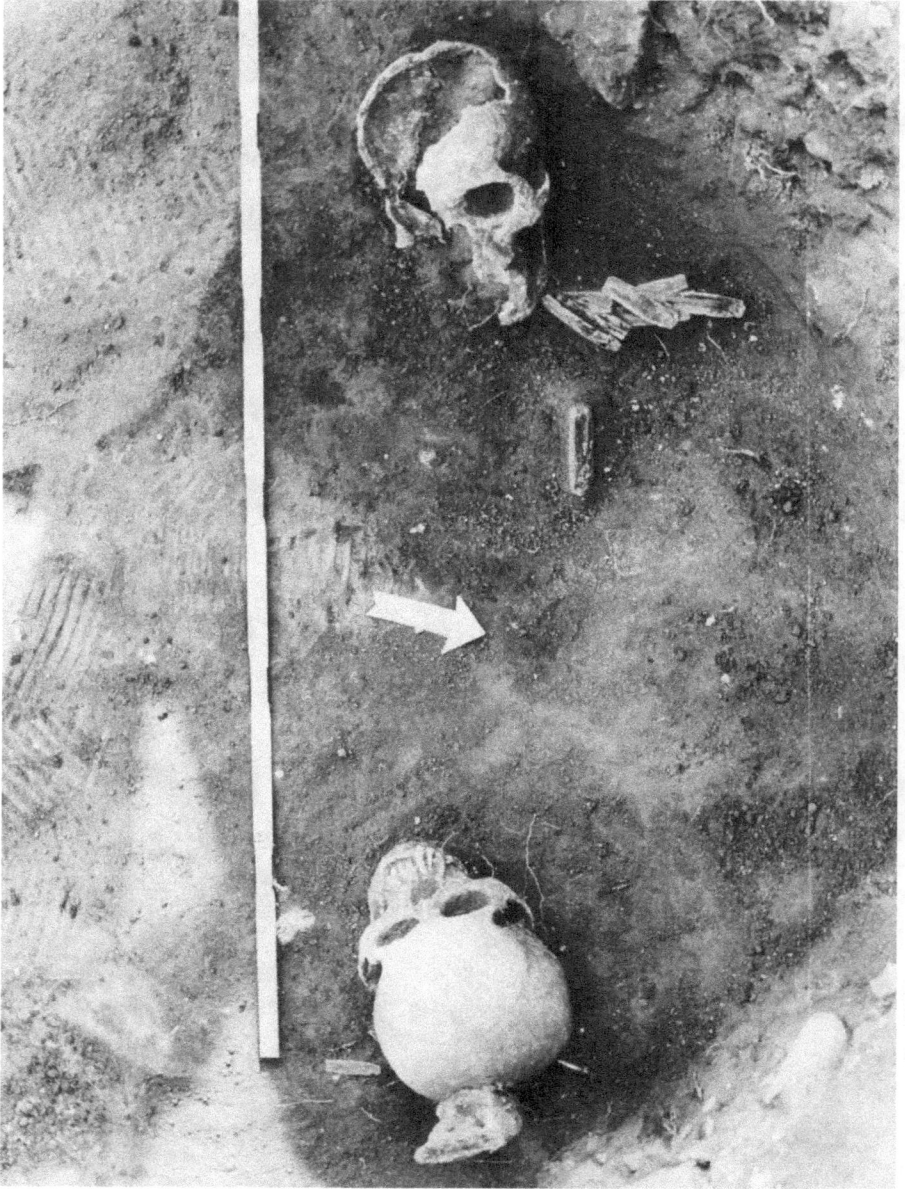

Fig. 9.25. Crania No. 14 *(top)* and No. 23 with Associated Obsidian Blades

Fig. 9.26. Crania Nos. 25 and 26

Fig. 9.27. Crania Nos. 30 *(bottom)*, 31 *(middle)*, and 32

Fig. 9.28. Cranium No. 32 with Associated Obsidian Blades (published previously in Guillemin 1965a: 52; republished by permission of the Instituto de Antropología e Historia de Guatemala)

Fig. 9.29. Cranium No. 34 and Hole from which Cranium No. 20 was Removed (rear wall of Structure 104 visible at top of plate)

Fig. 9.30. Crania Nos. 36–41 (*Left:* No. 36 and Nos. 38–40; *upper right:* No. 41; *lower right:* No. 37)

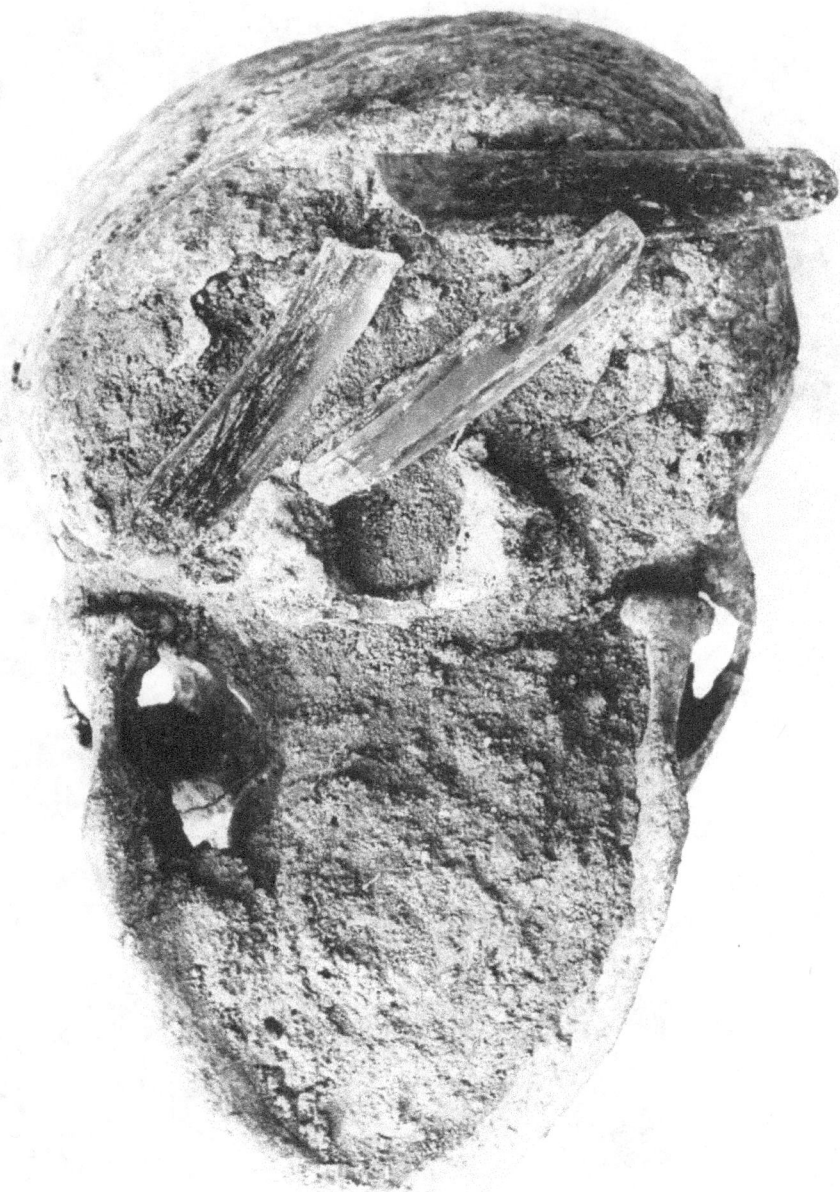

Fig. 9.31. Base of Cranium No. 36 Showing Cervical Vertebra and Obsidian Blades *in situ* (published previously in Guillemin 1969: 30; republished by permission of the Société Suisse des Américanistes)

Fig. 9.32. Crania Nos. 43 *(left)*, 44 *(bottom)*, and 45

10

ᴨᴨᴨᴨᴨᴨ

Analysis of Human Skeletal Material
Excavated by Guillemin

During the years between when Guillemin excavated Iximché and the skeletons were studied, many bones became separated from tags and bags marked with their provenience, and bones from different individuals became mixed together. Even when both cranial and postcranial bones from any one individual are present, it is now rarely possible to reassociate them. Thus, discussions of the analysis of cranial and postcranial bones generally will be presented separately, except for cervical vertebrae, which often were still associated with crania. (See appendix C for a list of cranial remains and their archaeological context, age, sex, and paleopathology.)

Number of Individuals Represented by Cranial Elements

At least 66 whole and partial crania are in the human skeletal sample from Iximché. This number is based on elements which still form units (for example, occipital-parietal-temporal). Groupings of cranial elements which belong together were compared to unassociated elements to determine whether or not they might belong to a single individual. If two groupings each contained the same element, then the possibility that they came from the same individual was rejected. If they were distinct in their makeup, however, then an attempt was made to find adjacent elements which physically joined. In the absence of an area of physical attachment, the groupings were compared for age, robusticity, and preservation, and a decision was made about whether or not they might belong together. Eventually, a minimum of 66 groupings of cranial elements representing distinct individuals emerged and were assigned IX numbers. Early in the project, another six IX numbers (8, 8-i, 14, 15, 18, 35) were assigned erroneously and do not represent individuals. Cranial bones that could not be assigned to any of the 66 groupings are identified by the bag in which they were found. The determination that at least 66 crania are in the sample was made independently of knowledge gleaned later from Guillemin's field notes concerning the number of skeletons he excavated (see chap. 9).

No single cranial element (for example, frontal) is present for every one of the 66 individuals, if only elements with more than 50% of their structures preserved are counted. The body of the right mandible, identified 60 times, is the most common element represented. Counts of less than 66 indicate elements were either broken into small fragments that could not be reconstructed, were lost in storage, or were not present when excavated.

Archaeological Context of Crania

Only 17 of the 66 crania could be visually matched with excavation photos of crania which Guillemin identified as decapitations. These are considered to be confirmed Decapitations. Most of them have damage identified as arising from the process of decapitation on the cranial bones or on associated cervical vertebrae (see discussion of Trauma below). The majority came from the group of 48 decapitated crania deposited together adjacent to Structure 104 in Plaza C, which Guillemin identified as a skull rack (Guillemin 1969: 26-27; 1977: 258).

Fourteen of the 66 are Possible Decapitations, which are classified into one of four categories. For 11, damage identified as arising from the process of decapitation appears on the crania or associated cervical vertebrae, but these could not be matched with crania in excavation photos. In one case, documentation found with the bones appears to be reliable and places the cranium within the group of 48 decapitations, although the cranium could not be matched to an excavation photo and no decapitation damage appears. In one case, the cranium was associated with postcranial bones, but decapitation damage also appears. Finally, in one case, a cranium with decapitation damage was matched to excavation photos showing it associated with a complete postcranial skeleton, which could not be located in storage. This is Burial 27-A/I, one of the three complete individuals thrown face-down into the burial pit with the gold-crowned individual tentatively identified by Guillemin as Chopená Tziquín Uqá. Figure 9.3 clearly shows that the cranium of Burial 27-A/I was out of anatomical position, suggesting that the individual had been decapitated before burial.

Three of the 66 are Possible Nondecapitations. For these individuals provenience information found with the crania indicated they were part of burials of intact bodies, but the postcranial bones had become separated in storage and could no longer be identified with certainty. Decapitation damage does not appear on these crania.

Four of the 66 are Nondecapitations, crania from intact or nearly intact skeletons which exhibit no signs of decapitation.

There is no physical or documentary evidence of the archaeological context of the remaining 28 crania. Contextual information is also lacking for cranial bones which could not be assigned to any of the 66 groupings. The only exception is a fragmentary bracelet made of a human occipital which was found on the right arm of Burial 27-A/IV.

Determination of Sex and Age for Crania

Since many crania were fragmentary after their years in storage, a methodology for determining sex was developed with the goal of reducing bias to a minimum. Simple presence or absence of 17 traits, 8 characteristic of female crania and 9 characteristic of male crania, according to Bass (1971), were recorded for each individual. No attempt was made to record degree of expression of the traits. As many traits were evaluated as possible, given each individual's state of fragmentation. If 8 or more traits could be evaluated and at least 75% of them pointed to one sex the individual was evaluated as Male or Female. If 8 or more traits could be evaluated and 67% to 74% of them pointed to one sex, the individual was evaluated as Male? or Female? If between 4 and 7 traits could be evaluated and all of them pointed to one sex, the individual again was evaluated as Male? or Female? Using these criteria, 10 crania were identified as Female and 11 were Male, 7 were Female? and 10 were Male? An additional bone which could not be attributed to any of the larger cranial groupings was Female? and a second was Male?

It was determined that five crania came from Subadults (younger than age 15) as indicated by their small, thin bones and the state of their dental development and tooth eruption. Ubelaker's (1989: 64) standards for dentition in Amerindians were used for designating the age of subadults. An additional six bones which could not be matched with any of the larger cranial groupings also came from subadults. Eleven crania and six additional bones which could not be associated with any larger groupings had third molars with incompletely formed roots. The best estimate of the ages of these individuals is approximately 15 to 21, and they can be called Young Adults. The remaining individuals can only be classified as Adults (age 15 or older). The Adult and Young Adult categories overlap. It is likely that some Young Adults are classified as Adults because they lack dentitions, have third molars with incomplete root development hidden within mandibles or maxillas, or had root closure occur at a relatively young age. Despite this, the average age of Young Adults undoubtedly is lower than the average age of Adults.

Table 10.1 shows the number of individual crania classified into different categories of age, sex, and context. The data are much too sparse to allow meaningful statistical analysis of patterns, but a few aspects of the table are worth noting. The characteristics of individuals identified as Decapitations provide some insights into Late Postclassic Highland warfare and human sacrifice. Although most of the victims were males, at least some appear to have been females. A large proportion of victims are classified into the Young Adult category. Since the skull may become slightly more robust as a person ages, there is a modest danger that crania from gracile young males were classified Female and crania from robust older females were classified Male.

Paleopathological Analysis of Crania

Trauma

Physical evidence of decapitation on the base of the skull, the vertebrae, or both appears on all but 1 of the 17 crania visually matched to crania in excavation photos Guillemin identified as decapitations. Damage typically occurs on some or all of the foramen magnum margin, mastoid process, inferior surface of the occipital, and posterior angles of the mandible (fig. 10.1), with jagged edges left adjacent to areas of missing bone. Cervical vertebrae deposited with the cranium frequently have articulations or parts of the body missing or even cut completely through, once again with jagged edges left adjacent to areas of missing

Table 10.1. Age, Sex, and Archaeological Context for Iximché Crania

	Decapitation			Possible Decapitation			Possible Nondecapitation			Nondecapitation			Unknown		
	Adult	Young Adult	Sub-adult	Adult	Young Adult	Sub-adult	Adult	Young Adult	Sub-adult	Adult	Young Adult	Sub-adult	Adult	Young Adult	Sub-adult
Male	3	1	0	2	1	0	0	0	0	0	0	0	4	0	0
Male?	4	2	0	2	0	0	0	0	0	0	0	0	2	0	0
Female?	0	2	0	1	0	0	1	0	0	1	0	0	2	0	0
Female	1	1	0	3	2	0	0	0	0	1	0	0	2	0	0
Unknown	2	1	0	2	1	0	1	0	1	0	0	2	16	0	2

bone (fig. 10.2). Cut marks made by thin, straight-edged tools are rare. The form of damage is so standardized that some crania, despite not being matched with excavation photos, can be categorized with high probability as decapitations. Trauma apparently associated with decapitation occurs on the cranial bones or vertebrae of 29 of the 66 individual crania. It also occurs on 12 mandibles and 1 temporal which could not be matched to any of the 66 (table 10.2). Trauma was found on 16 of 17 individuals identified as Decapitations (one could not be evaluated) and on 13 of 14 individuals identified as Possible Decapitations (one has an axis with possible, but not definite, damage).

The process of decapitation was neither quick nor neat. The tool of choice appears to have been a stone knife or ax with a jagged, almost serrated edge (fig. 10.3). Decapitation is one of the common forms of sacrifice depicted in Classic period (A.D. 250–925) Maya art (Schele 1984) and pressure-flaked stone axes and leaf-shaped stone knives frequently appear in painted and sculpted sacrificial scenes throughout Mesoamerica (Boone 1984).

Warfare apparently resulted in some damage to bones other than that directly related to decapitation. Perimortem cuts with well-defined edges that were made by straight-edged blades mark two left parietals, two frontals (one right side, one side unknown), and two left zygomatics (fig. 10.4). Most of the injuries are on the left side of the body, indicating that the cuts were usually made by a weapon held in the right hand.

The ectocranial surface of three frontals (two left side, one midline) and three left parietals from five individuals are marked by well-defined, slightly depressed areas with rough or smooth undulating surfaces at the bottom of the depressions (fig. 10.5). These represent healed trauma which occurred long before death. Saul (1972) believed such "dents" at Altar de Sacrificios possibly resulted from blows to the head. Hooton (1940) reported similar old, healed, and depressed circular lesions in various locations on the crania of three of eight female and two of ten male sacrificial victims recovered from the Postclassic Sacred Cenote at Chichén Itzá. He "suggested that the adult denizens of the Sacred Cenote may not have been generally beloved in their pre-sacrificial careers" (Hooton 1940: 277). On low-status individuals from Classic period Copán, however, Whittington (1989) attributed such lesions to trauma related to artificial cranial deformation. At Iximché it is unlikely that the lesions on three of the five individuals (IX-33, IX-42, and IX-62) have any connection with cranial deformation, as they are

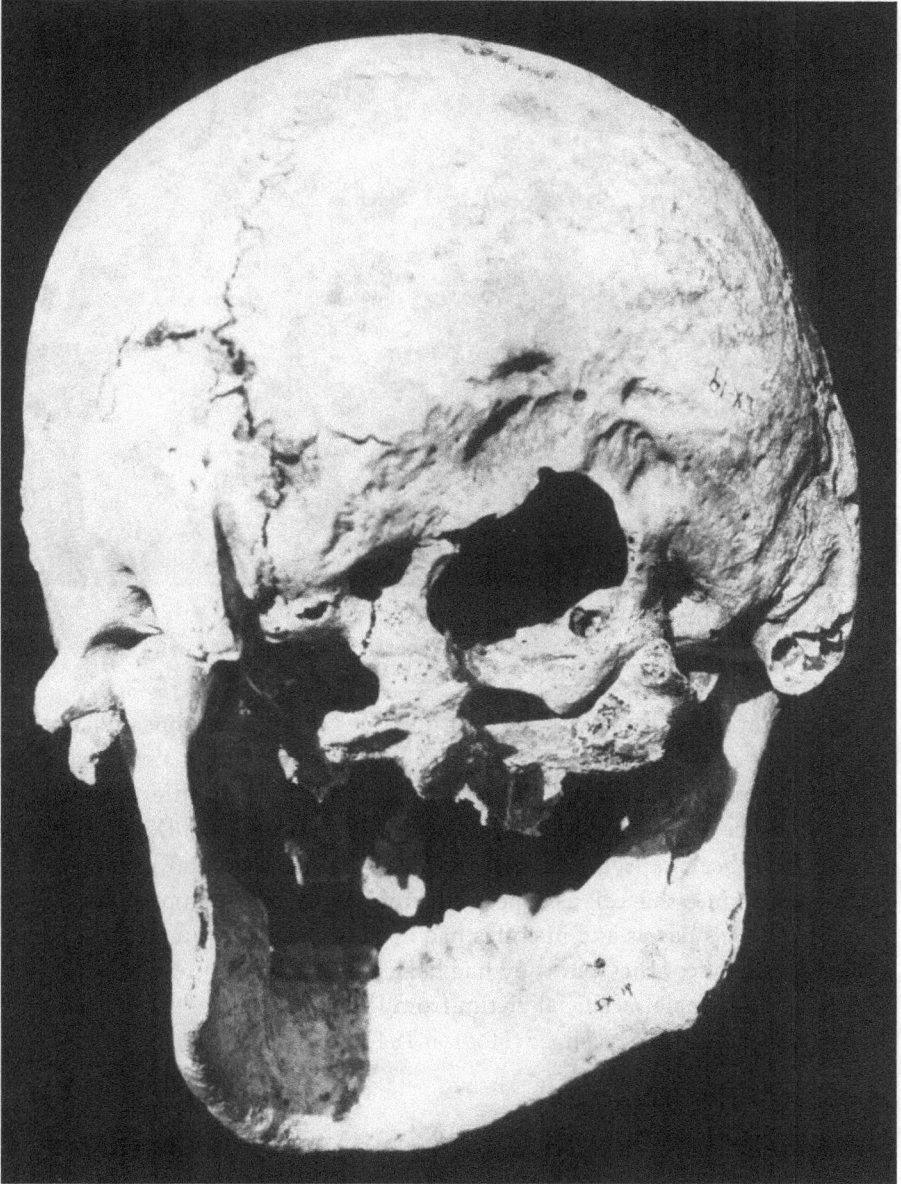

Fig. 10.1. Decapitation Damage to Angles of Mandible, Cervical Vertebrae, Occipital, and Possibly Mastoid Processes of IX-19

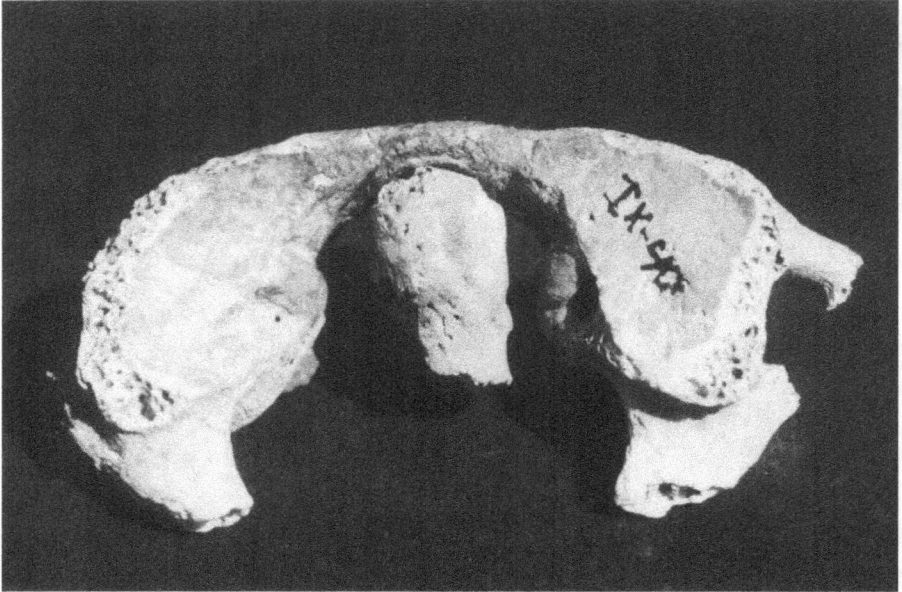

Fig. 10.2. Decapitation Damage to Atlas and Axis of IX-40

located on individuals without it or on bones or areas of bones not affected by it (see Cultural Modification below). These lesions may have been the result of blows to the head caused by accidents, interpersonal conflicts, or warfare. Lesions on two individuals (IX-27 and IX-65) may also have been caused by blows, but artificial deformation cannot be ruled out, since the lesions appear on bones affected by that process.

A female's nasals and maxillas had been fractured by an accident or interpersonal conflict, but they had healed by the time she was decapitated. One female sacrificial victim from the Sacred Cenote at Chichén Itzá also had a fractured nose (Hooton 1940).

Cultural Modification

Artificial cranial deformation is present in at least 48 individuals. Twenty-two have modification to both the frontal and occipital bones, and 26 have modification only to the occipital, although in 8 of these individuals it was not possible to evaluate frontal deformation. In 3 individuals with only occipital deformation the modification is so slight that it may have been an unintentional side effect of some other action, such as habitually sleeping in one position. The majority of individuals

Table 10.2. Decapitation damage at Iximché

Identi-fication	Decapi-tation?	Mandib. angle	Atlas	Axis	Mastoid	Inferior occip.	Mandib. ramus	Other
IX-2	Yes	X						
IX-4	Yes	X	X	X	X	X		
IX-5	Yes	X	X	X				
IX-6	Possible	X	X	X	P			
IX-7	Yes		X	X			X	
IX-9	Possible	X						Inferior body of mand.
IX-10	Yes	P	X					
IX-11	Yes	X	X		P			
IX-12	Yes	X			X			
IX-13	Yes	X	X	X				
IX-16	Yes	X	X		P			
IX-19	Yes	X	X		P	X		
IX-20	Yes	X	X					
IX-21	Yes	X	X		P	P		
IX-22	Yes	X			P			Occip. condyle (possible)
IX-23	Possible	X			P	X		
IX-28	Possible	X				P		
IX-29	Possible	X						
IX-33	Yes			X				Third cervical vert.
IX-40	Possible		X	X	X			
IX-41	Yes	X						
IX-43	Possible	X						
IX-46	Yes	X						
IX-47	Possible	X						
IX-50	Possible	X						
IX-51	Possible	X			P			
IX-52	Possible	X			P			
IX-53	Yes							
IX-54	Possible	X	X	X				
IX-56	Possible			X				
IX-68	Possible			P				
50-iii	Possible	X						
106	Possible	X						
176#1	Possible						T	
176#2	Possible	X						
206-N	Possible	X						
2290#8	Possible				T			
263	Possible	X						
270-i	Possible	T						
270-ii	Possible	X						
Str. 39-i	Possible	X						
Str. 39-iii	Possible	X						
Str. 45-ii	Possible	X						
Str. 45-iii	Possible	X						

1. X = Present, P = Possible, T = Thin, straight cuts present.

Fig. 10.3. Obsidian Bifaces Found in Bag with Human Skeletal Remains from Iximché

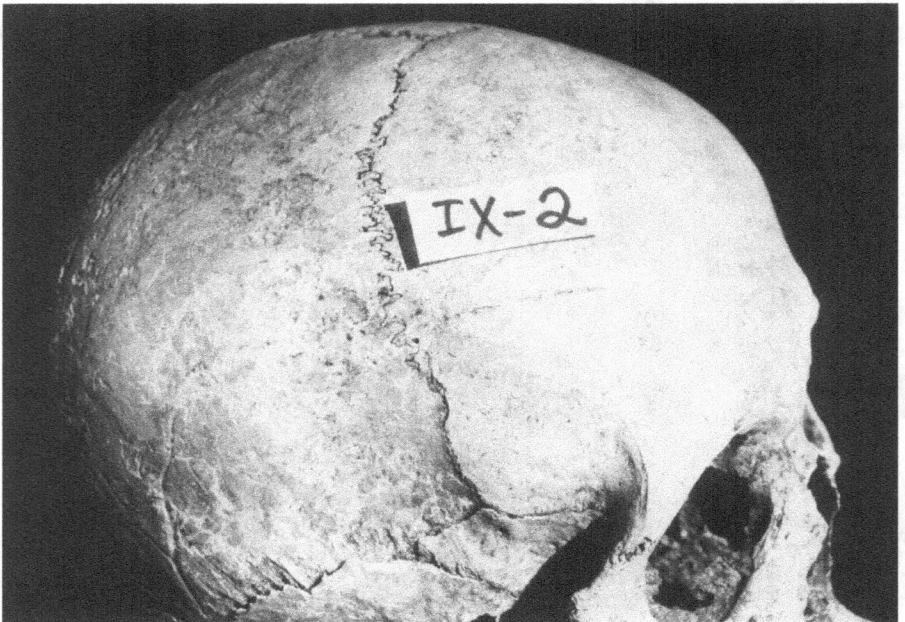

Fig. 10.4. Perimortem Cut from Edged Weapon to Right Side of Frontal of IX-2

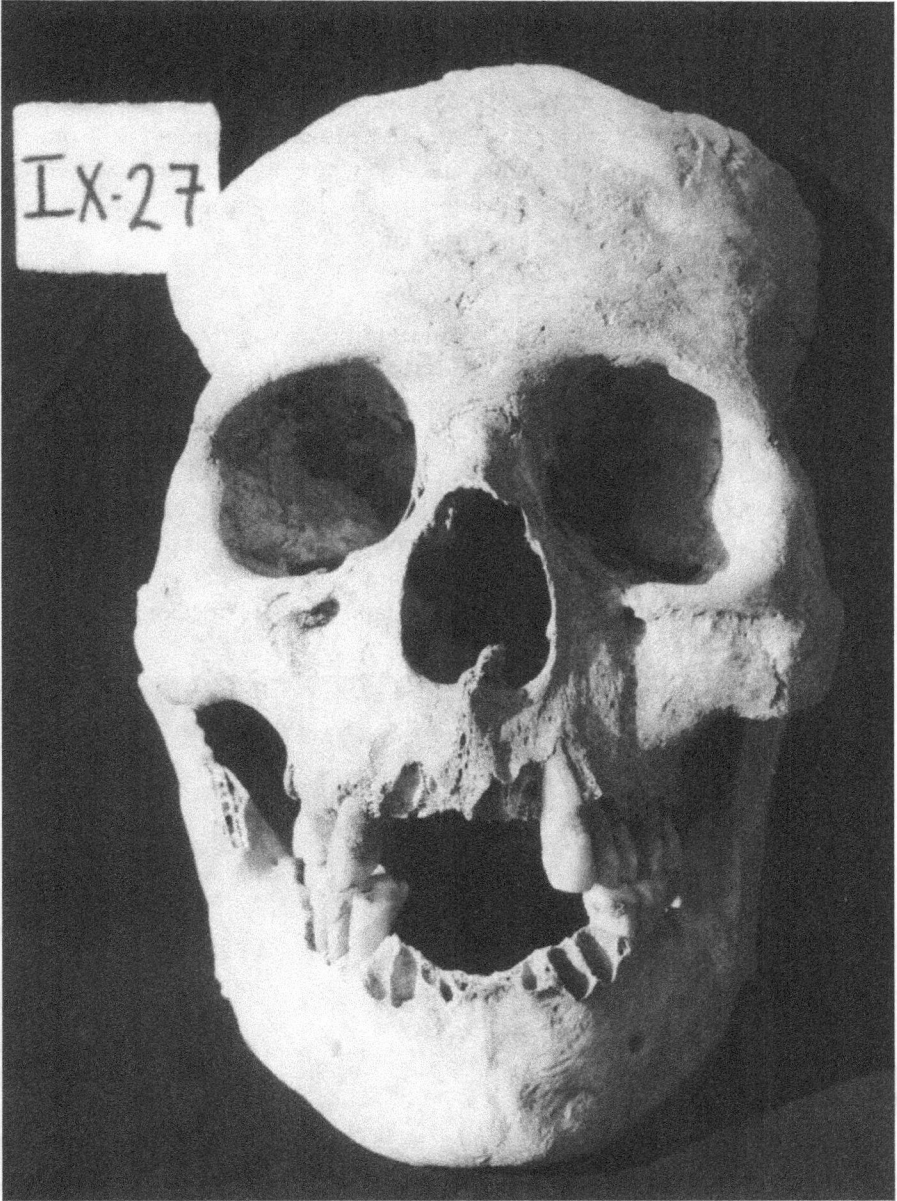

Fig. 10.5. "Dent" on Left Side of Frontal of IX-27; Individual also has Deviated Septum

exhibit markedly asymmetrical deformation, known as plagiocephaly (fig. 10.6), which has been noted in crania from the Highland Mam capital of Zaculeu (Weiss 1967) and Mixco Viejo (Gervais-Cloris 1985–1986). Guillemin (1969: 30) mentioned that cranium no. 36 from Structure 104 was deformed unilaterally, which he suggested was an unintentional result of the mother carrying her baby enveloped in a piece of textile which pressed on the infant's skull.

Diseases

Porotic hyperostosis is a pathological condition associated with cranial lesions characterized by expansion of the cancellous part, or diploë, and thinning of the outer table to the extent that small holes pierce the cortex and communicate with the underlying cancellous bone (El-Najjar and Robertson 1976; Hooton 1930; Ortner and Putschar 1985; Roberts 1987). Lesions appearing in the roofs of the eye orbits are termed cribra orbitalia. Osteoporotic pitting and spongy hyperostosis are lesions found on the frontal, parietals, or occipital in areas where muscles do not attach (El-Najjar et al. 1976). Cribra and vault lesions both may be

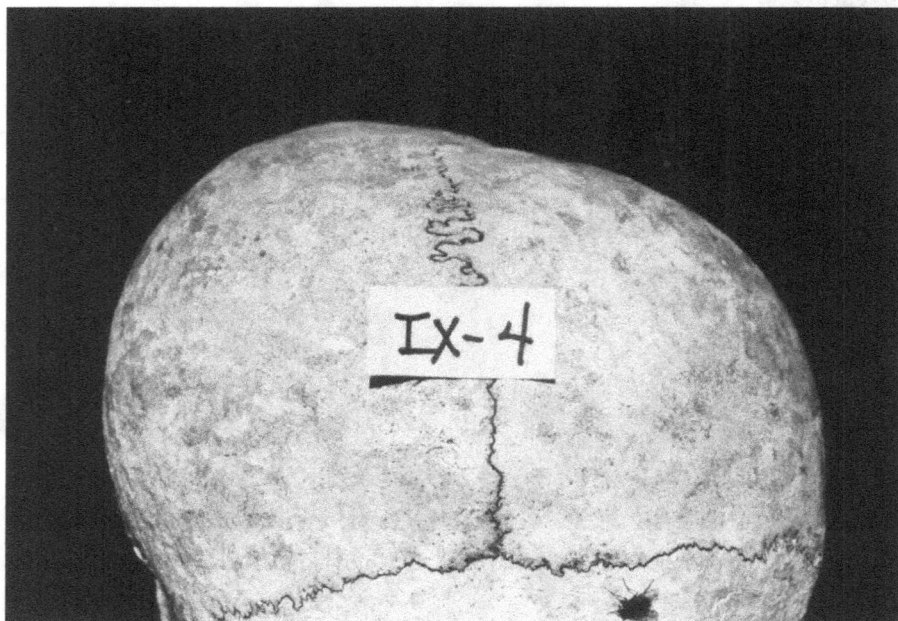

Fig. 10.6. Cranium of IX-4 Exhibiting Plagiocephaly *(viewed from above)*

found in a single skull, but each may occur separately (Ortner and Putschar 1985: 259).

Saul (1977) distinguished between active and healed porotic hyperostosis. Active lesions are those with significant diploic expansion and sharp-edged holes in the cortex; they indicate presence of disease at the time of death. Healed lesions also involve thickened diploë, but the holes may be partially filled in, smaller, and have rounded edges caused by bone remodeling. Healed lesions demonstrate that the individual survived a pathological state sometime before death occurred (Stuart-Macadam, 1985).

Steinbock (1976) concluded that most porotic hyperostosis in the Prehispanic New World was caused by iron deficiency anemia. The frequency of lesions of porotic hyperostosis observed in a population can be considered to represent a minimum estimate of iron deficiency anemia because bone changes in modern cases of iron deficiency anemia are rare (Ortner and Putschar 1985), with duration, rather than severity, apparently the critical factor (Perou 1964).

Iron deficiency anemia can have a variety of causes. It is more often the result of poor absorption and heavy iron losses than of an iron-deficient diet (Wing and Brown 1979). Iron in vegetables is much less readily absorbed than that in meat (Baker and Mathan 1975), and maize contains phytates, chemicals that interfere with iron absorption (Fleming 1977). Diseases of the digestive system may be accompanied by internal blood loss and impaired iron absorption (Layrisse and Roche 1964). *Ancylostoma*, the variety of hookworm that causes the greatest blood loss, existed in the Maya area before European contact (Shattuck 1938). Chronic diarrhea related to parasitic infection can cause further iron absorption problems (Saul 1972). Anemia and infection have a synergistic relationship, one aspect of which is that infection depresses appetite and causes iron to be diverted from the plasma to the liver and other organs (Lallo et al. 1977; Scrimshaw and Tejada 1970; Wing and Brown 1979).

Evidence of iron deficiency anemia is present in the form of pitting of porotic hyperostosis on the ectocranial surface of at least one cranial bone from seven individuals: six adults, and one subadult (fig. 10.7). The only two individuals whose sex could be determined were males. The most common location of the pitting is the occipital, with seven cases, followed by the parietals, with four cases on each side. No pitting was observed on frontals or in eye orbits, usual locations for expression in other populations. All cases have pits with rounded edges, indicating that they were healed at time of death and that the individual had survived whatever disease had caused the pitting earlier in life. If we standardize results by considering only parietals with more than 50% of the ectocranial surface preserved, then either pitting or a very rough surface in association with occipital pitting is present on 2 of 33 left (6.1%) and 1 of 30 right (3.3%). For occipitals with more than 50% of the ectocranial surface preserved, 5 of 32 (15.6%) are affected, which seems a reasonable estimate for the frequency of lesions in the population as a whole. Dividing the population by age, none of 4 Subadults and Young Adults and 5 of 28 Adults (17.9%) have lesions.

Stuart-Macadam (1987) reviewed evidence of anemia in various populations and found that orbital lesions occurred at frequencies as high as 69% in children and 45% in adults, with average values of 38% and 16%, respectively. Vault lesions reached frequencies as high as 31%. In a more recent review of anemia in skeletal series from around the world, the frequency of porotic hyperostosis (including cribra orbitalia) in subadults ranges from 23.3% to 88.0%, while that in adults

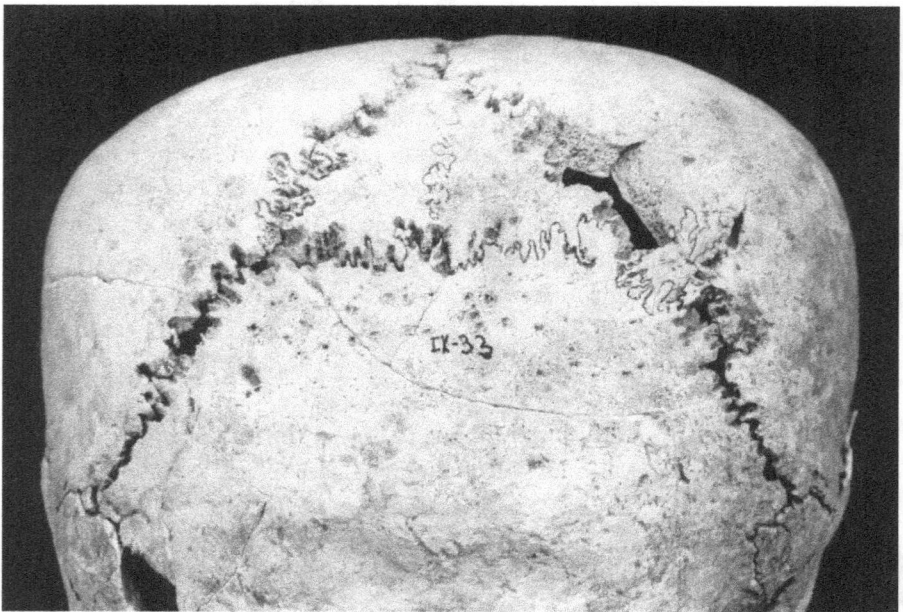

Fig. 10.7. Pitting of Healed Porotic Hyperostosis on Occipital of IX-33

ranges from 14.9% to 67.8% (Wright and White 1996). The frequency of porotic hyperostosis at Iximché is near the low end of the scale in comparison to these populations.

Comparison with other Maya skeletal series is confusing because of the lack of consistent patterns within the data, even when only Post-classic and Historic series are considered (table 10.3). Frequencies of lesions for the Postclassic range from 0% to 96.3%. The range for the Historic period is 17.0% to 80.0%. Much of this variability may be the result of differences between observers and in the way they report their results. The frequencies most directly comparable are those from Classic Copán, since the same methodology was used there as at Iximché. Lesions of anemia are much less common in skeletons at Iximché than at Copán. Given other osteological and archaeological evidence at Copán, the relatively high frequency of lesions at that site may reflect poor health and diet. However, Wood et al. (1992) pointed out the difficulty of interpreting differences in frequencies of lesions between populations. A lower frequency of lesions of anemia does not necessarily mean a healthier population or a better diet. Even if the low frequency at Iximché does reflect better health than at Copán, the explanation for the difference could relate to a number of potentially overlapping factors: social status, diet, synergism with infection, parasite load, altitude above sea level, and a host of others.

Periosteal reactions are bone lesions produced by two disease processes: periostitis and osteomyelitis. It is not always possible to distinguish between the two in dry bone. Periostitis is inflammation of the periosteum, a membrane overlying the surface of the bone. Primary periostitis is caused by either trauma or infection, whereas secondary periostitis is related to processes of certain specific diseases, such as the treponemal diseases syphilis and yaws (Ortner and Putschar 1985). Periostitis is a valuable indicator of stress (Mensforth et al. 1978). Osteomyelitis involves destructive invasion of bone periosteum and marrow by pyogenic microorganisms (Luck 1950). Infection may be caused by direct extension from adjacent tissues, or it may come from the bloodstream (Knaggs 1926).

Periostitis usually is associated with pathological changes in which new bone is laid down on the surface of the underlying cortex. Periosteal bone tends to be porous fiber bone that is superficial to the normal cortex. When it is deposited over a long period as a response to inflammation, it tends to be unevenly distributed, not involve the entire

Table 10.3. Lesions of Anemia in Maya Skeletal Series

Site	Period[1]	Cases	n	%	Notes	Source
National Museum (Mexico)	?	52	54	96.3		Saul 1977
Seibal	?	7	21	33.3	Adults	Cohen et al. 1994
Cuello	I	2	49	4.1		Saul & Saul 1997
Pasión	I–III	10	18	55.5	Subadults	Wright & White 1996
Pasión	I–III	53	81	65.4	Adults	Wright & White 1996
Caracol	I–III	7	317	2.2		Chase 1997
Sta. Rita Corozal	I–IV	3	165	1.8		Chase 1997
Tayasal	I–IV	0	59	0.0		Chase 1997
Altar de Sacrificios	I–IV	7	8	87.5	Subadults	Saul 1977
Altar de Sacrificios	I–IV	25	28	89.3	Adults	Saul 1977
Jaina	II?	5	19	26.3		Saul 1977
Copán	II–III	4	6	66.7	Subadults	Whittington 1989
Copán	II–III	10	16	62.5	Adults	Whittington 1989
Copán	II–III	9	36	25.0	Cribra	Whittington & Reed 1997
Copán	II–III	28	47	59.6	Porotic hyperostosis	Whittington & Reed 1997
Pasión	III	30	46	65.2	Adults	Wright 1997
Playa del Carmen	IV	4	10	40.0	Cribra	Márquez, Peraza, Gamboa, & Miranda 1982
Playa del Carmen	IV	12	24	50.0	Porotic hyperostosis	Márquez, Peraza, Gamboa, & Miranda 1982
Altar de Sacrificios	IV	8	16	50.0	Minimum estimate	Saul 1972
Chichén Itzá	IV	14	18	77.8	Cenote children	Hooton 1940
Chichén Itzá	IV	9	17	52.9	Cenote adults	Hooton 1940
Chichén Itzá	IV	34	36	94.4	Cenote	Márquez 1987
Chichén Itzá	IV	52	54	96.3	Cenote?	Márquez 1987
Chichén Itzá	IV	9	109	8.3	Ossuary minimum estimate	Márquez & Harrington 1981
Chichén Itzá	IV	24	36	66.7	Peabody Museum	Saul 1977
Cozumel	IV	0	88	0.0	Cribra	Peña 1985
Cozumel	IV	3	88	3.4	Porotic hyperostosis	Peña 1985
Lamanai	IV	5	53	9.0		White et al. 1994
Lamanai	V	17	100	17.0		White et al. 1994
Tancah	V	8	10	80.0		Saul 1982
Tipu	V	38	106	35.8	Children	Cohen et al. 1994
Tipu	V	36	185	19.5	Adults	Cohen et al. 1994
Tipu	V	49	214	22.9	Cribra	Cohen et al. 1997
Tipu	V	168	304	55.3	Porotic hyperostosis	Cohen et al. 1997
Sarteneja	V	2	13	15.4	Minimum estimate	G. E. Kennedy 1983

Notes. 1. I = Preclassic, II = Classic, III = Terminal Classic, IV = Postclassic, V = Historic

bone, and have an irregular surface, variable thickness, and marked and uneven hypervascularity. Eventually, such a deposit may be remodeled into smooth, compact, lamellar bone and integrated into the cortex (Ortner and Putschar 1985).

Periosteal reactions are present on one or more cranial vault bones of eight individuals, as well as on a fragment which might represent another individual. The most common location is the parietals, with six cases, followed in decreasing frequency by the frontal (four cases), temporals (three cases), and occipital (two cases). Most lesions occur on the ectocranial surface of the bones, but one is on the endocranial surface of an occipital. One individual, who also appears to have had osteomalacia (see discussion below), has an active reaction on the surface of each temporomandibular joint. Reactions which were active at time of death generally have sharply defined edges, rough surfaces, and a gray appearance (fig. 10.8), whereas those which were healed have rounded or ill-defined edges, smoother surfaces, and a color like that of the surrounding bone (fig. 10.9). The periosteal reactions were active at time of death in four cases and healed in five cases. Affected bones came from Adults in six cases, Young Adults in two cases, and one Subadult. All four individuals for whom sex could be determined were males. One individual is a Nondecapitation, one is a Decapitation, and two are Possible Decapitations.

Bony reactions involving the maxillas deserve separate treatment because of their different characteristics and etiology. When the periosteum becomes involved in sinusitis resulting from upper respiratory tract infection or dental infection bony changes may develop (Boocock et al. 1995: 487). Six individuals and another fragmentary maxilla show abnormal bony changes within the maxillary sinuses. Four are characterized by a very thin layer of smooth bone with well-defined edges lying atop the normal bone surface (fig. 10.10). Boocock et al. (1995: 486) referred to this as spicule-type bone formation. Bony growths within two sinuses are similar to what Boocock et al. (1995: 490) called lobules of new bone. One is a rough lump of bone within a right sinus and appears on a maxilla also exhibiting spicule-type bone around the palatine suture, which may be related to similar bone found in the sinuses of other maxillas. The other is an area of exuberant bony growth occurring within a left maxillary sinus (fig. 10.11) and is associated with a rough depressed area on the outer surface of the maxilla. An infection within another maxillary sinus is related to a periapical abscess of the second

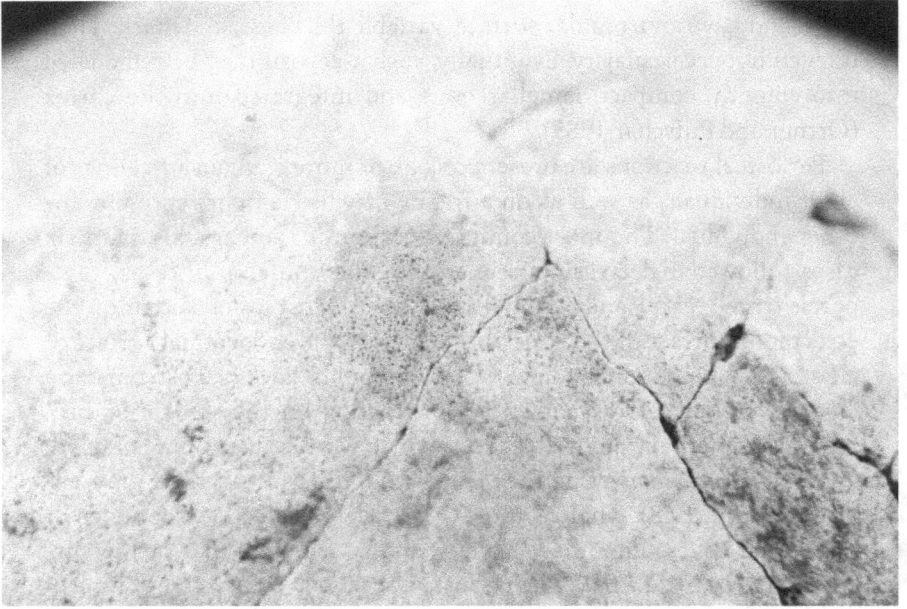

Fig. 10.8. Gray Patch of Bone in Center is Slight, Active Periosteal Reaction on Frontal of IX-33

Fig. 10.9. Pitted, Rough Surfaces of Frontal and Parietals of IX-62 are Healed Periosteal Reaction

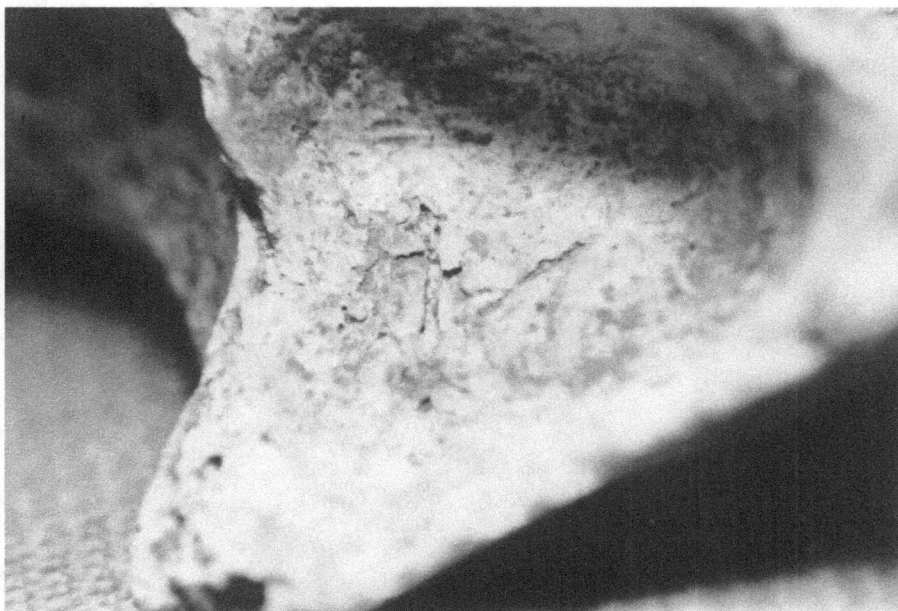

Fig. 10.10. Spicule-type Bone Formation in Maxillary Sinus of IX-68

premolar but does not exhibit spicule-type bone formation. All individuals with sinusitis are Adults; two are males and one is probably female.

Reactions within sinuses were evaluated only in individuals whose maxillary bones were broken, so it is not possible to calculate an accurate frequency of sinusitis within the population. The frequency appears to be fairly high, however, in agreement with reports that respiratory infections were common in Highland Guatemala during the fifteenth century (Goff 1953a). Many upper respiratory tract infections are viral and are contracted by droplet infection, but poor housing and general health, drying winds, cold, overcrowding, high population density, smoke and underventilation, and overheating all contribute to development of sinusitis (Boocock et al. 1995). For Medieval British skeletal populations whose maxillary sinuses were studied through endoscopy, frequencies were 39% for a rural cemetery and 55% for an urban cemetery (Lewis et al. 1995).

An Adult female has spicule-type bone formation associated with the suture between the palatine and maxilla but no visible sinus involvement. Although it has the same characteristics as abnormal bone appearing in sinuses, its location means it is not evidence of sinusitis per

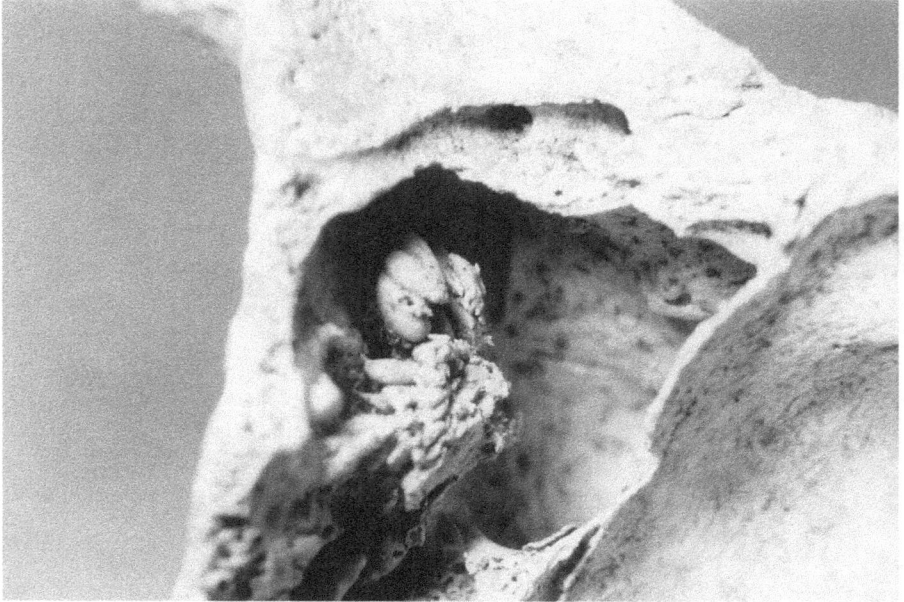

Fig. 10.11. Exuberant Bony Growth in Sinus of Maxilla 229#2

se. A reaction closely resembling a standard periosteal reaction appears within the nasal passage and on the outer surface of a left maxilla near the nasal aperture of a Young Adult. A possible cause is syphilis (Ortner and Putschar 1985: 208), although the reaction may be related to a heterotopic right maxillary canine which projects through the maxilla near the midline below the nasal passage (see discussion below).

Frequencies of periosteal reactions on cranial bones with more than 50% of various surfaces preserved are presented in figure 10.12. The highest frequency of lesions occurs on the right parietal ectocranial surface (13.3%). In comparison, the frequency of cranial periosteal reactions in Postclassic samples from other sites varies from 25.0% to 50.0% (table 10.4). The frequency of ectocranial periosteal reactions at Iximché is similar to the frequency in adults from a deposit of skulls at Terminal Classic Colha that has some similarities to the deposit of 48 crania at Iximché. As with porotic hyperostosis, the population that is the most comparable to Iximché in frequency of cranial periosteal reactions is from Classic Copán because the same observer studied both samples. One cannot, however, automatically equate the higher frequency of cranial periosteal reactions at Iximché with poorer health, because there are inherent paradoxes in interpretation of lesions on skeletons, which Wood et al. (1992) treated at length. The higher frequency at Iximché may actually reflect a robust population composed of individuals who survived infections long enough for lesions to mark their bones, in contrast to individuals at Copán who died quickly, before infections left marks on their bones.

Bony reactions were noted on 11 occipitals at muscle attachment areas. Such reactive bone is associated with use or overuse of muscles or

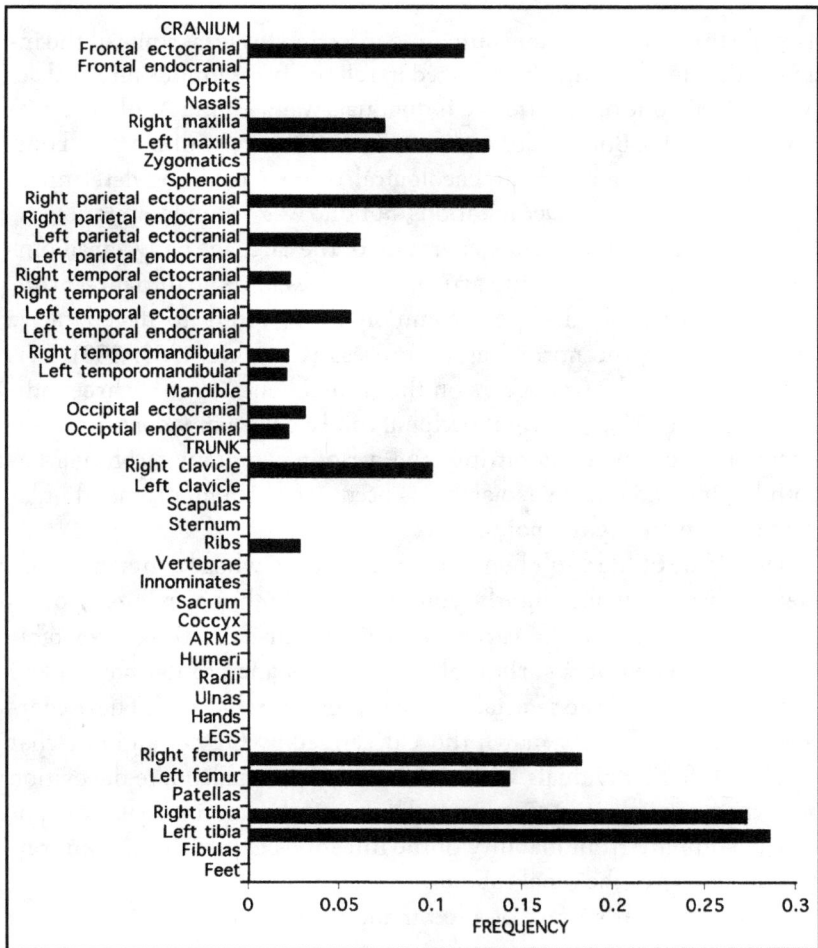

Fig. 10.12. Periosteal Reactions on Bones with More than 50% Preservation

Table 10.4. Cranial periosteal reactions in Maya skeletal series

Site	Period[1]	Cases	n	%	Notes	Source
Altar de Sacrificios	I–IV	5	14	35.7		Saul 1972
Altar de Sacrificios	II	2	3	66.7		Saul 1972
Copán	II–III	3	36	8.3	Ectocranium	Whittington 1989
Colha	III	3	20	15.0	Adult	Massey & Steele 1997
Playa del Carmen	IV	7	15	46.7	Maxilla (alveolus)	Márquez, Peraza, Gamboa, & Miranda 1982
Playa del Carmen	IV	6	12	50.0	Mandible (alveolus)	Márquez, Peraza, Gamboa, & Miranda 1982
Altar de Sacrificios	IV	1	4	25.0		Saul 1972

Notes. 1. I = Preclassic; II = Classic; III = Terminal Classic; IV = Postclassic

damage to connective tissue but not to infection. At least some of the individuals buried at Iximché engaged in relatively strenuous physical activities. Only one of the affected individuals was a Young Adult; the others were Adults. Both males and females had this type of reactive bone. Most of those for whom archaeological context could be determined came from deposits of Decapitations, but one was a Nondecapitation.

Arthritis is the gradual degeneration of the cartilage between adjoining bones in a joint, allowing articular surfaces to come into direct contact. Osteoarthritis, the most common form, refers to degenerative changes during the normal aging process (Ubelaker 1989: 108). Evidence of osteoarthritis appears on the cranial bones of only three individuals (fig. 10.13). One right occipital condyle has bony deposits, a left mandibular condyle has pitting, and a right mandibular condyle has both lipping and pitting. No arthritis occurs in the temporomandibular joint surface on any temporal.

The diploë of the vault bones of one Subadult, whose dental development indicates an age slightly younger than 15, has a spongy appearance. In cross section the parietals have an unusually thin outer table (fig. 10.14). The outer surface of the parietals and frontal have many pinprick holes, and the sagittal suture is prematurely fused. These characteristics most closely match those described by Ortner and Putschar (1985: 28) for individuals with osteomalacia, or inadequate deposition of calcium or vitamin D. Osteomalacia can result from inadequate exposure to sunlight, from inability of the intestines to resorb, or from congenital defects of the renal tubules.

On the interior surface of a left mandibular ramus is a well-defined .7 cm × .1 cm brown bony lump overlying the normal cortex. It appears

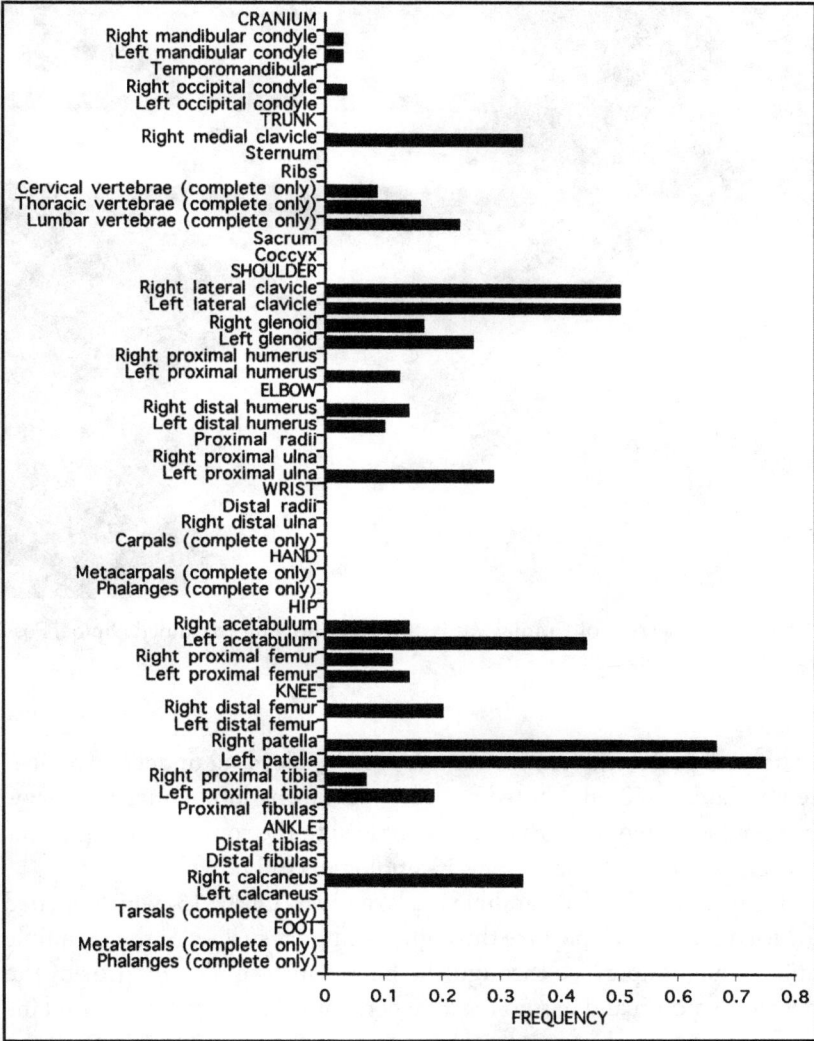

Fig. 10.13. Arthritis on Articulations with More than 50% Preservation. Data for IX-1, GU, and JI were deleted from calculation of frequencies owing to errors in recording. Frequency for ribs could not be calculated because state of preservation was not recorded for articulations

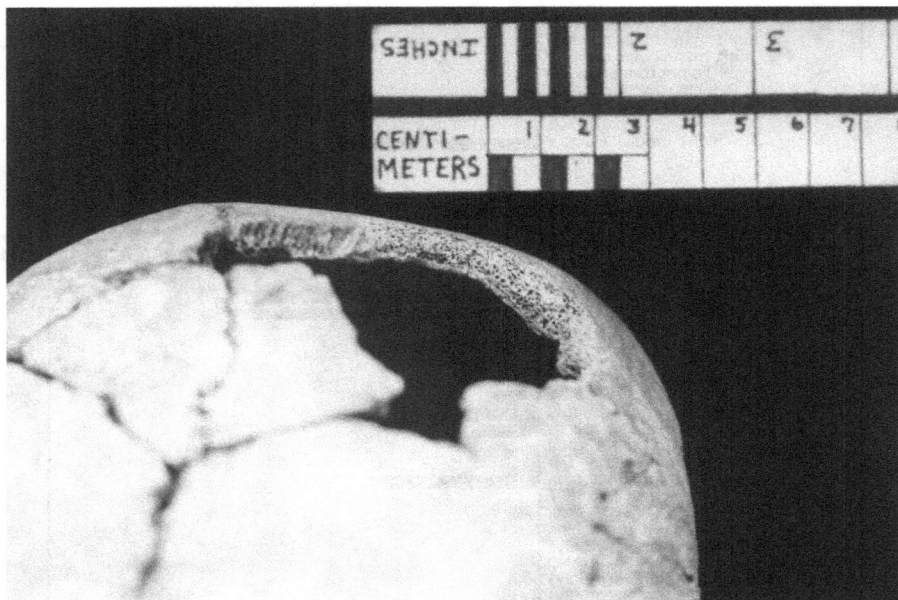

Fig. 10.14. Cross Section of Cranial Vault of IX-44 Showing Expanded Diploë, Possibly Associated with Osteomalacia

to be a subperiosteal hemorrhage, caused by bleeding under the periosteum. Saul (1972) attributed such lesions on the long bones to scurvy, but the location of this lesion does not lead to the conclusion that it was caused by vitamin C deficiency. Its etiology is unknown.

In the left body of a mandible is a large cyst (fig. 10.15) which opened a 2.6-cm × 1.4-cm aperture through the lingual surface of the mandible and a smaller aperture through the buccal surface. The interior of the defect is smooth and has no reactive bone or sharp edges that would indicate rapid growth. A small secondary cyst posterior to the first is .6 cm in diameter. These may be unicameral bone cysts, benign, tumorlike lesions that tend to be located below the nerve canal when they occur in the mandible (Ortner and Putschar 1985: 437).

The ectocranial surface of a right parietal has a 3.9-cm × 2.8-cm area of large lumps with rough, undulating, ivorylike surfaces rising above the surrounding normal bone. The lumps are probably button osteomas, benign border-line-neoplastic lesions (Ortner and Putschar 1985: 368).

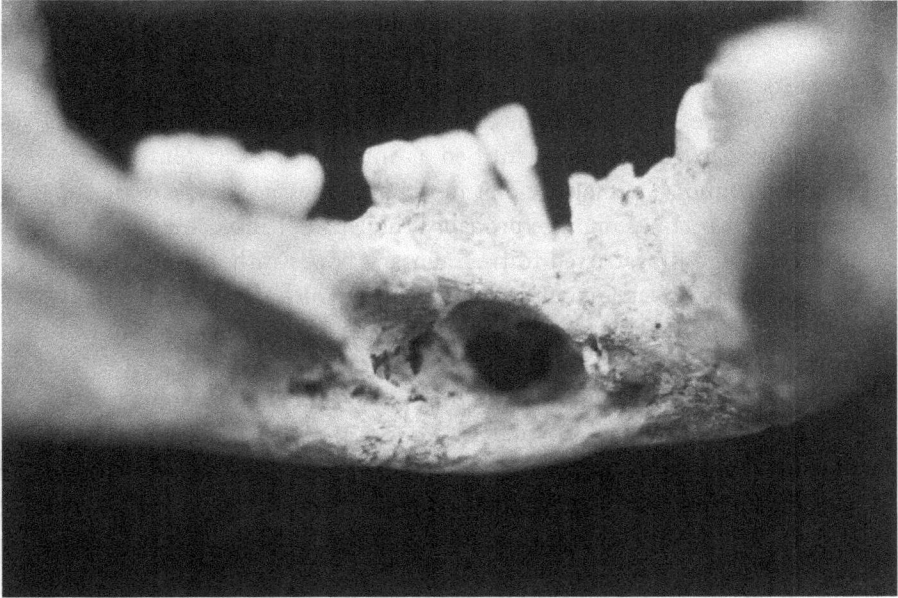

Fig. 10.15. Lingual View of Mandible No. 1 from Bag Marked "Str. 45" Showing Possible Unicameral Bone Cyst

Small lumps with smooth surfaces slightly raised above the surrounding cortex and generally ranging in diameter from 15 mm to 40 mm were noted individually or in groups of two or three on various bones. They appear on the ectocranial surface of four frontals, one right parietal, one left temporal, and one occipital; the endocranial surface of three left temporals and one occipital; the left ramus of one mandible, the left bodies of two mandibles, and the right bodies of two mandibles; the right orbital surface of a frontal; and a sphenoid. When located on the cortex they probably represent insignificant variations in bone architecture. However, similar lumps on the right condyle of a mandible and in the sinus of a right maxilla may be associated with arthritis or sinusitis.

Congenital and Developmental Anomalies

Congenital and developmental anomalies occur in a few crania. Three individuals have deviated nasal septums and another has the left temporal and parietal fused.

Postmortem Modification of Cranial Bones

Rodents and insects damaged various cranial bones. Shallow, parallel grooves in the surface of bones, generally located where adjacent surfaces form an edge, were identified as marks left by rodent incisors. Shallow, round, cup-shaped holes in the outer surface of the cortex appear on a few bones and are probably the work of insects. Rodent and insect damage is restricted to fragmentary bones rather than to those still relatively intact. Given the conditions to which the bones were subjected after excavation, the damage may have occurred while they were in storage.

In some cases bones have been burned. Part of the temporal and occipital of one individual, a Nondecapitation, are burned black. The body of a mandible from another individual is also partially burned. The significance of the burning, which occurred at low temperature, is unknown. It is possible that it somehow occurred after Guillemin had excavated the bones.

Individuals were occasionally buried with pieces of copper jewelry which, after the flesh had decomposed, left green stains on the bones with which they came in contact. Stains on two left parietals, a left temporal, and the inside surface of a left mandible were probably caused by copper earrings. In some cases, copper stains aided in tying skeletal remains to burial descriptions in Guillemin's field notes.

A cut, drilled, and polished fragmentary bracelet found on the right arm of Burial 27-A/IV was made of what may be a human occipital. This artifact may represent a trophy taken from the body of an enemy.

Paleopathological Analysis of the Dentition

See appendix D for a list of dentitions and their archaeological context, age, sex, and paleopathology.

Trauma

Figure 10.16 shows the mean amount of occlusal surface wear (fig. 10.17) for all permanent teeth according to the Molnar (1971) 1 to 6 scale. The mean amount of wear on this scale is 2.54. Patterson (1984: 183, 225, 269) reported figures of 2.38 to 3.55 for three Ontario populations, although he used a modified Molnar system and figures are not perfectly comparable. Degree of wear is greater near the front of the mouth, undoubtedly reflecting the smaller occlusal surface area of the anterior teeth. Fine grit left in food from the process of grinding maize with stones probably was responsible for the degree of wear recorded.

Larger pieces of grit, small stones, or other hard materials must also have entered the mouth, since small chips and other types of ante-mortem damage to the teeth are quite common (fig. 10.17). Ante-mortem damage was identified as chips and fractures in the enamel which show clear evidence of post-traumatic wear on the edges of the damage. Overall, 32.8% of all permanent teeth have at least one chip caused by antemortem trauma. For comparison, see Milner and Larsen's (1991: 368–369) table of trauma in archaeological populations from the U.S. and Canada. The rate in permanent teeth in eight populations ranged from 4.5% to 49.2%, with a mean of 19.6% and a median of 22.2%. Clearly, the amount of chipping at Iximché is above average. Trauma frequency is slightly higher in molars than in other teeth (fig. 10.18), and the pattern generally is similar to the pattern for wear.

Cultural Modification

In 19 mandibles, 16 from individuals assigned IX numbers and 3 from loose mandibles, one or more mandibular incisors or canines exhibit polishing of the labial surface (fig. 10.19; table 10.5). Architectural features and enamel defects normally visible on the labial surface have

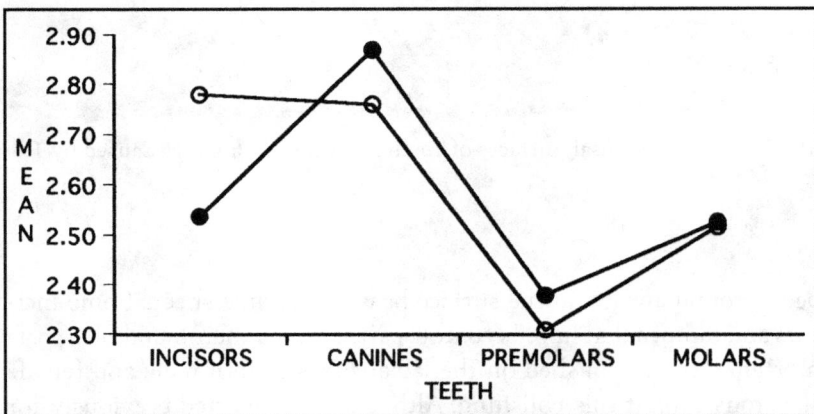

Fig. 10.16. Mean Amounts of Wear on Tooth Classes at Iximché on Molnar Scale. Solid circles represent maxillary teeth; open circles represent mandibular teeth

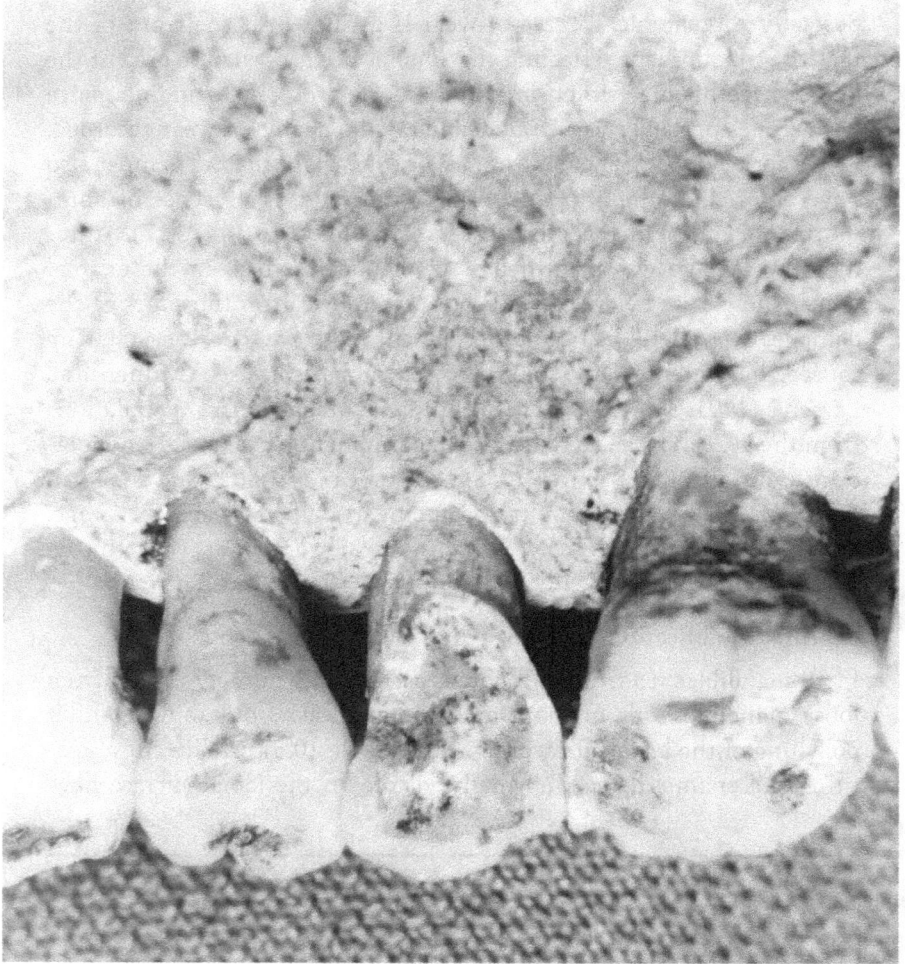

Fig. 10.17. Wear of Occlusal Surfaces of Teeth and Chips in Enamel Caused by Trauma in Right Maxilla of IX–55

been ground away, and the surface has a mirrorlike sheen. Some incisors and canines that have become separated from their mandibles postmortem also are polished on the labial surface. Both male and female skeletons exhibit this polishing. Although not reported previously for the Maya, similar polishing caused by use of lip plugs has been reported for adult dentitions from a Rupert Harbour, British Columbia, skeletal series (Milner and Larsen, 1991: 370). No labrets were excavated at Ix-

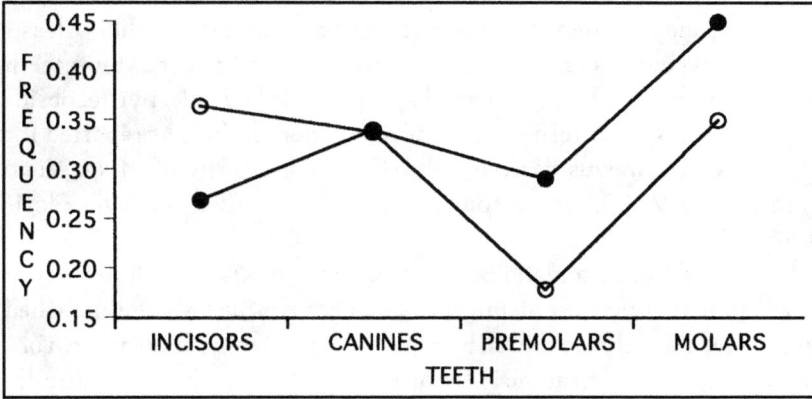

Fig. 10.18. Frequencies of Trauma for Tooth Classes at Iximché. Solid circles represent maxillary teeth and open circles, mandibular teeth

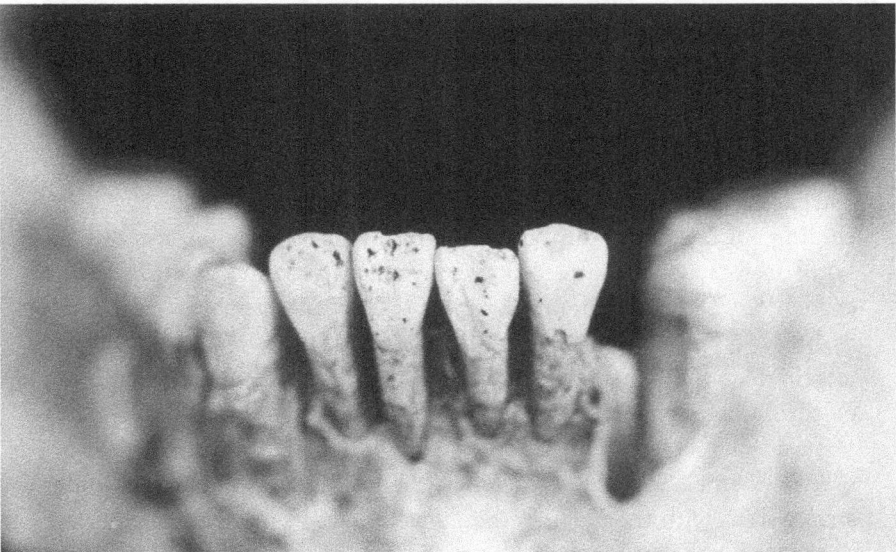

Fig. 10.19. Polishing of Labial Surfaces of Mandibular Incisors of IX-45 Caused by Labret

imché, but Carmack (1981: 262) reported an amber labret from a burial excavated at Utatlán, the Quiché capital. Perhaps significantly, all of the Iximché individuals with incisor or canine polishing whose type of burial can be determined are Decapitations or Possible Decapitations, and none are Nondecapitations. Decapitations with incisor or canine polishing may represent high-status Quiché captives. Unlike Classic period Lowland Maya, the skeletons from Iximché never exhibit teeth artificially modified with either filed edges or inlaid jade, pyrite, obsidian, or coral. The pattern at Iximché also differs from that reported for the contemporaneous Eastern Cakchiquel (Akajal) site of Mixco Viejo (Jilotepeque Viejo), where some teeth had been filed (Gervais-Cloris 1985–1986).

One loose tooth, a mandibular premolar, exhibits an additional type of cultural modification, an interproximal groove. Such shallow polished grooves apparently are caused by repeatedly inserting a hard pointed object between the teeth at the junction between the crown and root to alleviate discomfort related to caries or periodontal disease (Ubelaker 1989: 100), both of which were present at Iximché (see discussion below).

Diseases

Enamel hypoplasias are defects in the dental enamel which can be caused by systemic, local, or hereditary factors. Those of systemic origin are termed "chronologic" because they are found as horizontal features in the areas of the teeth where enamel was formed during the metabolic disturbance. They are nonspecific stress indicators which reflect episodes of severe metabolic upset (Sarnat and Schour 1941, 1942), including episodes caused by nutrition or disease (El-Najjar et al. 1978). Local factors usually affect single teeth and have no relation to the chronology of development. Hereditary factors affect enamel of all teeth as diffuse or vertical anomalies (El-Najjar et al. 1978; Yaeger 1980).

Nineteen individuals were studied for the presence and distribution of chronologic enamel hypoplasias (fig. 10.20). For this analysis, hypoplasic enamel was defined as a visibly depressed transverse line or region of enamel. Some areas of deficient enamel were visible only under strong light with the help of a hand-held magnifying lens. These were not scored, under the assumption that they resulted from minor, unimportant stress episodes. No other attempt was made to differentiate the degree of severity of the stresses which caused defects.

The enamel of the mandibular permanent lateral incisors, canines, and second premolars was evaluated for hypoplasias. Presence of hypoplastic enamel in these teeth indicates that serious stress occurred sometime during the first seven years of life, when the enamel is forming. These particular teeth were chosen because of their known susceptibility to defect formation. Some researchers prefer the maxillary central incisors to the mandibular lateral incisors, but looking only at

Table 10.5. Age, sex, and archaeological context for Iximché mandibles with labret polishing of anterior teeth

	Decapitation			Possible Decapitation			Possible Nondecapitation			Nondecapitation			Unknown		
	Adult	Young Adult	Sub-adult	Adult	Young Adult	Sub-adult	Adult	Young Adult	Sub-adult	Adult	Young Adult	Sub-adult	Adult	Young Adult	Sub-adult
Male	2	1	0	1	0	0	0	0	0	0	0	0	0	0	0
Male?	3	2	0	1	0	0	0	0	0	0	0	0	0	0	0
Female?	0	2	0	0	0	0	0	0	0	0	0	0	0	0	0
Female	1	1	0	0	0	0	0	0	0	0	0	0	3	0	0
Unknown	1	0	0	1	0	0	0	0	0	0	0	0	0	0	0

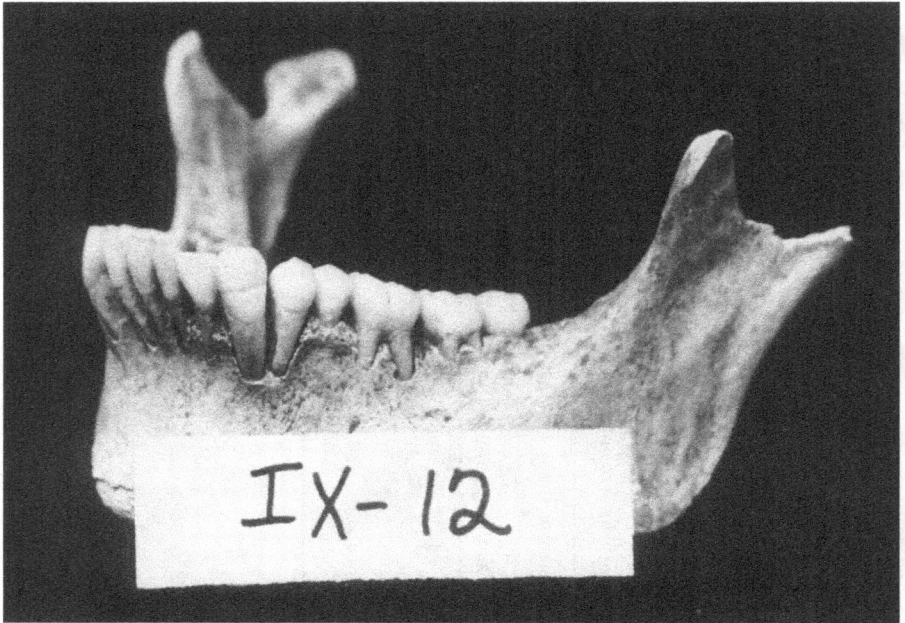

Fig. 10.20. Transverse Linear Enamel Hypoplasia on Left Mandibular Canine of IX-12

mandibular teeth made it more likely that all six teeth belonging to an individual would be found, since mandibles and maxillas could not always be matched at Iximché.

Needle-nosed calipers were used to measure the distance in tenths of millimeters from the cemento-enamel junction to the center of acute hypoplasias or to the upper and lower margins of chronic or continuous hypoplasias. Ensor and Irish (1995: 508) defined acute hypoplasias as thin transverse grooves resulting from acute stress episodes and chronic hypoplasias as incompletely formed enamel over a large portion of the crown surface caused by longer durations of stress than the acute variety. Occasionally, acute hypoplasias appeared as wide grooves, and they were recorded in the same manner as chronic hypoplasias. The crown height of each tooth was also measured to control for differences in amount of wear between individuals and between teeth.

Sections of enamel formed during six-month periods were scored for defects. Goodman et al. (1980) presented an enamel mineralization diagram for determining when a particular section of enamel was formed for any tooth. Maya teeth have considerably higher crown heights than the population on which Goodman et al. based their diagram, so unworn or very slightly worn crowns from Classic Copán were measured and used as the basis for a table specific to the Maya (Whittington 1992). This table was applied to teeth from Iximché. A section was scored as having a defect if any part of one entered it. However, a section which lacked 50% or more of its enamel owing to breakage or wear was not scored.

A distribution of ages at which defects occurred was created for each individual. If two or more enamel sections formed during a given six-month period on different teeth had transverse hypoplasias, then the period was scored as positive, since such a pattern of defects indicates stress-related etiology rather than local or hereditary etiology. It was scored as negative if at least two enamel sections were present and no more than one had a linear defect. It was not scored if fewer than two enamel sections were present.

Hypoplasias are present in 89% of the sample of 19 individuals, suggesting most children were exposed to severe stresses during their first seven years of life. This high frequency is similar to that observed in other ancient Maya samples, including some close in time to Iximché: Seibal, Tancah, Tipu, and Sarteneja (table 10.6). An average of 29% of enamel sections have defects. The frequency of defects is highest in enamel formed between 4 and 4.9 years of age (fig. 10.21). At least one serious episode of stress was experienced during that period of life by 58% of the individuals studied. This pattern is similar to that reported for other ancient Maya populations, including Altar de Sacrificios (Saul 1972) and Tipu (Cohen et al. 1997). Saul (1972) attributed the peak in defects around this age to stresses associated with weaning. Other researchers (Judkins and Baker 1996; Katzenberg et al. 1996) have asserted that hypoplasias do not reflect weaning age well. Recent studies of stable isotopes in teeth and bones from Maya sites, however, support a late weaning age. Children were breast-fed until at least 3 or 4 years of age and as late as 6 years of age at Kaminaljuyú and Altun Ha (White et al. 2001; Wright and Schwarcz 1998, 1999).

Figure 10.22 shows the frequency of dental caries in all permanent teeth from Iximché, including those found loose and not associated with jaws. In general, frequency increases with distance from the front of the mouth, and mandibular teeth are more likely to be carious than are maxillary teeth. Overall, 8.5% of the teeth exhibit caries (fig. 10.23). Compared to samples from seven Maya sites from various time periods,

Table 10.6. Enamel Hypoplasia in Maya Skeletal Series

Site	Period[1]	Cases	n	%	Notes	Source
Cuello	I			59.0		Saul & Saul 1997
Pasión	I–III	33	88	37.5	Maxillary central incisor	Wright 1997
Pasión	I–III	51	107	47.7	Maxillary canine	Wright 1997
Pasión	I–III	59	100	59.0	Mandibular canine	Wright 1997
Caracol	I–III			16.0		Chase 1997
Tayasal	I–IV	1	59	1.7		Chase 1997
Seibal	I–IV	36	39	92.3	Adults	Saul 1973
Altar de Sacrificios	I–IV	37	40	92.5	Adults	Saul 1972
Xcan	II	1	7	14.3	Mandibles	Márquez, Benavides, & Schmidt 1982
Xcan	II	3	8	37.5	Maxillas	Márquez, Benavides, & Schmidt 1982
Copán	II–III	19	19	100.0	Mandibles	Whittington 1992
Lubaantun	II	19	24	79.2	Minimum estimate	Saul 1977
Colha	III	2	9	22.2	Subadults	Massey & Steele 1997
Colha	III	7	20	35.0	Adults	Massey & Steele 1997
Pasión	III	16	40	40.0	Maxillary central incisor	Wright 1997
Pasión	III	23	44	52.3	Maxillary canine	Wright 1997
Pasión	III	30	45	66.7	Mandibular canine	Wright 1997
Altar de Sacrificios	IV	6	16	37.5	Minimum estimate	Saul 1972
Cozumel	IV	0	88	0.0		Peña 1985
Seibal	IV	19	21	90.5	Adults	Saul 1973
Tancah	V	10	11	90.9		Saul 1982
Tipu	V	100	105	95.2		Cohen et al. 1997
Sarteneja	V			100.0		G. E. Kennedy 1983

Notes. 1. I = Preclassic, II = Classic, III = Terminal Classic, IV = Postclassic, V = Historic

the frequency of caries at Iximché is lower than the rates at all but two (table 10.7). Compared to 14 archaeological sites in Ontario studied by Patterson (1984: 313), Iximché's caries rate is most similar to the rates for five populations relying on hunting and gathering, which range from 0% to 7.7%, and is lower than the 10.8% rate for one horticultural population relying to a fair degree on hunting and gathering or fishing. Compared to samples from Ohio sites studied by Schneider (1986), Iximché's rate is a little lower than the 9.7% rate for a population relying on a mixed subsistence base of meat, maize, beans, and nuts. However, before drawing conclusions about the implications of Iximché's low caries rate for Late Postclassic Highland subsistence, it is

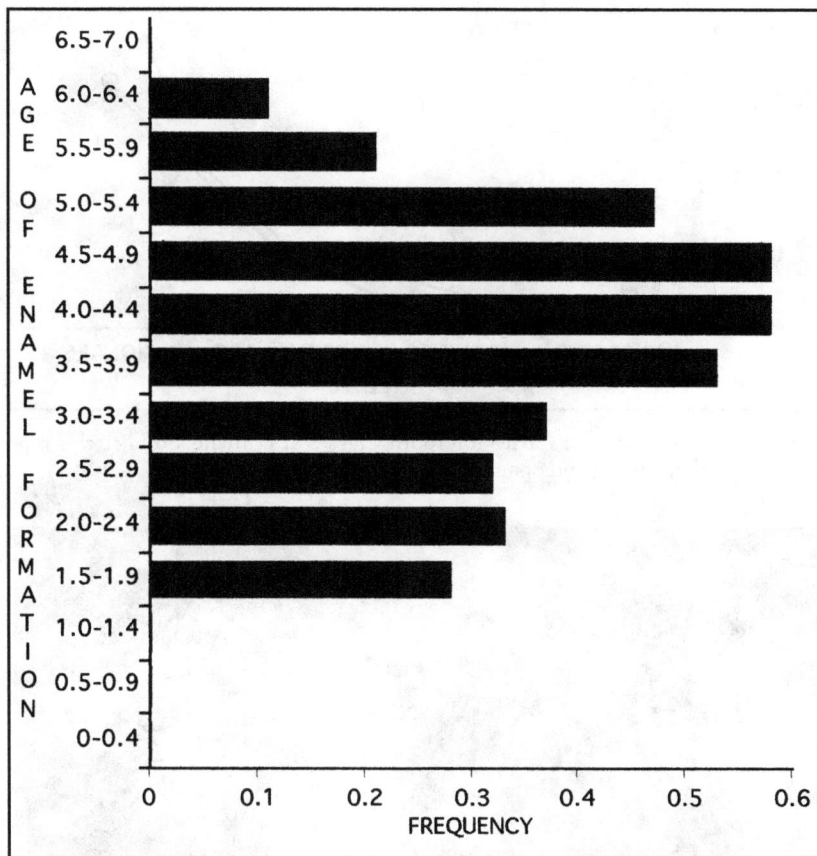

Fig. 10.21. Distribution of Enamel Hypoplasias by Age of Formation in 19 Individuals

important to note that a low caries frequency can be related to either a low proportion of carbohydrates in the diet or infrequent consumption of carbohydrates during the course of the day (Bibby 1961).

The frequency of antemortem loss (fig. 10.23) for permanent teeth associated with jaws is 3.4%, a calculation which does not include unerupted or congenitally absent teeth. This frequency is lower than that for two other Maya samples for which comparable data are available (table 10.7). The rate is lower than that found at any of seven Ontario sites studied by Patterson (1984: 308), including an 8.0% rate at a nonhorticultural site. Antemortem loss was age-dependent in the Maya population from Copán (Whittington 1999), so the low rate at Iximché may reflect the relatively large number of Young Adults. Comparing

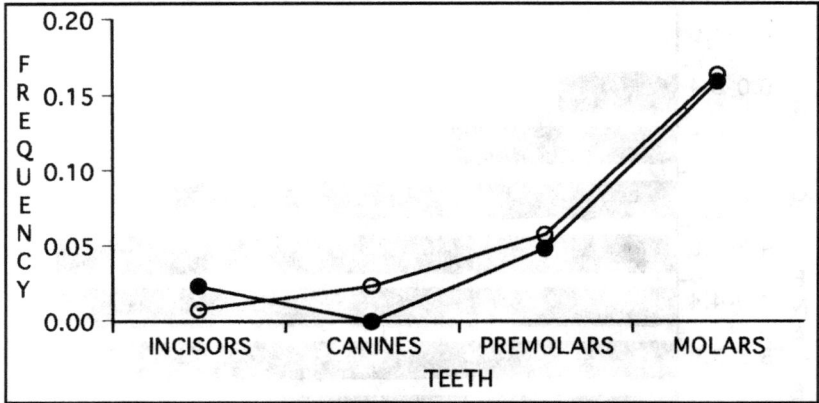

Fig. 10.22. Frequencies of Caries for Tooth Classes at Iximché. Solid circles represent maxillary teeth and open circles, mandibular teeth

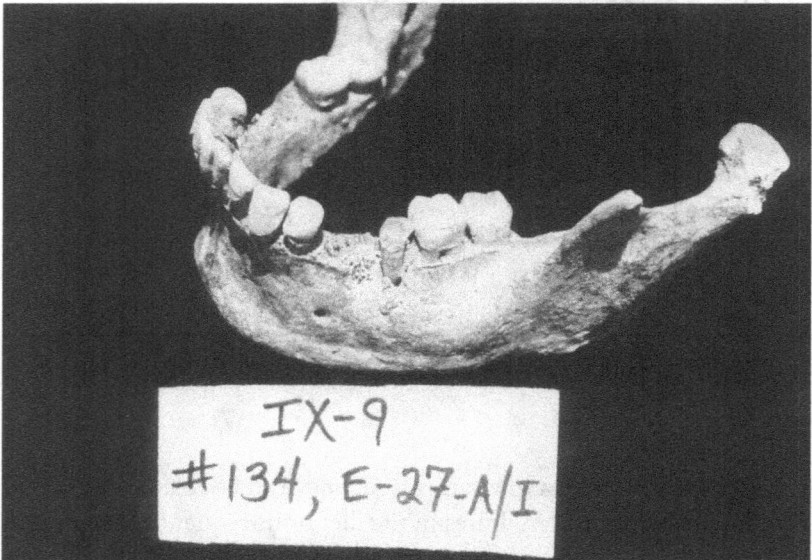

Fig. 10.23. Dental Caries, Antemortem Tooth Loss, Dental Calculus, and Alveolar Resorption in Mandible of IX-9

tooth classes, mandibular incisors stand out for their high frequency of loss. The general pattern is a high rate of loss for incisors, a low rate for canines, and then increasing rates toward the posterior of the mouth (fig. 10.24). Except for the incisors, loss is more common in the maxilla. This is at variance with the pattern found at seven Ontario sites studied

Table 10.7. Caries and Antemortem Loss in Maya Skeletal Series

Site	Period[1]	Caries, %		Loss, %		Notes	Source
		Teeth	Indiv.	Teeth	Indiv.		
Cuello	I	12.0		57.1			Saul & Saul 1997
Xcan	II		75.0			Maxillas	Márquez, Benavides, & Schmidt 1982
Xcan	II		28.6			Mandibles	Márquez, Benavides, & Schmidt 1982
Xcan	II		61.5				Márquez, Benavides, & Schmidt 1982
Lubaantun	II		71.4				Saul 1977
Tancah	II		60.0				Saul 1982
Copán	II–III	17.9	68.2	9.3	37.2	Permanent	Whittington 1999
Colha	III		75.0		55.0	Adults	Massey & Steele 1997
Colha	III		77.8			Juveniles	Massey & Steele 1997
Lamanai	III	1.8				Mean %	White 1997
Lamanai	IV	17.6				Mean %	White 1997
Playa del Carmen	IV		31.3			Maxillas	Márquez, Peraza, Gamboa, & Miranda 1982
Playa del Carmen	IV		38.5			Mandibles	Márquez, Peraza, Gamboa, & Miranda 1982
Altar de Sacrificios	IV		50.0		87.5	Minimum estimate (caries)	Saul 1972
Tayasal	IV	50.0				Mean of means	Evans 1973
Mayapán	IV		14.3		75.0		Fry 1956
Cozumel	IV		4.5				Peña 1985
Tancah	V		18.5			Minimum estimate	Saul 1982
Lamanai	V	20.5				Mean %	White 1997
Sarteneja	V	5.0		7.7			G. E. Kennedy 1983

Notes. 1. I = Preclassic, II = Classic, III = Terminal Classic, IV = Postclassic, V = Historic

by Patterson (1984: 308). Causes of loss may include periodontal disease and dental abscesses (see discussion below).

The amount of calculus, which is mineralized dental plaque (fig. 10.23), was recorded for all permanent teeth, using a scale of 0 to 4 developed by Evans (1973). The average amount at Iximché is .98. For comparison, an Early Postclassic Lowland Maya population from the Tayasal area had a value of 2.40 (Evans 1973). Research has shown that a soft diet enhances calculus formation, whereas a coarse diet reduces it; that the less a tooth is used in mastication, the heavier the calculus deposit; and that whatever factor predisposes individuals to calculus seems

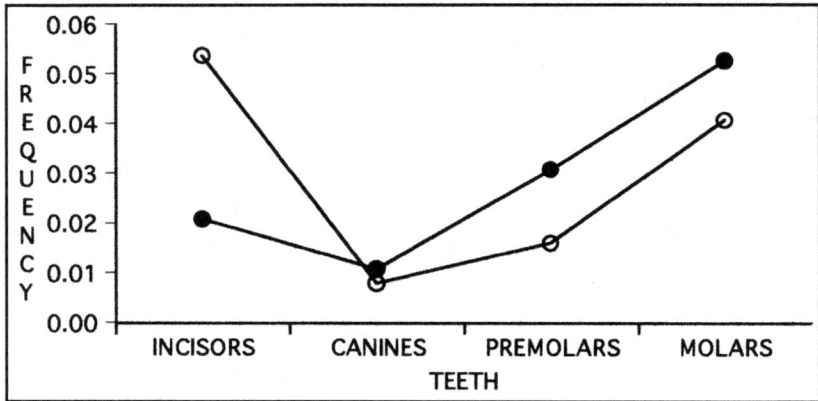

Fig. 10.24. Frequencies of Antemortem Loss for Tooth Classes at Iximché. Solid circles represent maxillary teeth and open circles, mandibular teeth

to inhibit caries (Evans 1973). In general, the amount of calculus on teeth at Iximché is inversely related to the frequency of caries. The amount of calculus decreases with increasing distance from the front of the mouth and is generally greater on mandibular teeth (fig. 10.25). Two of three Ontario populations studied by Patterson (1984: 292) also had more calculus on the mandibular teeth than on the maxillary teeth.

Irritation of gums by calculus is one cause of resorption of alveolar bone around teeth (fig. 10.23), or periodontal disease, which was found to various degrees in virtually 100% of the individuals (fig. 10.26). This rate is somewhat higher than has been reported for any other Maya site (table 10.8), but may partly reflect the different way resorption was recorded at Iximché. The amount of resorption was recorded as the distance between the cemento-enamel junction and the alveolar margin on the buccal side of the tooth. Measurements were taken with needle-nosed calipers in tenths of millimeters for all teeth in sockets where the alveolus was intact. The mean amount of resorption at Iximché is 2.30 mm. Resorption decreases with increasing distance from the front of the mouth, following the pattern seen for calculus. Resorption is greater in the mandible than in the maxilla. At three Ontario sites studied by Patterson (1984: 174, 217, 260), mandibular resorption also was greater than maxillary resorption.

Two types of dental abscesses with different etiologies are periapical and alveolar abscesses. Periapical abscesses (fig. 10.27), located in the bone of the jaw near root tips, generally result from infection arising

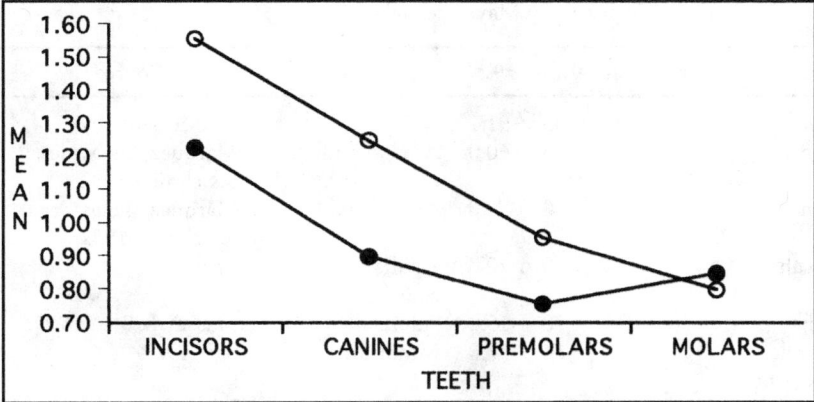

Fig. 10.25. Mean Amounts of Calculus for Tooth Classes at Iximché on the Evans Scale. Solid circles represent maxillary teeth and open circles, mandibular teeth

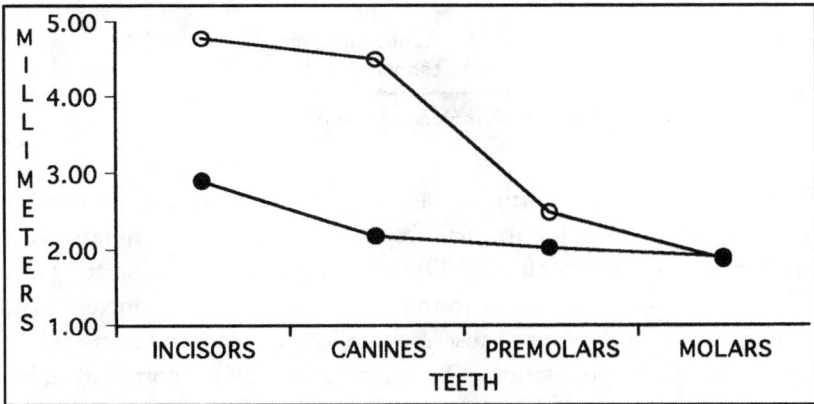

Fig. 10.26. Mean Amounts of Alveolar Resorption for Tooth Classes at Iximché (in mm). Solid circles represent maxillary teeth and open circles, mandibular teeth

from tooth pulp exposure by caries or heavy wear. Alveolar abscesses (fig. 10.28) generally represent pockets of pus within the bone immediately beneath gums affected by periodontal disease. No locations of unerupted or congenitally absent teeth are included in the calculation of frequencies of alveolar and periapical abscesses at tooth locations in the bone of the jaws. The overall frequency of alveolar abscesses is 1.3% and of periapical abscesses, 1.0%. No abscesses are associated with tooth locations of canines. At other locations frequency increases as distance

Table 10.8. Periodontal disease in Maya skeletal series

Site	Period[1]	n	Cases	%	Notes	Source
Cuello	I	41	45	91.1		Saul & Saul 1997
Xcan	II	3	5	60.0	Adult mandibles	Márquez, Benavides, & Schmidt 1982
Xcan	II	7	10	70.0	Adult maxillas	Márquez, Benavides, & Schmidt 1982
Tancah	II	4	10	40.0	Adults minimum estimate	Saul 1982
Colha	III	3	20	15.0	Adults	Massey & Steele 1997
Altar de Sacrificios	IV	10	16	77.0	Minimum estimate	Saul 1972
Playa del Carmen	IV	14	16	87.5	Mandibles	Márquez, Peraza, Gamboa, & Miranda 1982
Playa del Carmen	IV	15	17	88.2	Maxillas	Márquez, Peraza, Gamboa, & Miranda 1982
Mayapán	IV	5	7	71.4	Alveolar border resorption	Fry 1956
Tancah	V	6	18	33.3	Adults minimum estimate	Saul 1982

Notes. 1. I = Preclassic, II = Classic, III = Terminal Classic, IV = Postclassic, V = Historic

from the front of the mouth increases, and abscesses are more common in the maxilla, except for alveolar abscesses in mandibular molars, with the highest frequency (fig. 10.29). In general, the patterns for both types of abscesses are similar to those for caries and antemortem loss.

The rates of both types of abscesses are lower than for Ontario populations. For three populations, Patterson (1984: 296) reported alveolar abscess rates of 10.0% to 24.7%, with higher rates in the mandible. Periapical rates for seven populations ranged from 4.7% to 14.1% (Patterson 1984: 315), five of which had higher rates in the maxilla, as at Iximché. The low frequency of periapical abscesses at Iximché is probably related to the low frequency of caries.

Maxillary tori occur on the lingual surface of the alveolus of two maxillas. Tori, characterized by series of well-defined lumps of bone with smooth surfaces and diameters of approximately 19 mm, are bony reactions believed to reflect high levels of masticatory stress (Roberts and Manchester 1995: 54).

Correlations of Pathological Dental Traits

Table 10.9 presents the Pearson coefficients of correlation for various dental traits. Calculations involve only teeth associated with jaws.

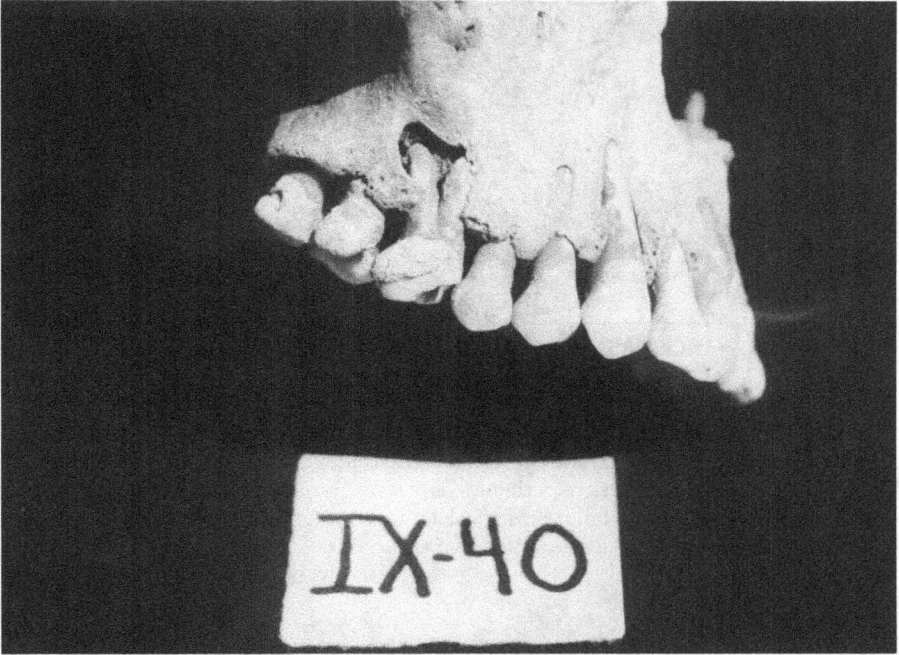

Fig. 10.27. Periapical Abscess in Right Maxilla of IX-40

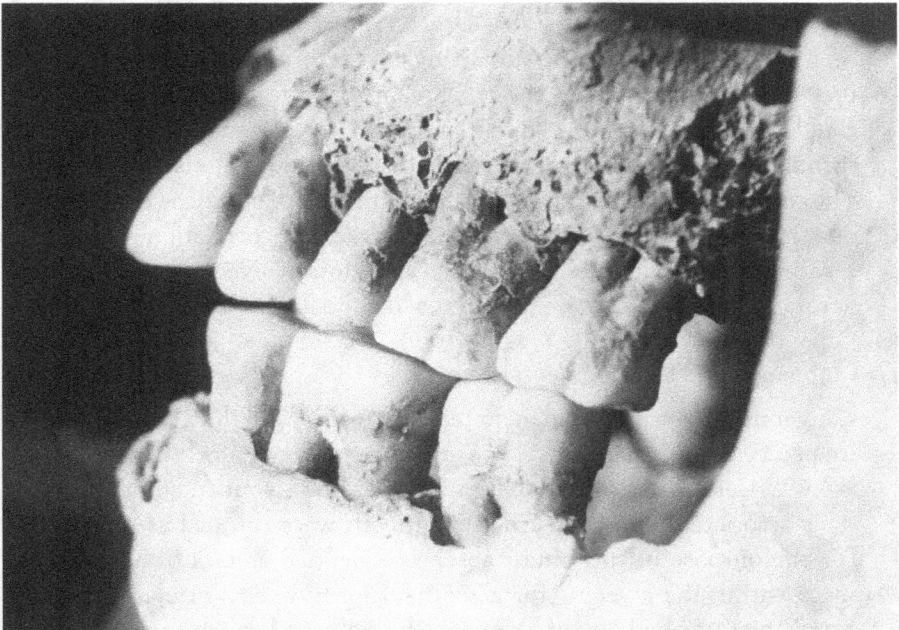

Fig. 10.28. Alveolar Abscesses around Mandibular Molar Roots of IX-27

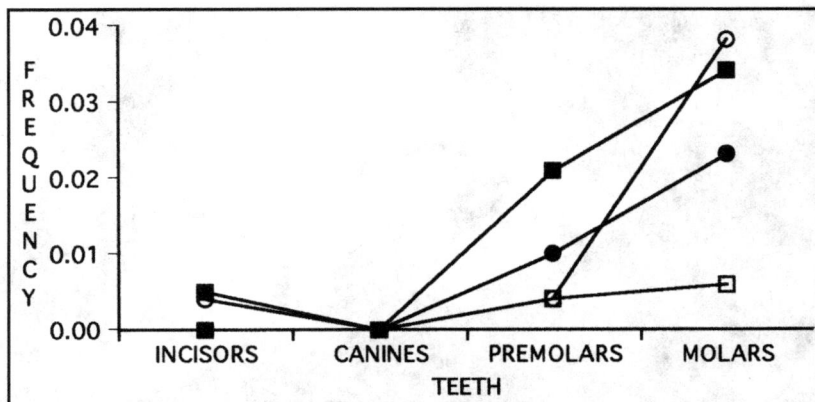

Fig. 10.29. Frequencies for Abscesses for Tooth Classes at Iximché. Solid shapes represent maxillary teeth and open shapes, mandibular teeth. Circles are alveolar abscesses and squares are periapical abscesses. Symbols for maxillary alveolar abscesses and mandibular periapical abscesses overlap for incisors and produce what appears to be a solid square on the x-axis

Correlations having statistical significance at the .05 level (Bonferroni-adjusted probability; Wilkinson et al. 1992) within the matrix of dental traits are between mean amount of wear and mean amount of trauma; between mean amount of alveolar resorption and mean amount of wear; and between mean amount of alveolar resorption and mean number of teeth lost antemortem. The correlation between wear and trauma could reflect use of poor quality grinding stones which crumbled through time and left particles larger than grit in otherwise soft food. The correlation between alveolar resorption and wear may be the result of a third variable which influenced them: age. The correlation between resorption and antemortem loss is logical, as loss of alveolar bone would naturally loosen teeth and increase the likelihood of loss.

Congenital and Developmental Anomalies

Congenital absence of permanent teeth is restricted to third molars. The frequency for the maxilla is 3.9%, and the frequency for the mandible is 4.6%. Calculation of frequencies includes only teeth and tooth locations associated with jaws. Unerupted teeth were counted as present. For the purpose of this study, absence is defined as lack of adequate space within the alveolus for a tooth to form or lack of evidence of a tooth within the bone of a jaw which had been broken through the

Table 10.9. Pearson correlation matrix for dental traits

	Alveolar Abscess	Periapical Abscess	Caries	Trauma	Calculus	Wear	Loss	Resorption	Hypoplasia
Alveolar Abs.	1.00								
Periapical Abs.	.08	1.00							
Caries	.09	.11	1.00						
Trauma	.25	.01	.16	1.00					
Calculus	.21	.16	-.01	.25	1.00				
Wear	.32	.15	.02	.41*	.27	1.00			
Loss	.29	.12	.29	.00	.16	.30	1.00		
Resorption	.36	.01	.25	.06	.34	.52*	.82*	1.00	
Hypoplasia	.10	.11	-.16	-.09	-.15	.34	.06	.04	1.00

* $p < .05$.

normal tooth location. Evaluations were based on visual inspection only and were not confirmed through X-rays.

Other dental anomalies are an individual with a supernumerary maxillary incisor, an unerupted maxillary right central incisor, and a deformed maxillary left central incisor (fig. 10.30); five individuals with peg-shaped teeth (two maxillary right lateral incisors, one mandibular right lateral incisor, one maxillary premolar, one maxillary left third molar); and one individual with a barrel-shaped upper incisor. Four individuals retained one or more deciduous teeth or roots past the age at which they normally are lost (one maxillary right first molar, both maxillary canines, one maxillary right second molar, one maxillary molar root). The individual who retained the deciduous maxillary right first molar also had a heterotopic permanent right maxillary canine.

Number of Individuals Represented by Postcranial Elements

Postcranial elements which still form units, either because they articulate or because they come from opposite sides of the body but match in terms of preservation, surface color, size, morphology, robusticity, and degree of epiphyseal union, were assigned two-letter designations, unless they were found bagged with cranial elements having an IX designation. Relatively complete single postcranial bones which are independent of groupings were also assigned two-letter designations. Small postcranial fragments are identified by the bag in which they were found. (See appendix E for a list of postcranial remains and their archaeological context, age, sex, and paleopathology.)

It is possible to estimate the number of postcranial skeletons by counting individual elements with more than 50% of their structure present, regardless of their membership in groupings. Not surprisingly, the larger long bones were the most frequently identified and counted. The most common element is the shaft of the left femur, counted 26 times. The next most common element is the shaft of the right tibia, counted 20 times. Except for cervical vertebrae found with 22 decapitated crania, it generally is not possible to match cranial with postcranial material.

Archaeological Context of Postcranial Bones

Cervical vertebrae accompanied the crania of 10 of the 17 confirmed Decapitations. The majority came from the group of 48 decapitated

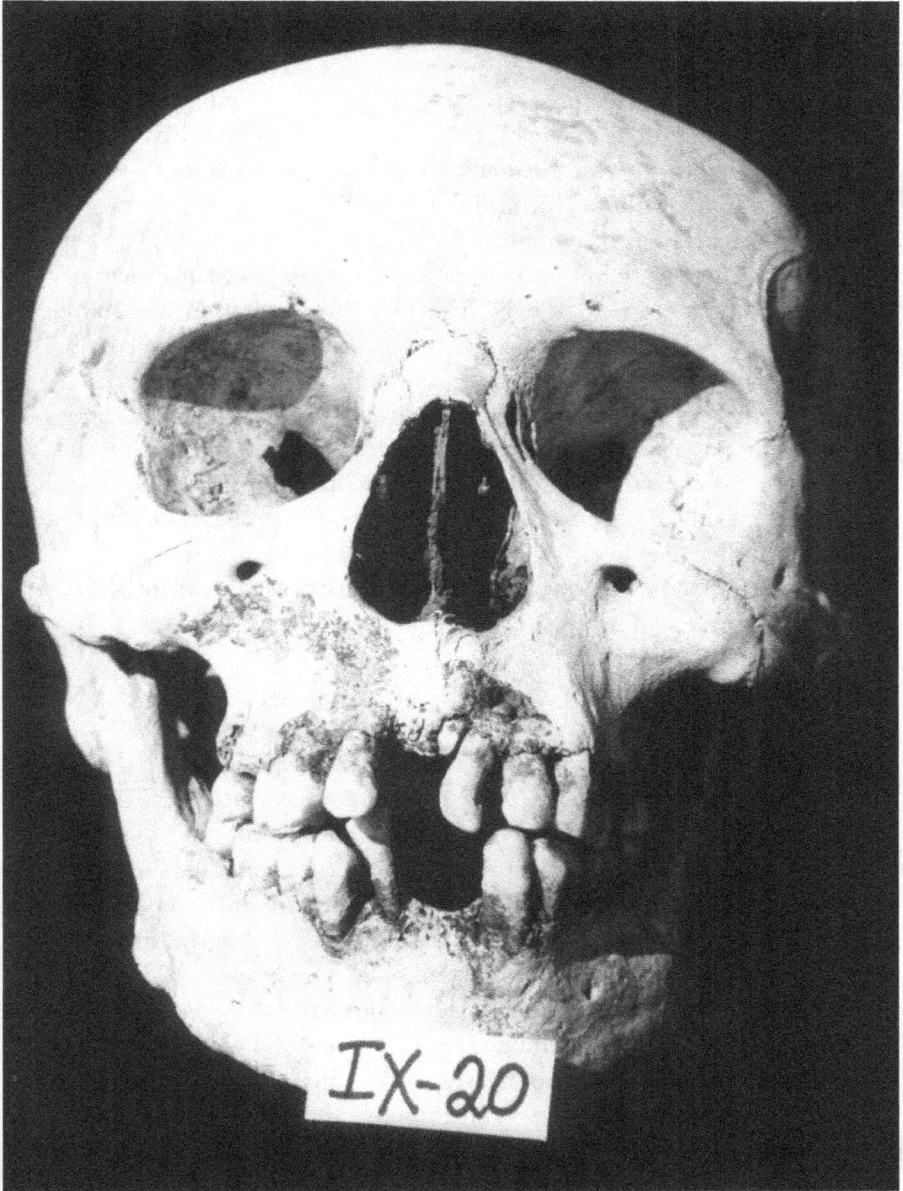

Fig. 10.30. Maxillas of IX-20 have Supernumerary Incisor, Unerupted Incisor, and Deformed Incisor

crania deposited together adjacent to Structure 104 in Plaza C (see discussion above).

Postcranial bones were associated with 7 of the 14 crania identified as Possible Decapitations. In six cases, just cervical vertebrae accompanied the crania, but in one case, the majority of a postcranial skeleton was associated with a cranium which exhibited decapitation damage.

Three postcranial skeletons are Possible Nondecapitations. They apparently were part of burials of intact bodies but had become separated from their crania in storage. No evidence of decapitation was found. These may be associated with the three crania identified as Possible Nondecapitations, but confirmation is not possible.

Four intact or nearly intact postcranial skeletons with no signs of decapitation are associated with the crania identified as Nondecapitations.

Three postcranial bones which had been modified to create musical instruments and an artifact of unknown function probably came from contexts other than burials.

There is not enough information to reconstruct context for the remaining postcranial bones.

Determination of Sex and Age for Postcranial Bones

The same methodology for determining sex that was applied to the cranium was also applied to the pelvis. Presence or absence of 15 traits, 8 characteristic of the female pelvis and 7 characteristic of the male pelvis, according to Bass (1971), were recorded for each individual. Using the same criteria for evaluating sex as with the cranium, three left and two right pelvises were identified as Female, one left and two right were Female?, and two left and two right were Male?

Age for the innominate was based on auricular surface seriation (Lovejoy et al. 1985), a methodology for placing individuals into five-year intervals on the basis of age-related changes to the iliac articular surface of the sacroiliac joint. Whittington and Bradley Adams seriated the bones independently and compared results. Inability to agree on which five-year interval various innominates belonged in led to placing some individuals in ten-year intervals.

Subadult postcranial bones were identified on the basis of their small size and lack of epiphyseal union. In only two cases were postcranial bones associated with dentitions from which accurate age determinations could be made. Not enough material was available for the remainder for age to be determined through size seriation.

Table 10.10 shows the number of innominates from each side classified into different categories of age and sex. The table includes only those bones which could be categorized for either age or sex. The majority of innominates are from individuals aged 35 or older and few are from individuals that might be classified as Young Adults (aged 15–21). Most innominates which could be sexed come from Females and Females?, but a large proportion could not be sexed. No innominates are from undoubted Males, but whether this is significant cannot be determined. It appears, however, that innominates and crania have different age and sex patterns, probably because they came from different populations.

Paleopathological Analysis of Postcranial Bones

Trauma

Evidence of interpersonal conflict, possibly warfare, appears on some postcranial bones. Puncture wounds of the type caused by the thrust of a pointed weapon appear on the pelvic bones of two individuals (fig. 10.31) and the ventral surface of a lumbar vertebra of a female. This woman would have been somewhat lame and an easy target for attackers because she was afflicted by chronic dislocation of the head of the left femur from the acetabulum, with the result that the flattened head of the femur formed a shallow new articulation adjacent to the acetabulum (fig. 10.32). The shafts of the left tibia and femur are osteoporotic and have smaller diameters than those on the right side. The left sciatic notch is extremely wide, as well. Osteoarthritis in the woman's right hip and knee may be the result of her putting more weight on the right leg when she walked. Zivanovic (1982: 152) presented a case of chronic

Table 10.10. Age and sex for Iximché innominates

	Age Range in Years[1]									
	15–24	20–29	25–34	30–34	30–39	35–39	35–44	40–44	50+	Unknown
Male	0	0	0	0	0	0	0	0	0	0
Male?	0	0	0	0	0	1L, 1R	1R	0	0	1L
Female?	0	0	0	0	0	0	0	1L, 1R	0	1R
Female	1L	0	1R	1L	0	0	1L, 1R	0	0	0
Unknown	0	1L	0	1R	1L	2L, 1R	2L, 2R	0	1R	—

Note. 1. L = Left; R = Right

Fig. 10.31. Three Puncture Wounds in Right Ilium HL

dislocation with similar characteristics which he attributed to trauma early in life.

Perimortem cuts with well-defined edges made by blades mark one left femur shaft and one right femur distal articulation. Accidents or interpersonal conflicts long before death resulted in evidence of healed fractures of a left clavicle, a rib, and a humerus (fig. 10.33). Osteoporosis led to development of a compression fracture of the centrum of a female's vertebra (see discussion below under Diseases).

Cultural Modification

Two right metatarsals show evidence of alterations which Ubelaker (1989: 103) argued might be caused by prolonged hyperdorsiflexion of the toes during kneeling. They have been reported for members of both sexes in various populations in the Americas.

Diseases

The most common postcranial location for periosteal reactions is the shaft of the right femur (four cases), followed by the right tibia (three cases), left tibia (two cases), and left femur, right clavicle, and inner sur-

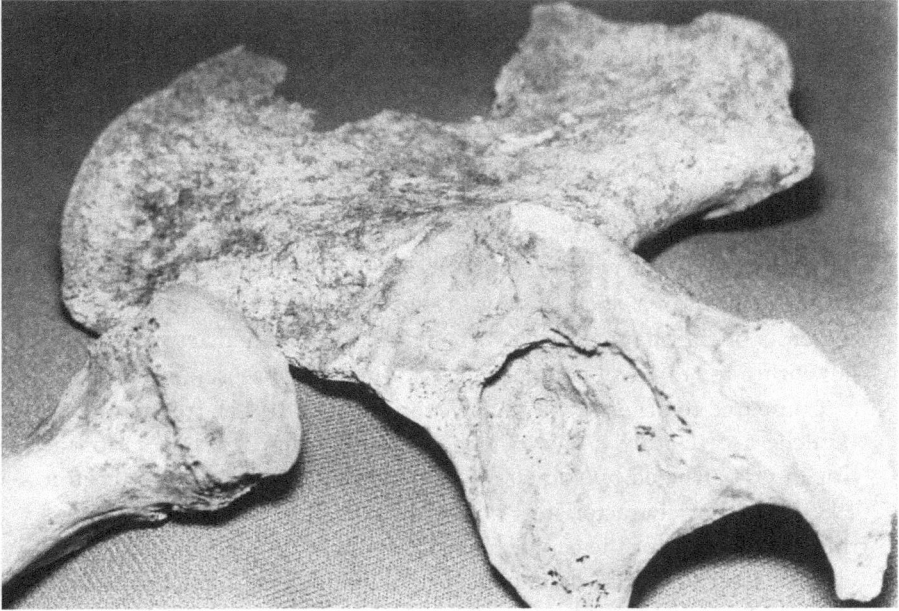

Fig. 10.32. Chronic Dislocation of Head of Left Femur of IX-6 Showing Formation of New Articulation Adjacent to Acetabulum

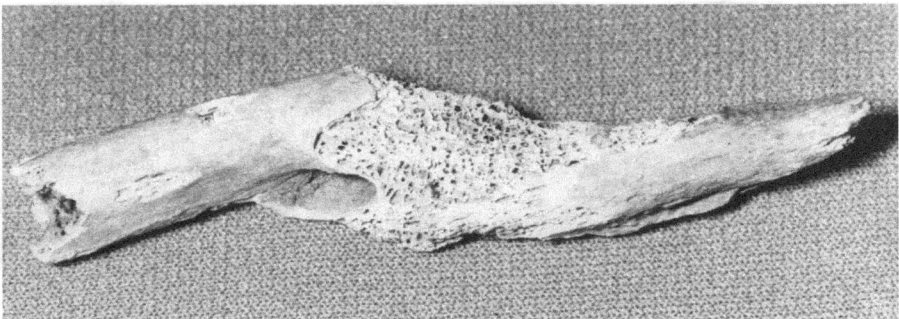

Fig. 10.33. Misaligned but Healed Fracture of Left Clavicle JI

face of a rib (one case each). One individual has healed reactive bone on the right tibia and both femurs. The frequency of periosteal reactions varies by bone. Frequencies of reactions on postcranial bones with more than 50% of cortical surfaces preserved are presented in figure 10.12. The highest frequency of lesions occurs on the tibias, followed in order of decreasing frequency by the femurs, right clavicle, and ribs. Such patterning within the skeleton is typical of a variety of diseases. The left tibia has the highest frequency of periosteal reactions, 28%, of any cranial or postcranial bone. This frequency seems reasonable as an estimate of the level of bony lesions of infection for the population as a whole. The frequency of periosteal reactions on the right femur is 18%.

Wright and White (1996) tabulated frequencies of periosteal reactions from skeletal series around the world. Frequencies on the femur range from 3.4% to 60.0%; frequencies on the tibia range from 12.6% to 84.4%. Series for which frequencies are high are those in which treponemal infections, such as yaws or syphilis, have been diagnosed on the basis of the characteristics of bone lesions. Frequencies at Iximché fall within the range of populations without these diseases.

Compared to other Maya skeletal series (table 10.11), frequencies at Iximché are relatively low. Evidence suggests that the population at Copán was afflicted by some sort of treponemal disease (Whittington 1989). Neither characteristics nor frequencies of lesions indicate that this was the case for the people buried at Iximché, which is surprising in view of Goff's (1953b) diagnosis of syphilis in pre-Contact skeletons from the Mam area, not far from Iximché.

Table 10.11. Postcranial Periosteal Reactions in Maya Skeletal Series

Bone	Site	Period[1]	Cases	n	%	Notes	Source
Tibia							
	Cuello	I	33	59	55.9	Cortical expansion	Saul & Saul 1997
	Pasión	I–III	51	75	68.0	Adult	Wright & White 1996
	Altar de Sacrificios	I–IV	6	10	60.0		Saul 1972
	Pasión	II	16	27	59.3		Wright 1997
	Altar de Sacrificios	II	5	36	13.9	Minimum estimate	Saul 1972
	Copán	II–III	22	48	45.8		Whittington 1989
	Pasión	III	17	20	85.0		Wright 1997
	Altar de Sacrificios	IV	0	1	0.0		Saul 1972
	Tipu	V	59	704	8.4		Cohen et al. 1994
Femur							
	Pasión	I–III	28	75	37.3	Adult	Wright & White 1996
	Altar de Sacrificios	I–IV	5	24	20.8		Saul 1972
	Pasión	II	9	32	28.1		Wright 1997
	Altar de Sacrificios	II	2	6	33.3		Saul 1972
	Copán	II–III	21	55	38.2		Whittington 1989
	Pasión	III	10	26	38.5		Wright 1997
	Altar de Sacrificios	IV	0	4	0.0		Saul 1972

Notes. 1. I = Preclassic, II = Classic, III = Terminal Classic, IV = Postclassic, V = Historic.

Reactive bone at attachment areas for ligaments, tendons, and muscles was noted on one left tibia and one left fibula. A bony growth on a sacrum near the right sacroiliac articulation is probably also a related condition.

In the postcranial skeleton, the most common location for osteoarthritis is the left acetabulum, with five cases. Three cases occur for the right acetabulum, left patella, left glenoid, and sacrum. Two cases each occur for the right glenoid, proximal articulation of the left tibia, proximal articulation of the left femur, distal articulation of the right femur, right patella, proximal articulation of the left ulna, and dorsal articulation of the rib. One case appears at each of the following locations: proximal articulation of the right tibia, distal articulation of the left femur, proximal articulation of the right femur, proximal and distal articulations of the left humerus, distal articulation of right humerus, lateral articulation of the left and right clavicles, medial articulation of the right clavicle, sternum, hand phalanx, right calcaneus, and right metatarsal. Arthritis also occurs on the centra and articulations of cervical, thoracic, and lumbar vertebrae. Characteristics of arthritic lesions on and around the surfaces of articulations are pitting, lipping (osteophytes), deposits of bone, and eburnation (fig. 10.34). In addition, some arthritic vertebrae display Schmorl's nodes, herniation which develops when intervertebral disc contents exert pressure on vertebral body surfaces and cause marked depressions (Roberts and Manchester 1995: 107).

The distribution of osteoarthritis in body joints can be used to reveal aspects of occupation and handedness in a population (Merbs 1983). However, the number of articular surfaces with at least 50% preservation is relatively low at Iximché, hiding fine-grained differences between joints and producing patterns without statistical significance. The postcranial joint with the highest frequency of osteoarthritis, based only on articulations with more than 50% preservation, is the knee, followed, in order of decreasing frequency, by the shoulder, hip, sterno-clavicular and ankle (tie), and elbow (see fig. 10.13). The frequency is low for joints of the wrist, hand, and foot. Within the vertebrae, frequency of arthritis increases with distance from the cranium. In comparing differences between joints and sides of the body, no clear patterns emerge that can be explained in behavioral terms.

An older woman at Iximché shows evidence of septic arthritis, probably resulting from bacteria spread to joints via the bloodstream. Joints clearly involved are the right elbow, shoulder, and hip. In the elbow, the proximal ulna and distal humerus have large lytic foci, and mutilating

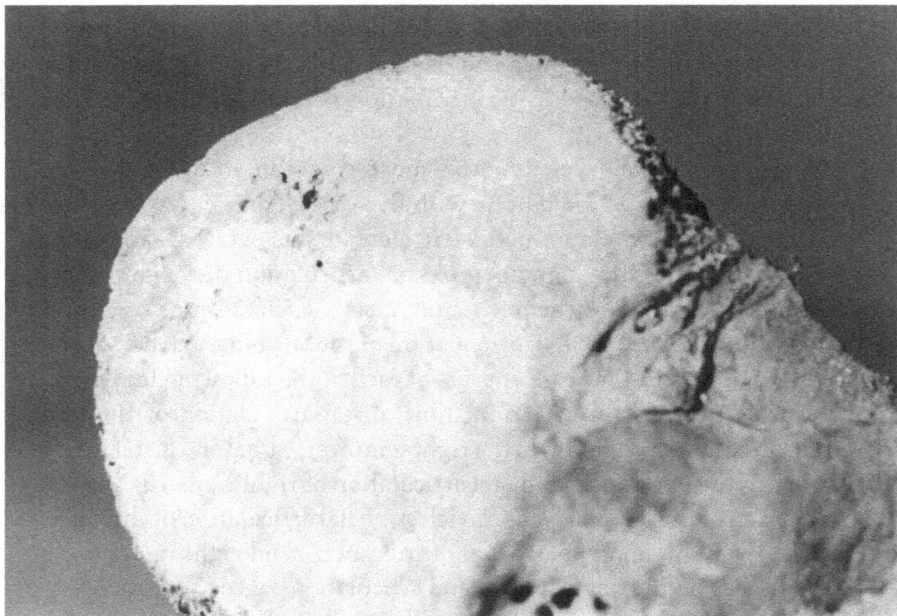

Fig. 10.34. Osteoarthritic Eburnation and Pitting of Proximal Articulation of Left Tibia AD

arthritis has destroyed the proximal end of the radius (fig. 10.35). The proximal head of the humerus and glenoid of the scapula are markedly deformed, as well as pitted and lipped. Lytic lesions have destroyed much of the acetabulum of the hip, which is also lipped.

Although superficially similar to tubercular arthritis, certain characteristics of this woman's condition allow that diagnosis to be ruled out. Tubercular arthritis primarily affects children, usually involves only one joint, and is more destructive of joint surfaces. It often involves the vertebrae through abscess formation within the body, collapse, and subsequent bony fixation resulting in angular deformity of the spine, known as Pott's disease (Roberts and Manchester 1995: 115, 138). Although the woman's fifth thoracic vertebra did collapse (fig. 10.36), it is clearly the result of a compression fracture related to advanced osteoporosis. All of the woman's postcranial bones have very thin cortices and porous trabeculae, and are very light in weight. The osteoporosis is especially marked in the bones of the right arm, probably owing to disuse related to the septic arthritis.

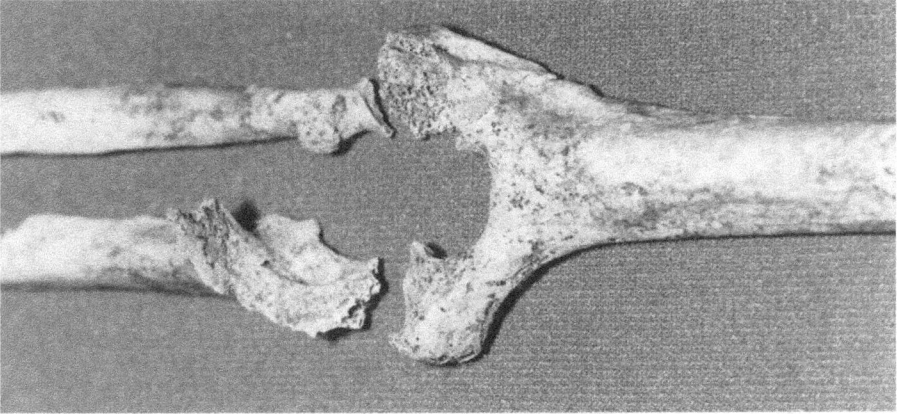

Fig. 10.35. Septic Arthritis of Right Elbow of IX-1

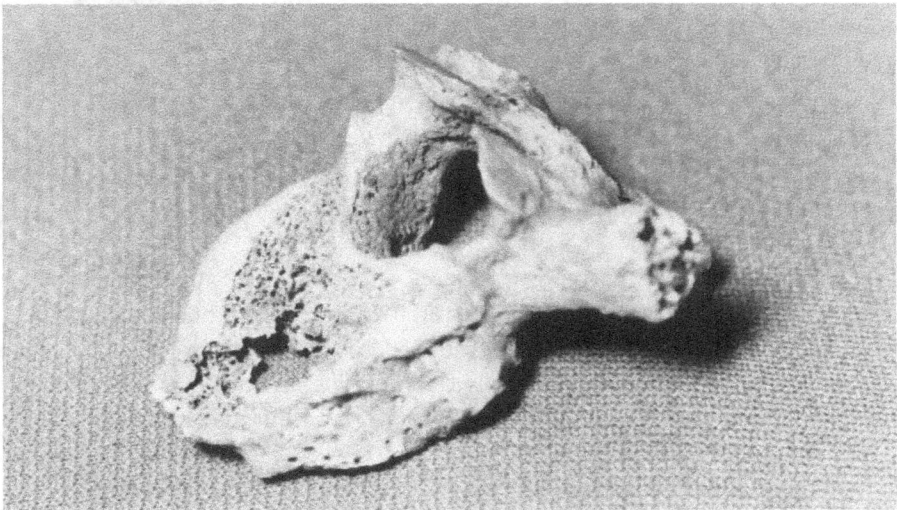

Fig. 10.36. Compression Fracture of Thoracic Vertebra of IX-1; Woman with Extensive Osteoporosis

A small smooth-walled cyst appears in the inferior surface of the arch of an atlas and could represent an aneurysmal bone cyst (Ortner and Putschar 1985: 366). Other small smooth-walled cysts are located in the distal articulations of two right humeri (fig. 10.37) and a right acetabulum. The locations and characteristics of these three defects suggest that they might represent chondroblastomas, benign tumors occurring mainly in adolescents and young adults, especially in

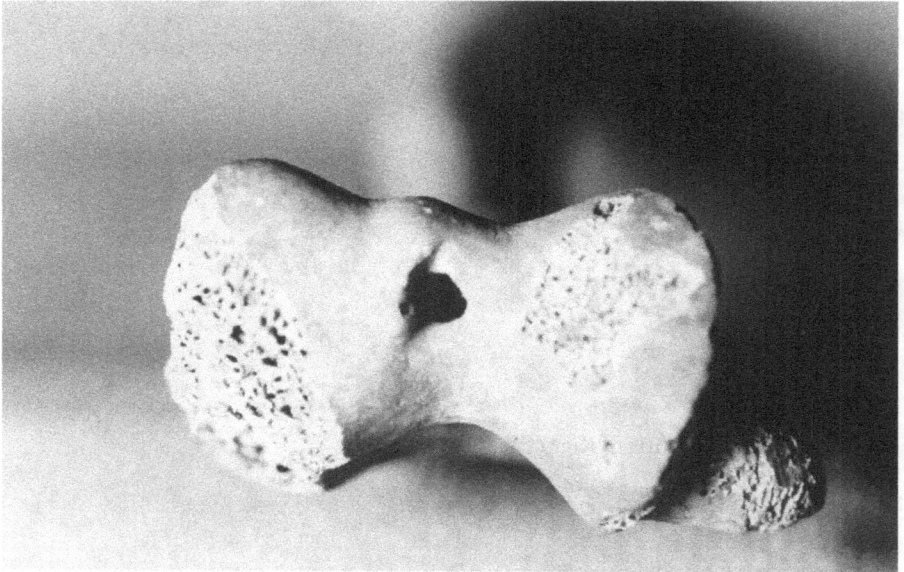

Fig. 10.37. Possible Chondroblastoma of Distal Articulation of Right Humerus EU

males, most commonly in the epiphyses of the long bones (Ortner and Putschar 1985: 373).

Small lumps with smooth surfaces slightly raised above the surrounding cortex, identical in characteristics and size to those on cranial bones, are on the surface of one left tibia, two left fibulas, two right fibulas, one right radius, one right clavicle, four ribs, and one hand phalanx. As with the cranial versions, they probably represent insignificant variations in bone architecture.

There are long smooth ridges along the length of the outer surfaces of three ribs of one individual (fig. 10.38). Their etiology is unknown.

Congenital and Developmental Anomalies

One individual possesses a ninth thoracic vertebra with a single rib facet, a characteristic normally found on the tenth through twelfth thoracic vertebrae. The inferior articular surfaces of the twelfth thoracic vertebra from another individual do not take on the normal lumbar pattern. Three cases of fused postcranial bones were noted: a right proximal radius and ulna (congenital radioulnar synostosis) (fig. 10.39) and two cases in which the fifth lumbar vertebra is fused to the sacrum (sacralization) (fig. 10.40).

Fig. 10.38. Long Smooth Ridge on Outer Surface of Rib of IX-1

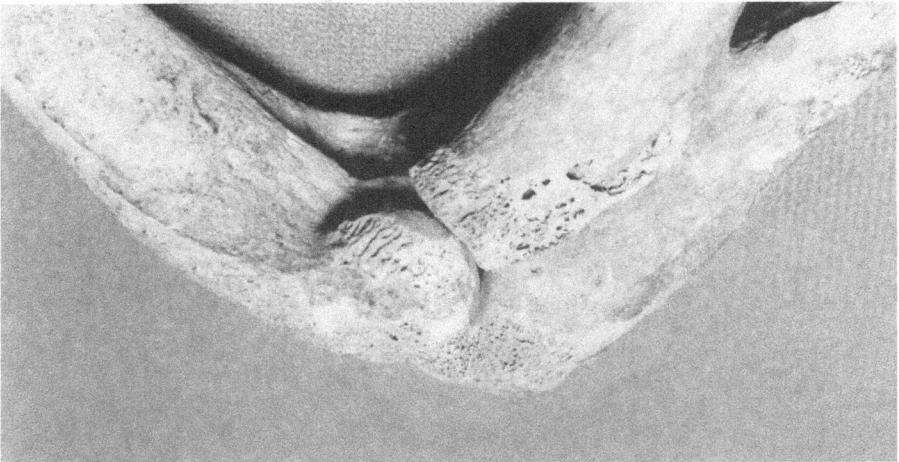

Fig. 10.39. Congenital Radioulnar Synostosis of GM

Postmortem Modification of Postcranial Bones

Rodents and insects damaged various postcranial bones, as they did cranial bones. Low-temperature burning occurred to part of the innominate and sacrum of a Nondecapitation whose temporal and occipital were also burned, as well as a tibia, a femur, two fibulas, a humerus, a radius, and a rib of other individuals. As with burning of cranial bones, the

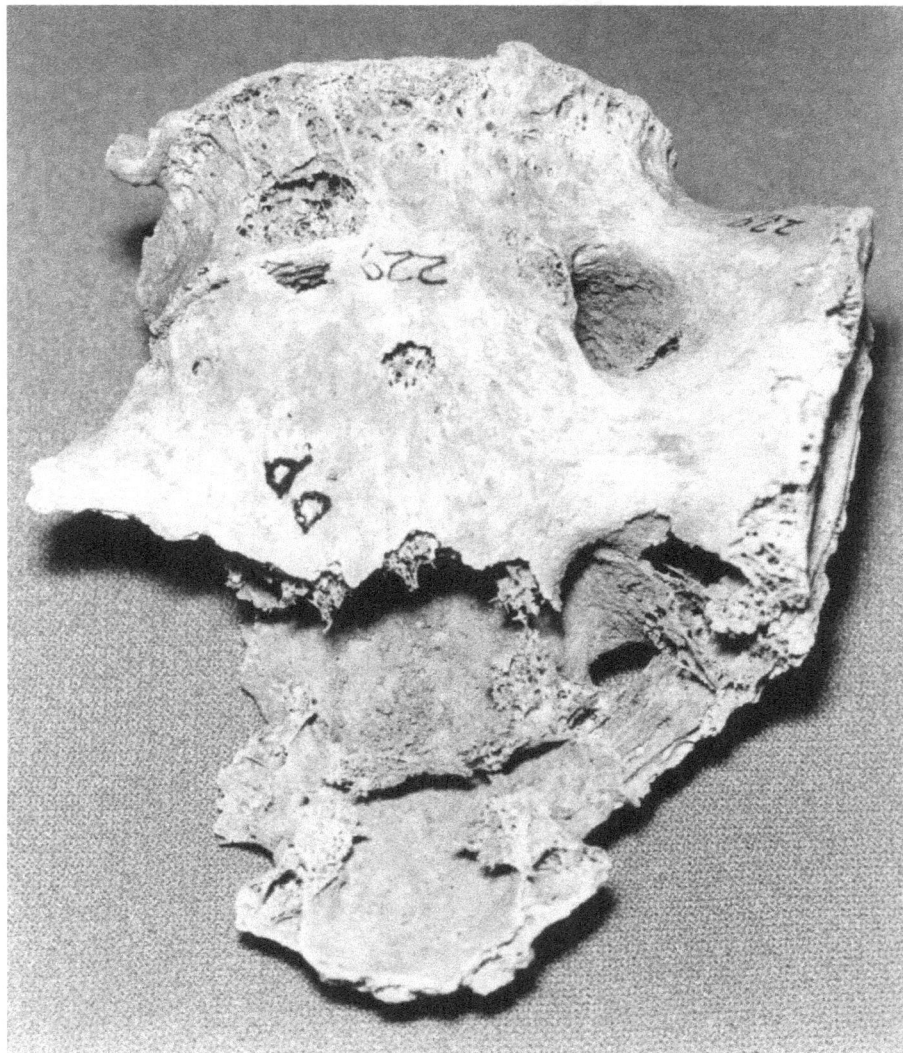

Fig. 10.40. Congenital Lumbar Sacralization of DP

significance is unknown. A left ulna, right radius, and distal right femur have copper staining, the ulna and radius probably from bracelets and the femur from a displaced earspool buried with the body.

One right ulna is marked by parallel cuts made by a knife. This may be evidence of defleshing, either soon after death or after the body had partially decomposed. It may have been associated with making a trophy of part of the body of a vanquished foe or with moving ancestral bones from a primary burial to a secondary burial or shrine, a practice which seems to be depicted on Altar 5 from Classic period Tikal (Freidel et al. 1995: 263).

Some postcranial bones have been purposely modified and should be classified as artifacts. A carved and polished right femur fragment represents part of a musical rasp. A right humerus was cut, drilled, and polished to produce a flute. A left humerus was cut, incised, and polished to produce an object of unknown function.

Stable Isotope Analysis

Analysis of stable isotopes of carbon and nitrogen in the nonmineral portion of bone, called collagen (DeNiro and Epstein 1978, 1981), and stable isotopes of carbon in apatite, a crystalline mineral in bones (Gerry and Krueger 1997), together with paleopathological and social interpretations derived from the archaeological record, provide a direct method of determining diet. Bone collagen is partially composed of carbon preferentially derived from proteins in the diet (Ambrose and Norr 1993; Tieszen and Fagre 1993).

The turnover of collagen in bones means that stable isotope values derived from collagen reflect diet during the last few years before an individual's death. Tooth enamel is structurally similar to bone apatite and is partially composed of carbon representative of the whole diet (Ambrose and Norr 1993). Unlike apatite in bone, it is not subject to continuous replacement after enamel formation is complete. Therefore, the carbon isotopic composition of enamel reflects diet at the time of enamel formation as a child, regardless of the individual's age at death.

Measures of isotopic composition of a material are expressed in per-mil (‰) as the deviation, or delta δ of the ratio of heavy to light isotopes in the sample from the ratio in a reference sample. For carbon the reference sample is the rostrum of the Cretaceous Pee Dee Belemnite (PDB) formation. The reference used to calculate delta for nitrogen is ambient air (AIR).

Carbon isotopic ratios can be related to terrestrial plants (DeNiro 1987). Terrestrial plants can be divided into types, based on type of photosynthesis, each with its own carbon isotopic signature (Coleman and Fry 1991). Leafy C_3-based plants, including legumes, have a worldwide average carbon isotope ratio of –26‰. C_4-based plants, including tropical grasses such as maize, have an average carbon isotope ratio of –12‰.

Nitrogen isotopes in collagen can be used to distinguish between marine animals and terrestrial plants and between legumes and nonlegumes in the diet (DeNiro 1987). The average nitrogen isotope ratio for marine animals is greater than 12‰ and the average nitrogen isotope ratio for terrestrial plants is less than 10‰. The ratio for legumes, all of which are C_3-based, is 1‰; the ratio for nonlegumes is 9‰.

David Reed subjected 18 human ribs, a dog mandible, and a pig humerus from bags of Iximché artifacts to stable isotope analysis at the Mass Spectrometry Laboratory at Penn State University. Preliminary results have been published previously (Whittington and Reed 1994, 1998). A summary of these publications follows, along with final results, with minor corrections, as presented by Reed and Whittington (1995) and Whittington et al. (1996, n.d.).

In Guatemala, Reed sorted all ribs found together in a storage bag by morphology, preservation, size, side, and location within the rib cage. He chose fragments of the first rib for analysis in an attempt to avoid sampling individuals twice. When a skeleton that appeared not to have been sampled had no first rib, he took fragments of another rib. He also took fragments of the dog mandible and the pig humerus to compare the diets of local animals. The dog may have lived at Iximché before the arrival of Spaniards, and the pig probably was a post-Contact domesticated animal whose bone somehow became mixed with the artifacts.

After analysis at Penn State, Reed discarded the results for five rib samples, three because they were likely duplicate samples and two (IX-69 and 229-i) because they were extreme outliers (table 10.12). The latter two samples might represent some subgroup, but the individuals share no obvious social, demographic, or pathological characteristics. For the remaining 13 human ribs, nitrogen values range from 6.9‰ to 9.2‰, with a mean value of 8.0‰, and carbon values range from −9.3‰ to −7.4‰, with a mean value of −8.0‰. The pig bone has a nitrogen value of 7.3‰ and a carbon value of −8.5‰. The dog bone has a nitrogen value of 7.4‰ and a carbon value of −6.1‰. The nitrogen and carbon values of the post-Contact pig are within the ranges for humans, meaning that it ate a diet similar to the diet of some individuals buried at Iximché. The dog has a carbon value that falls outside of the range of humans and that may reflect a diet composed of both maize and meat from other animals eating C_4-based plants.

Wright and White (1996) summarized isotopic composition of human collagen at 14 Maya sites, including Iximché. Wright and Schwarcz

Table 10.12. Stable carbon and nitrogen isotope ratio measurements from Iximché bone collagen

Burial ID	Burial Type	Sex	Age	$\delta^{13}C_{PDB}$	$\delta^{15}N_{AIR}$	Notes
IX-1	Nondecapitation	Female	Adult	−8.8	7.6	Right rib
IX-24	Nondecapitation	Unknown	Subadult	−7.4	8.3	Right rib
IX-34	Nondecapitation	Female?	Adult	−7.6	8.1	Rib
IX-69	Nondecapitation	Unknown	Subadult	−6.0	10.7	Ribs; extreme
50-i	Unknown	Unknown	Adult?	−7.7	7.2	Rib
50-ii	Unknown	Unknown	Adult?	−8.1	8.3	Rib
129-i	Unknown	Unknown	Adult?	−8.0	7.9	Right rib
129-ii	Unknown	Unknown	Adult?	−8.0	7.8	Left rib; duplicate?
129-iii (GO)	Nondecapitation?	Unknown	Adult	−7.8	8.6	Ribs
224-i	Unknown	Unknown	Adult?	−7.5	7.8	First left rib
224-ii	Unknown	Unknown	Adult?	−7.7	7.4	First right rib
224-iii	Unknown	Unknown	Adult?	−8.1	7.6	Right rib; duplicate?
224-iv	Unknown	Unknown	Adult?	−8.4	7.6	Rib; duplicate?
229-i	Unknown	Unknown	Adult?	−6.3	3.8	First left rib; extreme
229-ii	Unknown	Unknown	Adult?	−8.5	7.9	First left rib
229-iii	Unknown	Unknown	Adult?	−9.3	9.2	First right rib
229-iv (GP)	Nondecapitation?	Unknown	Subadult	−7.7	6.9	Rib
263	Nondecapitation?	Unknown	Adult	−7.7	8.4	Rib
175	Pig (humerus)			−8.5	7.3	
229	Dog (mandible)			−6.1	7.4	

(1998, 1999) published stable isotope values for Highland Kaminaljuyú, geographically and environmentally closer to Iximché than any other site for which data are available and thus more ecologically comparable than Lowland sites. White et al. (2001) published carbon and nitrogen values for the Lowland site of Altun Ha, near the Caribbean. The mean nitrogen value for Iximché is low in comparison to most other sites, except Itzán, Copán, and Kaminaljuyú. Itzán is a Lowland Petén site, but Copán (600 m), Kaminaljuyú (1500 m), and Iximché (2200 m) have higher altitudes and environments more dominated by coniferous trees than do the other sites. Mean nitrogen isotope values indicate that individuals from the sites at higher elevations ate exclusively terrestrial diets and consumed less meat than residents of most Lowland sites. Residents of some coastal sites included a marine animal component in their diets. A high proportion of higher altitude diets consisted of nonleguminous terrestrial plants.

The bone collagen from Iximché skeletons has a more positive mean carbon isotope ratio than skeletons from any other site presented by Wright and White (1996), Wright and Schwarcz (1989, 1999), or White et al. (2001). Compared to individuals from other sites, it appears that individuals buried at Iximché were more dependent on dietary maize. White et al. (2001) found that maize was highly valued as a status food at Postclassic Altun Ha. High-status Altun Ha individuals consumed a high proportion of C_4-based foods and obtained protein from C_4-fed terrestrial animals, such as deer or dogs; low-status individuals ate little maize and obtained protein from marine animals. The high proportion of maize in the diet of those whose postcranial remains were buried in the elite part of Iximché also flags their high status. There is no correlation between carbon and nitrogen values at Iximché (Pearson's $r = -.39$), similar to the situation at Altun Ha, which White et al. (2001) interpreted as meaning that the diet was not protein deficient.

In addition to dietary differences between sites and ecosystems, differences in carbon isotope values possibly reflect Iximché's 2200-m altitude, which is higher than any other Maya site yet sampled. The carbon isotope composition of plants shifts toward more positive values with increasing altitude (Körner et al. 1988; Marino and McElroy 1991; Polley et al. 1993), although the shift is greatest for C_3-based plants. That the Lowland sites of Mojo Cay (−8.5‰), Itzán (−9.2‰), and Dos Pilas (−9.1‰) have carbon values more similar to Iximché's than do either of the sites at higher altitude, Copán (−9.3‰) and Kaminaljuyú (−9.8‰), demonstrates that multiple variables influence carbon values.

Robert Tykot performed stable carbon isotope analysis of 43 human teeth from Iximché at the University of South Florida. Tykot et al. (2000) presented preliminary results. A more complete treatment of the project is in preparation (Whittington et al. n.d.), but a summary and final results are presented below.

Third molars, whose enamel typically forms between the ages of 9 and 12 years in humans, were removed from skeletons in Guatemala for analysis in the United States. We attempted to sample Iximché individuals only once by preferentially removing a mandibular third molar, when available. A maxillary molar had to be taken from some individuals lacking mandibular molars because of antemortem loss, congenital absence, or inability to locate the mandible. Possibly some individuals were sampled twice, once from a maxilla and once from a mandible that had not been matched to the rest of the cranium, but this should have minimal impact on this study. The diets reflected in stable carbon isotopes in the enamel represent what juveniles in the Highlands were eating.

The mean value for carbon in the 43 tooth samples tested is −2.1‰, with values ranging from −5.2‰ to .1‰ (table 10.13). Based on empirically observed differences between diet and bone apatite in large herbivores (Lee-Thorp and van der Merwe 1987), these values should be shifted by −12‰, so that the mean is −14.1‰ and the values range from −17.2‰ to −11.9‰. These values imply moderate to high reliance on maize in the diet.

Four individuals (IX-2, IX-4, 224-v, and 270-i) have extreme values relative to the Iximché mean and had adolescent diets different from other individuals buried at the site. IX-2 and IX-4 are Decapitations and 270-i is a Possible Decapitation. Values for three of the individuals (IX-4, 224-v, and 270-i) are extreme in the negative direction. Possible explanations for these three include living in areas with more abundant C_3-based foods or access to a greater variety of foods because of social status. This is similar to Lowland Altun Ha, where dedicatory burials are dietarily distinct, exhibiting the greatest C_3-based plant consumption and degree of herbivory, and may come from elsewhere (White et al. 2001).

Comparison of stable isotope ratios between subpopulations at Iximché reveals patterns that help in reconstructing Late Postclassic Highland society. Sixteen Decapitations have values ranging from −4.3‰ to .1‰ and a mean of −1.9‰. The value for the one Nondecapitation that was sampled is −2.0‰, close to the mean value for Decapitations. No dietary differences between types of burials can be discerned among individuals whose burial type could be determined with confidence.

Values for seven Males extend from −3.7‰ to −.9‰, a range of 2.8, whereas values for six Females extend from −2.2‰ to −.3‰, a range of 1.9. The greater Male range indicates that juvenile males apparently had access to more food choices because they migrated more, represent a greater range of social statuses, or came from a wider range of locations. The pattern is similar to that for stable carbon isotopes in collagen extracted from the bones of low-status inhabitants of Classic Copán (Whittington and Reed 1997). The mean carbon value for Iximché Males is −2.1‰, and the mean for Females is −1.5‰. Although the difference is not statistically significant according to the independent samples t-test, which tests the equality of group means, the more negative Male value mean may indicate less reliance on maize in the diet.

Table 10.13. Stable carbon isotope ratio measurements from Iximché teeth

Burial ID	Burial Type	Sex	Age	$\delta^{13}C_{PDB}$	Notes
IX-1	Nondecapitation	Female	Adult	−2.0	Right mandible
IX-2	Decapitation	Male?	Adult	0.1	Right maxilla
IX-4	Decapitation	Male?	Adult	−4.3	Right mandible
IX-5	Decapitation	Male	Young adult	−0.9	Left mandible
IX-6	Decapitation?	Female	Young adult	−2.2	Left maxilla
IX-7	Decapitation	Male?	Young adult	−2.2	Right maxilla
IX-8-i*	Unknown	Unknown	Adult	−1.8	Right mandible
IX-9	Decapitation?	Female?	Adult	−1.9	Right mandible
IX-10	Decapitation	Male	Adult	−2.2	Left maxilla
IX-11	Decapitation	Female?	Young adult	−1.9	Right mandible
IX-12	Decapitation	Female	Adult	−2.0	Left maxilla
IX-13	Decapitation	Male	Adult	−2.3	Right maxilla
IX-15*	Unknown	Female?	Young adult	−3.3	Left mandible
IX-16	Decapitation	Male?	Adult	−3.1	Right maxilla
IX-17	Nondecapitation?	Unknown	Adult	−2.4	Left mandible
IX-18*	Unknown	Unknown	Adult	−2.5	Left mandible
IX-19	Decapitation	Unknown	Young adult	−0.9	Right maxilla
IX-20	Decapitation	Male?	Adult	−0.8	Right maxilla
IX-21	Decapitation	Male?	Young adult	−1.9	Left maxilla
IX-22	Decapitation	Unknown	Adult	−1.6	Right maxilla
IX-23	Decapitation?	Female	Adult	−2.0	Right maxilla
IX-33	Decapitation	Male	Adult	−3.7	Left maxilla
IX-41	Decapitation	Female	Young adult	−0.3	Right mandible
IX-43	Decapitation?	Male	Young adult	−2.3	Right maxilla
IX-45	Unknown	Unknown	Adult	−1.8	Left mandible
IX-46	Decapitation	Female?	Young adult	−2.4	Left mandible
IX-47	Decapitation?	Male?	Adult	−1.5	Right mandible
IX-50	Decapitation?	Female	Young adult	−0.7	Right mandible
IX-51	Decapitation?	Male	Adult	−1.5	Left mandible
IX-52	Decapitation?	Male	Adult	−1.7	Left mandible
Str. 39-i	Decapitation?	Unknown	Adult	−1.8	Left mandible
Str. 39-ii	Unknown	Unknown	Adult	−2.3	Right mandible
Str. 39-iii	Decapitation?	Unknown	Young adult	−3.2	Left maxilla
Str. 39-iv	Unknown	Unknown	Young adult	−3.5	Right mandible
Str. 39-v	Unknown	Unknown	Young adult	−2.3	Right mandible
Str. 45-ii	Decapitation?	Unknown	Adult	−1.4	Left mandible
Str. 45-iii	Decapitation?	Unknown	Adult	−2.2	Left mandible
50-iii	Decapitation?	Unknown	Adult	−1.3	Right mandible
176#1	Decapitation?	Male?	Adult	−1.1	Left mandible
206-N	Decapitation?	Unknown	Adult	−2.9	Right mandible
224-v	Unknown	Unknown	Adult	−5.0	Right mandible
270-i	Decapitation?	Unknown	Adult	−5.2	Right mandible
270-ii	Decapitation?	Unknown	Young adult	−1.6	Right mandible

*Should not have been assigned an IX number.

Few other results of stable carbon isotope analysis of teeth from the Maya area have been published for comparison with results from Iximché. Stable carbon isotopes in teeth have been studied at the sites of Lamanai, Pacbitun, and Kaminaljuyú.

Coyston et al. (1999) analyzed teeth from Lamanai and Pacbitun in Belize. Three teeth from Lamanai dating from between A.D. 1000 and A.D. 1675 have isotopic values that overlap those from Iximché. Two others with earlier dates have more negative values but may not represent diet because of postmortem alteration (diagenesis). For three teeth from Pacbitun from the Tzib phase (A.D. 700–900) and an undated postabandonment phase, one isotopic value falls within the range of values from Iximché, and two are more negative. These patterns suggest that Highland and Lowland subadult diets were similar during the Postclassic, although earlier subadult Lowland diets may have been less dependent on maize.

Wright and Schwarcz (1998) analyzed 25 third molars from within and near Highland Kaminaljuyú in the Valley of Guatemala, dating from the Middle Preclassic to the Late Postclassic (700 B.C.–A.D. 1500). Their data, with values ranging from $-4.3‰$ to $-.4‰$, fall completely within the range observed for Iximché. The Kaminaljuyú average of $-2.5‰$, based on 24 third molars not suspected of diagenesis or contamination, is close to that of Iximché but somewhat more negative. Individuals buried at Iximché had been more dependent on maize in their diets when they were adolescents. However, the greater range of values at Iximché indicates that the individuals buried there had more diverse adolescent diets than did the individuals buried at Kaminaljuyú, despite the much shorter time span in which burials occurred at Iximché. This could relate to sacrificial victims at Iximché coming from a wider variety of geographic locations with different food resources or a wider variety of social statuses.

Archaeological phases for a subset of third molars from the vicinity of Kaminaljuyú can be determined from published data (Wright and Schwarcz 1998, 1999). The average carbon value for the late Early Classic (A.D. 400–600) is $-2.8‰$ (n = 6), for the Late Classic (A.D. 600–900) is $-2.6‰$ (n = 2), and for the Late Postclassic (ca. A.D. 1500) site of Belek is $-2.2‰$ (n = 2). All are close to the Iximché mean but more negative, reflecting slightly less reliance on maize in the diet. Only one Late Postclassic value of $-.4‰$ is as positive as some contemporaneous values from Iximché. This comparison implies that adolescent diets in the

Highlands remained relatively stable for approximately one thousand years.

Differences in isotope ratios for Iximché and Kaminaljuyú for bone collagen but not tooth apatite could reflect differences between subadult and adult diets, but they could also suggest a possible dietary shift in the Highlands during the approximately one thousand years between the Early Classic and the Late Postclassic, primarily in the source of protein. Such a shift could be explained by decreased availability through time of wild animals because of shrinking forest coverage or increased consumption through time of maize-fed domesticated animals.

11

⊓⊔⊓⊔⊓⊔

Settlement Plan and Architecture

Although Guillemin (1977) believed that Great Palaces I and II were residences for the two ruling kings of Iximché, ceramic distributions described in chapters 8 and 9 suggest another possibility: that of the two, only Great Palace II served as a royal residence, and that Great Palace I functioned as a religious, not a political center. In this chapter, architecture and the site settlement plan are considered in view of these ceramic data. Also, regional implications will be drawn from the architecture and settlement layouts of other Late Postclassic sites in the Guatemalan Highlands.

Architectural Design Differences in the Great Palaces

Architectural differences between Great Palaces I and II detract from Guillemin's idea that both structures were royal residences. During its first occupation, the building phase for which archaeological reconstruction was most complete, Great Palace I had fewer and larger rooms than its counterpart and a single, large interior patio. Great Palace II had many rooms arranged around eight or nine interior patios. Certainly the latter structure seems more compatible with the many occupants and activities one would imagine for a royal residence.

The central patio of Great Palace I contained an elaborate roofed altar with basin, an altar which continued in use through all three phases of occupation (Guillemin 1977: 244). As discussed in chapter 4, Guillemin found at least three other altars during the excavation of Great Palace I but no altar within Great Palace II. Guillemin appreciated the significance of this contrast. Of Great Palace I, he wrote, "in the palace itself religion is omnipresent with altars in the interior patios associated with incense burners" (1977: 234) and implied (1977: 240) that the "lords" of Great Palace I were higher in the religious hierarchy than those of Great Palace II.

Another architectural difference between the two Great Palaces is that Great Palace I was built on an elevated platform, ca. 3 m high, during its final phase of occupation, whereas Great Palace II was much closer to ground level (cf. figs. 4.20 and 4.38). For the Postclassic Highlands, temples, that is, religious buildings, may tend to be more elevated than their secular counterparts. John Weeks, working at the Late Postclassic site of Chisalín, tested the hypothesis that elevated structures tended more to have religious functions. He summarized the distribution of censer sherds at Chisalín by structure class based on ratios of basal area to height and found significantly higher proportions of these vessel forms at relatively tall structures (Weeks 1980: tables 6 and 10; 1983: 42). The elevation differences between the two Iximché Great Palaces and their differing proportions of ceremonial types (censers) are consistent with Weeks's findings and support the idea that Great Palace I served primarily religious functions. This correspondence of censers and religious structures has long been recognized by archaeologists in the Maya Lowlands (Thompson 1957: 601).

In sum, architectural differences between Great Palaces I and II, considered alone, detract from Guillemin's interpretation. They also are compatible with ceramic differences between the structures. Both ceramic and architectural findings suggest that Great Palace I may have been a religious center, and, that of the two, only Great Palace II served as a royal residence.

Settlement Plan, Burials, and Iconography: An Interpretation

In Maya cosmology the east-west line is fundamental to religion and worldview and takes precedence over other geographical orientations (B. Tedlock 1992: 172–173). East is the paramount direction. In the east, time and direction come together each morning as the sun rises from the underworld, the Maya spirit world. This orientation is considered by Classic Maya archaeologists when they study the possible impact of this fusion of time and the cardinal directions on the planning of prehistoric settlements and the design of glyphs (see, for example, Coe [1965] and Coggins [1980]).

East is the direction to Tulán, the mythical home of the Cakchiquel people and their rulers (Recinos and Goetz 1953: 45; 55–56). East is the direction of birth (life coming from the underworld), and a case can be made that east is also the direction of political power and the state. West, on the other hand, is the direction of death (life following the sun back to the underworld), organized religion, and human spirituality. Gucumatz (the Maya plumed serpent; Quetzalcoatl in Mexico), who lived in the east, was the archetypical god-king of Mesoamerica. Mythologically he was both deity and mortal and took the guise of either man or animal (serpent or feathered serpent, among other forms).

At Iximché, Great Palace II with its secular architecture and higher proportion of utility pottery is east of Great Palace I with its more religious architecture and ceremonial ceramics. The whole site of Iximché is aligned along a narrow east-west trending ridge, and the locality might have been chosen, in part, for the trend of its topography. In Plazas A and C, the major temple platforms (2 and 3; 4 and 5) are aligned east to west. Also, the cruciform architecture of all temple substructures and of some altars suggests preoccupation with the cardinal directions. For Chisalín, stairways accessing platform summits are usually on the east or west sides, occasionally on the south but rarely to the north (Weeks 1980: 112). The same is true of excavated and restored portions of Iximché. Temple pyramidal bases all have stairways on their east or west faces. Only lower platforms have stairs on their southern sides, and no structure has stairs providing access from the north.

The two temples (2 and 4) associated with human sacrifice are both on the western edge of their respective plazas. Las Casas (1958, 4: 152) held that sacrifice was accompanied by ceremonial cannibalism and indicates this to have been a most religious act. The larger of the two facing temples in Plaza A is Temple 2, to the west of Temple 3, whereas the larger in Plaza C, Temple 5, faces Temple 4 from the east (Guillemin 1977: 234). If Plazas A and B (west of Plaza C) constituted a religious compound, then the predominance of Temple 2 is compatible with that idea, just as the predominance of the eastern Temple 5 over Temple 4 in Plaza C is in accord with the view that Plaza C and Placita C together were a political center for Iximché and the Cakchiquel state based there.

Considered next are the two elaborate burials from Iximché. Burial 27-A/IV, in Plaza A, was west of the larger pyramid, Temple 2, and on the western periphery of the Plaza; Burial 39-A was in an obverse position in

Plaza C, on the eastern periphery and just east of the larger of the two pyramids there. If political power emanated from the east, this would have been an ideal place to bury a deceased political leader, and if spiritual power and authority derived from the west, then to inter a religious leader on the western edge of Plaza A would have been just as fitting.

Moreover, grave goods accompanying the skeletal remains of the two individuals seem to turn this exercise in logic into a plausible interpretation. Guillemin (1961: 105) estimated that the principal interment (27-A/IV) in the Structure 27 crypt was possibly the remains of Chopená Tziquín Uqá, one of nine sons of Vukubatz, an early king of Iximché. The high status of the person in this burial was indicated by the presence of gold ornaments and a copper nose ornament. (Guillemin's ideas on this burial are reviewed in chapter 9.) The individual's skull had been crushed, and he evidently had died from this blow to the head (Guillemin 1961; chap. 9). Although there can be no doubt of the person's eminence in Iximché society, some artifacts do point to an association with death and spirituality.

The same individual wore a collar decorated with ten small jaguar heads of cast gold (see fig. 9.20). Marqusee (1980: 203–206), discussing the iconography of this artifact, pointed to the powerful role of the jaguar in Mesoamerican and South American religion. A guardian spirit, or *nahual*, relationship between jaguars and shamans commonly exists. The term *balam* means both "jaguar" and "sorcerer" in many Maya languages, including those of the Quiché group. Also, in his study of Late Postclassic Highland iconography, Marqusee found that jaguar effigies often occur on funerary urns and cited several examples from Iximché in the Museo Nacional de Arqueología y Etnología. In a detailed study, Marqusee (1980: 86–93) recorded jaguar effigy handles on 17 (63‰) of 27 essentially complete crematory urns from Mixco Viejo. The jaguar, then, is associated with death, spirituality, and religious practitioners.

Political leaders probably associated themselves with the jaguar image, but less often than did those in the religious hierarchy. The term *balam* appears rarely in the *Annals of the Cakchiquels* and was not a title associated directly with Cakchiquel kings in that book. In one of the early post-Conquest Quiché sources, the *Title of the Lords of Totonicapán* (Chonay and Goetz 1953), the four earliest Quiché kings are discussed and the *Balam* title is assigned to three of them (Balam-Quitzé, Balam-Agab, Mahucutah, and Iqi-Balam), but they are submerged in mythology (for example, those who came from the east are specifically referred to as *Nahuales*, or guardian spirits). The same names appear in the *Popol Vuh*, where they designate the first four men created by the "Bearer, Begetter, the Makers, Modelers named Sovereign Plumed Serpent" (D. Tedlock 1985: 163). In the *Popol Vuh*, they were the first to perform penitence, committing auto-sacrifice as well as animal and human sacrifice, and acted as intermediaries between humans and the gods. Ximénez commented on Balam-Quitzé in his guise as king: "This first King Balamquitzé meaning smiling jaguar or jaguar of the lethal smile like a poison which harms everyone. This king apparently was the one who originated human sacrifice to the idol Tohil" (Ximénez 1929, 1: 72). Las Casas (1958, 4: 344) stated that "they burned whoever was a sorcerer [*brujo o bruja*], calling them in their language *balan* which is to say, tiger. . . . these caused much harm, and they burned them for this, and the same thing was done of those found among Christians."

A final note regarding the association of jaguars with Burial 27-A/IV: It is possible that jaguar teeth were recovered from this burial. An unpublished photo taken by Guillemin shows a grouping of Burial 27-A/IV artifacts and jaguar teeth.

Another item in the same grave also carries strong ties to death and religion (that is, religious sacrifice): an incised bracelet, which, according to Guillemin, was fashioned from a human calvarium (Guillemin 1967: 34; see also chapter 10). Finally, the individual in Burial 27-A/IV wore a gold headband; Las Casas (1958, 4: 151) wrote of high priests ("at the hour of sacrifice") wearing crowns of gold, silver, or other metal, "the most precious they were able to have." These grave goods, then, are consonant with interment on the western edge of Plaza A.

According to the *Annals of the Cakchiquels* (Recinos and Goetz 1953: 100), Chopená Tziquín Uqá was killed in warfare, but another scenario seems at least as plausible. If the individual were a priest or priest-shaman, he might have been executed by clubbing. This was the exact penalty for the crime of witchcraft, specified according to indigenous law (Las Casas 1958, 4: 356).

By contrast, Burial 39-A from the eastern edge of Plaza C contained a necklace of cast gold bells and spherical beads. Gold was rare in the Highlands (Woodbury 1965: 176; Shook 1952: 25), and the artifact certainly connotes wealth and prestige. However, obvious symbolism having to do with death, sacrifice, and spirituality appears (from an admittedly distant vantage point) to be missing. Close to the grave were two large sculpted stone artifacts which may have been broken deliberately at the death of this personage, a Late Classic ball game yoke and a stone cylindrical phallus (probably the artifact in fig. 4.43). A sculpted face and cap make the latter a personified (or deified) phallus. There is mention of a phallic idol in the *Título Coyoi* (Guillemin 1977: 243; Carmack 1973: 319), and Maya gods associated with male sexuality tend to be affiliated with the earth, plant growth, and fertility (Thompson 1970: 294–297).

All of this is reminiscent of present-day Quiché diviners in Momostenango. "When a day keeper prays, he or she may begin, by facing east" (B. Tedlock 1992: 140). This is the direction of "descendents, divination . . . present, future/birth," while to the diviner's back, the west has to do with "past/death . . . Death Ceremony, Ancestors" (B. Tedlock 1992: fig. 26). One major point of contrast between Iximché and Momostenango, however, is that for the former, religion and politics were intertwined. The king or kings identified with the east, the source of life and fertility. In communion with the gods, the well-being of Cakchiquel kings was inextricably linked to that of their subjects. To the west, the sorcerers, the priests of Iximché, contended with the religion of death, with human sacrifice, and communication with ancestral spirits.

Other burials exhumed at Iximché are described in chapter 9. Most significant, however, are the 48 skulls from the base of the Temple 4 Annex (Structure 104), which is situated on the western edge of Plaza C. Although their interment in Plaza A would have simplified this narrative, their actual provenience does lead to consideration of another important dimension of Cakchiquel culture. Certainly political success and community well-being depended upon more than just the harmony Cakchiquel kings maintained with their gods. We are here confronted by one of those factors: military effectiveness. Probably war captives (chap. 9; see Las Casas (1958, 4: 353) on the preference for captives as sacrificial victims), these individuals were sacrificed in the compound of the dominant Cakchiquel king. Secular affairs must have taken precedence over religion at Iximché, given the demands of warfare if for no other reason, but in the practice of human sacrifice, religion, warfare, and political power were all closely intertwined. For the province of Verapaz, Las Casas wrote that although the principal priest had vassals subject to him, he was also inferior to the governing monarch. The principal priest, though, was the person most esteemed and revered by the king, the lesser lords, and the general populace (Las Casas 1958, 4: 351). The honor and prestige of the king, then, were enhanced and commemorated by these acts of sacrifice in his own ceremonial plaza.

Other fragments from the archaeological record contribute to this general interpretive reconstruction. First, Guillemin must have believed that the association of colors and directions on the painted walls of the Structure 1 temple was significant (blue with west-southwest and yellow with south-southwest). This is indicated in the brief passage from his field notes quoted in chapter four. Thompson (1970: 178, 211, 304, 308), citing Landa and other sources, related that blue was a sacred color associated with sacrifice and the rain gods, and yellow was associated with the direction south and death. These painted wall remnants add further support to the idea that the cardinal directions did hold sacred qualities for the inhabitants of Iximché.

Second, mention can be made of a ceramic figure which Guillemin regarded as a representation of Gucumatz. This large incensario fragment (Guillemin 1977: fig. 8) was found in front of the blocked-off steps to Patio I, Great Palace II (chap. 4). Its identification as Gucumatz was based on a subconical cap, typical of those found on Central Mexico portrayals of Quetzalcoatl as a human (Guillemin 1977: 256–257; cf. Burland 1968: 149, fig. 7d). This Great Palace II effigy of Gucumatz, the god of fertility and of the east, then, had been left in a fitting locality: in the eastern of the two major plaza complexes and at the political center of Iximché.

Settlement Design: A Colonial Perspective

Fuentes y Guzmán visited the ruins of Iximché in the late seventeenth century and left a sketch map and a detailed written description of the site (Sáenz de Santa Maria 1969: 333–335; Maudslay 1889–1902: pl. 73). He wrote that according to tradition commoners resided west (that is, northwest) of the defensive moat and nobility to the east within the protected portion of the town. His 1690 map shows many houses situated both east and west of this line (map 11.1). With this in mind, our hypothesis allows us to suggest a series of social filters operative at Iximché. In other words, the moat and physical barriers between Plazas A and B and between B and C may have functioned on a daily basis and not only while the town was under siege. Indeed, such attacks may have been rare events. During one recorded Prehispanic invasion of Iximché, the Cakchiquel army intercepted the invading Quiché somewhere in front of the town (Recinos and Goetz 1953: 102–103). In the only other recorded battle, that of the Tukuché revolt in 1492, the Tukuché attack began at the bridge over the Iximché moat. In the *Annals,* subsequent details of the fighting are confusing, except that the Tukuché were ultimately defeated (Recinos and Goetz 1953: 108–109). Following Fuentes y Guzmán, then, the moat separated nobility from commoners who may have been allowed only occasional visits across the bridge into Plaza A. If access to the large religious edifice in Plaza B was further limited, possibly only the most privileged or those in direct service to the monarch(s) would have entered the royal compound, Plaza C (or what may have been the two royal compounds of Plazas C and D, an idea developed below).

Richard Blanton offered a similar interpretation for the Classic period Monte Albán in Oaxaca, Mexico. He assumes that whereas civic buildings would lack "obvious architectural impediments to the general flow of traffic . . . Elite residences, facing inward on an enclosed patio were designed to restrict traffic flow or permit the selection of entrants" (Blanton 1978: 61). He then described the North Platform at Monte Albán as having both an accessible public platform facing the Main Plaza and a highly secluded elite component consisting of clustered mounds surrounding a small patio, "the single most secluded feature. . . in all of Monte Albán" (Blanton 1978: 61–62). Blanton suggests that this small mound group was the residence of the highest ranking household in the city.

There are obvious problems with the Fuentes y Guzmán sketch (map 11.1), but it is still interesting that he depicted within the Iximché precinct two adjacent plazas, one with a palace (labeled *"Plaza del Palacio"*) and the other with a temple (*"Plaza del Adoratorio"*). The problems concern the positions of these plazas within the site and how the site is oriented to the cardinal directions. Fuentes y Guzmán laid out the site's long axis due east and west instead of northwest to southeast as accurately recorded by Guillemin (see fig. 1.1). Also, Fuentes y Guzmán positioned these two important plazas so that they are aligned at right angles to the site's long axis instead of parallel to it. Finally, he shows the Plaza del Palacio as north of the Plaza del Adoratorio. In the interpretation offered here, however, the palace (Great Palace II) is south and southeast of the temple (Great Palace I).

In the text which accompanied his map, Fuentes y Guzmán seems to have been more concerned with accuracy (Sáenz de Santa María 1969, 1: 333–335). For example, he points out that the bridge over the moat was on the western side of the elite precinct with some orientation to

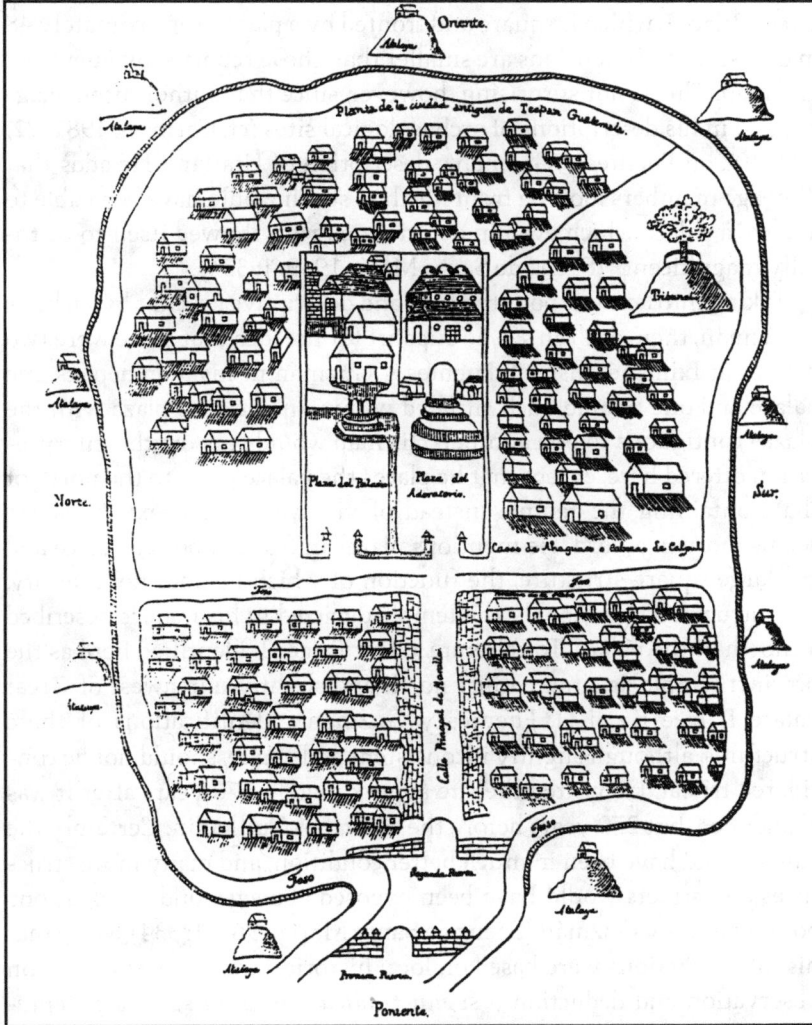

Map 11.1. Fuentes y Guzmán Sketch Map of Iximché (reproduced from A. P. Maudslay, 1889–1902, 2: plate 73)

the northwest ("*con alguna declinación at Noroeste*"). He describes at Iximché the ruins of a "serious and magnificent" building, whose length is 100 *pasos geométricos*. Assuming that a *paso geométrico* was the same length in the late seventeenth century as it is today, this structure would have been 139.3 m long. Fuentes y Guzmán further described this as a perfectly square stone masonry structure with a large square plaza in front of it. The largest edifice in the Iximché precinct is

Great Palace I, which is square and fronted by a plaza. Approximately 48 m on a side, its dimensions are smaller than those reported by Fuentes y Guzmán. This is not surprising, however, since that author often exaggerated in his descriptions of archaeological sites (cf. Carmack 1981: 22, 292–302 on Fuentes y Guzmán's description of Utatlán). He adds that "lineage members looking from north to south would have been able to admire a palace which even in deteriorated ruin showed itself to be totally magnificent" (Sáenz de Santa María 1969, 1: 334).

Taking into account both the map and descriptive account by Fuentes y Guzmán, then, one can see no support for the idea that there were two palaces at Iximché. Instead, Fuentes y Guzmán in his map depicts one palace and one temple, each situated within an enclosed plaza with the plazas contiguous to one another. His map would support the interpretation offered here, except that he places the palace plaza to the north of that containing the temple instead of vice versa. His text, however, seems more in accord. He mentions plazas in front of both a palace and the large square structure, the function of which he does not identify. This structure, presumably the temple depicted in his map, is described as north of the palace. To reiterate, Great Palace I, identified here as the precinct temple, is situated just north and slightly northwest of Great Palace II (see fig. 1.1). Fuentes y Guzmán's identifications of these structures, although slightly inconsistent and vague, should not be considered trivial. He visited the site approximately 170 years after it was abandoned, but 270 years before the arrival of Guillemin. Certainly the ruins would have been in much better condition, and many more structures and streets would have been exposed aboveground. Also, at one point Fuentes y Guzmán (Sáenz de Santa María 1969, 1: 334) wrote that his interpretations were based on local historical tradition as well as on observation and deduction (*"segun tradición y lo qu se deja patentemente conocer por su ostentación"*). Possibly, this tradition derived from local accounts perpetuated since the Conquest.

Early Ethnohistory

Is the idea of a temple of such imposing size and as centrally located as Great Palace I compatible with the earliest Spanish accounts of the Highland Maya? Miles, in an ethnohistorical reconstruction of Pokomam culture, tells us that Pokomam nobility "filled the offices of lords, priests of the upper brackets" and that "only boys of the first families were trained at the temples as writers and historians" (Miles 1957: 766). She also relates that all boys received instruction at the temple. At least temporary service may have been required, as many boys seem to have lived there along with priests (Miles 1957: 763). Miles adds, however, that the Spanish sources are weak on the roles of priests and their place in Pokomam social structure. She does suggest that a high priest, in effect, may have shared power with a town's political leader. The *Annals of the Cakchiquels* is mute on this point, and although reference is often made to the two co-rulers of Iximché, there is no mention of the religious responsibilities of either. We must emphasize that very little is known of Maya religious organization or the role of priests in the Prehispanic Maya community. This is true for the Lowlands (Thompson 1970: 167–168) as well as the Guatemalan Highlands (Carmack 1973: 86). As discussed in chapter 1, the authors of the *Annals of the Cakchiquels* either feared Spanish sanctions or had developed a strong aversion to their native religion. The *Annals* must provide a biased view of Cakchiquel culture, emphasizing secular, political figures over the religious leadership.

Such biases and the general paucity of ethnohistorical information may have led to distortions in the archaeological literature. Although Mesoamericanists tend to view temples as limited to one- or two-room structures atop steep-sided pyramids (e.g., Marcus 1983; Smith 1965: 85–86), there are at least several early Spanish accounts which suggest that in addition there were larger and more complex religious structures. Tomás López Medel (Medel 1941: 221) wrote in 1612 of sumptuous temples with many priests and contrasted these to very high square pyramids with broad bases which narrowed at their summits to a platform "which could accommodate a half dozen or a dozen men" and which were employed for human sacrifice. Another account, written by Alonso de Zorita sometime after his return to Spain in 1566, describes temple fields cultivated by aristocratic youth engaged in religious training. The harvest of maize, beans, chilies, and other cultigens was all stored in "graneries and rooms of the temples that were designated for this purpose" (Zorita 1963: 262).

Regarding the town plan, Miles believed that the principal lord's house, the temple, and the ball court all would have been centrally located. Based largely on the writing of Las Casas, Miles's reconstruction is not incompatible with the idea that the temple at Iximché would have been large, imposing, and situated near the center of the site.

The Second Palace

It seems unlikely that both of the co-ruling kings of Iximché resided at Great Palace II. At least the ceramic data presented in the preceding chapter do not support that idea. Great Palace I, as discussed earlier, also seems an unlikely candidate. Since the *Annals of the Cakchiquels* is quite clear that for most the town's history Iximché had two principal political leaders, the question of a second palace should be explored. Plaza D, immediately east of Great Palace II, contains a structure which Guillemin named Palace III (see fig. 1.1). Although Guillemin (1977: 244) saw Palace III as "very modest in comparison with the two already described," this room complex and Great Palace II architecturally have more in common with each other than either does with Great Palace I. In view of the ceramic data discussed above, Palace III deserves reconsideration as the second ruler's home.

Palace III has three small interior patios separated by intervening rooms and like Great Palace II (and in contradistinction to Great Palace I) lacks evidence of a central altar (Guillemin 1977: 244). Also, the size of Palace III, expanding more than 800 m², is not inconsiderable. If the royal apartment in Great Palace II occupied only the rooms surrounding Patios N and NE, then that portion of Great Palace II and Palace III are comparable enough. Finally, Palace III occupied its own large Plaza (D), apparently a scaled-down version of the Plaza A-Plaza B and Plaza C-Placita C complexes (described in chap. 4).

One might not expect palaces of equal grandeur, at any rate. The two Cakchiquel rulers had different titles, *Ahpop* and *Ahpop Qamahay*, and, according to Recinos, the latter was second in importance to the former and was slated to succeed him (footnote 37 in Recinos and Goetz 1953: 52).

Settlement Design at Chisalín and Iximché Compared

Chisalín is a Late Postclassic Quiché settlement which was intensively excavated and reported by John Weeks (1980; 1983). It is located on a small irregularly shaped plateau, surrounded by *barrancas* like Iximché but with access from the northeast. The single ceremonial plaza is configured much like Plazas A and B at Iximché: Facing pyramids are aligned east and west, and a ball court stands on the southwest corner.

Weeks identified four palaces at Chisalín, west, east, southeast, and south of the ceremonial plaza. Although all four structures are broad and relatively low platforms, two of these structures, 1B-3 and 4B-2, are large U-shaped platforms, each with an associated altar and with remnants of elongated buildings on one or two of the three summit segments. A third platform, 4D-3, is also large and U-shaped. It is described as follows: "[s]everal terraces were constructed to form interior courtyards or patios. Buildings with masonry foundations and either *adobe* or pole and thatch upper zones were built on these terraces and faced onto the courtyards" (Weeks 1983: 148). The fourth structure, 3D-4, has a broad rectangular summit surface and two small rectangular interior patios adjacent to one another of the type described for Great Palace II. Evidence for rooms surrounding these patios is absent, but they do connote the type of elite domicile suggested here for Iximché. This last structure occupies the southern, narrow side of and faces onto a rectangular courtyard which is bordered by elongated platforms (Weeks 1983: fig. 10). The entire structure-courtyard complex is much like that for Palace III at Iximché on the southern border of Plaza D. These two large Chisalín platforms with interior patios are situated south (3D-4) and southeast (4D-3) of the ceremonial plaza.

Weeks believes there was a dual social organization at Chisalín, and the presence of only two palaces would be compatible with that idea (Weeks 1983: 56–58). If just the two platforms with interior patios were actually palaces, instead of the larger group of four suggested by Weeks (and deleting the two structures with altars), there are definite parallels between the settlement organization of Chisalín and Iximché:

1. Ceremonial plazas contain east-west facing pyramids, and ball courts are on their southwest corners.
2. Residences of the political elite consisted of complexes of rooms situated around secluded patios.
3. Residences of the political elite were two in number and were situated south or southeast of the ceremonial plaza(s).

Differences between the centers can be explained partially in terms of their regional importance. Chisalín was a satellite to and about a kilometer to the south of Utatlán, the Quiché capital (Carmack 1981: fig. 8.2), whereas Iximché was the major Cakchiquel capital. This may explain the absence of a major temple at Chisalín and the lack of an expanded palace there.

Continuity in the Western Highlands

Very few Late Postclassic Highland sites have been investigated thoroughly. Chronological assignments based on surface ceramic collections can be misleading as can architectural reconstructions based on unexcavated structures. Nevertheless, some comparisons are warranted. Fox (1981) has identified an architectural divide separating the Quiché-Cakchiquel region on the west from the Pokomam-Rabinal region on the east, with the dividing line at Longitude 90°43′ W. He regarded the region east of this line as the Mesoamerican frontier zone, and although this interpretation presents some difficulties (see Arnauld 1981: 334–335 and Kennedy 1981: 338), architectural differences, east to west, are real enough.

Generally for the Late Postclassic, there are many shared architectural features between Highland Guatemala and Central Mexico (Smith 1965: 93), and these similarities are more pronounced for this eastern Highland region than for the Quiché-Cakchiquel region to the west. Features prevalent in the east include twin pyramids and, on many structures, multiple stairways set off by balustrades with vertical upper zones (see discussion in Fox 1981). Because they participated less in this pan-Mesoamerican architectural tradition, the western Highlands, then, appear to have been more conservative.

On the other hand, the Cakchiquel inhabitants of Iximché do seem to have been more open to these design ideas than were their contemporaries at other centers in the western Highlands. Consider the pyramidal temple bases at Iximché. Smith (1965: 87) wrote that for this period, "the substructures supporting temples are usually square and almost always rise in vertical terraces," and that, "they are flanked by balustrades with a vertical upper zone." The temple bases at Iximché lacked balustrades and are not square but have a modified cruciform outline. The interior corners of the cross are filled with small square projections which Guillemin (1959 field notes) referred to as "bastions." However, continuity is evidenced by what Smith considered a more typical design, and one which definitely is typical at sites to the east, such as Cahyup and Chutinamit in Baja Verapaz, which were described by Smith (1955), and at El Jocote and Cauinal in the same general region (near the confluence of the Río Rabinal and the Río Negro; Ichon 1979; Ichon and Grignon 1981). At Iximché, one can still imagine balustrades on either side of the stairs—on Temple 2, for example (see fig. 4.5)—except they are now so massive that they protrude to form one arm of the cross. That is, angled facing walls (vertical above outward-sloping sections) are still present on both sides of the stairway. The "bastions" of vertical-walled terraces represent the original square form of the pyramid. For the other three arms of the cross the end walls are composed of upper vertical and lower sloping sections (also representations of the balustrade form). In the future, this architectural form may be found commonly at other western Highland sites, but this will require extensive excavation and restoration efforts. The form does occur in the ceremonial plaza at Utatlán, where the western temple pyramid, as drawn in Wallace (1977), appears very likely to be the same structure illustrated as "*El Sacrificatorio*" by Catherwood (Stephens 1969: 184 ff).

Parenthetically, Stephens (1969: 184) mentioned that this structure "had been ornamented with painted figures," and that "in one place we made out part of the body of a leopard, well drawn and colored." We have, then, for Utatlán surviving as legend and in the form of art what was determined at Iximché through archaeology: the association of both the jaguar and human sacrifice with the direction west within a ceremonial plaza. Fuentes y Guzmán (1932–1933, 2: 415, 422) visited Utatlán in 1672 and described the *sacrificadero* as in tact and "toward the western part."

This architectural form as a structure base, however, was not described for Chisalín, which was intensively excavated by Weeks (1980; 1983). Low altars with this outline form were described for Chisalín (Weeks 1980: 346) and also have been recorded at Iximché (e.g., fig. 4.22), elsewhere in the vicinity of Utatlán (Babcock 1979: fig. 19a), and at other sites (distribution reviewed in Weeks 1980).

Other evidence of this pan-Mesoamerican architecture (cf. Smith 1965: 93) at Iximché includes the round altar in Plaza B; the double stairway on the upper portion of Temple 5; enclosed ball courts; and a low, bordering batter of cement which Guillemin described for the exterior wall of the Temple 2 superstructure (1959 field notes; 47 cm high $\times$ 29 cm wide at the base).

It remains to consider other sites within the western Highlands proper. Taken as a group, these sites may have their own distinguishing characteristics. Considered here briefly is a small group of sites with striking settlement-design parallels to Iximché: Chutixtioc and Tenam-Aguacatán on the upper Río Negro; the Quiché capital, Utatlán, and two of its outliers, Chisalín and Resguardo; and Pueblo Viejo Chichaj, also in the central Quiché region. Keeping in mind the tenuous nature of these comparisons, all six sites have plazas demarcated by facing pyramids aligned east and west and with enclosed-end ball courts in their southwest corners (see site plans and descriptions in Fox 1978; Ichon 1975;

Smith 1955; Wallace 1977; and Weeks 1977 and 1983). Among these sites, however, Iximché is unique in possessing two such plazas contiguous to one another. It also appears to be unique in having large residential structures appended to the ceremonial plazas, each with its own smaller courtyard (Plaza B and Placita C).

For the six comparable sites under discussion, it may be significant that in every case but one, the eastern pyramid is either reported to be higher or appears from plan-view drawings to be the more substantial of the two. (The exception is Utatlán, but there one of the two facing pyramids has been torn down completely, and the assessment is based on historical accounts and drawings summarized in Carmack 1981: 264–274.) This seems compatible with interpretations of Iximché's settlement plan offered above. In a town center with only a single plaza, one would expect civil concerns to have outweighed religious matters within the plaza and authority of political leadership to have taken precedence there. One would also expect that political authority would have taken precedence in the entire community, at least in the long run. In fact, the tallest structure at Iximché is Temple 5, the eastern pyramid in Plaza C.

It seems, then, that the planners of Iximché took the ceremonial plaza concept with its primarily political orientation and replicated it for the purely religious realm as well. Based on the sparse evidence at hand, this may not have occurred at other centers in the western Highlands.

12

꘏꘏꘏꘏꘏

Conclusion

In the foregoing chapters we examined the site of Iximché, focusing primarily on two classes of archaeological materials: ceramics and human skeletal remains. In many ways this has been an exercise in recent history—the history of an archaeological project carried out more than 30 years ago by George Guillemin. We have attempted to understand the surviving record of this project (in artifacts, in bones, and on paper) in order to illuminate the greater historical or archaeological question: what was the nature of the community which once resided on this small ravine-enclosed peninsula?

Much of this work has been descriptive. This is what we could glean from what Guillemin excavated at Iximché. Our work is also a summary of his observations of the ruins and burials, as he excavated and then restored platforms, mounds, and floors within the site's ceremonial center. We found much of this information in his notes and manuscripts.

Although circumstances have limited the value of the collections we studied, they still are of considerable import. The skeletal remains constitute the first Highland Maya collection fully analyzed using modern methods, and the study provides a baseline for assessing prehistoric health for this region of Mesoamerica. Ceramics from the two "Great Palaces" are in all likelihood the only significant artifactual record that will ever be obtained from these two preeminent structures at Iximché, regardless of the variety of fine-grained archaeological projects conducted there in the future.

Moving beyond Guillemin and his work, and moving beyond the material remains, we come to Iximché, the community, and its place in the life and times of fifteenth-to-sixteenth-century Guatemala. Part of our understanding of Iximché must derive from the ethnohistorical record, from characterizations of Highland Maya culture by the authors of the *Annals of the Cakchiquels,* by the chroniclers Francisco Ximénez, Antonio de Remesal, Francisco Vasquez, and Bartolomé de Las Casas, and other of their Colonial contemporaries, and by more recent scholars as well. We find that insights also come from a reconstructed history of Iximché based on these documents, the city's dealings with contemporary Highland cultures over several centuries. The ethnohistorical study which comprises chapter 2 is the first English language synthesis of early regional Cakchiquel history, and it helps to place the city of Iximché in a larger context. In chapter 3, we employed this literature to partially reconstruct Iximché culture as it existed just before the Conquest.

Every archaeologist is obligated to interpret data generated in the course of research, but in offering interpretations here, we have been acutely aware of the limitations of the ethnohistorical record as well as the flawed archaeological picture from Iximché. Also, there is a surprising lack of archaeological research on Highland Postclassic sites. The interpretations we offer here are only hypotheses to be tested in future research.

Ceramic Research

A broad view of ceramic trends and the ideas of George Guillemin can be reconsidered with all data now at hand. As stated above, Guillemin believed that the ceramics from Great Palace II represented a temporary post-Contact occupation and were not associated with the original occupation. He concluded that most of the sherds are from utilitarian ceramics (Guillemin 1977: 239). His conclusions seem reasonable, as an intuitive, overall assessment. In chapter 8, we reported higher percentages of thick, utilitarian pottery for Great Palace II, compared to Great Palace I.

However, recent work at the Classic site of Copán indicates that elite residences may tend to produce higher than expected quantities of utilitarian pottery, suggesting "food storage, preparation, and feasting" (Webster et al. 1998: 339). That is, high proportions of utilitarian pottery actually may be typical of palaces.

A patio-by-patio analysis of Great Palace II showed considerable variability by patio and that Patio NE was atypical within the Palace, owing to its higher proportions of thin, well-finished ceramics and also to the high frequency of sherds found there. But, the question remains, how do the ceramics of Patio NE compare with the collection from Great Palace I? As revealed in table 12.1, the two collections are similar, with neither standing out as more indicative of utilitarian, commoner activities. The most significant differences, predictably enough, seem to be the greater proportion of ceremonial ware in Great Palace I and the greater proportion of bichrome ware in Patio NE. A comparison of rare or potentially exotic types for the two showed a higher overall percentage for Patio NE (6.75% vs. 4.40% for Great Palace I), but much of this can be attributed to large proportions of two types in Patio NE: Orange on Gray-Buff and Red Bands on White.

If Guillemin were correct that the ceramics of Great Palace II are post-Contact in date, one would not expect to find sherd frequency increasing with inferred status. In a small refugee group, elite ceramics might be isolated but more likely would consist of a small minority, compared with other localities in the palace.

In sum, the ceramics as distributed at Great Palace II do not suggest the degraded assemblage of refugees, but the normal household activities one might expect of a residing elite family and its supporting personnel.

Guillemin's ideas on the functions of the two Great Palaces, however, are not so easily dismissed. These could have been the two major palaces, with the king in Great Palace I having more to do with religious activities, as Guillemin suggested. The idea is attractive in its simplicity: two kings (according to the *Annals of the Cakchiquels*), two major palaces, and two very similar compounds, one for each. Still, Guillemin's interpretation does not deal with architectural differences between the two structures or overall ceramic differences. The reader's

Table 12.1. Ceramics Compared: Patio NE vs. Great Palace I

Variable	G. P. I	Patio NE
Thickness (% thick)	44.14%	42.81%
Polish (both surfaces)	34.75%	17.77%
Slip (both surfaces)	28.34%	27.94%
Handle width (% wide)	48.35%	50.00%
Paste color (% dark)	64.20%	62.50%
Utility types	68.55%	67.04%
Ceremonial types	11.45%	5.86%
Monochrome SP types	12.00%	10.36%
Bichrome types	2.38%	5.71%

own evaluation will hinge on weightings assigned to the various forms of evidence: the importance of the elevated nature of Great Palace I, for example, and also of Weeks's correlation of ceremonial pottery and elevated structures at Chisalín. Then there is this important issue: the extent to which one accepts as bias the lack of documentation in the *Annals* for a priesthood. On this point hinges the interpreted priestly presence at the center of Iximché.

Future research may help decide the issue. The horseshoe curve in the correspondence analysis of chapter 7 may represent a progression of types from those affiliated with political activities at one end to those having to do with religion at the other. It actually appears to be based, of course, on differences in type composition between the two Great Palaces. The curve might come to appear in ceramic data for other Late Postclassic Highland sites, and future archaeological work might establish a regularly appearing dichotomy. The importance of organized religion at the center of these sites might then be interpreted both from the size of the structures involved and the intensity of occupation represented at both ends of the continuum.

A Note on Methodology

Computers have been used for many years in ceramic analyses for Southeastern Mesoamerica, but detailed provenience data, such as those discussed above, are not often reported. One impediment to generating such data in the past may relate to the tedium of recovering and summarizing provenience data after the sherds have been sorted physically by type. To go back through piles of hundreds of sherds and to use sherd catalogue numbers to tabulate the number of sherds by type from each excavation unit or site locality can involve hundreds of hours of work. Modern microcomputers and comprehensive software packages can take much of the labor out of this process.

For example, at Iximché each large plastic bag found in the store room was given an arbitrary lot number (in the data set PROVNO), and smaller bags inside larger ones were identified by letter, "a," "b," et cetera. (In the data set these small bag designations were later converted to numbers; for BAGNO, a = 1, b = 2, et cetera.) Individual sherds might be numbered "IX258a-1," "IX258a-2," et cetera.

In almost all cases, Guillemin assigned proveniences to large bags; included smaller bags had the same provenience. Sometimes many large bags (PROVNO's) had the same provenience, that is, Guillemin had written the same information on different bag labels. For example, 17 PROVNO's have the provenience, "Great Palace II, Patio N-E." After the collection had been sorted by type, each sherd was re-examined, and the catalogue number (recorded by CATNO, BAGNO, and PROVNO) for each was listed by type. For the Iximché research, other attribute data were listed at the same time, for THICK, SLIP, POLISH, and so forth. This resulted in a large data set with 9508 data lines, one for each potsherd.

The real time-saving device is the "Merge" procedure in comprehensive software packages. SAS (Statistical Analysis System) software was used for the work at Iximché. The procedure provides for merging two data sets on the basis of a common variable.

One data set was the large one mentioned above. The second data set was, in effect, an archaeological catalogue. Each PROVNO was listed along with its provenience designation, which was named NEWPROV. Thus, there was a small two-variable data set consisting of all PROVNO's and corresponding NEWPROV's. This second data set had 174 data lines, one for each large plastic bag of artifacts (PROVNO) included in this research. The 27 NEWPROVS are listed in chapter 5. The merge procedure, then, linked the appropriate NEWPROV value to each data line in the larger data set on the basis of the common variable, PROVNO. Finally, with TYPE and NEWPROV listed for each sherd in the expanded data set, it was a simple matter to generate a two-way table of type by provenience (see appendix A).

Critical Overview

This research represents an effort to salvage information from the Guillemin collection of Iximché potsherds. One major problem was the lack of stratigraphic control. Ceramic differences across various structures at the site to some extent could be the product of time and culture change. In fact, Guillemin (1977) suggested this as an explanation for ceramic differences between Great Palaces I and II; that is, they were the result of the presence of Prehispanic and refugee post-Contact populations. Guillemin recognized three or more stages of construction in some of the structures he excavated, so the potential exists for a site ceramic sequence. At the same time, the *Annals of the Cakchiquels* indicates a relatively brief history for the site, and virtually all of the pottery appears to be of the Late Postclassic period. Any ceramic sequence probably would involve minor differences in type morphological attributes, but that remains to be determined through further excavations at Iximché.

With this and other limitations in mind, types as defined in this study were not viewed as immutable entities. They were not given formal names, and it is believed the typology will be refined through future research. The rationale for this approach was expressed succinctly by Robert Wauchope 30 years ago, and conditions in the vicinity of Iximché have not changed appreciably since: "In the case of pottery from intensively investigated limited areas, perhaps we are justified in using the type-variety nomenclature; this is certainly not yet the case with Protohistoric pottery of the Guatemala Highlands except as a convenient tentative classification subject to year-to-year modifications" (Wauchope 1970: 100).

Conclusions

What, then, can be said of this investigation of Iximché ceramics? We have moved toward establishing a site ceramic typology and thereby contributed to the definition of late prehistoric/protohistoric complexes which might prove co-extensive with territories of historic Maya ethnolinguistic groups in the Highlands. The typological study, combined with attribute analysis, allowed re-evaluation of Guillemin's functional assessments for the two major structures on the site, Great Palaces I and II. Now, with ceramic and architectural evidence combined, and especially in view of Weeks's (1980, 1983) findings from Chisalín, a case can be made that Great Palace I was more likely the major temple at Iximché. The attribute and typological distributions among the patios of Great Palace II led to the identification of one of these patios, NE, as the center of one king's apartment.

The attribute study augmented that of type distributions, and the sherd thickness variable was identified as a potentially useful tool in Late Postclassic research. Weeks (1980, 1983) in his study of Chisalín discovered a kind of signature for ceremonial structures: a distinctive architectural attribute (that is, elevated platform) coupled to relatively high proportions of ceremonial type pottery. Work at Iximché suggests this signature can be expanded: possibly thicker utility ware at domiciliary structures and thicker ceremonial ware at ceremonial structures. Other signatures may well be developed, as suggested by ceramics patterns across the patios of Great Palace II. Characteristic ceramic profiles linked to distinctive architectural features (for example, altars, the presence of interior patios) may lead to reasonable and detailed reconstructions on a structure-by-structure and site-by-site basis.

Human Remains

Guillemin noted that several ancient and contemporary groups in the Americas deserted or destroyed a house after a deceased person was buried there, and villages were abandoned after the death of the chief. Abandoning an entire ceremonial center was impractical. "I am inclined to believe that such customs can also explain a good part of the superpositions and transformations of Mesoamerican ceremonial buildings, from diverse epochs and cultures, which also show parallels and common features with the funeral customs observed in Iximché" (Guillemin n.d.f).

At Iximché, many of the burials of individuals who were not sacrificial victims were "intrusive," that is, they were located underneath house platforms. It seemed notable to Guillemin that the two house platforms producing the most burials (Structures 27 and 39) were located behind the main temple of each of the two principal complexes. Skeletons generally were in a squatting position but had no standard orientation. A broken obsidian biface (knife or projectile point) was frequently found with the dead (Guillemin n.d.d: 13; 1965a: 32; 1966: 11; 1967: 33; 1977: 243). Las Casas (1958, 4: 362), referring to burial customs in Verapaz, described interments as seated with faces "turned toward the south." Pieces of jade or jade beads were also common, possibly reflecting the custom of rubbing the face with a precious stone to capture the departing spirit of the dead (Las Casas 1958, 4: 361) or the Classic period practice of placing a bead in the mouth of the deceased.

Many, but not all, of the artifacts described in association with human remains were found in bags with bones in the storage facility at Iximché. A few bones and burial goods are on display in the Museo Nacional de Arqueología y Etnología in Guatemala City. The gold crown and necklace worn by Individual IV in Burial 27-A are rumored to have disappeared from the town hall of Tecpán in the aftermath of a destructive earthquake (Vinicio García, personal communication, 17 August 1992).

The minimum number of individuals represented by skeletal remains is 66, the number of distinct groupings of cranial bones. The maximum number is 92, the number of cranial groupings plus the number of the most common postcranial element: the shaft of the left femur. The actual number probably lies somewhere between those extremes. It is possible to lower the maximum by assuming (1) Guillemin's identification of 50 crania as decapitations (see chap. 9) is correct, (2) all of them are represented among the 66 groupings of cranial bones, (3) none of them is associated with a left femur, and (4) all 16 of the remaining crania are associated with left femurs. This leaves 50 crania without femurs, 16 crania with femurs, and 10 femurs without crania, for a total of 76 individuals. In reality, some of the decapitated crania may have been associated with left femurs; figures 8.20 and 8.22 show postcranial bones lying within the deposit of 48 crania. Conversely, some of the remaining 16 crania may *not* have been associated with left femurs; Guillemin reported one incomplete and two secondary burials. In conclusion, the number of individuals represented by skeletons is no less than 66 and probably not much greater than 76.

It is not clear in most cases what social status a person whose skeletal remains were recovered at Iximché might have held in life. The rare Nondecapitations accompanied by gold offerings almost certainly were members of the Cakchiquel royalty, important priests, or other nobility. The individuals sometimes accompanying them are more problematical: Were they high-status wives, slaves, or war captives sacrificed to accompany the powerful person into the realm of death? Welsh (1988: 173) interpreted evidence from Classic Lowland burials to mean that such individuals were slaves, killed to serve their masters in the afterlife. However, stable isotope evidence that the diet of individuals whose postcranial remains were buried at Iximché included a high proportion of maize, a status food, supports their identification as high status. The social status of Decapitations, confirmed sacrificial victims, is also open to debate. Ethnohistoric accounts (see below) relate that high-status individuals from rival polities were sometimes captured and executed. Other accounts suggest that some victims were of lower status. The dentitions of some Decapitations exhibit traces of labret polishing; these may have been high-status individuals. The social status of Decapitations lacking such traces cannot be determined with certainty from evidence currently available. The surprising range of stable carbon isotope values in Iximché teeth, given the short span of time during which burials occurred, can be interpreted as indicating diversity in either geographic origin or social status.

Clearly, all damage associated with warfare and human sacrifice in this sample from Iximché was caused by stone weapons. Our expectation that direct evidence of the Spanish Conquest would be found in the marks of metal weapons on human bones was not met. However, evidence of the Conquest did come to light in the form of bones of a butchered horse, an iron horseshoe, and an aborted copper lance point, which were found in bags of artifacts during the search for human remains.

There were ample opportunities for people at Iximché to obtain both sacrificial victims and battle injuries without going far from home. While Oxlahuh Tzíi and Cablahuh Tihax were ruling Iximché, the city resisted an attack by the Quichés whose kings Tepepul and Itzayul, many court dignitaries, and warriors were captured and later executed (Recinos 1988: 86). The Akajal king Ychal, his principal lords, and warriors also were killed when they came to Iximché (Recinos 1988: 87–88). On May 18, 1493, the Tukuché, who were in revolt, attacked Iximché but were defeated (Recinos 1988: 88–90). In 1517, when Hunyg and Lahuh Noh ruled Iximché, the Quichés were again defeated and many prisoners were taken (Recinos 1988: 94–95).

It is logical that sacrificial victims chosen from among captive warriors or noncombatants from settlements within enemy territory would have been the most physically fit and attractive members of society, and many victims appear to have been young adults.

Not all females who died as sacrificial victims or with battle-related injuries were necessarily bystanders, though. Four women of Iximché, disguised for battle as young warriors in cotton cloaks, armed themselves with bows to fight against the Tukuché revolt (Recinos 1988: 90). After the battle their bodies were carried to the district of the Zotzils and Xahils, from which they came.

Many presumed decapitations are known from other Maya sites (Welsh 1988: 167–173), but the deposit of decapitated skulls most directly comparable to the one at Iximché is the Terminal Classic skull pit at Colha, Belize (Massey and Steele 1997). At that site, 30 crania were placed in two layers in a 20-cm-deep pit whose extent was 110 cm × 80 cm. Although human sacrifices at Colha and Iximché share superficial similarities, their demographic and physical characteristics differ. The Colha skulls were all deposited in a single event. More than one-half of the individuals whose sex can be determined are females. One-third are children, but none of the individuals is between the ages of 7 and 18. Massey and Steele reported damage from the process of decapitation on only two vertebrae, although cervical vertebrae accompanied most crania. They did not note decapitation damage on any mandibles or skull bases but reported extensive cut marks on the skulls, interpreted as evidence of defleshing. Tooth filing, wear, caries, alveolar abscesses, enamel hypoplasias, calculus, periodontal disease, ante-mortem loss, and malformations (notching on the edges of incisors and fusion or gemination) were found. Bone disorders include infection, joint deformation, developmental anomalies, and cribra orbitalia (ane-mia). Cranial deformation was practiced, and some bones were charred. Massey and Steele concluded that the impetus for creation of the skull pit may have been religious sacrifice, political defeat, or both, but they did not feel comfortable drawing firm conclusions.

The Colha sacrifices are earlier than those at Iximché. The Terminal Classic was a period of extensive social upheaval and political and de-mographic collapse. Although continuous warfare with surrounding groups and internal revolts might suggest that a degree of social up-heaval also existed at Iximché, it is clear that the Cakchiquel kingdom was politically strong and undergoing a period of rapid and aggressive expansion on the eve of the Spanish Conquest. Differences in the char-acteristics of sacrificial deposits between Colha and Iximché may reflect differences in the source of victims: internal revolt versus external con-quest. They may also reflect differences in overall growth potential of the polities involved owing to underlying social realities.

Frequencies of lesions that are important indicators of diet and health—porotic hyperostosis, periosteal reactions, and dental caries—are relatively low at Iximché in comparison with other Maya and non-Maya skeletal series. It is appealing to equate this with good health and diet among members of Late Postclassic Highland society. This may in-deed be the explanation, but it is difficult to draw strong conclusions based on differences in frequencies of lesions between populations alone. Stable isotopes indicate that both subadults and adults depended heavily on maize for food. Although maize may have been a status food, heavy reliance on it argues against good health and diet. High frequen-cies of enamel hypoplasias and tooth trauma and presence of depressed cranial lesions and reactions at muscle and connective tissue attachment areas also suggest that life was not always easy for people at Iximché.

Ethnohistory

Because we have included both documentary and archaeological evi-dence in this volume, it is appropriate to review briefly some possible interrelationships between the two types of evidence. Ethnohistory is sometimes narrowly defined as the study of the past using non-Western indigenous historical materials. However, most ethnohistorians would also include in this definition all the information about indigenous peoples, many of whom had no written language, written by the earliest Europeans to travel, and eventually settle, among them. This is certainly the case with the Maya of Highland Guatemala who, at Spanish Contact, did not have a written language. Only in the early Colonial period did Cakchiquel elites, such as the authors of the *Annals of the Cakchiquels*, learn to record their oral history and genealogies. These two authors, Francisco Oxlahuh and Francisco Díaz, were members of the Xajilá lineage and direct descendants of the Iximché ruler Oxlahuh (Recinos and Goetz 1953: 11, 15). Although such accounts probably existed as oral history before the Conquest, early Colonial period native elites were motivated to write their histories. They were attempting to acquire for themselves *cacique* privileges, awarded by the Spanish Crown to those who could demonstrate direct descent from Prehispanic indigenous rulers (Carmack 1973: 50).

The term "historical archaeology" is most often used to describe sites somewhat later than Iximché. Examples would include sites that existed during the Colonial period after Spanish control had been established and colonization begun, and about which much more has been written. The profusion of documentary sources available for Guatemala later in the Colonial period begins at Spanish Contact with a mere trickle, and only gradually expands with subsequent colonization into a significant body of written evidence. Little (1992: 1–5) applies the term "text-aided archaeology" to include sites, even prehistoric ones, about which anything at all has been written, even if only in modern times. Contributors to this volume address relationships among the various available sources (archaeology, documents, ethnography, and oral history), and focus on the ways in which many kinds of historical documents can be used to help interpret archaeological data. For societies such as the "protohistoric" Iximché Cakchiquel, who lived immediately before the historic period but about whom some historical documentation exists, the term "text-aided archaeology," as broadly interpreted by Little, is appropriate. However, much information we wish we had is simply not available, and it has been difficult to tease "history" out of the relatively few relevant sources which can be brought to bear upon the site of Iximché.

In her introduction, Little (1992: 4) states that documentary and archaeological data may be thought of as "interdependent and complementary or as independent and contradictory." Some historical archaeologists see the documentary and archaeological records as independent sources of data to be "played off" against each other. Thus, the goal is not simply to fill in the gaps, but where there is poor fit between the two data sets, to identify anomalies that will lead to further questions. Other contributors to Little's volume, fortunate to have both rich documentary and rich archaeological resources, find that the two bodies of data fit much better and are thus more interdependent and complementary. Though the two approaches appear contradictory, both can provide useful material for the archaeologist, depending upon the richness of the types of evidence involved.

Because of the paucity of direct historical information about Iximché, it is a site that must be examined using primarily prehistoric archaeological techniques. This is true even for Lowland Maya sites for which deciphered hieroglyphic texts are available. The elite bias inherent in such documents requires that the more egalitarian and democratic techniques of prehistoric archaeology be used to illuminate the lives of the people of all classes and statuses who made up such a complex society.

Historical, or text-aided, archaeology began as a North American phenomenon and has only recently begun to be productively practiced in Latin America. Thus, it is not surprising that George Guillemin did not design his original excavations at Iximché as a project in historical archaeology. Neither should readers be surprised that in reworking the Iximché materials we would attempt to utilize more historical sources than Guillemin himself used.

In chapter 2 we have provided a reconstruction of Cakchiquel protohistory and a summary of what is known about Iximché and the Cakchiquels in the early Colonial period, with comments about the significance of the site in modern times. The city of Iximché has been placed in a regional context, especially regarding its military struggles with other competing groups both inside and outside the Cakchiquel region. We now know that during the 50 years before Spanish contact the Iximché Cakchiquel had attempted to extend their control over the entire Cakchiquel region, including the obsidian mines in Jilotepeque and at nearby El Chayal as well as the rich cacao fields along the Pacific coast. Iximché clearly constituted the "heartland" and Tzololá, Jilotepeque, and Sacatepéquez the "hinterland" in terms of power relationships. Between about 1517 and the arrival of the Spanish in 1524 the Iximché Cakchiquel had defeated the rebellious Sacatepéquez Cakchiquel, which finally put them in control of the entire Cakchiquel region.

Further expansion by Iximché was perhaps only temporarily curtailed by equally strong and warlike neighbors to the north (Quichés and Rabinals), west (Tzutujils), and south (Pipils), who competed for the same resources, and whom the Iximché Cakchiquel often fought. The elites of Iximché might well have continued to expand their power and influence in the region had Spanish conquest not intervened. Acting briefly as allies to the Spaniards against their old rivals the Quichés, the Cakchiquel eventually revolted against the abusive treatment they received at the hands of the foreigners. Pockets of resistance continued to plague the conquerors for many more years until they finally executed the last of the Iximché Cakchiquel kings in 1540.

In chapter 3 the relevant published sources have been scoured for any clues that might assist in drawing conclusions from the archaeological data about this important site. These sources, which contain tantalizing yet elusive bits of information, constitute an opportunity for the archaeologist at the same time that they create a dilemma. As has been discussed above, if it could be demonstrated that the archaeological and documentary data for Iximché were equally rich, they would be more interdependent and complementary, and they could be given equal weight in the final analysis. For Iximché, however, the documentary record is less rich and less well-corroborated than we would like. For example, the *Annals of the Cakchiquels* was written soon after the Conquest. In addition to its elite bias, this important source contains relatively little discussion of several topics of interest to the researcher such as native religion, undoubtedly the result of culture contact and the Spanish policy of directed culture change.

Similarly, although the *Apologética Historia* of Las Casas is extremely detailed and was written between 1527 and 1550 (Hanke 1951: 66), more than 100 years before the next Spanish Colonial account of the Highland Maya, ethnohistorians encounter significant problems with this source. Las Casas does not claim to be an eyewitness to much about what he wrote in the *Apologética*, in contrast to such claims in many of his other works (Wagner 1967: 201–202). He may not have spoken an indigenous language, and by his own admission he relied on the accounts of other ecclesiastics, mostly Dominicans, who did speak native languages. Las Casas was also a polemical figure who generated much controversy during his lifetime and since, and who wrote with his own agenda in mind. The *Apologética Historia* is also problematic because it stands without ethnohistorical corroboration, and, because, as mentioned above, it cannot be demonstrated to apply specifically to the Cakchiquel.

Admitting these shortcomings, Las Casas's account is still important because it purports to describe Maya society as it existed before Spanish influence and because Las Casas theoretically was in a position to do so. Carmack (1973: 100) regards the *Apologética Historia* as "the most important Spanish source on prehispanic Quichean culture," and later Spanish Colonial writers often relied on Las Casas for information on traditional Maya culture (Miles 1957: 736).

What can be done under the circumstances is to attempt to evaluate the Las Casas account, as it might apply to Iximché, by looking for both support and inconsistencies in the archaeological record. There we do find limited support from archaeological Iximché: the importance of bird symbolism, the practice of auto-sacrifice, and human sacrifice through decapitation. Also, we have identified no inconsistencies. Future archaeological research will continue to explore this problem. In sum, given the limitations of the ethnohistorical sources, it is appropriate in our final interpretation of the site of Iximché that greater reliance has been placed upon the archaeological data.

And Finally ...

We are left, then, with final impressions of Iximché. Here was a political, economic, and ceremonial center which grew quickly from its founding. Its citizens and leaders stood ready to expand their borders militarily in order to secure their own independence, to expand economic opportunities, and to appease their gods and, we would imagine, their own restless dispositions.

The arts and building crafts prospered and were often dedicated to public ceremonies, sometimes involving human sacrifice and/or the funeral of a deceased public figure. And, people from surrounding towns were drawn to Iximché to witness or participate in these events and to negotiate other matters of importance. Much of this is preserved archaeologically in the human skeletal remains and the elaborate building platforms, pyramids, ball courts, and plazas at Iximché, or it can be surmised from the study of historical documents. It also can be seen in the ceramic industry. The incensarios reflect both artistic and technical excellence but so do the remains of utility vessels for everyday use. There was an artistic sensibility at work here.

With the Spanish invasion and ultimate conquest, the picture is one of profound change: the sudden abandonment of Iximché; the end of a vigorous state; cessation of elaborate pageantry; and demographic catastrophe caused by epidemic disease and Spanish oppression. Severe retrenchment in the building and ceramic crafts occurred as well. It is no wonder that to this day Highland Maya commemorate the Conquest through their poignant dances.

Today the Cakchiquel participate not only in local affairs, but provide leadership in government at the national level. Their folk art thrives in the weaving of the famed women's blouses known as *huipiles* (Hendrickson 1995), while some painters are known internationally for their work in the greater artistic traditions. Weekly markets at Tecpán and Comalapa are crowded with those selling home-grown produce, while other Cakchiquel entrepreneurs conduct their business by E-mail and FAX.

Altogether, these people understand Iximché as a place of great historical significance, as do other Guatemalans. It is a national landmark they are willing to share with visitors. The site certainly beckons other ethnohistorians, physical anthropologists, and archaeologists. Given the enormity of the task ahead, the odyssey into the ethnohistory and archaeology of protohistoric Guatemala is just beginning.

Appendix A. Type Distributions by Provenience at Iximché: Table of Newprov by Type (Chapter 5)

NEWPROV Frequency Percent Row Pct	TYPE							Total (Types 1–47)
	1	2	3	4	5	6	7	
1	320	17	4	1	1	1	0	792
	3.37	0.18	0.04	0.01	0.01	0.01	0.00	8.33
	40.40	2.15	0.51	0.13	0.13	0.13	0.00	
2	212	20	9	5	0	1	0	534
	2.23	0.21	0.09	0.05	0.00	0.01	0.00	5.62
	39.70	3.75	1.69	0.94	0.00	0.19	0.00	
3	427	35	9	39	3	2	0	1332
	4.49	0.37	0.09	0.41	0.03	0.02	0.00	14.01
	32.06	2.63	0.68	2.93	0.23	0.15	0.00	
4	93	7	4	4	0	0	0	318
	0.98	0.07	0.04	0.04	0.00	0.00	0.00	3.34
	29.25	2.20	1.26	1.26	0.00	0.00	0.00	
5	142	5	1	9	2	1	0	407
	1.49	0.05	0.01	0.09	0.02	0.01	0.00	4.28
	34.89	1.23	0.25	2.21	0.49	0.25	0.00	
6	33	3	0	0	0	0	0	93
	0.35	0.03	0.00	0.00	0.00	0.00	0.00	0.98
	35.48	3.23	0.00	0.00	0.00	0.00	0.00	
7	28	6	0	0	0	0	0	118
	0.29	0.06	0.00	0.00	0.00	0.00	0.00	1.24
	23.73	5.08	0.00	0.00	0.00	0.00	0.00	
8	368	15	5	10	0	0	0	901
	3.87	0.16	0.05	0.11	0.00	0.00	0.00	9.48
	40.84	1.66	0.55	1.11	0.00	0.00	0.00	
9	443	42	11	8	1	4	0	1528
	4.66	0.44	0.12	0.08	0.01	0.04	0.00	16.07
	28.99	2.75	0.72	0.52	0.07	0.26	0.00	
10	299	37	2	21	2	4	1	1038
	3.14	0.39	0.02	0.22	0.02	0.04	0.01	10.92
	28.81	3.56	0.19	2.02	0.19	0.39	0.10	
11	112	6	0	3	0	1	0	373
	1.18	0.06	0.00	0.03	0.00	0.01	0.00	3.92
	30.03	1.61	0.00	0.80	0.00	0.27	0.00	
12	81	5	0	0	0	2	0	254
	0.85	0.05	0.00	0.00	0.00	0.02	0.00	2.67
	31.89	1.97	0.00	0.00	0.00	0.79	0.00	
13	23	1	6	0	0	0	0	147
	0.24	0.01	0.06	0.00	0.00	0.00	0.00	1.55
	15.65	0.68	4.08	0.00	0.00	0.00	0.00	

NEWPROV Frequency Percent Row Pct	TYPE							Total (Types 1–47)
	1	2	3	4	5	6	7	
14	16	1	0	2	0	0	0	67
	0.17	0.01	0.00	0.02	0.00	0.00	0.00	0.70
	23.88	1.49	0.00	2.99	0.00	0.00	0.00	
15	8	1	0	0	0	0	0	28
	0.08	0.01	0.00	0.00	0.00	0.00	0.00	0.29
	28.57	3.57	0.00	0.00	0.00	0.00	0.00	
16	72	4	0	2	2	2	0	177
	0.76	0.04	0.00	0.02	0.02	0.02	0.00	1.86
	40.68	2.26	0.00	1.13	1.13	1.13	0.00	
17	0	0	0	0	0	0	0	7
	0.00	0.00	0.00	0.00	0.00	0.00	0.00	0.07
	0.00	0.00	0.00	0.00	0.00	0.00	0.00	
18	35	3	0	1	0	0	0	79
	0.37	0.03	0.00	0.01	0.00	0.00	0.00	0.83
	44.30	3.80	0.00	1.27	0.00	0.00	0.00	
19	45	7	4	0	0	0	0	159
	0.47	0.07	0.04	0.00	0.00	0.00	0.00	1.67
	28.30	4.40	2.52	0.00	0.00	0.00	0.00	
20	91	2	3	1	0	0	0	304
	0.96	0.02	0.03	0.01	0.00	0.00	0.00	3.20
	29.93	0.66	0.99	0.33	0.00	0.00	0.00	
21	41	3	0	16	0	0	0	163
	0.43	0.03	0.00	0.17	0.00	0.00	0.00	1.71
	25.15	1.84	0.00	9.82	0.00	0.00	0.00	
22	100	4	8	1	0	4	0	360
	1.05	0.04	0.08	0.01	0.00	0.04	0.00	3.79
	27.78	1.11	2.22	0.28	0.00	1.11	0.00	
23	2	0	0	0	0	0	0	4
	0.02	0.00	0.00	0.00	0.00	0.00	0.00	0.04
	50.00	0.00	0.00	0.00	0.00	0.00	0.00	
25	27	3	0	1	0	0	0	65
	0.28	0.03	0.00	0.01	0.00	0.00	0.00	0.68
	41.54	4.62	0.00	1.54	0.00	0.00	0.00	
26	6	0	3	0	0	0	0	42
	0.06	0.00	0.03	0.00	0.00	0.00	0.00	0.44
	14.29	0.00	7.14	0.00	0.00	0.00	0.00	
27	73	4	2	2	0	0	0	218
	0.77	0.04	0.02	0.02	0.00	0.00	0.00	2.29
	33.49	1.83	0.92	0.92	0.00	0.00	0.00	
Total (Newprovs 1–27)	3097	231	71	126	11	22	1	9508
	32.57	2.43	0.75	1.33	0.12	0.23	0.01	100.00

(continued)

(continued)

NEWPROV Frequency Percent Row Pct	TYPE							Total (Types 1–47)
	8	9	10	11	12	13	14	
1	2 0.02 0.25	0 0.00 0.00	19 0.20 2.40	0 0.00 0.00	0 0.00 0.00	0 0.00 0.00	0 0.00 0.00	792 8.33
2	14 0.15 2.62	0 0.00 0.00	1 0.01 0.19	0 0.00 0.00	0 0.00 0.00	1 0.01 0.19	0 0.00 0.00	534 5.62
3	24 0.25 1.80	0 0.00 0.00	28 0.29 2.10	1 0.01 0.08	1 0.01 0.08	1 0.01 0.08	0 0.00 0.00	1332 14.01
4	2 0.02 0.63	1 0.01 0.31	5 0.05 1.57	11 0.12 3.46	0 0.00 0.00	0 0.00 0.00	0 0.00 0.00	318 3.34
5	7 0.07 1.72	0 0.00 0.00	7 0.07 1.72	0 0.00 0.00	0 0.00 0.00	0 0.00 0.00	0 0.00 0.00	407 4.28
6	0 0.00 0.00	0 0.00 0.00	0 0.00 0.00	0 0.00 0.00	1 0.01 1.08	0 0.00 0.00	0 0.00 0.00	93 0.98
7	2 0.02 1.69	0 0.00 0.00	1 0.01 0.85	0 0.00 0.00	0 0.00 0.00	0 0.00 0.00	0 0.00 0.00	118 1.24
8	17 0.18 1.89	0 0.00 0.00	17 0.18 1.89	0 0.00 0.00	0 0.00 0.00	0 0.00 0.00	0 0.00 0.00	901 9.48
9	17 0.18 1.11	0 0.00 0.00	35 0.37 2.29	4 0.04 0.26	1 0.01 0.07	0 0.00 0.00	0 0.00 0.00	1528 16.07
10	17 0.18 1.64	0 0.00 0.00	18 0.19 1.73	1 0.01 0.10	0 0.00 0.00	0 0.00 0.00	0 0.00 0.00	1038 10.92
11	0 0.00 0.00	0 0.00 0.00	18 0.19 4.83	0 0.00 0.00	0 0.00 0.00	0 0.00 0.00	0 0.00 0.00	373 3.92
12	1 0.01 0.39	0 0.00 0.00	8 0.08 3.15	0 0.00 0.00	0 0.00 0.00	0 0.00 0.00	1 0.01 0.39	254 2.67
13	1 0.01 0.68	0 0.00 0.00	1 0.01 0.68	0 0.00 0.00	0 0.00 0.00	0 0.00 0.00	0 0.00 0.00	147 1.55

NEWPROV Frequency Percent Row Pct	TYPE							Total (Types 1–47)
	8	9	10	11	12	13	14	
14	1	0	3	0	0	0	0	67
	0.01	0.00	0.03	0.00	0.00	0.00	0.00	0.70
	1.49	0.00	4.48	0.00	0.00	0.00	0.00	
15	0	0	0	0	0	0	0	28
	0.00	0.00	0.00	0.00	0.00	0.00	0.00	0.29
	0.00	0.00	0.00	0.00	0.00	0.00	0.00	
16	2	0	3	0	0	2	2	177
	0.02	0.00	0.03	0.00	0.00	0.02	0.02	1.86
	1.13	0.00	1.69	0.00	0.00	1.13	1.13	
17	0	0	0	0	0	0	0	7
	0.00	0.00	0.00	0.00	0.00	0.00	0.00	0.07
	0.00	0.00	0.00	0.00	0.00	0.00	0.00	
18	0	0	0	1	0	0	0	79
	0.00	0.00	0.00	0.01	0.00	0.00	0.00	0.83
	0.00	0.00	0.00	1.27	0.00	0.00	0.00	
19	3	0	0	0	0	0	0	159
	0.03	0.00	0.00	0.00	0.00	0.00	0.00	1.67
	1.89	0.00	0.00	0.00	0.00	0.00	0.00	
20	2	0	8	0	0	0	0	304
	0.02	0.00	0.08	0.00	0.00	0.00	0.00	3.20
	0.66	0.00	2.63	0.00	0.00	0.00	0.00	
21	1	0	2	0	0	3	0	163
	0.01	0.00	0.02	0.00	0.00	0.03	0.00	1.71
	0.61	0.00	1.23	0.00	0.00	1.84	0.00	
22	1	0	17	0	0	0	0	360
	0.01	0.00	0.18	0.00	0.00	0.00	0.00	3.79
	0.28	0.00	4.72	0.00	0.00	0.00	0.00	
23	0	0	0	0	0	0	0	4
	0.00	0.00	0.00	0.00	0.00	0.00	0.00	0.04
	0.00	0.00	0.00	0.00	0.00	0.00	0.00	
25	0	0	2	0	0	0	0	65
	0.00	0.00	0.02	0.00	0.00	0.00	0.00	0.68
	0.00	0.00	3.08	0.00	0.00	0.00	0.00	
26	0	0	0	0	0	0	0	42
	0.00	0.00	0.00	0.00	0.00	0.00	0.00	0.44
	0.00	0.00	0.00	0.00	0.00	0.00	0.00	
27	2	0	2	0	0	0	0	218
	0.02	0.00	0.02	0.00	0.00	0.00	0.00	2.29
	0.92	0.00	0.92	0.00	0.00	0.00	0.00	
Total (Newprovs 1–27)	116	1	195	18	3	7	3	9508
	1.22	0.01	2.05	0.19	0.03	0.07	0.03	100.00

(continued)

(continued)

NEWPROV Frequency Percent Row Pct			TYPE					Total (Types 1–47)
	15	16	17	18	19	20	21	
1	0 0.00 0.00	0 0.00 0.00	2 0.02 0.25	0 0.00 0.00	0 0.00 0.00	3 0.03 0.38	25 0.26 3.16	792 8.33
2	0 0.00 0.00	0 0.00 0.00	1 0.01 0.19	0 0.00 0.00	0 0.00 0.00	1 0.01 0.19	16 0.17 3.00	534 5.62
3	0 0.00 0.00	0 0.00 0.00	1 0.01 0.08	1 0.01 0.08	3 0.03 0.23	44 0.46 3.30	52 0.55 3.90	1332 14.01
4	0 0.00 0.00	0 0.00 0.00	4 0.04 1.26	11 0.12 3.46	0 0.00 0.00	3 0.03 0.94	18 0.19 5.66	318 3.34
5	0 0.00 0.00	0 0.00 0.00	4 0.04 0.98	1 0.01 0.25	0 0.00 0.00	20 0.21 4.91	4 0.04 0.98	407 4.28
6	0 0.00 0.00	0 0.00 0.00	2 0.02 2.15	0 0.00 0.00	0 0.00 0.00	4 0.04 4.30	2 0.02 2.15	93 0.98
7	0 0.00 0.00	0 0.00 0.00	0 0.00 0.00	0 0.00 0.00	0 0.00 0.00	0 0.00 0.00	10 0.11 8.47	118 1.24
8	1 0.01 0.11	0 0.00 0.00	0 0.00 0.00	0 0.00 0.00	0 0.00 0.00	23 0.24 2.55	31 0.33 3.44	901 9.48
9	0 0.00 0.00	0 0.00 0.00	2 0.02 0.13	0 0.00 0.00	0 0.00 0.00	53 0.56 3.47	71 0.75 4.65	1528 16.07
10	0 0.00 0.00	0 0.00 0.00	3 0.03 0.29	0 0.00 0.00	0 0.00 0.00	44 0.46 4.24	44 0.46 4.24	1038 10.92
11	0 0.00 0.00	0 0.00 0.00	0 0.00 0.00	0 0.00 0.00	0 0.00 0.00	19 0.20 5.09	23 0.24 6.17	373 3.92
12	0 0.00 0.00	0 0.00 0.00	0 0.00 0.00	0 0.00 0.00	0 0.00 0.00	11 0.12 4.33	9 0.09 3.54	254 2.67
13	0 0.00 0.00	0 0.00 0.00	0 0.00 0.00	0 0.00 0.00	0 0.00 0.00	13 0.14 8.84	6 0.06 4.08	147 1.55

NEWPROV Frequency Percent Row Pct	TYPE							Total (Types 1–47)
	15	16	17	18	19	20	21	
14	0	0	0	0	0	1	0	67
	0.00	0.00	0.00	0.00	0.00	0.01	0.00	0.70
	0.00	0.00	0.00	0.00	0.00	1.49	0.00	
15	0	0	0	0	0	0	0	28
	0.00	0.00	0.00	0.00	0.00	0.00	0.00	0.29
	0.00	0.00	0.00	0.00	0.00	0.00	0.00	
16	0	0	0	0	0	2	2	177
	0.00	0.00	0.00	0.00	0.00	0.02	0.02	1.86
	0.00	0.00	0.00	0.00	0.00	1.13	1.13	
17	0	0	0	0	0	0	0	7
	0.00	0.00	0.00	0.00	0.00	0.00	0.00	0.07
	0.00	0.00	0.00	0.00	0.00	0.00	0.00	
18	0	0	0	0	0	0	2	79
	0.00	0.00	0.00	0.00	0.00	0.00	0.02	0.83
	0.00	0.00	0.00	0.00	0.00	0.00	2.53	
19	0	0	0	0	0	7	8	159
	0.00	0.00	0.00	0.00	0.00	0.07	0.08	1.67
	0.00	0.00	0.00	0.00	0.00	4.40	5.03	
20	0	0	0	0	0	4	12	304
	0.00	0.00	0.00	0.00	0.00	0.04	0.13	3.20
	0.00	0.00	0.00	0.00	0.00	1.32	3.95	
21	0	1	0	0	0	4	5	163
	0.00	0.01	0.00	0.00	0.00	0.04	0.05	1.71
	0.00	0.61	0.00	0.00	0.00	2.45	3.07	
22	0	0	0	0	0	0	12	360
	0.00	0.00	0.00	0.00	0.00	0.00	0.13	3.79
	0.00	0.00	0.00	0.00	0.00	0.00	3.33	
23	0	0	0	0	0	0	0	4
	0.00	0.00	0.00	0.00	0.00	0.00	0.00	0.04
	0.00	0.00	0.00	0.00	0.00	0.00	0.00	
25	0	0	0	0	0	0	0	65
	0.00	0.00	0.00	0.00	0.00	0.00	0.00	0.68
	0.00	0.00	0.00	0.00	0.00	0.00	0.00	
26	0	0	1	0	0	5	1	42
	0.00	0.00	0.01	0.00	0.00	0.05	0.01	0.44
	0.00	0.00	2.38	0.00	0.00	11.90	2.38	
27	0	0	0	0	0	4	4	218
	0.00	0.00	0.00	0.00	0.00	0.04	0.04	2.29
	0.00	0.00	0.00	0.00	0.00	1.83	1.83	
Total (Newprovs 1–27)	1	1	20	13	3	265	357	9508
	0.01	0.01	0.21	0.14	0.03	2.79	3.75	100.00

(continued)

(continued)

NEWPROV Frequency Percent Row Pct	TYPE							Total (Types 1–47)
	23	24	25	26	27	28	29	
1	3	3	0	0	3	0	0	792
	0.03	0.03	0.00	0.00	0.03	0.00	0.00	8.33
	0.38	0.38	0.00	0.00	0.38	0.00	0.00	
2	6	6	0	0	9	0	0	534
	0.06	0.06	0.00	0.00	0.09	0.00	0.00	5.62
	1.12	1.12	0.00	0.00	1.69	0.00	0.00	
3	7	7	1	1	41	1	0	1332
	0.07	0.07	0.01	0.01	0.43	0.01	0.00	14.01
	0.53	0.53	0.08	0.08	3.08	0.08	0.00	
4	3	1	1	0	11	2	1	318
	0.03	0.01	0.01	0.00	0.12	0.02	0.01	3.34
	0.94	0.31	0.31	0.00	3.46	0.63	0.31	
5	2	2	0	0	7	0	1	407
	0.02	0.02	0.00	0.00	0.07	0.00	0.01	4.28
	0.49	0.49	0.00	0.00	1.72	0.00	0.25	
6	0	0	0	0	0	0	0	93
	0.00	0.00	0.00	0.00	0.00	0.00	0.00	0.98
	0.00	0.00	0.00	0.00	0.00	0.00	0.00	
7	0	1	0	0	0	0	0	118
	0.00	0.01	0.00	0.00	0.00	0.00	0.00	1.24
	0.00	0.85	0.00	0.00	0.00	0.00	0.00	
8	8	8	1	1	21	0	0	901
	0.08	0.08	0.01	0.01	0.22	0.00	0.00	9.48
	0.89	0.89	0.11	0.11	2.33	0.00	0.00	
9	24	21	0	0	21	5	6	1528
	0.25	0.22	0.00	0.00	0.22	0.05	0.06	16.07
	1.57	1.37	0.00	0.00	1.37	0.33	0.39	
10	6	14	2	0	23	4	0	1038
	0.06	0.15	0.02	0.00	0.24	0.04	0.00	10.92
	0.58	1.35	0.19	0.00	2.22	0.39	0.00	
11	2	0	0	0	6	0	1	373
	0.02	0.00	0.00	0.00	0.06	0.00	0.01	3.92
	0.54	0.00	0.00	0.00	1.61	0.00	0.27	
12	1	0	0	0	4	0	0	254
	0.01	0.00	0.00	0.00	0.04	0.00	0.00	2.67
	0.39	0.00	0.00	0.00	1.57	0.00	0.00	
13	1	2	0	0	4	0	0	147
	0.01	0.02	0.00	0.00	0.04	0.00	0.00	1.55
	0.68	1.36	0.00	0.00	2.72	0.00	0.00	

NEWPROV Frequency Percent Row Pct	TYPE							Total (Types 1–47)
	23	24	25	26	27	28	29	
14	2	0	0	0	2	0	0	67
	0.02	0.00	0.00	0.00	0.02	0.00	0.00	0.70
	2.99	0.00	0.00	0.00	2.99	0.00	0.00	
15	0	0	0	0	0	0	0	28
	0.00	0.00	0.00	0.00	0.00	0.00	0.00	0.29
	0.00	0.00	0.00	0.00	0.00	0.00	0.00	
16	7	1	0	0	2	1	0	177
	0.07	0.01	0.00	0.00	0.02	0.01	0.00	1.86
	3.95	0.56	0.00	0.00	1.13	0.56	0.00	
17	0	0	1	0	0	0	0	7
	0.00	0.00	0.01	0.00	0.00	0.00	0.00	0.07
	0.00	0.00	14.29	0.00	0.00	0.00	0.00	
18	1	1	0	0	2	0	0	79
	0.01	0.01	0.00	0.00	0.02	0.00	0.00	0.83
	1.27	1.27	0.00	0.00	2.53	0.00	0.00	
19	0	0	0	11	7	0	0	159
	0.00	0.00	0.00	0.12	0.07	0.00	0.00	1.67
	0.00	0.00	0.00	6.92	4.40	0.00	0.00	
20	5	2	3	0	4	1	0	304
	0.05	0.02	0.03	0.00	0.04	0.01	0.00	3.20
	1.64	0.66	0.99	0.00	1.32	0.33	0.00	
21	3	1	0	0	4	0	0	163
	0.03	0.01	0.00	0.00	0.04	0.00	0.00	1.71
	1.84	0.61	0.00	0.00	2.45	0.00	0.00	
22	2	0	0	0	5	0	0	360
	0.02	0.00	0.00	0.00	0.05	0.00	0.00	3.79
	0.56	0.00	0.00	0.00	1.39	0.00	0.00	
23	0	0	0	0	0	0	0	4
	0.00	0.00	0.00	0.00	0.00	0.00	0.00	0.04
	0.00	0.00	0.00	0.00	0.00	0.00	0.00	
25	0	1	0	0	2	0	1	65
	0.00	0.01	0.00	0.00	0.02	0.00	0.01	0.68
	0.00	1.54	0.00	0.00	3.08	0.00	1.54	
26	1	0	0	0	2	0	0	42
	0.01	0.00	0.00	0.00	0.02	0.00	0.00	0.44
	2.38	0.00	0.00	0.00	4.76	0.00	0.00	
27	1	5	0	0	8	1	0	218
	0.01	0.05	0.00	0.00	0.08	0.01	0.00	2.29
	0.46	2.29	0.00	0.00	3.67	0.46	0.00	
Total (Newprovs 1–27)	85	76	9	13	188	15	10	9508
	0.89	0.80	0.09	0.14	1.98	0.16	0.11	100.00

(continued)

(continued)

NEWPROV Frequency Percent Row Pct	TYPE							Total (Types 1–47)
	30	31	32	34	35	36	37	
1	0	0	0	0	0	0	0	792
	0.00	0.00	0.00	0.00	0.00	0.00	0.00	8.33
	0.00	0.00	0.00	0.00	0.00	0.00	0.00	
2	0	0	0	0	0	0	0	534
	0.00	0.00	0.00	0.00	0.00	0.00	0.00	5.62
	0.00	0.00	0.00	0.00	0.00	0.00	0.00	
3	0	0	0	0	0	0	0	1332
	0.00	0.00	0.00	0.00	0.00	0.00	0.00	14.01
	0.00	0.00	0.00	0.00	0.00	0.00	0.00	
4	0	0	0	0	0	0	0	318
	0.00	0.00	0.00	0.00	0.00	0.00	0.00	3.34
	0.00	0.00	0.00	0.00	0.00	0.00	0.00	
5	0	0	0	0	0	0	0	407
	0.00	0.00	0.00	0.00	0.00	0.00	0.00	4.28
	0.00	0.00	0.00	0.00	0.00	0.00	0.00	
6	0	0	0	0	0	0	0	93
	0.00	0.00	0.00	0.00	0.00	0.00	0.00	0.98
	0.00	0.00	0.00	0.00	0.00	0.00	0.00	
7	0	0	0	0	0	0	0	118
	0.00	0.00	0.00	0.00	0.00	0.00	0.00	1.24
	0.00	0.00	0.00	0.00	0.00	0.00	0.00	
8	9	0	0	0	0	0	0	901
	0.09	0.00	0.00	0.00	0.00	0.00	0.00	9.48
	1.00	0.00	0.00	0.00	0.00	0.00	0.00	
9	0	0	0	0	0	0	0	1528
	0.00	0.00	0.00	0.00	0.00	0.00	0.00	16.07
	0.00	0.00	0.00	0.00	0.00	0.00	0.00	
10	0	0	1	4	0	0	8	1038
	0.00	0.00	0.01	0.04	0.00	0.00	0.08	10.92
	0.00	0.00	0.10	0.39	0.00	0.00	0.77	
11	0	0	0	0	2	0	0	373
	0.00	0.00	0.00	0.00	0.02	0.00	0.00	3.92
	0.00	0.00	0.00	0.00	0.54	0.00	0.00	
12	0	0	0	0	0	0	0	254
	0.00	0.00	0.00	0.00	0.00	0.00	0.00	2.67
	0.00	0.00	0.00	0.00	0.00	0.00	0.00	
13	0	0	0	0	0	0	0	147
	0.00	0.00	0.00	0.00	0.00	0.00	0.00	1.55
	0.00	0.00	0.00	0.00	0.00	0.00	0.00	

NEWPROV Frequency Percent Row Pct	TYPE							Total (Types 1–47)
	30	31	32	34	35	36	37	
14	0	0	0	0	0	0	0	67
	0.00	0.00	0.00	0.00	0.00	0.00	0.00	0.70
	0.00	0.00	0.00	0.00	0.00	0.00	0.00	
15	0	0	0	0	0	0	0	28
	0.00	0.00	0.00	0.00	0.00	0.00	0.00	0.29
	0.00	0.00	0.00	0.00	0.00	0.00	0.00	
16	0	0	0	0	1	0	0	177
	0.00	0.00	0.00	0.00	0.01	0.00	0.00	1.86
	0.00	0.00	0.00	0.00	0.56	0.00	0.00	
17	0	0	0	0	0	0	0	7
	0.00	0.00	0.00	0.00	0.00	0.00	0.00	0.07
	0.00	0.00	0.00	0.00	0.00	0.00	0.00	
18	0	0	0	0	0	0	0	79
	0.00	0.00	0.00	0.00	0.00	0.00	0.00	0.83
	0.00	0.00	0.00	0.00	0.00	0.00	0.00	
19	0	0	0	0	0	0	0	159
	0.00	0.00	0.00	0.00	0.00	0.00	0.00	1.67
	0.00	0.00	0.00	0.00	0.00	0.00	0.00	
20	0	0	0	0	0	0	0	304
	0.00	0.00	0.00	0.00	0.00	0.00	0.00	3.20
	0.00	0.00	0.00	0.00	0.00	0.00	0.00	
21	0	2	0	0	0	1	0	163
	0.00	0.02	0.00	0.00	0.00	0.01	0.00	1.71
	0.00	1.23	0.00	0.00	0.00	0.61	0.00	
22	0	0	0	0	0	0	0	360
	0.00	0.00	0.00	0.00	0.00	0.00	0.00	3.79
	0.00	0.00	0.00	0.00	0.00	0.00	0.00	
23	0	0	0	0	0	0	0	4
	0.00	0.00	0.00	0.00	0.00	0.00	0.00	0.04
	0.00	0.00	0.00	0.00	0.00	0.00	0.00	
25	0	0	0	0	0	0	0	65
	0.00	0.00	0.00	0.00	0.00	0.00	0.00	0.68
	0.00	0.00	0.00	0.00	0.00	0.00	0.00	
26	0	0	0	0	0	0	0	42
	0.00	0.00	0.00	0.00	0.00	0.00	0.00	0.44
	0.00	0.00	0.00	0.00	0.00	0.00	0.00	
27	0	0	0	0	0	0	0	218
	0.00	0.00	0.00	0.00	0.00	0.00	0.00	2.29
	0.00	0.00	0.00	0.00	0.00	0.00	0.00	
Total (Newprovs 1–27)	9	2	1	4	3	1	8	9508
	0.09	0.02	0.01	0.04	0.03	0.01	0.08	100.00

(continued)

(continued)

NEWPROV Frequency Percent Row Pct	TYPE							
	38	39	40	41	42	43	44	**Total (Types 1–47)**
1	108	9	130	88	19	19	8	792
	1.14	0.09	1.37	0.93	0.20	0.20	0.08	8.33
	13.64	1.14	16.41	11.11	2.40	2.40	1.01	
2	40	6	86	26	3	62	0	534
	0.42	0.06	0.90	0.27	0.03	0.65	0.00	5.62
	7.49	1.12	16.10	4.87	0.56	11.61	0.00	
3	167	21	172	98	29	92	10	1332
	1.76	0.22	1.81	1.03	0.31	0.97	0.11	14.01
	12.54	1.58	12.91	7.36	2.18	6.91	0.75	
4	65	4	30	20	9	2	2	318
	0.68	0.04	0.32	0.21	0.09	0.02	0.02	3.34
	20.44	1.26	9.43	6.29	2.83	0.63	0.63	
5	57	8	51	45	14	8	1	407
	0.60	0.08	0.54	0.47	0.15	0.08	0.01	4.28
	14.00	1.97	12.53	11.06	3.44	1.97	0.25	
6	17	1	16	9	3	0	0	93
	0.18	0.01	0.17	0.09	0.03	0.00	0.00	0.98
	18.28	1.08	17.20	9.68	3.23	0.00	0.00	
7	16	0	36	12	5	0	0	118
	0.17	0.00	0.38	0.13	0.05	0.00	0.00	1.24
	13.56	0.00	30.51	10.17	4.24	0.00	0.00	
8	91	11	115	66	7	25	6	901
	0.96	0.12	1.21	0.69	0.07	0.26	0.06	9.48
	10.10	1.22	12.76	7.33	0.78	2.77	0.67	
9	258	80	224	123	18	25	3	1528
	2.71	0.84	2.36	1.29	0.19	0.26	0.03	16.07
	16.88	5.24	14.66	8.05	1.18	1.64	0.20	
10	136	29	133	73	6	39	4	1038
	1.43	0.31	1.40	0.77	0.06	0.41	0.04	10.92
	13.10	2.79	12.81	7.03	0.58	3.76	0.39	
11	54	12	50	28	10	7	2	373
	0.57	0.13	0.53	0.29	0.11	0.07	0.02	3.92
	14.48	3.22	13.40	7.51	2.68	1.88	0.54	
12	35	5	28	23	5	0	0	254
	0.37	0.05	0.29	0.24	0.05	0.00	0.00	2.67
	13.78	1.97	11.02	9.06	1.97	0.00	0.00	
13	9	12	19	21	2	0	0	147
	0.09	0.13	0.20	0.22	0.02	0.00	0.00	1.55
	6.12	8.16	12.93	14.29	1.36	0.00	0.00	

NEWPROV Frequency Percent Row Pct	TYPE							Total (Types 1–47)
	38	39	40	41	42	43	44	
14	9	0	12	8	1	4	1	67
	0.09	0.00	0.13	0.08	0.01	0.04	0.01	0.70
	13.43	0.00	17.91	11.94	1.49	5.97	1.49	
15	5	0	8	5	0	0	0	28
	0.05	0.00	0.08	0.05	0.00	0.00	0.00	0.29
	17.86	0.00	28.57	17.86	0.00	0.00	0.00	
16	24	3	12	13	2	5	1	177
	0.25	0.03	0.13	0.14	0.02	0.05	0.01	1.86
	13.56	1.69	6.78	7.34	1.13	2.82	0.56	
17	3	0	3	0	0	0	0	7
	0.03	0.00	0.03	0.00	0.00	0.00	0.00	0.07
	42.86	0.00	42.86	0.00	0.00	0.00	0.00	
18	4	0	10	7	0	0	0	79
	0.04	0.00	0.11	0.07	0.00	0.00	0.00	0.83
	5.06	0.00	12.66	8.86	0.00	0.00	0.00	
19	26	5	15	9	4	0	0	159
	0.27	0.05	0.16	0.09	0.04	0.00	0.00	1.67
	16.35	3.14	9.43	5.66	2.52	0.00	0.00	
20	62	6	59	19	4	2	3	304
	0.65	0.06	0.62	0.20	0.04	0.02	0.03	3.20
	20.39	1.97	19.41	6.25	1.32	0.66	0.99	
21	20	5	33	8	5	1	0	163
	0.21	0.05	0.35	0.08	0.05	0.01	0.00	1.71
	12.27	3.07	20.25	4.91	3.07	0.61	0.00	
22	77	9	75	20	11	9	0	360
	0.81	0.09	0.79	0.21	0.12	0.09	0.00	3.79
	21.39	2.50	20.83	5.56	3.06	2.50	0.00	
23	0	0	2	0	0	0	0	4
	0.00	0.00	0.02	0.00	0.00	0.00	0.00	0.04
	0.00	0.00	50.00	0.00	0.00	0.00	0.00	
25	4	0	6	6	3	7	0	65
	0.04	0.00	0.06	0.06	0.03	0.07	0.00	0.68
	6.15	0.00	9.23	9.23	4.62	10.77	0.00	
26	12	3	3	3	2	0	0	42
	0.13	0.03	0.03	0.03	0.02	0.00	0.00	0.44
	28.57	7.14	7.14	7.14	4.76	0.00	0.00	
27	22	3	41	14	6	22	0	218
	0.23	0.03	0.43	0.15	0.06	0.23	0.00	2.29
	10.09	1.38	18.81	6.42	2.75	10.09	0.00	
Total (Newprovs 1–27)	1321	232	1369	744	168	329	41	9508
	13.89	2.44	14.40	7.82	1.77	3.46	0.43	100.00

(continued)

(continued)

NEWPROV Frequency Percent Row Pct	TYPE			
	45	46	47	**Total (Types 1–47)**
1	7 0.07 0.88	0 0.00 0.00	0 0.00 0.00	792 8.33
2	9 0.09 1.69	0 0.00 0.00	0 0.00 0.00	534 5.62
3	13 0.14 0.98	1 0.01 0.08	0 0.00 0.00	1332 14.01
4	4 0.04 1.26	0 0.00 0.00	0 0.00 0.00	318 3.34
5	8 0.08 1.97	0 0.00 0.00	0 0.00 0.00	407 4.28
6	2 0.02 2.15	0 0.00 0.00	0 0.00 0.00	93 0.98
7	1 0.01 0.85	0 0.00 0.00	0 0.00 0.00	118 1.24
8	45 0.47 4.99	0 0.00 0.00	0 0.00 0.00	901 9.48
9	28 0.29 1.83	0 0.00 0.00	0 0.00 0.00	1528 16.07
10	62 0.65 5.97	0 0.00 0.00	1 0.01 0.10	1038 10.92
11	17 0.18 4.56	0 0.00 0.00	0 0.00 0.00	373 3.92
12	35 0.37 13.78	0 0.00 0.00	0 0.00 0.00	254 2.67
13	26 0.27 17.69	0 0.00 0.00	0 0.00 0.00	147 1.55
14	4 0.04 5.97	0 0.00 0.00	0 0.00 0.00	67 0.70

NEWPROV Frequency Percent Row Pct	TYPE			
	45	46	47	**Total (Types 1–47)**
15	1 0.01 3.57	0 0.00 0.00	0 0.00 0.00	28 0.29
16	10 0.11 5.65	0 0.00 0.00	0 0.00 0.00	177 1.86
17	0 0.00 0.00	0 0.00 0.00	0 0.00 0.00	7 0.07
18	12 0.13 15.19	0 0.00 0.00	0 0.00 0.00	79 0.83
19	8 0.08 5.03	0 0.00 0.00	0 0.00 0.00	159 1.67
20	11 0.12 3.62	0 0.00 0.00	0 0.00 0.00	304 3.20
21	4 0.04 2.45	0 0.00 0.00	0 0.00 0.00	163 1.71
22	5 0.05 1.39	0 0.00 0.00	0 0.00 0.00	360 3.79
23	0 0.00 0.00	0 0.00 0.00	0 0.00 0.00	4 0.04
25	2 0.02 3.08	0 0.00 0.00	0 0.00 0.00	65 0.68
26	0 0.00 0.00	0 0.00 0.00	0 0.00 0.00	42 0.44
27	2 0.02 0.92	0 0.00 0.00	0 0.00 0.00	218 2.29
Total (Newprovs 1–27)	316 3.32	1 0.01	1 0.01	9508 100.00

Appendix B

Ceramic Paste Characteristics by Type

Introduction

Detailed observations of paste color and temper were made on sherd samples from each type; each sherd was studied under a low-power binocular microscope. Paste characteristics were not included in the sherd classification, but some variation was found in paste by type. Fine-ware sherds tend to have finer-textured temper. Dark-surfaced sherds (e.g., of the Black Polished Utility type) tend to have darker paste, whereas the opposite is true of light-surfaced sherd types (e.g., Red Bands on White).

Most sherds are believed to have been tempered with sand of igneous origin, although for many types several sherds were recorded as having crushed (igneous) rock temper. Also, in several scattered sherds the temper had eroded away, leaving small holes in the paste. These "hole-tempered" sherds may have been tempered originally with crushed limestone.

Temper texture, or grain size, was described as fine, medium, or coarse, and temper abundance as sparse, moderate, or abundant.

(1) Unpolished Utility

Sample: 22 sherds

Temper tends to be medium sand in moderate amounts. Paste color is variable: black to dark gray (2.5 YR 2.5/0, 3/0, 4/0), reddish brown (2.5 YR 4/4, 5/4), light reddish brown (2.5 YR 6/4), and red (2.5 YR 5/6, 4/6).

(2) Black Slipped and Polished

Sample: 22 sherds

Temper appears to be crushed igneous rock, igneous sand, or quartz sand; it tends to be of medium texture and present in moderate amounts. Paste color generally varies from red (2.5 YR 4/6) to reddish brown (5 YR 5/4) to yellowish red (5 YR 5/6).

(3) Gray Slipped and Polished

Sample: 22 sherds

Temper for the most part is igneous sand, although several sherds contain crushed rock. One sherd may have had limestone temper. The paste tends to be dark-colored, varying from black and very dark gray (2.5 YR 3/0) to dusky red (2.5 YR 3/2), although some are reddish brown (5 YR 5/4) or light red (2.5 YR 6/6).

(4) Orange on Gray / Buff

Sample: 22 sherds

Although temper for several sherds is crushed rock, most are tempered with sand of medium texture generally present in moderate amounts. Paste color tends to be more uniform than for other types. The predominant color is red (2.5 YR 4/6, 5/6), and most other sherds are reddish brown (2.5 YR 5/4) or reddish yellow (5 YR 6/6).

(5) Black and Red on White

Sample: 11 sherds

One sherd appears to be tempered with grog and sand, one with crushed rock, and the remaining nine with fine or medium sand. Temper is present in moderate amounts. Paste color tends to be pink (5 YR 7/4), light reddish brown (2.5 YR 6/4), or red (2.5 YR 5/6).

(6) White on Red

Sample: 20 sherds

Temper is mostly sand with a minority appearing to have crushed rock temper. Paste color tends to vary from light reddish brown (2.5 YR 6/4) to red (2.5 YR 5/6), but a broad range is represented, from very dark grey (2.5 YR 3/0) to yellowish red (5 YR 5/8).

(7) Gray on Red

Sample: 2 sherds

Temper is medium sand in moderate amounts. Paste color is light reddish brown (5 YR 6/4) and very dark grey (5 YR 3/1).

(8) Red Bands on White

Sample: 8 sherds

Temper is medium sand, either scarce or in moderate amounts. Paste color tends to vary from light reddish brown (5 YR 6/4) to pink (5 YR 7/4).

(9) Red on Orange

Sample: 1 sherd

Temper is a small amount of very fine sand. Paste color is light reddish brown (5 YR 6/4).

(10) Red Slipped and Polished

Sample: 22 sherds

Temper for the most part is fine to medium sand in moderate amounts. Paste color tends to be light red (2.5 YR 6/6), light reddish brown (2.5 YR 6/4), or red (2.5 YR 5/6) but varies from very dark gray (2.5 YR 3/0) to pinkish gray (5 YR 7/2).

(11) Cacao Pod Effigy Vessel

Sample: 12 sherds

Temper is fine to medium sand in moderate to sparse amounts. Paste color for most sherds is reddish brown (2.5 YR 5/4) to red (2.5 YR 5/6).

(12) Brown Slipped and Polished Incised

Sample: 2 sherds

Temper is crushed rock of medium texture in moderate amounts. Paste color was recorded as black (5 YR 2.5/1).

(13) Brown-Black on Buff

Sample: 7 sherds

Temper is coarse to medium sand in sparse to moderate amounts. Paste color tends to be very dark gray (2.5 YR 3/0) or red (2.5 YR 4/6).

(14) Reed Punctate

Sample: 3 sherds

Temper is medium sand in moderate amounts. Paste color is reddish brown (2.5 YR 5/4) to red (2.5 YR 5/6).

(15) Other Punctate

Sample: 1 sherd

This sherd is tempered with a moderate amount of fine sand. Paste color is reddish gray (5 YR 5/2).

(16) Unique Black Slipped Incised

Sample: 1 sherd

This sherd has a moderate amount of medium sand temper. The paste is red (2.5 YR 4/6).

(17) Polished Brown-Black Incised

Sample: 20 sherds

These sherds tend to have medium sand temper in moderate amounts. Most sherds are very dark gray (2.5 YR 3/0) or reddish brown (2.5 YR 5/4, 5 YR 5/3).

(18) Fine-Incised Beaker

Sample: 3 sherds

Temper consists of fine sand in moderate amounts. Paste color is dark grey (2.5 YR 4/0) and very dark gray (5 YR 3/1).

(19) Zoned Crosshatched Incised

Sample: 3 sherds

Fine sand is present in moderate amounts. Paste color was recorded for all sherds as light reddish brown (5 YR 6/4).

(20) Ladle Incensario

Sample: 22 sherds

Most sherds contain moderate amounts of medium sand temper; others contain crushed rock of medium texture. Paste color for most sherds is red (2.5 YR 5/6, 4/6).

(21) Brown Slipped and Polished

Sample: 22 sherds

Most sherds are sand-tempered, although some contain crushed quartz or other crushed rock. Temper tends to be present in moderate quantities and in size (texture) varies from fine to moderate. Paste color varies from yellowish red (5 YR 4/6) and reddish brown (5 YR 4/4) to red (2.5 YR 4/6).

(22) Streaky White Slip (Type combined with Red Bands on White)

Sample: 22 sherds

Most of these sherds have moderate quantities of medium sand temper. Most have red paste (2.5 YR 4/6 to 2.5 YR 5/8); others are pale to weak red (2.5 YR 4/2 to 2.5 YR 6/2).

(23) Buff Slipped and Polished

Sample: 22 sherds

Temper is fine to medium sand in moderate amounts. Paste colors tend to be high in value, ranging from light reddish brown (2.5 YR 6/4) to pink (5 YR 7/3), although several sherds have dark cores (2.5 YR 3/0).

(24) Gray-Brown Slipped

Sample: 22 sherds

Most sherds are tempered with fine to medium sand in moderate amounts. Paste color is highly variable: some sherds are red (2.5 YR 4/6); others range in color from very dark gray (2.5 YR 3/0) to pink (5 YR 7/4).

(25) Orange Polished

Sample: 7 sherds

Temper for most is medium sand in sparse to moderate amounts. Paste color varies from light reddish brown (2.5 YR 6/4) to light red (2.5 YR 6/6) and from reddish yellow (5 YR 6/6) to pink (5 YR 7/3).

(26) Micaceous Paste

Sample: 10 sherds

Temper is fine to medium sand in sparse to moderate amounts. Paste color is mostly dark gray (2.5 YR 4/0, 5 YR 4/1) to very dark gray (2.5 YR 3/0), but grades to dusky red (2.5 YR 3/2) and weak red (2.5 YR 4/2, 5/2).

(27) Thick, White Painted

Sample: 22 sherds

Temper is medium to fine sand in moderate amounts. Several of these sherds have dark cores, black (2.5 YR 2.5/1) to dark gray (5 YR 4/1). Other paste colors are red (2.5 YR 5/6, 4/6), light red (2.5 YR 6/6), reddish brown (5 YR 5/3), and light reddish brown (2.5 YR 6/4).

(28) Nonslipped, Nonpolished Fine Ware

Sample: 4 sherds

Temper is fine sand in sparse amounts. Paste colors are generally dark: black (2.5 YR 2.5/0) to dusky red (2.5 YR 3/2).

(29) Micaceous Slip

Sample: 22 sherds

Temper is medium sand in moderate amounts. Paste color is highly varied, from black (2.5 YR 2.5/0, 5 YR 2.5/1) and dark gray (5 YR 4/1) to light reddish brown (5 YR 6/4), yellowish red (5 YR 5/6), and red (2.5 YR 5/6).

(30) Black on Red

Sample: 2 sherds

From the same vessel, these sherds exhibit fine sand temper in sparse quantities. Paste color is red (2.5 YR 4/6).

(34) Orange, Matte-Finish

Sample: 2 sherds

Temper is fine to medium sand in moderate amounts. Paste color for the two sherds is red (2.5 YR 5/6) and light red (2.5 YR 6/8).

(35) Unique Bichrome and Polychrome

Sample: 3 sherds

Temper is fine-textured sand or crushed rock in sparse to abundant amounts. Paste color is red (2.5 YR 4/6, 5/6) or black (2.5 YR 2.5/0).

(36) Red Slipped Incised

Sample: 1 sherd

The sherd is tempered with medium sand in sparse amount. Paste color is pink (5 YR 7/4).

(37) Brown Polished Punctate

Sample: 8 sherds

These sherds are mostly tempered with fine sand in moderate amounts. Paste color for most is dark reddish gray (2.5 YR 4/2) or reddish brown (2.5 YR 4/3).

(38) Brown Polished Utility

Sample: 22 sherds

Most sherds contain a moderate amount of medium sand temper. Paste color varies from black (2.5 YR 2.5/0) and very dusky red (2.5 YR 2.5/2) to red (2.5 YR 4/6, 5/6) and reddish brown (2.5 YR 4/4, 5/4).

(39) Small Micaceous-Slip Dish

Sample: 22 sherds

Temper is mostly medium sand in moderate amounts. Paste color tends to be light reddish brown (2.5 YR 6/4), pale red (2.5 YR 6/2), or, for several sherds, lighter colors: pinkish gray (5 YR 7/2) or pink (5 YR 7/3, 7/4).

(40) Micaceous Paste Utility

Sample: 22 sherds

All of these sherds contain temper of medium micaceous sand, although several appear to be tempered with a mixture of crushed rock and micaceous sand. Temper is present in moderate to abundant amounts. Several sherds have dark paste colors, black (2.5 YR 2.5/0) to very dark gray (5 YR 3/1); most others are reddish brown (5 YR 5/4) to light reddish brown (5 YR 6/3).

(41) Red Polished Utility

Sample: 22 sherds

Temper for most sherds is composed of medium sand in moderate amounts. Paste color tends to be reddish brown (2.5 YR 4/4, 5/4) or light reddish brown (2.5 YR 6/4). Several sherds are light red (2.5 YR 6/6) or dark gray (2.5 YR 4/1).

(42) Black Polished Utility

Sample: 23 sherds

Temper consists mostly of medium sand in moderate amounts. Paste color tends to be dark: black (2.5 YR 2.5/0), very dark gray (2.5 YR 3/0), or dusky red (2.5 yr 3/2). Some sherds manifest a red (2.5 YR 4/4) or reddish brown (5 YR 5/3) paste.

(44) Thick Black and White Painted

Sample: 21 sherds

Temper is medium sand in moderate to sparse amounts. Paste color varies from very dark gray (2.5 YR 3/0) to red (2.5 YR 5/6) to reddish brown (2.5 YR 4/4) and to light red (2.5 YR 6/6).

(45) Thick Beaker Incensario

Sample: 22 sherds

These sherds for the most part have medium sand temper in moderate amounts. Paste colors are mostly reddish brown (2.5 YR 4/4, 5/4 and 5 YR 4/4, 5/4) and red (2.5 YR 4/6, 5/6). Several sherds are dark gray (2.5 YR 4/0, 5 YR 4/1), and several others are lighter in color (e.g., light red, 2.5 YR 6/6).

Appendix C. Cranial bones[1] with notable demographic or paleopathological features

Ident.	Guillemin ID No.	Burial Type	Sex	Age	Decap. Damage		Other Trauma	Cranial Deform.		Plagio-cephaly	Porotic Hyper.	Periosteal Reactions	Attachment Area Reactions	Smooth Lumps	Gnawing	Miscellaneous
					Cranium	Vert.		Frontal	Occip.							
IX-1	E39-C	Nondecap.?	F	Adult	N	N		Y	Y	Right						Burning
IX-2	#36	Decap.	M?	Adult	Y	Y	F (cut)	N	Y	Left				F		
IX-3				Adult				N	Y	Left	P, O					
IX-4	#28	Decap.	M?	Adult	Y	Y		N	Y	Left						
IX-5	#47		M	15–21	Y	?		N	Y	Left						
IX-6		Decap.?	F	15–21	Y			Y	Y	Right						
IX-7	#17	Decap.	M?	15–21	Y	Y		N	Y	Right						Copper stain (P)
IX-8				Adult												Should not have IX number
IX-8-i				Adult												Should not have IX number
IX-9	E27-A/l	Decap.?	F?	Adult	Y	Y		Y	Y	Symmet.			O			
IX-10	Str. 74	Decap.	M	Adult	N	Y		N	Y	Symmet.						
IX-11	#12	Decap.	F?	15–21	Y	N		N	Y	Left						Arth. dep. (O condyle)
IX-12	#10	Decap.	F	Adult	Y		Mx, N (fracture)						O			
IX-13	#29	Decap.	M	Adult	Y	N		N	Y	Left						Should not have IX number
IX-14				Adult										Mn		Should not have IX number
IX-15			F?	15–21	N											
IX-16	#32	Decap.	M?	Adult	Y	Y		Y	Y	Right						
IX-17	E_Q_?	Nondecap.?		Adult	N			Y	Y	Right						
IX-18				Adult												Should not have IX number
IX-19	#38	Decap.		15–21	Y	Y						Mx (active, nasal)				
IX-20	#15	Decap.	M?	Adult	Y	Y		Y	Y	Symmet.			O			
IX-21	#21	Decap.	M?	15–21	Y	Y		Y	Y	Right			O			Arth. pits (Mx condyle)
IX-22	#23	Decap.		Adult	Y			N	Y	Symmet.						
IX-23		Decap.?	F	Adult	Y			Y	Y	Left						
IX-24		Nondecap.		13–14	N	N		Y	Y	Left						

Specimen	ID	Status	Sex	Age		Cut marks			Side					Animal	Comments
IX-25			F	Adult			Y	Y	Symmet.		Mx (sinusitis)	O (endo.)			
IX-26			F?	Adult			N	Y	Left		Mx (spicules, nasal)				
IX-27		Decap.?	M	Adult		E, P (dent)	Y	Y	Right						Deviated septum
IX-28			F	Adult	Y				Left						
IX-30	E38-A/II?	Nondecap.?	F?	Adult			Y	Y	Right		Mx (sinusitis)	O			GQ?
IX-31			M	Adult			Y	Y	Left			O			Deviated septum
IX-32			M	Adult	N	F (dent)	N	Y	Right						
IX-33	#11	Decap.	M	Adult	N				Symmet.	P, O	E, P, O (active), Mx (sinusitis)				Copper stain (P, T)
IX-34	E27-D	Nondecap.	F?	Adult	N			Y	Left		T (healed), Mx (sinusitis; spicules, nasal)	T (endo.)			
IX-35				Adult											Should not have IX number
IX-36				Adult		P (cut)		Y	Symmet.	P, O		O			
IX-37			M?	Adult											Fused T and P
IX-38				Adult											
IX-39				Adult			Y	Y	Right			O			
IX-40		Decap.?	M?	Adult	N	F, Z (cut)	Y	Y	Right						
IX-41	#37	Decap.	F	15–21	Y		N	Y			P, T (healed)				
IX-42			M	Adult	N	P (dent)	N	N			E, P (active)				
IX-43		Decap.?	M	15–21	Y		N	Y	Left		T (active, TMJ)				Deviated septum
IX-44				14	Y										Osteomalacia
IX-45				Adult										Rodent (F)	
IX-46	#20	Decap.	F?	15–21	Y		N	Y	Left						
IX-47		Decap.?	M?	Adult	Y		Y	Y	Right			O		Insect (O)	
IX-48			F	Adult				Y	Left				F	(O)	Large lumps (P)
IX-49				Adult											
IX-50		Decap.?	F	15–21	Y		N	Y							
IX-51		Decap.?	M	Adult	Y		N	Y					T, S		
IX-52		Decap.?	M	Adult	Y		N	Y	Right				Mx (sinus)	Rodent (F, P)	
IX-53	#34	Decap.		Adult				Y	Symmet.					Rodent (O)	
IX-54		Decap.?		Adult	Y		Y	Y	Right					Rodent (Mn)	

1. Does not include all cranial bones present.
F = frontal; Mn = mandible; M = maxilla; N = nasal; Mx = maxilla; O = occipital; P = parietal; S = sphenoid; T = temporal; Z = zygomatic

(continued)

(*Appendix C continued*)

Ident.	Guillemin ID No.	Burial Type	Sex	Age	Decap. Damage Cranium	Vert.	Other Trauma	Cranial Deform. Frontal	Occip.	Plagio-cephaly	Porotic Hyper.	Periosteal Reactions	Attachment Area Reactions	Smooth Lumps	Gnawing	Miscellaneous
IX-55				Adult								Mx (sinusitis)				
IX-56		Decap.?		15–21	N	Y			Y			O (active, endocranial)			Insect (O)	
IX-57				Adult										P		
IX-58				Adult												
IX-59				Adult					Y							
IX-60			M?	Adult												
IX-61				Adult												
IX-62			M	Adult			F (dent)	Y	Y	Right	O	E, P (healed)			Rodent (P, O)	
IX-63				Adult					Y	Symmet.					Rodent (P)	
IX-64				Adult				N	Y	Symmet.	O					
IX-65				Adult			P (dent)	Y	Y	Right	P, O		O		Rodent (F)	
IX-66			F?	Adult				Y	Y	Symmet.					Rodent (P)	
IX-67				Adult		?	P (cut)		Y	Symmet.		P (healed)	O			
IX-68	#46?	Decap.?		Adult	N	N						Mx (sinusitis)				
IX-69		Nondecap.		1–1.5												
IX-70		Nondecap.?		Child												
IX-71				13–14												GP?
50-iii		Decap.?		Adult	Y									Mn (condyle)		
106		Decap.?		Adult	Y											
157(229)				Adult							E, P (healed)		F			
176				Adult												Occipital bracelet
176#1		Decap.?	M?	Adult	Y											
176#2		Decap.?		10	Y										Insect (Mn)	Copper stain (Mn)

Specimen	Decap.	Age						
206-N	Decap.?	Adult	Y			Mn		Burning (Mn)
224-v		Adult						
229#1		15–21			Mx (sinusitis)			
229#2	Decap.?	Adult						
229#8	Decap.?	Adult	Y				Rodent (Mn)	
263		Adult	Y					
270#1		15–21						
270#3		Adult				Mn	Rodent (Mn)	Subper. hemorrhage (Mn)
270#17		Adult				F, O	Rodent (Mn)	
270-i	Decap.?	Adult	Y				Rodent (Mn)	
270-ii	Decap.?	15–21	Y			Mn		
294#1		15–21				Mx		
294#2		Adult				O		
294#7		Adult				T (endo.)		
294#10		Adult						
294#15		Subadult						
321		15–21		O				
P-II		1.5–2						
Str. 39-i	Decap.?	Adult	Y				Insect (Mn)	
Str. 39-ii		Adult					Rodent (Mn)	
Str. 39-iii	Decap.?	15–21	Y					
Str. 39-iv		15–21						
Str. 39-v		15–21					Rodent (Mn)	
Str. 45-i		Adult						Arth. pits, lip. (Mx con.) Cyst (Mn)
Str. 45-ii	Decap.?	Adult	Y					
Str. 45-iii	Decap.?	Adult	Y					
Str. 45(270)		Adult					Rodent (Mn)	

1. Does not include all cranial bones present.

F = frontal; Mn = mandible; Mx = maxilla; N = nasal; O = occipital; P = parietal; S = sphenoid; T = temporal; Z = zygomatic

Appendix D. Dentitions[1] with Notable Demographic or Paleopathological Features

Ident.	Guillemin ID No.	Burial Type	Sex	Age	Labret Polish	Alveolar Abscesses	Periapical Abscesses	Caries	Trauma	Antemortem Absence	Congenital Absence	Calculus Mean	Wear Mean	Resorption Mean (cm)	Hypoplasias 6 Mo. Per.	Hypoplasias in 4th Yr.	Miscellaneous
IX-1	E39-C	Nondecap.	F	Adult		1/31	0/31	5/25	4/25	0/31	1/32	2.44	2.64	0.34			
IX-2	#36	Decap.	M?	Adult	Y	1/32	0/32	2/32	3/32	0/32	0/32	1	2.38	0.25	0/13	N	
IX-3				Adult													
IX-4	#28	Decap.	M?	Adult	Y	0/31	0/31	3/30	9/30	0/31	1/32	1.13	2.53	0.24	6/14	Y	
IX-5	#47	Decap.	M	15–21	Y	0/30	0/30	0/30	3/30	0/30	2/32	1.03	2.4	0.16	5/13	Y	
IX-6		Decap.?	F	15–21		0/32	0/32	0/32	6/32	0/32	0/32	1.34	2.19	0.15	1/13	N	Peg-shaped 1
IX-7	#17	Decap.	M?	15–21	Y	0/30	0/30	3/30	2/30	0/30	2/32	1.47	2.2	0.16	2/13	Y	Should not have IX number
IX-8				Adult		0/11	0/11	1/2	2/2	0/11	0/11	0.5	3				Should not have IX number
IX-8-i				Adult		0/4	0/4	0/3	2/3	0/4	0/4	0.67	3	0.15			
IX-9	E27-A/1	Decap.?	F?	Adult		1/32	2/32	3/29	3/28	1/32	0/32	1.93	2.75	0.33	3/12	N	
IX-10	Str. 74	Decap.	M	Adult		0/32	1/32	0/32	7/32	0/32	0/32	1.47	3.13	0.25	7/12	Y	
IX-11	#12	Decap.	F?	15–21	Y	0/31	0/31	0/28	0/28	0/31	1/32	0.75	2.21	0.31	6/13	Y	
IX-12	#10	Decap.	F	Adult	Y	0/32	0/32	0/32	1/32	0/32	0/32	1.09	2.41	0.21	2/13	Y	
IX-13	#29	Decap.	M	Adult	Y	0/29	0/29	1/29	3/29	0/32	0/32	2.04	2.36	0.12	2/13	N	
IX-14				Adult													Should not have IX number
IX-15			F?	15–21		0/16	0/16	3/15	1/14	0/16	0/16	0.64	2.14	0.07	3/11	Y	Should not have IX number
IX-16	#32	Decap.	M?	Adult	Y	0/32	0/32	0/31	4/31	0/32	0/32	0.35	2.87	0.21	4/13	Y	
IX-17	E_Q_?	Nondecap.?		Adult		0/30	0/30	1/14	3/14	2/30	2/32	1.07	2.36	0.3	2/8	Y	
IX-18				Adult		0/16	0/16	0/13	2/13	0/16	0/16	1.15	2.77	0.24	5/12	N	Should not have IX number; peg-shaped 1
IX-19	#38	Decap.		15–21		0/31	0/31	2/30	2/30	0/31	0/32	0.33	2.13	0.28	0/14	N	Retained m; unerupted C
IX-20	#15	Decap.	M?	Adult		0/31	0/31	1/28	10/26	4/31	0/32	1.35	2.96	0.37	5/13	Y	Unerupted I and supernumerary I; deformed I
IX-21	#21	Decap.	M?	15–21	Y	1/32	0/32	0/31	0/31	0/32	0/32	0.45	2.19	0.15	10/13	Y	
IX-22	#23	Decap.		Adult	Y	0/32	0/32	0/32	7/32	0/32	0/32	0.41	2.44	0.16	4/13	Y	

Specimen	Field No.	Status	Sex	Age	Y										4/13	Y	Notes
IX-23		Decap.?	F	Adult		0/32	0/32	12/32	2/32	0/32	0/32	1.28	2.38	0.16	4/13	Y	2 retained c
IX-24		Nondecap.		13–14		0/28	0/28	1/24	0/24	0/28	0/32	0.21	2.29	0.12			
IX-25			F	Adult		0/20	0/20	5/15	4/15	0/21	0/21	0	2.33	0.24			
IX-26			F?	Adult		0/31	0/31	0/29	8/29	2/31	1/32	0.03	2.69	0.14			
IX-27			M	Adult		10/31	1/31	2/15	12/15	3/31	0/31	1.93	3.8	0.48			
IX-28		Decap.?	F	Adult		0/28	0/28	2/28	1/28	0/28	4/32	0.82	2.5	0.26			
IX-29		Decap.?	F	Adult		0/32	0/32	0/4	0/4	0/32	0/32	0.5	2				
IX-30	E38-A/II?	Nondecap.?	F?	Adult		0/22	0/22	1/17	0/15	5/26	0/26	1	3.06	0.55			GQ?
IX-31			M	Adult		0/15	0/15	0/2	2/2	2/15	0/15	2	3.5	0.54			
IX-32																	
IX-33	#11	Decap.	M	Adult	Y	0/32	0/32	6/30	15/30	0/32	0/32	1.9	2.77	0.22			
IX-34	E27-D	Nondecap.	F?	Adult		1/29	1/29	3/6	1/6	21/29	0/29	1.17	3.17	1.06			
IX-35				Adult	Y												Should not have IX number
IX-36				Adult													
IX-37				Adult													
IX-38			M?	Adult													
IX-39																	
IX-40		Decap.?	M?	Adult	Y	0/16	5/16	3/14	4/14	1/18	0/18	1.29	2.79	0.2			
IX-41	#37	Decap.	F	15–21		0/31	0/31	2/31	11/31	0/32	0/32	0.61	2.13	0.13			Retained m
IX-42			M	Adult		0/31	0/31	1/23	9/23	0/32	0/32	1.09	2.48	0.33			
IX-43		Decap.?	M	15–21	Y	0/29	0/29	0/28	5/28	0/29	2/32	0.57	2.54	0.13			
IX-44				14		0/17	0/17	1/14	1/14	3/31	1/19	0.64	2.14	0.08			Retained m root
IX-45				Adult	Y	0/30	0/30	5/27	14/27	3/31	0/31	0.89	2.78				
IX-46	#20	Decap.	F?	15–21	Y	0/31	0/31	0/30	4/30	0/32	0/32	0.27	2.13	0.08			
IX-47		Decap.?	M?	Adult		0/21	1/21	2/9	6/9	0/21	1/22	1	2.44	0.17			
IX-48			F	Adult													
IX-49																	
IX-50		Decap.?	F	15–21		0/24	0/24	0/6	0/6	0/24	0/24	0.33	2.17	0.37			
IX-51		Decap.?	M	Adult		0/31	0/31	2/13	5/13	0/31	1/32	0	2.92	0.12			
IX-52		Decap.?	M	Adult	Y	0/23	0/23	6/17	6/17	0/23	0/23	0.76	2.18	0.18			
IX-53	#34	Decap.		Adult													
IX-54		Decap.?	F?	Adult	Y	0/31	0/31	0/18	8/18	1/31	0/31	0.5	2.94	0.15			Peg-shaped I
IX-55				Adult		0/16	2/16	2/7	1/7	2/16	2/16	1.14	3.86	0.28			
IX-56		Decap.?		15–21		0/2	0/2	0/1	0/1	0/2	0/2	0	2	0.03			
IX-57				Adult													

1. Does not include all fragments of maxillas and mandibles present.

C = permanent canine; c = deciduous canine; I = permanent incisor; I-P = inter-proximally; M = permanent molar; m = deciduous molar; P = permanent premolar

(continued)

364

(Appendix D continued)

Ident.	Guillemin ID No.	Burial Type	Sex	Age	Labret Polish	Alveolar Abscesses	Periapical Abscesses	Caries	Trauma	Antemortem Absence	Congenital Absence	Calculus Mean	Wear Mean	Resorption Mean (cm)	Hypoplasias 6 Mo. Per.	Hypoplasias in 4th Yr.	Miscellaneous
IX-58				Adult													
IX-59				Adult													
IX-60			M?	Adult													
IX-61				Adult													
IX-62			M	Adult													
IX-63				Adult													
IX-64				Adult													
IX-65				Adult													
IX-66				Adult													
IX-67			F?	Adult													
IX-68	#46?	Decap.?		Adult				0/9	7/9	0/9	0/9	1	2.56				
IX-69		Nondecap.		1–1.5							0/5						Mostly deciduous teeth (not in freqs) GP?
IX-70		Nondecap.?		Child													
IX-71				13–14		0/15	0/15	1/4	2/4	0/15	0/16	0.75	2.5	0.13			
50-iii		Decap.?		Adult		0/16	0/16	1/9	4/9	0/16	0/16	1.11	2.33	0.14			
106		Decap.?		Adult		0/8	0/8			0/8	0/8						
157				Adult		0/4	0/4			0/4	0/4						
176#1		Decap.?	M?	Adult	Y	0/6	0/6	1/9	3/9	0/10	0/10	1.11	2.22				
176#2		Decap.?		10		0/15	0/15			0/15	0/16						Some deciduous teeth (not in freqs)
206-D				Adult		0/2	0/2			0/2	0/2						
206-G				Adult		1/12	0/12	1/3	2/3	1/12	1/13	1	4	0.4			
206-N		Decap.?		Adult		0/12	0/12	1/1		1/12	0/12		2				
206-P				Adult		0/14	0/14			0/14	0/14						
224-v				Adult	Y	3/16	0/16	2/11	7/11	3/16	0/16	1.18	3.09	0.58			
229#1				15–21		0/7	0/7	0/2	1/2	0/7	0/8	1.5	2	0.17			
229#2				Adult		0/16	1/16	0/1	0/1	2/16	0/16	1	2				
229#3				Adult		0/8	0/8			0/8	0/8						
263		Decap.?		Adult		2/14	1/14	3/7	5/6	3/14	2/16	1.67	2.83	0.24			
270				Adult		0/2	0/2			0/2	0/2						
270#1				15–21		0/4	0/4	0/4	2/4	0/4	0/5	0.75	2	0.01			

Specimen	Decap.?	Age											Comment
270#2		Adult		1/7	0/7	0/3	2/3	0/7	1/8	0.33	2.33	0.11	
270#3		Adult		0/3	0/3	0/1	1/1	0/3	1/4	1	2		
270#4		Adult		0/6	0/6	0/2	0/2	0/6	0/6	1	2	0.11	
270#5		Adult		0/6	0/6	0/2	1/2	0/6	0/7	2	3		
270#6		Adult		0/7	0/7	0/5	4/5	0/7	1/8	0.8	3.4	0.12	
270-i	Decap.?	Adult		0/19	0/19	1/15	3/15	0/19	0/19	1.73	2.6	0.19	Maxillary torus
270-ii	Decap.?	15–21		0/6	0/6	1/2	0/2	0/6	0/6	0	2		Maxillary torus
294#1		15–21		0/8	0/8	1/3	3/3	0/8	0/8		2.67	0.18	
294#2		Adult		0/6	0/6	0/4	3/4	0/7	0/7	1.5	2.25		
294#3		Adult		0/5	0/5			0/5	0/5				
321		15–21		0/3	0/3	2/3	1/3	0/3	0/3	0.33	1.67	0.11	
IX133		Adult		0/6	0/6	0/4	3/4	0/6	0/6	1	4.5		
P-II		1.5–2		0/1	0/1		3/4	0/1	0/2				Mostly deciduous teeth (not in freqs)
Str. 39-i	Decap.?	Adult		0/30	0/30	4/12	8/12	0/30	0/30	0.83	2.92	0.17	
Str. 39-ii		Adult		0/16	0/16	2/10	6/10	0/16	0/16	1	3.44	0.29	
Str. 39-iii	Decap.?	15–21		0/32	0/32	0/18	3/18	0/32	0/32	1.06	2.17	0.2	Peg-shaped M
Str. 39-iv		15–21		0/23	0/23	0/9	3/9	0/23	0/23	0.56	2.33	0.06	
Str. 39-v		15–21		0/16	0/16	2/11	3/11	0/16	0/16	0.55	2.09	0.08	
Str. 39(229)		Adult	Y	0/11	0/11	2/6	1/6	0/11	2/13	0.5	2.33	0.15	
Str. 45#1		Adult		0/16	0/16	2/13	2/13	0/16	0/16	0.85	2.69	0.08	
Str. 45#2		Adult		0/12	0/12	0/4	3/4	0/12	1/13	0.25	2.25	0.09	
Str. 45#3		Adult		0/8	1/8	1/6	4/6	0/8	0/8	1	2.5	0.09	
Str. 45#4		Adult		0/8	0/8	1/4	4/4	0/8	0/8	3	2.67	0.21	Maxillary torus
Str. 45-ii	Decap.?	Adult		0/16	0/16	0/10	3/10	0/16	0/16	0.8	2.9	0.17	
Str. 45-iii	Decap.?	Adult		0/6	0/6	1/4	3/4	0/6	0/6	1	2.25		
Str. 45(270)		Adult		0/13	0/13	1/4	2/4	0/13	0/13	0	3	0.14	
Unnumbered		Adult		0/3	0/3	0/1	1/1	0/3	0/3	1	3		
Loose Teeth			Y	0/3	0/3	5/135	5/135	133/146	133/146	1.03		2.5	1-P grooved P; peg-shaped P; barrel-shaped l

1. Does not include all fragments of maxillas and mandibles present.
C = permanent canine; c = deciduous canine; I = permanent incisor; I-P = inter-proximally; M = permanent molar; m = deciduous molar; P = permanent premolar

Appendix E. Postcranial Bones[1] with Notable Demographic or Paleopathological Features

Ident.	Guillemin ID No.	Burial Type	Age	Sex	Bone	Side/Type	Trauma	Periosteal Reactions	Osteoarthritis	Gnawing	Miscellaneous
IX-1	E39-C	Nondecap.	35–39		Clavicle	L			Pits (lateral)		
IX-1	E39-C	Nondecap.	35–39		Femur	L			Deposit (prox.)		
IX-1	E39-C	Nondecap.	35–39		Femur	R			Deposit (prox.)		
IX-1	E39-C	Nondecap.	35–39		Fibula	L					Smooth lump
IX-1	E39-C	Nondecap.	35–39		Fibula	R			Pits, lipping (dist.)		Smooth lump
IX-1	E39-C	Nondecap.	35–39		Foot	R			Pits, lipping (calcaneus, metatarsal)		
IX-1	E39-C	Nondecap.	35–39		Hand	L/R			Pits, lipping (phalanges)		
IX-1	E39-C	Nondecap.	35–39		Humerus	R					Septic arthritis (prox., dist.)
IX-1	E39-C	Nondecap.	35–39		Innominate	L			Lipping (acetab.)		
IX-1	E39-C	Nondecap.	35–39		Innominate	R					Septic arthritis (acetab.); burning
IX-1	E39-C	Nondecap.	35–39		Patella	L			Lipping		
IX-1	E39-C	Nondecap.	35–39		Patella	R			Pits, lipping		
IX-1	E39-C	Nondecap.	35–39		Radius	R					Septic arthritis (prox.)
IX-1	E39-C	Nondecap.	35–39		Ribs	?					Long smooth ridges on 3
IX-1	E39-C	Nondecap.	35–39		Sacrum	R					Burned
IX-1	E39-C	Nondecap.	35–39		Scapula	L			Lipping		Septic arthritis (glenoid)
IX-1	E39-C	Nondecap.	35–39		Tibia	R		Healed			
IX-1	E39-C	Nondecap.	35–39		Ulna	C					Septic arthritis (prox.)
IX-1	E39-C	Nondecap.	35–39		Vertebra	L			Eburnation, herniation		
IX-1	E39-C	Nondecap.	35–39		Vertebra	T	Break (healed)		Pits, lipping, herniation		
IX-1	E39-C	Nondecap.	35–39		Vertebra	C	Cut		Lipping, herniation		
IX-4	#28	Decap.	Adult		Vertebra	C	Cut				
IX-5		Decap.	Adult		Vertebra	L					
IX-6		Decap.?	15–24	F	Femur				Lipping (prox.)		Congenital dislocation (prox.)
IX-6		Decap.?	15–24	F	Fibula	R					Smooth lump

Specimen	Field no.	Decapitation	Age	Sex	Element[1]	Side	Cut marks	Lesion	Status	Rodent	Notes
IX-6		Decap.?	15–24		Innominate	L		Lipping (acetab.)			Congenital dislocation (acetab.)
IX-6		Decap.?	15–24	F	Ulna	L	Cut?				Copper stain
IX-6		Decap.?	15–24	F	Vertebra	C	Puncture				
IX-6		Decap.?	15–24	F	Vertebra	C	Cut				
IX-7	#17	Decap.	Adult		Vertebra	C	Cut	Pits			
IX-10	Str. 74	Decap.	Adult		Vertebra	C	Cut				
IX-11	#12	Decap.	Adult		Vertebra	C	Cut				
IX-13	#29	Decap.	Adult		Vertebra	C	Cut				
IX-16	#32	Decap.	Adult		Vertebra	C	Cut				Cyst (arch)
IX-19	#38	Decap.	Adult		Vertebra	C	Cut				
IX-20	#15	Decap.	Adult		Vertebra	C	Cut				
IX-21	#21	Decap.	Adult		Vertebra	C	Cut				
IX-24		Nondecap.	13–14		Rib	R		Pits (dorsal)			
IX-33	#11	Decap.	Adult		Vertebra	C	Cut			Rodent	
IX-34	E27-D	Nondecap.	Adult		Femur	L				Rodent	
IX-34	E27-D	Nondecap.	Adult		Humerus	L		Lipping			
IX-34	E27-D	Nondecap.	Adult		Patella	?					Smooth lump
IX-34	E27-D	Nondecap.	Adult		Rib	L					
IX-34	E27-D	Nondecap.	Adult		Scapula	L		Lipping (glenoid)			
IX-40		Decap.?	Adult		Vertebra	C	Cut				
IX-54		Decap.?	Adult		Vertebra	C	Cut				
IX-56		Decap.?	Adult		Vertebra	C	Cut				
IX-68	#46?	Decap.?	Adult		Vertebra	C	Cut?				
IX-69		Nondecap.	1–1.5								
AB			Adult		Tibia	L		Pits, eburnation (prox.)	Active	Rodent	Attachment area reaction
AD			Adult		Tibia	L		Pits, deposit (prox.)			
AF			Adult		Tibia	L					
AM			Adult		Tibia	L				Rodent	
AR			Adult		Tibia	R				Rodent	
AW			Adult		Tibia	R		Pits, deposit (prox.)	Healed		

1. Does not include all postcranial bones present.

C = cervical; L = left or lumbar; R = right; T = thoracic

(continued)

(*Appendix E continued*)

Ident.	Guillemin ID No.	Burial Type	Age	Sex	Bone	Side/Type	Trauma	Periosteal Reactions	Osteoarthritis	Gnawing	Miscellaneous
BB			Adult		Fibula	L					Attachment area reaction
BB			Adult		Tibia	R		Active			Burned
BE			35–44	F	Innominate	R			Pits (acetab.)		Cyst (acetab.)
BE			35–44	F	Innominate	R					Burned
BI			Adult		Fibula	R					
CA			Adult		Femur	R		Healed			
CD			Adult		Femur	L	Cut (shaft)				
CE			Adult		Femur	L				Rodent	
CF			Adult		Femur	L					Burned
CM			Adult		Femur	L				Rodent	
CP			Adult		Femur	L				Rodent	
CX			Adult		Femur	R			Pits, lipping (dist.)		
CZ			Adult		Femur	R	Cut (dist. artic.)	Healed		Insect	
DA			Adult		Femur	R				Rodent	
DC			Adult		Femur	R				Rodent	
DE			Adult		Femur	R		Healed			
DE			50+		Innominate	R			Lipping (acetab.)		Same as DY?
DL			35–44		Innominate	R					
DM			30–34	F	Innominate	L					
DM			Adult		Sacrum						Fused
DM			Adult		Vertebra	L					Fused
DO			Adult		Femur	L		Healed			
DO			Adult		Femur	R		Healed	Pits, lipping, eburnation (dist.)		
DO			Adult		Tibia	R		Healed			Smooth lump
DP			Adult		Sacrum						Fused
DP			Adult		Vertebra	L			Lipping		Fused
DS			Adult		Sacrum				Pits		
DT			35–44		Innominate	L					
DU			35–39	M?	Innominate	L					Same as EF?
DV			20–29		Innominate	L					

DW	35–39		Innominate	L			
DX	30–39		Innominate	L			
DY	40–44	F?	Innominate	L	Pits (acetab.)		Same as DL?
DZ	35–44		Innominate	L			
EA	Adult	M?	Innominate	L	Lipping (acetab.)		
EB	Adult		Innominate	R			
ED	35–44		Innominate	R			
EE	40–44	F?	Innominate	R	Lipping (acetab.)		Same as DU?
EF	35–39	M?	Innominate	R		Insect	
EG	Adult		Innominate	R			
EH	25–34	F	Innominate	R			
EI	Adult		Innominate	R			
EJ	30–34	F?	Innominate	R			
EK	Subadult?		Humerus	?			
EP	Adult		Humerus	L		Rodent	
ES	Adult		Humerus	L		Rodent	
EU	Adult		Humerus	R			Cyst (dist.)
FB	Adult		Humerus	?			Burned
FG	Adult		Ulna	L		Insect	
FH	Adult		Ulna	L	Pits (prox.)	Rodent	
FK	Adult		Ulna	R			
FP	Adult		Scapula	L	Pits (glenoid)	Rodent	
FV	Adult		Ulna	R		Rodent	
FW	Adult		Radius	R			Smooth lump
GE	Adult		Humerus	L	Pits (dist.)		
GE	Adult		Humerus	R	Pits, deposit (dist.)		
GE	Adult		Ulna	L	Deposit (prox.)		
GF	Adult		Humerus	R			Cyst (dist.)
GF	Adult		Radius	R			Fused (prox.); copper stain
GF	Adult		Ulna	R			Fused (prox.)
GK	Adult		Humerus	L		Rodent	
GK	Adult		Radius	L		Rodent	
GK	Adult		Ulna	L		Rodent	

1. Does not include all postcranial bones present.
C = cervical; L = left or lumbar; R = right; T = thoracic

(continued)

(*Appendix E continued*)

Ident.	Guillemin ID No.	Burial Type	Age	Sex	Bone	Side/Type	Trauma	Periosteal Reactions	Osteoarthritis	Gnawing	Miscellaneous
GO	E38-A/I	Nondecap.?	Adult		Clavicle	R			Pits (medial)		Copper stain
GO	E38-A/I	Nondecap.?	Adult		Femur	R					Gold beads
GO	E38-A/I	Nondecap.?	Adult		Ribs	?					Smooth lump (phalanges)
GO	E38-A/I	Nondecap.?	Adult		Hand	?					
GO	E38-A/I	Nondecap.?	Adult		Sternum				Pits		IX-70?
GP		Nondecap.?	Child								IX-30?
GQ	E38-A/II	Nondecap.?	Adult								
GR			35–44	M?	Clavicle	R			Pits (prox.)		
GR			35–44	M?	Humerus	L		Active		Rodent	
GR			35–44	M?	Innominate	R					
GU			Adult		Vertebra	T			Lipping		
GV			Adult		Scapula	R			Lipping (glenoid)		
GY			Adult		Scapula	L			Lipping (glenoid)		
HB			Adult		Clavicle	R			Pits (lateral)		Smooth lump
HC			Adult		Vertebra	T					Abnormal configuration
HK			Adult		Innominate	R	Puncture				
HL			Adult		Innominate	R	Puncture				
IA			Adult		Scapula	R			Pits (glenoid)		
ID			Adult		Scapula	L				Rodent	
IH			Adult		Vertebra	L			Lipping		
IH			Adult		Vertebra	T			Pits, lipping		Abnormal configuration
JJ			Adult		Vertebra	T			Lipping, deposit		
IK			Adult		Vertebra	C			Pits, lipping, eburnation		
IL			Adult		Vertebra	C	Cut				
IV			Adult		Humerus	L					Artifact
IZ			Adult		Sacrum						Bony growth
JC			Adult		Humerus	L				Rodent	
JG			Child		Tibia	L				Rodent	
JH			Adult		Sacrum				Lipping		

JI	Adult	Clavicle	L	Break (healed)	Active		Rodent	
JI	Adult	Rib	?					
JI	Adult	Vertebra	T			Pits, lipping		
JL	Adult	Innominate	R			Pits (acetab.)		
JO	Adult	Tibia	L			Lipping	Rodent	
KH	Adult	Patella	L			Lipping		
KI	Adult	Patella	L					
KL	Adult	Fibula	?				Rodent	
KM	Adult	Fibula	?					Burned
KN	Adult	Humerus	?	Break (healed)				
KP	Adult	Humerus	R					Flute
KR	Adult	Femur	R					Musical rasp
LA	Adult	Ulna	R					Defleshing cuts
LB	Subadult	Ulna	?					
50	Subadult	Femurs (2)	?					Kneeling facets (metatarsals)
50	Adult	Foot	R					
50	Adult	Rib	?					Burned
50	Subadult	Ribs (2)	?					Burned
50	Adult	Vertebra	C			Lipping		
50	Adult	Vertebra	L			Lipping		
50	Subadult	Vertebrae (4)	T					
50-ii	Adult	Rib	?					
129	Subadult	Hand phalanx	?					Smooth lumps
129-ii	Adult	Rib	L			Pits (dorsal)		
206-L	Adult	Vertebra	C			Pits		
224	Subadult	Hand phalanx	?					
224	Subadult	Metacarpals (2)	?					
224	Subadult	Metatarsal	?					
224	Adult	Rib	?	Break (healed)			Rodent	
224	Adult	Vertebra	C			Lipping		
224	Adult	Vertebra	L			Pits, lipping, herniation		

1. Does not include all postcranial bones present.

C = cervical; L = left or lumbar; R = right; T = thoracic

(continued)

(Appendix E continued)

Ident.	Guillemin ID No.	Burial Type	Sex	Age	Bone	Side/Type	Trauma	Periosteal Reactions	Osteoarthritis	Gnawing	Miscellaneous
224				Subadult	Vertebrae (2)	L			Pits, lipping		
224				Adult	Vertebra	T					
224				Subadult	Vertebrae (5)	T					
224-iv				Adult	Rib	?					Smooth lump
229				Subadult	Metacarpal	L					
229				Subadult	Metatarsal	?					
229				Adult	Radius	R					Burned
229				Adult	Rib	?					Smooth lump
229				Subadult	Ribs (22)	?				Rodent	
229				Adult	Vertebra	C			Lipping		
229				Subadult	Vertebrae (4)	C					
229				Adult	Vertebra	L			Lipping, herniation		
229				Subadult	Vertebrae (2)	T					
229				Adult	Vertebra	T			Lipping		
229				Subadult	Vertebrae (7)	T					
229				Subadult	Vertebrae (4)	?					
263				Adult	Vertebra	C			Lipping		
263				Adult	Vertebra	L			Lipping		
263				Subadult	Vertebra	T					
Unnumbered				Adult	Fibula	L					Smooth lump; found with IX-15
Unnumbered				Subadult	Sternum						
Unnumbered				Subadult	Vertebra	T					

1. Does not include all postcranial bones present.

C = cervical; L = left or lumbar; R = right; T = thoracic

Bibliography

Alvarado, P. de

1969   Another Account Given by Pedro Alvarado to Hernando Cortés. trans., S. J. Mackie, pp. 86–90. In *Documents and Narratives Concerning the Discovery and Conquest of Latin America*, No. 3. Kraus Reprint, New York.

Ambrose, S. H., and L. Norr

1993   Experimental Evidence for the Relationship of the Carbon Isotope Ratios of Whole and Dietary Protein to Those of Bone Collagen and Carbonate. In *Prehistoric Human Bone: Archaeology at the Molecular Level*, edited by J. Lambert and G. Grupe, pp. 1–37. Springer-Verlag, Berlin.

Arnauld, M. C.

1981   Comments on "The Late Postclassic Frontier of Mesoamerica: Cultural Innovation along the Periphery" by John W. Fox. *Current Anthropology* 22 (4): 334–335.

Arnold, D. E.

1978   Ethnography of Pottery Making in the Valley of Guatemala. In *The Ceramics of Kaminaljuyú*, edited by R. K. Wetherington, pp. 327–400. Pennsylvania State University, University Park.

Babcock, T. F.

1979   "Prehistoric Community Organization of a Quiché Center: Investigations in the Utatlán Residence Zone." Ph.D. diss., Tulane University, New Orleans.

Baker, S. J., and V. I. Mathan

1975   Prevalence, Pathogenesis, and Prophylaxis of Iron Deficiency in the Tropics. In *Iron Metabolism and Its Disorders*, edited by H. Kief, pp. 145–157. Excerpta Medica, Amsterdam.

Bass, W. M.
1971   *Human Osteology: A Laboratory and Field Manual of the Human Skeleton.* Missouri Archaeological Society, Columbia.

Bernal, I., and L. Gamio
1974   *Yagul: El Palacio de los Seis Patios.* Instituto de Investigaciones Antropológicas, Universidad Nacional Autónoma de México, México.

Bibby, B. G.
1961   Cariogenicity of Foods. *Journal of the American Medical Association* 177: 316–321.

Blanton, R. E.
1978   *Monte Albán: Settlement Patterns at the Ancient Zapotec Capital.* Academic Press, New York.

Blasius, J.
1994   Correspondence Analysis in Social Science Research. In *Correspondence Analysis in the Social Sciences,* edited by M. Greenacre and J. Blasius, pp. 23–52. Academic Press, London.

Bølviken, E., E. Helskog, K. Helskog, I. M. Holm-Olsen, L. Solheim, and R. Bertelsen
1982   Correspondence Analysis: An Alternative to Principal Components. *World Archaeology* 14 (1): 41–60.

Boocock, P., C. A. Roberts, and K. Manchester
1995   Maxillary Sinusitis in Medieval Chichester, England. *American Journal of Physical Anthropology* 98: 483–495.

Boone, E. H., ed.
1984   *Ritual Human Sacrifice in Mesoamerica.* Dumbarton Oaks, Washington, D.C.

Borg, B. E. J.
1986   "Ethnohistory of the Sacatepéquez Cakchiquel Maya, ca. 1450–1690 A.D." Ph.D. diss., University of Missouri, Columbia.

Borhegyi, S. F.
1959   The Composite or "Assemble-it-yourself" Censer, a New Lowland Maya Variety of the Three-Pronged Incense Burner. *American Antiquity* 25: 51–65.

Braswell, G. E.
1998   La Arqueología de San Martín Jilotepeque, Guatemala. *Mesoamérica* 35: 117–154.

Burland, C. A.
1968   *The Gods of Mexico.* Capricorn Books, New York.

Carmack, R. M.
1973   *Quichean Civilization: The Ethnohistoric, Ethnographic, and Archaeological Sources.* University of California Press, Berkeley.

1977   Ethnohistory of the Central Quiché: The Community of Utatlán. In *Archaeology and Ethnohistory of the Central Quiché*, edited by D. T. Wallace and R. M. Carmack, pp. 1–19. Publication No. 1. Institute for Meso-American Studies. State University of New York at Albany.

1979   La Verdadera Identificación de Mixco Viejo. In *Historia Social de los Quichés*, edited by R. M. Carmack, pp. 131–162. Ministerio de Educación, Editorial "Jose de Pineda Ibarra," Guatemala.

1981   *The Quiché Mayas of Utatlán, The Evolution of a Highland Guatemala Kingdom*. University of Oklahoma Press, Norman.

Carrasco, P.

1961   The Civil Religious Hierarchy of Mesoamerican Communities. *American Anthropologist* 63 (4): 483–497.

1964   Los Nombres de Persona en la Guatemala Antigua. *Estudios de Cultura Maya* 4: 323–334.

1967   Don Juan Cortéz, Cacique de Santa Cruz Quiché. *Estudios de Cultura Maya* 6: 251–267.

Chase, D. Z.

1997   Southern Lowland Maya Archaeology and Human Skeletal Remains: Interpretations from Caracol (Belize), Santa Rita Corozal (Belize), and Tayasal (Guatemala). In *Bones of the Maya: Studies of Ancient Skeletons*, edited by S. L. Whittington and D. M. Reed, pp. 15–27. Smithsonian Institution Press, Washington, D.C.

Chonay, D. J., and D. Goetz, trans.

1953   *Title of the Lords of Totonicapán*. University of Oklahoma Press, Norman.

Clouse, R. A.

1999   Interpreting Archaeological Data through Correspondence Analysis. *Historical Archaeology* 33 (2): 90–107.

Coe, M. D.

1965   A Model of Ancient Community Structure in the Maya Lowlands. *Southwest Journal of Anthropology* 21: 97–114.

1999   *The Maya*. 6th ed. Thames and Hudson, New York.

Coggins, C.

1980   The Shape of Time: Some Implications of a Four-Part Figure. *American Antiquity* 45: 727–739.

Cohen, M. N., K. O'Connor, M. Danforth, K. Jacobi, and C. Armstrong

1994   Health and Death at Tipu. In *In the Wake of Contact*, edited by C. S. Larsen and G. R. Milner, pp. 121–133. Wiley-Liss, New York.

1997   Archaeology and Osteology of the Tipu Site. In *Bones of the Maya: Studies of Ancient Skeletons*, edited by S. L. Whittington and D. M. Reed, pp. 78–86. Smithsonian Institution Press, Washington, D.C.

Coleman, D. C., and B. Fry
1991 *Carbon Isotope Techniques*. Academic Press, San Diego.

Contreras R., J. D.
1965 El Último Cacique de la Casa de Cavec. *Cuadernos de Antropología* 5: 37–48. Guatemala.

Coyston, S., C. D. White, and H. P. Schwarcz
1999 Dietary Carbonate Analysis of Bone and Enamel for Two Sites in Belize. In *Reconstructing Ancient Maya Diet*, edited by C. D. White, pp. 221–243. University of Utah Press, Salt Lake City.

Crespo, M.
1956 Títulos Indígenas de Tierras. Trasunto de un Título de los del Pueblo de San Martín Xilotepeque. *Antropología e Historia de Guatemala* 8(2): 13–15.

Danforth, M. E., S. L. Whittington, and K. P. Jacobi
1997 Appendix. An Indexed Bibliography of Prehistoric and Early Historic Maya Human Osteology: 1839–1994. In *Bones of the Maya: Studies of Ancient Skeletons*, edited by S. L. Whittington and D. M. Reed, pp. 229–259. Smithsonian Institution Press, Washington, D.C.

DeNiro, M. J.
1987 Stable Isotopy and Archaeology. *American Scientist* 75: 182–191.

DeNiro, M. J., and S. Epstein
1978 Influence of Diet on the Distribution of Carbon Isotopes in Animals. *Geochimica et Cosmochimica Acta* 42: 495–506.
1981 Influence of Diet on the Distribution of Nitrogen Isotopes in Animals. *Geochimica et Cosmochimica Acta* 45: 341–351.

Díaz del Castillo, B.
1927 *The True History of the Conquest of Mexico*, translated by M. Keatinge. Robert M. McBride, New York.

El-Najjar, M. Y., and A. L. Robertson, Jr.
1976 Spongy Bones in Prehistoric America. *Science* 193: 141–143.

El-Najjar, M. Y., M. V. DeSanti, and L. Ozbek
1978 Prevalence and Possible Etiology of Dental Enamel Hypoplasia. *American Journal of Physical Anthropology* 48: 185–192.

El-Najjar, M. Y., D. J. Ryan, C. G. Turner II, and B. Lozoff
1976 The Etiology of Porotic Hyperostosis among the Prehistoric and Historic Anasazi Indians of Southwestern United States. *American Journal of Physical Anthropology* 44: 477–488.

Ensor, B. E., and J. D. Irish
1995 Hypoplastic Area Method for Analyzing Dental Enamel Hypoplasia. *American Journal of Physical Anthropology* 98: 507–517.

Evans, D. T.
1973   A Preliminary Evaluation of Tooth Tartar among the Preconquest Maya of the Tayasal Area, El Petén, Guatemala. *American Antiquity* 38: 489–493.

Feldman, L. H.
1981   Definiendo Un Estado Pokam. *Anales de Academia de Geografía e Historia de Guatemala* 55: 7–22.
1985   *A Tumpline Economy*. Labyrinthos, Culver City, California.

Fleming, A. F.
1977   Iron-Deficiency in the Tropics. In *Ferastral. Iron-Poly (Sorbitol-Gluconic Acid) Complex*, edited by J. Fielding, pp. 315–321. *Scandinavian Journal of Haematology* Supplementum No. 32.

Fox, J. W.
1977   Quiché Expansion Processes: Differential Ecological Growth Bases within an Archaic State. In *Archaeology and Ethnohistory of the Central Quiché*, edited by D. T. Wallace and R. M. Carmack, pp. 82–97. Publication No. 1. Institute for Meso-American Studies, State University of New York, Albany.
1978   *Quiché Conquest: Centralism and Regionalism in Highland Guatemalan State Development*. University of New Mexico Press, Albuquerque.
1981   The Late Postclassic Eastern Frontier of Mesoamerica: Cultural Innovation along the Periphery. *Current Anthropology* 22 (4): 321–346.
1987   *Maya Postclassic State Formation: Segmentary Lineage Migration in Advancing Frontiers*. Cambridge University Press, New York.

Freidel, D., L. Schele, and J. Parker
1995   *Maya Cosmos: Three Thousand Years on the Shaman's Path*. William Morrow, New York.

Fry, E. I.
1956   Skeletal Remains from Mayapán. In *Current Reports no. 38, Department of Anthropology*, pp. 551–571. Carnegie Institution of Washington, Washington, D.C.

Fuentes y Guzmán, F. A. de
1932–1933   *Recordación Florida: Discurso Historial y Demostración Natural, Material, Militar y Política del Reino de Guatemala* (3 Vols.). Biblioteca "Goathemala" de la Sociedad de Geografía e Historia, Vols. 6–8. Guatemala.

Gall, F., comp.
1976   *Diccionario Geográfico de Guatemala* (16 Vols., 2nd ed.). Tipografía Nacional, Guatemala. (Vols. 3–16, original ms., in the collection of the Centro de Investigaciones Regionales de Mesoamérica, Antigua, Guatemala)

Gerry, J. P., and H. W. Krueger
1997   Regional Diversity in Classic Maya Diets. In *Bones of the Maya: Studies of Ancient Skeletons*, edited by S. L. Whittington and D. M. Reed, pp. 196–207. Smithsonian Institution Press, Washington, D.C.

Gervais-Cloris, V.
1985–1986 *Recherches sur l'anthropologie des populations maya. Paléoanthropologie d'une nécropole de Mixco Viejo (Guatemala)*. Memoire de maitrise d'espagnol, Université de Caen, Caen.

Gervais, V., and A. Ichon
1990   Paléoanthropologie des Cimetiéres de La Campana á Mixco Viejo (Guatemala). *Journal de Société de Americanistes* 76: 55–77.

Goff, C. W.
1953a   Anthropometry of a Mam-Speaking Group of Indians from Guatemala. In *The Ruins of Zaculeu, Guatemala*, Vol. 1, edited by R. B. Woodbury and A. S. Trik, pp. 288–294. William Byrd Press, Richmond, Virginia.
1953b   New Evidence of Pre-Columbian Bone Syphilis in Guatemala. In *The Ruins of Zaculeu, Guatemala*, Vol. 1, edited by R. B. Woodbury and A. S. Trik, pp. 312–319. William Byrd Press, Richmond, Virginia.

Gonzales, D. de, and R. K. Wetherington
1978   Incensarios and Other Ceremonial Forms at Kaminaljuyú. In *The Ceramics of Kaminaljuyú, Guatemala*, edited by R. K. Wetherington, pp. 279–298. Pennsylvania State University, University Park.

Goodman, A. H., G. J. Armelagos, and J. C. Rose
1980   Enamel Hypoplasias as Indicators of Stress in Three Prehistoric Populations from Illinois. *Human Biology* 52: 515–528.

Gorenstein, S., and H. P. Pollard
1983   *The Tarascan Civilization: A Late Prehispanic Cultural System*. Vanderbilt University Publications in Anthropology, No. 28. Nashville, Tennessee.

Guillemin, G. F.
n.d.a   Un Palais D'Iximché, Fouille de 1963. Unpublished manuscript on file at the Centro de Investigaciones Regionales de Mesoamérica, Antigua, Guatemala.
n.d.b   Iximché - Fouilles 1971–72. Unpublished manuscript on file at the Centro de Investigaciones Regionales de Mesoamérica, Antigua, Guatemala.
n.d.c   The Ancient Cakchiquel Capital of Iximché. Unpublished manuscript on file at the Centro de Investigaciones Regionales de Mesoamérica, Antigua, Guatemala.
n.d.d   Iximché, Ancient Capital City of the Cakchiquel-Maya, 12–23–66. Unpublished manuscript on file at the Centro de Investigaciones Regionales de Mesoamérica, Antigua, Guatemala.

n.d.e   Progress at Iximché, Guatemala-1963. Unpublished manuscript on file at the Centro de Investigaciones Regionales de Mesoamérica, Antigua, Guatemala.

n.d.f   Prácticas Funerarias en Iximché. Unpublished manuscript on file at the Centro de Investigaciones Regionales de Mesoamérica, Antigua, Guatemala.

n.d.g   Proyecto Iximché Dibujo No. 2. Unpublished drawing on file at the Centro de Investigaciones Regionales de Mesoamérica, Antigua, Guatemala.

n.d.h   Proyecto Iximché Dibujo No. 4. Unpublished drawing on file at the Centro de Investigaciones Regionales de Mesoamérica, Antigua, Guatemala.

1959   Iximché. *Revista de Antropología e Historia de Guatemala* 11: 22–43.

1961   Un Entierro Señorial en Iximché. *Anales de la Sociedad de Geografía e Historia de Guatemala* 34: 89–105.

1965a   *Iximché, Capital del Antigua Reino Cakchiquel*. Instituto de Antropología e Historia de Guatemala, Guatemala.

1965b   Iximché (Guatemala). *Bulletin de la Société Suisse des Américanistes* 29: 23–33.

1966   Iximché. *36th Congreso Internacional de Americanistas* 1: 373–384 (pagination of published reprint is 1–12).

1967   The Ancient Cakchiquel Capital of Iximché. *Expedition* (Winter): 22–35.

1968   La Sepulture d'un Chef a Iximché. *Archéologia* No. 23 (Summer): 70–73.

1969   Exploration du Groupe C d'Iximché (Guatemala). *Bulletin de la Société Suisse des Américanistes* 33: 23–33.

1971   Excavaciones e Investigaciones en Iximché, Hallazgos in la Nueva Temporada de Trabajo, 1970–71. Newspaper article in *El Imparcial*, July 26, 1971. Guatemala City.

1977   Urbanism and Hierarchy at Iximché. In *Social Processes in Maya Prehistory*, edited by N. Hammond, pp. 227–264. Academic Press, London.

Hanke, L.
1951   *Bartolomé de las Casas: An Interpretation of his Life and Writings*. Martinus Nijof, The Hague.

Hendrickson, C.
1995   *Weaving Identities. Construction of Dress and Self in a Highland Guatemala Town*. University of Texas Press, Austin.

Hill, R. M., II
1992   *Colonial Cakchiquels, Highland Maya Adaptations to Spanish Rule, 1600–1700*. Case Studies in Cultural Anthropology, general editors,

G. Spindler and L. Spindler. Harcourt, Brace, Jovanovich Publishers, Fort Worth, Tex.

1996   Eastern Chajomá (Cakchiquel) Political Geography: Ethnohistorical and Archaeological Contributions to the Study of a Late Postclassic Highland Maya Polity. *Ancient Mesoamerica* 7(1): 63–87.

Hill, R. M., II, and J. Monaghan

1987   *Continuities in Highland Maya Social Organization: Ethnohistory in Sacapulas.* University of Pennsylvania Press, Philadelphia.

Hooton, E. A.

1930   *The Indians of Pecos Pueblo.* Papers of the Southwest Expedition, No. 4. Yale University Press, New Haven.

1940   Skeletons from the Sacred Cenote of Sacrifice at Chichén Itzá. In *The Maya and Their Neighbors,* edited by C. L. Hay, R. L. Linton, S. K. Lothrop, H. L. Shapiro, and G. C. Vaillant, pp. 272–280. D. Appleton-Century, New York.

Ichon, A.

1975   Organización de un Centro Quiché Protohistórico: Pueblo Viejo Chichaj. *Instituto de Antropología e Historia de Guatemala.* Publicación Especial, No. 9.

1979   *Rescate Arqueológico en la Cuenca del Río Chixoy. 1. Informe Preliminar.* Misión Científica Franco-Guatemalteca, Guatemala.

Ichon, A., and R. Grignon

1981   *Archéologie de Sauvetage dans la Vallée du Río Chixoy. 3. El Jocote.* Centre National de la Recherche Scientifique, Institut d'Ethnologie, Paris.

Judkins, C. K., and J. E. Baker

1996   LEH and the Weaning Hypothesis: Too Good to Be True. *American Journal of Physical Anthropology* 22 (Supplement): 234–235.

Katzenberg. M. A., D. A. Herring, and S. R. Saunders

1996   Weaning and Infant Mortality: Evaluating the Skeletal Evidence. *Yearbook of Physical Anthropology* 39: 177–199.

Kennedy, G. E.

1983   Skeletal Remains from Sarteneja, Belize. In *Archaeological Excavations in Northern Belize, Central America,* edited by R. V. Sidreys, pp. 353–372. Monograph 17. Institute of Archaeology, University of California at Los Angeles.

Kennedy, N. C.

1981   Comments on "The Late Postclassic Eastern Frontier of Mesoamerica: Cultural Innovation along the Periphery" by John W. Fox. *Current Anthropology* 22 (4): 338.

Knaggs, R. L.

1926   *The Inflammatory and Toxic Diseases of Bone.* John Wright and Sons, Bristol, England.

Körner, Ch., G. D. Farquhar, and Z. Roksandic
1988   A Global Survey of Carbon Isotope Discrimination in Plants from High Altitude. *Oecologia* 74: 623–632.

Lallo, J. W., G. J. Armelagos, and R. P. Mensforth
1977   The Role of Diet, Disease, and Physiology in the Origin of Porotic Hyperostosis. *Human Biology* 49: 471–483.

Las Casas, B. de
1958   *Apologética Historia*. In *Obras Escogidas de Fray Bartolomé de Las Casas* (Vols. 3 and 4). Biblioteca de Autores Españoles, Vols. 105 and 106. Madrid.

Layrisse, M., and M. Roche
1964   The Relationship Between Anemia and Hookworm Infection. *American Journal of Hygiene* 79: 279–287.

Lee-Thorp, J. A., and N. J. van der Merwe
1987   Carbon Isotope Analysis of Fossil Bone Apatite. *South African Journal of Science* 83: 71–74.

Lehman, H.
1968   *Mixco Viejo*. Tipografía. Nacional, Guatemala

Lewis, M. E., C. A. Roberts, and K. Manchester
1995   Comparative Study of the Prevalence of Maxillary Sinusitis in Later Medieval Urban and Rural Populations in Northern England. *American Journal of Physical Anthropology* 98: 497–506.

Little, B. J.
1992   *Text-Aided Archaeology*. CRC Press, Boca Raton, Florida.

Lovejoy, C. O., R. S. Meindl, T. R. Pryzbeck, and R. P. Mensforth
1985   Chronological Metamorphosis of the Auricular Surface of the Ilium: A New Method for the Determination of Adult Skeletal Age at Death. *American Journal of Physical Anthropology* 68: 15–28.

Luck, J. V.
1950   *Bone and Joint Diseases*. Charles C. Thomas, Springfield, Illinois.

Lutz, C. H.
1994   *Santiago de Guatemala, 1541–1773*. University of Oklahoma Press, Norman.

MacLeod, M. J.
1973   *Spanish Central America: A Socioeconomic History, 1520–1720*. University of California Press, Berkeley.

Marcus, J.
1983   On the Nature of the Mesoamerican City. In *Prehistoric Settlement Patterns: Essays in Honor of Gordon R. Willey*, edited by V. Z. Vogt and R. M. Leventhal, pp.192–242. University of New Mexico Press and Peabody Museum of Archaeology and Ethnology, Harvard University, Cambridge.

Marino, B. D., and M. B. McElroy
1991   Isotopic Composition of Atmospheric CO_2 Inferred from Carbon in C_4 Plant Cellulose. *Nature* 349: 127–131.

Marquez de González, L., A. Benavides Castillo, and P. Schmidt
1982   *Exploración de la Gruta de Xcan, Yucatán*. Centro Regional del Sureste, Instituto Nacional de Antropología e Historia, Merida, Yucatán, México.

Márquez de González, L., and R. Harrington
1981   Spongy Hyperostosis and Cribra Orbitalia in a Maya Subadult Temple. *Paleopathology Newsletter* 35: 12–13.

Márquez Morfín, L.
1987   Qué sabemos de los mayas peninsulares, a partir de sus restos óseos. In *Memorias del Primer Coloquio Internacional de Mayistas*, pp. 43–56. Universidad Nacional Autónoma de México, México.

Márquez Morfín, L., M. E. Peraza, J. Gamboa, and T. Miranda
1982   *Playa del Carmen: una población de la costa oriental en el postclásico (un estudio osteológico)*. Colección Científica-Antropología Física No. 119. Instituto de Antropología e Historia, México.

Marqusee, S. J.
1980   "An Analysis of Late Postclassic Period Quichean Art from the Highlands of Guatemala." Ph.D. diss., State University of New York at Albany.

Massey, V. K., and D. G. Steele
1997   A Maya Skull Pit from the Terminal Classic Period, Colha, Belize. In *Bones of the Maya: Studies of Ancient Skeletons*, edited by S. L. Whittington and D. M. Reed, pp. 62–77. Smithsonian Institution Press, Washington, D.C.

Maudslay, A. P.
1889–1902 *Archeology*, Vol.2, *Biología Centrali-Americana* Published for the editors by R.H. Porter and Dulau and Co., London.

McBryde, F. W.
1947   *Cultural and Historical Geography of Southwest Guatemala*. Smithsonian Institution, Institute of Social Anthropology, Publication, No. 4. Washington, D.C.

Medel, T. L.
1941   Relación (1612)-Academia de Historia, Madrid, Papeles de Muños, Tomo 42, trans., A. M. Tozzer. In *Landa's Relación de las Cosas de Yucatán*. Papers of the Peabody Museum of American Archaeology and Ethnology, Vol. 18, pp. 221–229 (Appendix B). Harvard University, Cambridge.

Mensforth, R. P., C. O. Lovejoy, J. W. Lallo, and G. J. Armelagos
1978   The Role of Constitutional Factors, Diet, and Infectious Disease in the Etiology of Porotic Hyperostosis and Periosteal Reactions in Prehistoric Infants and Children. *Medical Anthropology*, Vol. 2, Issue 1, Part 2.

Merbs, C. F.
1983   *Patterns of Activity-Induced Pathology in a Canadian Inuit Population.* Paper No. 119. Archaeological Survey of Canada, National Museums of Canada, Ottawa.

Miles, S. W.
1957   The Sixteenth-Century Pokom Maya: A Documentary Analysis of Social Structure and Archaeological Setting. *Transactions of the American Philosophical Society,* No. 47, Pt. 2: 733–781.

Milner, G. R., and C. S. Larsen
1991   Teeth as Artifacts of Human Behavior: Intentional Mutilation and Accidental Modification. In *Advances in Dental Anthropology,* edited by M. A. Kelley and C. S. Larsen, pp. 357–378. Wiley-Liss, New York.

Molnar, S.
1971   Human Tooth Wear, Tooth Function and Cultural Variability. *American Journal of Physical Anthropology* 34: 175–190.

Nance, C. R.
1998   La Cerámica y Palacios de Iximché: Examen Prelminar de la Colección Guillemin Proveniente de la Capital Kaqchiquel. *Mesoamérica* 35: 199–215.

———, ed.
1988   Archaeology of the Rodgers-CETA Site: A Lamar Village on Talladega Creek. *Journal of Alabama Archaeology,* 34 (whole issue).

Navarette, C.
1961   La Ceramica de Mixco Viejo. *Humanidades, Universidad de San Carlos de Guatemala,* No. 3.

Neitzel, J. E.
1995   Elite Styles in Hierarchically Organized Societies: The Chacoan Regional System. In *Style, Society and Person, Archaeological and Ethnological Perspectives,* edited by C. Carr and J. E. Neitzel, pp. 393–417. Plenum Press, New York.

Orellana, S. L.
1984   *The Tzutuhil Mayas: Continuity and Change, 1250–1630.* University of Oklahoma Press, Norman.
1995   *Ethnohistory of the Pacific Coast.* Labyrinthos, Lancaster, California.

Ortner, D. J., and W. G. Putschar
1985   *Identification of Pathological Conditions in Human Skeletal Remains.* Reprinted. Smithsonian Contributions to Anthropology No. 28. Smithsonian Institution, Washington, D.C. Originally published 1981.

Patterson, D. K., Jr.
1984   *A Diachronic Study of Dental Paleopathology and Attritional Status of Prehistoric Ontario Pre-Iroquois and Iroquois Populations.* Paper No. 122. Archaeological Survey of Canada. National Museum of Man,

Mercury Series. National Museums of Canada, Ottawa.

Peña Saint Martín, F.

1985 Nutrición entre los mayas prehispánicos. Un estudio osteobiográfico. *Cuicuilco* 4(16): 5–16. Escuela Nacional de Antropología e Historia, México.

Perou, M. L.

1964 *Cranial Hyperostosis (Hyperostosis Cranii or H. C.).* Charles C. Thomas, Springfield, Illinois.

Polley, H. W., H. B. Johnson, B. D. Marino, and H. S. Mayeux

1993 Increase in C_3 Plant Water-Use Efficiency and Biomass over Glacial to Present CO_2 Concentrations. *Nature* 361: 61–64.

Polo, S. F.

1977 *Los Cakchiqueles en la Conquista de Guatemala.* Editorial "José de Pineda Ibarra," Ministerio de Educación, Guatemala.

Polo, S. F., trans.

1979 *Título de Alotenango.* Editorial "José de Pineda Ibarra," Ministerio de Educación, Guatemala.

Rands, R. L., and R. E. Smith

1965 Pottery of the Guatemalan Highlands. In *Archaeology of Southern Mesoamerica*, Part 1, edited by G. R. Willey, pp. 76–94. Handbook of Middle American Indians, Vol. 2, R. Wauchope, general editor. University of Texas Press, Austin.

Recinos, A., trans.

1950 *Memorial de Sololá: Anales de los Cakchiqueles, Título de los Señores de Totonicapán.* Fondo de Cultura Económica, Mexico.

1957 *Crónicas Indígenas de Guatemala.* Editorial Universitaria, Guatemala.

1988 *Memorial de Sololá, Anales de los Kaqchikeles, Título de los Señores de Totonicapán.* Editorial Piedra Santa, Guatemala.

Recinos, A., and D. Goetz, trans.

1953 *The Annals of the Cakchiquels.* University of Oklahoma Press, Norman.

Recinos, A., D. Goetz, and S. G. Morley, trans.

1950 *Popol Vuh, the Sacred Book of the Ancient Quiché Maya.* University of Oklahoma Press, Norman.

Reed, D. M., and S. L. Whittington

1995 *El análisis de isótopos estables de carbono y nitrógenoen los huesos de Iximché.* Final technical report submitted to the Instituto de Antropología e Historia, Guatemala.

Reina, R. E., and R. M. Hill

1978 *The Traditional Pottery of Guatemala.* University of Texas Press, Austin.

Remesal, A. D.

1932 *Historia General de las Indias Occidentales, y Particular de la Gobernación de Chiapa y Guatemala* (2 Vols.). Biblioteca "Goathemala" de la

Sociedad de Geografía e Historia, Vols. 4 and 5. Tipografía Nacional, Guatemala.

Rice, P. M.

1978 Ceramic Continuity and Change in the Valley of Guatemala: A Technological Analysis. In *The Ceramics of Kaminaljuyú*, edited by R. K. Wetherington, pp. 401–510. Pennsylvania State University, University Park.

Roberts, C. A.

1987 Case Report No. 9. *Paleopathology Newsletter* No. 57, pp. 14–15.

Roberts, C., and K. Manchester

1995 *The Archaeology of Disease*, 2nd ed. Alan Sutton, Stroud, England.

Sáenz de Santa María, C., ed.

1969–1972 *Recordación Florida*. In *Obras Históricas de Don Francisco Antonio de Fuentes y Guzmán*, Vols. 1–3. Biblioteca de Autores Españoles, Books 230, 251 and 259. Ediciones Atlas, Madrid.

Sarnat, B. G., and I. Schour

1941 Enamel Hypoplasia (Chronologic Enamel Aplasia) in Relation to Systemic Disease: A Chronologic, Morphologic and Etiologic Classification. *Journal of the American Dental Association* 28: 1989–2000.

1942 Enamel Hypoplasia (Chronologic Enamel Aplasia) in Relation to Systemic Disease: A Chronologic, Morphologic and Etiologic Classification. *Journal of the American Dental Association* 29: 67–75.

Saul, F. P.

1972 *The Human Skeletal Remains of Altar de Sacrificios: An Osteobiographic Analysis*. Papers, Vol. 63, No. 2. Peabody Museum of Archaeology and Ethnology, Harvard University, Cambridge.

1973 Disease in the Maya Area: The Pre-Columbian Evidence. In *The Classic Maya Collapse*, edited by T. P. Culbert, pp. 301–324. University of New Mexico Press, Albuquerque.

1977 The Paleopathology of Anemia in Mexico and Guatemala. In *Porotic Hyperostosis: An Enquiry*, edited by E. Cockburn, pp. 10–15, 18. Monograph No. 2. Paleopathology Association, Detroit, Mich.

1982 Appendix 2, The Human Skeletal Remains from Tancah, Mexico. In *On the Edge of the Sea: Mural Paintings at Tancah-Tulum*, edited by A. G. Miller, pp. 115–128. Dumbarton Oaks, Washington, D.C.

Saul, J. M., and F. P. Saul

1997 The Preclassic Skeletons from Cuello. In *Bones of the Maya: Studies of Ancient Skeletons*, edited by S. L. Whittington and D. M. Reed, pp. 28–50. Smithsonian Institution Press, Washington, D.C.

Schele, L.

1984 Human Sacrifice among the Classic Maya. In *Ritual Human Sacrifice in Mesoamerica*, edited by E. H. Boone, pp. 7–48. Dumbarton Oaks, Washington, D.C.

Schele, L., and P. Mathews
1998 *The Code of Kings: The Language of Seven Sacred Maya Temples and Tombs*. Scribner, New York.

Schneider, K. M.
1986 Dental Caries, Enamel Composition, and Subsistence among Prehistoric Amerindians of Ohio. *American Journal of Physical Anthropology* 71: 95–102.

Scrimshaw, N. S., and C. Tejada
1970 Pathology of Living Indians Seen in Guatemala. In *Physical Anthropology*, edited by T. D. Stewart, pp. 203–225. Handbook of Middle American Indians, Vol. 9, R. Wauchope, general editor. University of Texas Press, Austin.

Sharer, R. J.
1994 *The Ancient Maya*. Stanford University Press, Stanford, Calif.

Shattuck, G. C.
1938 *A Medical Survey of the Republic of Guatemala*. Publication No. 499. Carnegie Institution of Washington, Washington, D.C.

Sherman, W. L.
1979 *Forced Native Labor in Sixteenth-Century Central America*. University of Nebraska Press, Lincoln.

Shook, E. M.
1952 Lugares Arqueológicos del Altiplano Meridional Central de Guatemala. *Antropología e Historia de Guatemala* 1 (2): 3–39.

Smith, A. L.
1955 *Archaeological Reconnaissance in Central Guatemala*. Publication No. 608. Carnegie Institution of Washington, Washington, D.C.
1965 Architecture of the Guatemalan Highlands. In *Archaeology of Southern Mesoamerica, Part 1*, edited by G. R. Willey, pp. 76–94. Handbook of Middle American Indians, Vol. 9, R. Wauchope, general editor, University of Texas Press, Austin.

Steinbock, R. T.
1976 *Paleopathological Diagnosis and Interpretation: Bone Diseases in Ancient Human Populations*. Charles C. Thomas, Springfield, Illinois.

Stephens, J. L.
1969 *Incidents of Travel in Central America, Chiapas and Yucatan* (2 Vols.). Dover Publications, New York. (Unabridged replication of 1st ed. published by Harper and Brothers, New York, 1841).

Stewart, T. D.
1953 Skeletal Remains from Zaculeu, Guatemala. In *The Ruins of Zaculeu, Guatemala*, Vol. 1, edited by R. B. Woodbury and A. S. Trik, pp. 295–311. William Byrd Press, Richmond, Virginia.

Stuart-Macadam, P.

1985   Porotic Hyperostosis: Representative of a Childhood Condition. *American Journal of Physical Anthropology* 66: 391–398.

1987   Porotic Hyperostosis: New Evidence to Support the Anemia Theory. *American Journal of Physical Anthropology* 74: 521–526.

Swezey, W. R.

1985   Cakhay: La Ubicación Original de Tecpán-Atitlán (Sololá). *Mesoamérica* 9: 154–169.

1998   El Primer Informe de Cakhay. *Mesoamérica* 35: 7–26.

Tedlock, B.

1992   *Time and the Highland Maya* (rev. ed.). University of New Mexico Press, Albuquerque.

Tedlock, D., trans.

1985   *Popol Vuh*. Simon and Schuster, New York.

Thompson, J. E. S.

1957   Deities Portrayed on Censers at Mayapán. In *Current Reports*, No. 40, pp. 599–632. Carnegie Institution of Washington, Washington, D.C.

1970   *Maya History and Religion*. University of Oklahoma Press, Norman.

Tieszen, L. L., and T. Fagre

1993   Effect of Diet Quality and Composition on the Isotopic Composition of Respiratory CO_2, Bone Collagen, Bioapatite, and Soft Tissues. In *Prehistoric Human Bone: Archaeology at the Molecular Level*, edited by J. Lambert and G. Grupe, pp. 121–155. Springer-Verlag, Berlin.

Tykot, R. H., S. L. Whittington, D. M. Reed, and J. W. Wilson

2000   Diet, Demography, and Decapitation in the Late Postclassic: Stable Isotope Analysis of Human Teeth from Iximché, Guatemala. Paper presented at the 65th Annual Meeting of the Society for American Archaeology, Philadelphia.

Ubelaker, D. H.

1989   *Human Skeletal Remains* (2nd ed.). Taraxacum, Washington, D.C.

Vásquez, F.

1937–1944 *Crónica de la Provincia del Santísimo Nombre de Jesús de Guatemala* (4 Vols., 2nd ed.). Tipografía Nacional, Guatemala.

Villacorta, C. J. A.

1926   *Monografía del Departamento de Guatemala*. Tipografía Nacional, Guatemala.

1934   *Memorial de Tecpán-Atitlán (Anales de Cakchiqueles)*. Tipografía Nacional, Guatemala.

Vogt, E. Z.

1990   *The Zinacantecos, a Modern Maya Way of Life* (2nd ed.). Case Studies in

Cultural Anthropology, general editors, G. Spindler and L. Spindler. Holt, Rinehart and Winston, Fort Worth, Texas.

Wagner, H. R., with collaboration by H. R. Parish

1967   *The Life and Writings of Bartolomé de las Casas*. University of New Mexico Press, Albuquerque.

Wallace, D. T.

1977   An Intra-site Locational Analysis of Utatlán: The Structure of an Urban Site. In *Archaeology and Ethnohistory of the Central Quiché*, edited by D. T. Wallace and R. M. Carmack, pp. 20–54. Institute for Mesoamérican Studies, Publication, No. 1. State University of New York at Albany.

Wauchope, R.

1949   Las Edades de Utatlán e Iximché. *Revista de Antropología e Historia de Guatemala*. 1(1): 10–22.

1970   Protohistoric Pottery of the Guatemala Highlands. In *Monographs and Papers in Maya Archaeology*, edited by W. R. Bullard, Jr., pp. 89–243. Papers, Vol. 61. Peabody Museum of Archaeology and Ethnology, Harvard University, Cambridge.

Webster, D., B. Fash, R. Widmer, and S. Zeleznik

1998   The Sky Band Group: Investigation of a Classic Maya Elite Residential Complex at Copán, Honduras. *Journal of Field Archaeology* 25(3): 319–343.

Weeks, J. M.

1977   Evidence for Metal Working on the Periphery of Utatlán. In *Archaeology and Ethnohistory of the Central Quiché*, edited by D. T. Wallace and R. M. Carmack, pp. 55–67. Institute for Mesoamerican Studies, Publication, No. 1. State University of New York at Albany.

1980   "Dimensions of Social Differentiation at Chisalín, El Quiché, Guatemala, A.D. 1400–1524." Ph.D. diss., State University of New York at Albany.

1983   *Chisalín, a Late Postclassic Settlement in Highland Guatemala*. B.A.R., Oxford.

Weiss, P.

1967   Ensayo de osteología cultural en Guatemala. *Antropología e Historia de Guatemala* 19: 14–26.

Welsh, W. B. M.

1988   *An Analysis of Classic Lowland Maya Burials*. International Series 409. B.A.R., Oxford.

West, R. C.

1964   The Natural Regions of Middle America. In *Natural Environment and Early Cultures*, edited by R. C. West, pp. 363–383, Handbook of Middle

American Indians, Vol. 1, R. Wauchope, general editor. University of Texas Press, Austin.

Wetherington, R. K.

1978   Postclassic Ceramics at Beleh. In *The Ceramics of Kaminaljuyú,* edited by R. K. Wetherington, pp. 173–184. Pennsylvania State University, University Park.

White, C. D.

1997   Ancient Diet at Lamanai and Pacbitun: Implications for the Ecological Model of Collapse. In *Bones of the Maya: Studies of Ancient Skeletons,* edited by S. L. Whittington and D. M. Reed, pp. 171–180. Smithsonian Institution Press, Washington, D.C.

White, C. D., D. M. Pendergast, F. J. Longstaffe, and K. R. Law

2001   Social Complexity and Food Systems at Altun Ha, Belize: The Isotopic Evidence. *Latin American Antiquity* 12: 371–393.

White, C. D., L. E. Wright, and D. M. Pendergast

1994   Biological Disruption in the Early Colonial Period at Lamanai. In *In the Wake of Contact: Biological Responses to Conquest,* edited by C. S. Larsen and G. R. Milner, pp. 135–145. Wiley-Liss, New York.

Whittington, S. L.

1989   "Characteristics of Demography and Disease in Low-Status Maya from Classic Period Copán, Honduras." Ph.D. diss., Pennsylvania State University, University Park.

1992   Enamel Hypoplasia in the Low Status Maya Population of Prehispanic Copán, Honduras. In *Recent Contributions to the Study of Enamel Developmental Defects,* edited by A. H. Goodman and L. L. Capasso, pp. 185–205. Journal of Paleopathology Monographic Publications No. 2. Associazione Antropologica Abruzze, Chieti, Italy.

1999   Caries and Antemortem Tooth Loss at Copán: Implications for Commoner Diet. In *Reconstructing Ancient Maya Diet,* edited by C. D. White, pp. 151–167. University of Utah Press, Salt Lake City.

Whittington, S. L., and D. M. Reed

1994   Los esqueletos de Iximché. In *7 Simposio de Investigacions Arqueológicas en Guatemala, 1993,* edited by J. P. Laporte and H. L. Escobedo, pp. 23–28. Museo Nacional de Arqueología y Etnología, Guatemala.

1997   Commoner Diet at Copán: Insights from Stable Isotopes and Porotic Hyperostosis. In *Bones of the Maya: Studies of Ancient Skeletons,* edited by S. L. Whittington and D. M. Reed, pp. 157–170. Smithsonian Institution Press, Washington, D.C.

1998   Evidencia de dieta y salud en los esqueletos de Iximché. *Mesoamérica* 35: 73–82.

Whittington, S. L., D. M. Reed, D. A. Merriwether, and B. Adams

1996   Rescue Osteology: Salvaging the Past at Iximché, Guatemala. Paper presented at the 61st Annual Meeting of the Society for American Archaeology, New Orleans.

Whittington, S. L., R. H. Tykot, and D. M. Reed

n.d.   Diet, Demography, and Death at Iximché, Guatemala: Stable Isotope Analyses of Late Postclassic Human Skeletal Remains from the Kaqchikel Maya Capital. In preparation.

Wilkinson, L., M. A. Hill, and E. Vang

1992   *SYSTAT: Statistics, Version 5.2 Edition.* SYSTAT, Evanston, Illinois.

Wing, E. S., and A. B. Brown

1979   *Paleonutrition: Method and Theory in Prehistoric Foodways.* Academic Press, New York.

Wobst, H. M.

1977   Stylistic Behavior and Information Exchange. In *For the Director: Research Essays in Honor of James B. Griffin,* edited by C. E. Cleland, pp. 317–342. Anthropological Paper No. 61, University Museum, University of Michigan, Ann Arbor.

Wood, J. W., G. R. Milner, H. C. Harpending, and K. M. Weiss

1992   The Osteological Paradox: Problems of Inferring Prehistoric Health from Skeletal Samples. *Current Anthropology* 33: 343–370.

Woodbury, R. B.

1965   Artifacts of the Guatemalan Highlands. In *Archaeology of Southern Mesoamerica, Part 1,* edited by G. R. Willey, pp. 163–179. Handbook of Middle American Indians, Vol. 2, R. Wauchope, general editor. University of Texas Press, Austin.

Woodbury, R. B., and A. S. Trik

1953   *The Ruins of Zaculeu, Guatemala* (2 Vols.). William Byrd Press, Richmond, Virginia.

Wright, L. E.

1997   Biological Perspectives on the Collapse of the Pasión Maya. *Ancient Mesoamerica* 8: 267–273.

Wright, L. E., and H. P. Schwarcz

1998   Stable Carbon and Oxygen Isotopes in Human Tooth Enamel: Identifying Breastfeeding and Weaning in Prehistory. *American Journal of Physical Anthropology* 106: 1–18.

1999   Correspondence between Stable Carbon, Oxygen and Nitrogen Isotopes in Human Tooth Enamel and Dentine: Infant Diets at Kaminaljuyú. *Journal of Archaeological Science* 26: 1159–1170.

Wright, L. E., and C. D. White

1996   Human Biology in the Classic Maya Collapse: Evidence from Paleopathology and Paleodiet. *Journal of World Prehistory* 10: 147–198.

Ximénez, F.
1929–1931 *Historia de la Provincia de San Vicente de Chiapa y Guatemala* (3 Vols.). Biblioteca "Goathemala" de las Sociedad de Geografía e Historia, Guatemala.

Yaeger, J. A.
1980 Enamel. In *Orban's Oral Histology and Embryology,* 9th ed., edited by S. N. Bhaskar, pp. 46–106. C. V. Mosby, St. Louis.

Zivanovic, S.
1982 *Ancient Diseases.* Methuen, London.

Zorita, A. de
1963 *Life and Labor in Ancient Mexico: The Brief and Summary Relation of the Lords of New Spain by Alonso de Zorita,* translated by B. Keen. Rutgers University Press: New Brunswick, New Jersey.

Index

C. Roger Nance is the author of *The Archaeology of La Calsada: A Rockshelter in the Sierra Madre Oriental, Mexico.*

Stephen L. Whittington is retired executive director of the National Mining Hall of Fame and Museum in Leadville, Colorado. He is coeditor of *Bones of the Maya: Studies of Ancient Skeletons.*

Barbara E. Borg is associate professor emerita of anthropology at College of Charleston, South Carolina.

Maya Studies
Edited by Diane Z. Chase and Arlen F. Chase

Salt: White Gold of the Ancient Maya, by Heather McKillop (2002)

Archaeology and Ethnohistory of Iximché, by C. Roger Nance, Stephen L. Whittington, and Barbara E. Borg (2003; first paperback edition, 2024)

The Ancient Maya of the Belize Valley: Half a Century of Archaeological Research, edited by James F. Garber (2004; first paperback edition, 2011)

Unconquered Lacandon Maya: Ethnohistory and Archaeology of Indigenous Culture Change, by Joel W. Palka (2005)

Chocolate in Mesoamerica: A Cultural History of Cacao, edited by Cameron L. McNeil (2006; first paperback edition, 2009)

Maya Christians and Their Churches in Sixteenth-Century Belize, by Elizabeth Graham (2011; first paperback edition, 2020)

Chan: An Ancient Maya Farming Community, edited by Cynthia Robin (2012; first paperback edition, 2013)

Motul de San José: Politics, History, and Economy in a Classic Maya Polity, edited by Antonia E. Foias and Kitty F. Emery (2012; first paperback edition, 2015)

Ancient Maya Pottery: Classification, Analysis, and Interpretation, edited by James John Aimers (2013; first paperback edition, 2014)

Ancient Maya Political Dynamics, by Antonia E. Foias (2013; first paperback edition, 2014)

Ritual, Violence, and the Fall of the Classic Maya Kings, edited by Gyles Iannone, Brett A. Houk, and Sonja A. Schwake (2016; first paperback edition, 2018)

Perspectives on the Ancient Maya of Chetumal Bay, edited by Debra S. Walker (2016)

Maya E Groups: Calendars, Astronomy, and Urbanism in the Early Lowlands, edited by David A. Freidel, Arlen F. Chase, Anne S. Dowd, and Jerry Murdock (2017; first paperback edition, 2020)

War Owl Falling: Innovation, Creativity, and Culture Change in Ancient Maya Society, by Markus Eberl (2017; first paperback edition 2024)

Pathways to Complexity: A View from the Maya Lowlands, edited by M. Kathryn Brown and George J. Bey III (2018; first paperback edition, 2021)

Water, Cacao, and the Early Maya of Chocolá, by Jonathan Kaplan and Federico Paredes Umaña (2018)

Maya Salt Works, by Heather McKillop (2019)

The Market for Mesoamerica: Reflections on the Sale of Pre-Columbian Antiquities, edited by Cara G. Tremain and Donna Yates (2019; first paperback edition, 2023)

Migrations in Late Mesoamerica, edited by Christopher S. Beekman (2019)

Approaches to Monumental Landscapes of the Ancient Maya, edited by Brett A. Houk, Barbara Arroyo, and Terry G. Powis (2020)

The Real Business of Ancient Maya Economies: From Farmers' Fields to Rulers' Realms, edited by Marilyn A. Masson, David A. Freidel, and Arthur A. Demarest (2020)

Maya Kingship: Rupture and Transformation from Classic to Postclassic Times, edited by Tsubasa Okoshi, Arlen F. Chase, Philippe Nondédéo, and M. Charlotte Arnauld (2021)

Lacandón Maya in the Twenty-First Century: Indigenous Knowledge and Conservation in Mexico's Tropical Rainforest, by James D. Nations (2023)

The Materialization of Time in the Ancient Maya World: Mythic History and Ritual Order, edited by David A. Freidel, Arlen F. Chase, Anne S. Dowd, and Jerry Murdock (2024)

El Perú-Waka': New Archaeological Perspectives on the Kingdom of the Centipede, edited by Keith Eppich, Damien B. Marken, and David Freidel (2024)